PERMUTATIONS OF ORDER

Permutations of Order makes an innovative and important contribution to current discussions about the relationship between religion and law, bringing together theoretically informed case studies from different parts of the world, relating to various types of politico-legal settings and religions. This volume also deals with contemporary legal/religious transfigurations that involve "permutations," meaning that elements of "legal" and "religious" acts of ordering are at times repositioned within each realm and from one realm to the other. These permutations of order in part result from the fact that, in ethnographic settings like those examined here, "legal" and "religious" realms are relational to – and in certain cases even constitutive of – each other, resulting in categoric transpositions and new social positionalities through which, among other things, "the legal" and "the religious" are blended. *Permutations of Order* is a work that transcends convention, identifies new and theoretically overarching themes and will be of strong interest to researchers and policy-makers seeking a comparative focus on the intersections and disjunctions of religion and law.

Permutations of Order

Religion and Law as Contested Sovereignties

Edited by

THOMAS G. KIRSCH

Goldsmiths College, University of London, UK

BERTRAM TURNER

Max Planck Institute for Social Anthropology, Germany

Routledge

Taylor & Francis Group

LONDON AND NEW YORK

First published 2009 by Ashgate Publishing

Published 2016 by Routledge
2 Park Square, Milton Park, Abingdon, Oxfordshire OX14 4RN
711 Third Avenue, New York, NY 10017, USA

First issued in paperback 2016

Routledge is an imprint of the Taylor & Francis Group, an informa business

British Library Cataloguing in Publication Data
Permutations of order : religion and law as contested
sovereignties. -- (Law, justice and power series)
1. Religion and law. 2. Sovereignty--Religious aspects.
I. Series II. Kirsch, Thomas G. III. Turner, Bertram.
201.7'2-dc22

Library of Congress Cataloging-in-Publication Data
Permutations of order : religion and law as contested sovereignties / edited by
Thomas Kirsch and Bertram Turner.
p. cm. -- (Law, justice and power)
Includes bibliographical references and index.
ISBN 978-0-7546-7259-3 -- ISBN 978-0-7546-8938-6 (ebook) 1.
Religion and law. 2. Legal polycentricity. 3. Customary law. I. Kirsch,
Thomas G. II. Turner, Bertram.

K3280.P47 2008
344' .096--dc22

2008052666

ISBN 13: 978-1-138-27640-6 (pbk)
ISBN 13: 978-0-7546-7259-3 (hbk)

Contents

List of Figures, Maps and Tables

Figure

Map

Tables

Notes on Contributors

Franz von Benda-Beckmann is professor emeritus and head of the Project Group "Legal Pluralism" at the Max Planck Institute for Social Anthropology in Halle/Saale, Germany. He is also Honorary Professor at the Universities of Leipzig and Halle. He did his PhD research on *Legal Pluralism in Malawi* (1970) and obtained his habilitation in anthropology at the University of Zurich (1979) with his book *Property in Social Continuity* (Martinus Nijhoff 1979), based on field research among the Minangkabau in West Sumatra, Indonesia. In the 1980s he did field research on social security and legal pluralism in the central Moluccas, Indonesia. Since 1999 he has been engaged in research on the effects of decentralization in West Sumatra. He has co-edited several books and published numerous articles and book chapters on issues of property rights, social (in)security and legal pluralism in developing countries and on legal anthropological theory. He co-edited, with Keebet von Benda-Beckmann and Anne Griffiths, *Mobile People, Mobile Law. Expanding Legal Relations in a Contracting World* (Ashgate 2005) and, with Keebet von Benda-Beckmann and Melanie G. Wiber, *Changing Properties of Property* (Berghahn Books 2006). He published, jointly with Keebet von Benda-Beckman, *Dynamics of Plural Legal Orders.* Special Issue of the *Journal of Legal Pluralism* 53/54 (Lit-Verlag 2006), and *Social Security between Past and Future: Ambonese Networks of Care and Support* (Lit-Verlag 2007).

Keebet von Benda-Beckmann is head of the Project Group "Legal Pluralism" at the Max Planck Institute for Social Anthropology in Halle/Saale, Germany. Since 2003 she has been Honorary Professor of Legal Anthropology at the University of Leipzig, and since 2004 Honorary Professor for Legal Pluralism at the University of Halle/Saale. She has carried out research in West Sumatra, on the Moluccan Island of Ambon, Indonesia and among Moluccan women in the Netherlands. She has published extensively on dispute resolution, social security in developing countries, property and water rights, decentralization, and theoretical issues in the anthropology of law. She co-edited, with Franz von Benda-Beckmann and Anne Griffiths, *Mobile People, Mobile Law: Expanding Legal Relations in a Contracting World* (Ashgate 2005) and, with Franz von Benda-Beckmann and Melanie G. Wiber, *Changing Properties of Property* (Berghahn Books 2006). She published, jointly with Franz von Benda-Beckmann, *Social Security between Past and Future: Ambonese Networks of Care and Support* (Lit-Verlag 2007).

Lorenzo Cañás Bottos, PhD (2004) University of Manchester. He is Professor at the Estonian Institute of Humanities, Tallinn University and occupies the Chair of Social and Cultural Anthropology. He has done research on identity, nation-making and the relationship between religion and politics in the Irish border area and among Old Colony Mennonites in Argentina and Bolivia. His publications include *Old Colony Mennonites in Argentina and Bolivia: Nation Making, Religious Conflict and Imagination of the Future* (Brill 2008); *Christenvolk: Historia y Etnografía de una Colonia Menonita* (Antropofagia 2005); and (as co-editor) *Political Transformation and National Identity Change* (Routledge 2008).

Anindita Chakrabarti works in the area of Sociology of Religion and Social Movements. After receiving her doctoral degree from the Department of Sociology, Delhi University, in 2007 she has joined the Department of Humanities and Social Sciences at the Indian Institute of Technology, Kanpur, as a Lecturer in Sociology. Her publications include "Assertive Religious Identities, the Secular Nation-State and the Question of Pluralism: The Case of the Tablighi Jamaat" in *Assertive Religious Identities: India and Europe*, edited by Satish Saberwal and Mushirul Hasan (Manohar 2006) and "Initiation, 'Re-birth' and the Emergent Congregation: An Analysis of the Svadhyaya Movement in Western India", forthcoming in *Ritual Matters*, edited by Christiane Brosius and Ute Hüsken (Routledge).

Nina Glick Schiller is the Director of the Research Institute for Cosmopolitan Cultures and Professor of Social Anthropology at the University of Manchester, UK. She serves as an Associate of the Max Planck Institute for Social Anthropology, Germany. Glick Schiller founded the journal *Identities: Global Studies in Culture and Power*. Her work on migration explores unequal globalization and transnational processes, the restructuring of cities, nationalism, ethnicity, and racialization, religion, citizenship, medical anthropology. Her most recent work on migration and cities is the focus of the co-authored article "Towards a Comparative Theory of Locality in Migration Studies: Migrant Incorporation and City Scale", *Journal of Migration and Ethnic Studies* 2009.

Anthony Good is Professor of Social Anthropology in Practice at the University of Edinburgh, and currently Head of its School of Social and Political Science. His principal overseas field research has been in Tamil Nadu, South India, focusing initially on family and kinship, especially domestic life-cycle ceremonies, and subsequently on the ceremonial economy linking gods, priests and worshippers in a Hindu temple. He has also carried out policy-related work as a senior consultant for the UK Department for International Development, and is now extensively involved as an expert witness in asylum appeals in the British courts, mainly involving Sri Lankan Tamils. Recent publications include *Worship and the Ceremonial Economy of a Royal South Indian Temple* (Edwin Mellen Press 2004) and *Anthropology and Expertise in the Asylum Courts* (Routledge 2007).

Thomas G. Kirsch is Lecturer at the Department of Anthropology at Goldsmiths College, University of London. Between 1993 and 2001, he conducted extensive ethnographic fieldwork in Zambia. He has published two books on African Christianity, one of them entitled *Spirits and Letters: Reading, Writing and Charisma in African Christianity* (Berghahn Books 2008) and articles in some of the major refereed journals for anthropology and sociology in Germany. Other articles were published in the journals *American Anthropologist* (2004), *Visual Anthropology* (2006) and *American Ethnologist* (2007). Since 2003, he has also conducted ethnographic fieldwork on issues of human safety, security and crime prevention in South Africa.

René Kuppe, Dr. iur., is Professor of Law at Vienna University Law School, Austria. He is doing research on indigenous peoples' rights, with a special focus on indigenous peoples' traditional knowledge and natural resources and indigenous peoples' religious freedom rights. Between 2001 and 2003 he worked as a legal adviser of the Standing Commission of Indigenous Affairs of the National Assembly of Venezuela, and in this function he was involved in the drafting process of a comprehensive national law on the rights of indigenous peoples. Currently he is the coordinator of an EU funded project on "Promotion of the indigenous peoples of Venezuela in the demarcation of their habitats and lands". Together with Richard Potz, he is the editor of *Law and Anthropology. International Yearbook for Legal Anthropology* (Brill).

Stephan Palmié (Dr. Phil, University of Munich 1989; Habilitation, University of Munich 1999) is Associate Professor of Anthropology at the University of Chicago. His research centres on Afro-Cuban religious formations and their relations to a wider Atlantic world, conceptions of embodiment and moral personhood, practices of historical representation and knowledge production, biotechnology, and constructions of race. He is the author of *Das Exil der Götter* (Peter Lang 1991) and *Wizards and Scientists: Explorations in Afro-Cuban Modernity and Tradition* (Duke University Press 2002); editor of *Slave Cultures and the Cultures of Slavery* (University of Tennessee Press 1995) and *Africas of the Americas: Beyond the Search for Origins in the Study of Afro-Atlantic Religions* (Brill 2008); and co-editor of a four volume edition of C.G.A. Oldendorp's late eighteenth-century manuscript on the history of the Moravian missions in the Danish Virgin Islands (VWB-Verlag für Wissenschaft und Bildung 2000, 2002).

Michaela Pelican is a postdoctoral fellow and lecturer in Social Anthropology at the University of Zurich. She has been a researcher with the Max Planck Institute for Social Anthropology in Halle/Saale, and received her PhD from the Martin Luther University Halle-Wittenberg with a thesis on interethnic relations and identity politics in northwest Cameroon. Her publications include articles and book chapters on Fulbe agro-pastoral economy, farmer-herder relations, interethnic friendship, citizenship and minority rights, and transnational relations of Cameroonian migrants. Her latest article “Complexities of indigeneity and autochthony: An African example” has just appeared in *American Ethnologist* 36(1).

Nahda Shehada is Senior Lecturer and convener of the Women, Gender and Development programme at the Institute of Social Studies (The Hague), where she teaches Gender, Culture and Development. She is currently coordinating a three-year research project entitled “Islamic Family Law in Palestine: Text and Context” in cooperation with Zurich and Bern Universities/Switzerland. Between 2005 and 2006, she was a researcher at (ISIM) in Leiden and is associate researcher at Birzeit University/Palestine and chercheure associée at the Laboratoire d’anthropologie urbaine (CNRS, Ivry-sur-Seine, France). Among her recent publications are *Justice without Drama* (Shaker Publishing B.V. 2005), “Le paradoxe du mariage precoce a Gaza” (2005), “Women’s Experience in the *Shari‘a* Court of Gaza City” (2005), “Religious Mediators in Palestine” (2006), “Equity vs. Predictability in Islamic Law” (2008, co-authored with E. Conte), “House of Obedience: Social Norms, Individual Agency and Historical Contingency” (forthcoming), and “Flexibility vs. Rigidity in the Practice of Islamic Family Law” (forthcoming).

Bertram Turner is Senior Researcher at the Max Planck Institute for Social Anthropology in Halle/Saale, Germany and member of the Research Group “Legal Pluralism”. He received his PhD in social anthropology in Munich in 1996 and was Assistant Professor at the Institute of Social Anthropology and African Studies in Munich between 1993 and 2001. He taught anthropology with special reference to religion and legal anthropology and held university teaching positions in Munich, Leipzig and Halle. He is mainly doing fieldwork in Morocco and Canada. Bertram Turner studies the management of natural resources, Islamic activism and conflict settlement in a plural legal configuration in South West Morocco. His recent research is on faith-based dispute management and cultural diversity in Canada. Recent book publication is on asylum and conflict: *Asyl und Konflikt* (Reimer 2005); recent edited volume (together with Günther Schlee) is on retaliation: *Vergeltung* (Campus 2008).

Jacqueline Vel is a research fellow at the Van Vollenhoven Institute for Law, Governance, and Development of Leiden University. Her book *Uma politics: An Ethnography of Democratization in West Sumba, Indonesia, 1986–2006*, appeared in August 2008 with KITLV Press. After gaining a MSc in agricultural economics (Wageningen Agricultural University, 1983) she worked as development worker and researcher on the island of Sumba in Indonesia from 1984 until 1990. She obtained her PhD at Wageningen University (1994) with a dissertation entitled *The Uma Economy: Indigenous Economics and Development Work in Lawonda, Sumba (Eastern Indonesia)* and afterwards moved into Asian Studies at the University of Amsterdam. She participated in two Modern Indonesia projects of KITLV in Leiden. Her current research (since 2006) concerns legal change in post-1998 Indonesia regarding natural resources, access to justice, and socio-legal aspects of bio-fuel production.

Acknowledgements

This volume resulted from an international conference on "The Legitimate and the Supernatural: Law and religion in a complex world" at the Max Planck Institute for Social Anthropology in Halle/Saale, Germany, 25–27 August 2005. The theme had emerged from the work of the Project Group Legal Pluralism at the Max Planck Institute in preparation of the research focus on "Religion in Disputes: Religious Belief, Law and Authority in Dispute Management". We are indebted to David Dichelle for language editing and Gesine Koch, Philipp Humpert and Titus Rebhann for preparing the manuscript and index.

Chapter 1
Law and Religion in Permutation of Order: An Introduction

Bertram Turner and Thomas G. Kirsch

Whatever historicity we attribute to the particularities of global social realities at the turn of the twenty-first century – whether they are assumed to be transient episodes or heralds of a new post-millennial era – observers have remarked that we are currently witnessing consequential transfigurations of which two have provided impetus for the present volume.

The first of these two transfigurations has been exposited eloquently by Jean and John L. Comaroff who in a number of recent publications suggest that – on a global scale, among highly diverse populations, and as part of what they call "millennial capitalism" – there is "a palpable intensification in the resort to legal ways and means" (2005: 12) that involves "the displacement of the political into the legal" (ibid.: 23) and a "fetishism of legalities" (Comaroff and Comaroff 2006: 31). This process, they argue, is signalled by the growing importance of international tribunals and special courts (see also Dembour and Kelly 2007, Politi 2008), the global boom in legal NGOs and rights-claiming movements (see also Rajagopal 2003, Richmond and Carey 2005, Santos and Rodriguez-Garavito 2005) and in human rights advocacy (see also Goodale and Merry 2007, Kurasawa 2007), and the heightened emphasis on constitutionalism after the end of the Cold War (see also Seidman 2006, Bellamy 2007, Waluchow 2007).[1]

The second transfiguration concerns the augmented prominence – some would say: visibility – of religion in many domains of life, in many countries around the world. From the striking role of Orthodox Christian religiosity in Eastern Europe's new democracies (Borowik 2006, Hann 2006), through to Buddhist acts of resistance to the military regime in Burma (Fink 2001, Jordt 2007; see also Houtman 1999), the strengthened transnational presence of Islamic movements (Wiktorowicz 2004, Rubin 2007), and the expansive portfolio of African-initiated proselytization in the global North (Adogame 2002, Simon 2003, Adogame, Gerloff

1 In addition, these transfigurations manifest themselves in the area of restorative justice (see for example Hadley 2001, Chapman and Spong 2003, Tierney 2006). For faith-based organizations (FBOs) with a rights-based approach, see Tyndale (2006); for the relationship between "religion" and human rights, see Barzilai (2007); and for the relationship between "religion" and politico-legal constitutions, see for example Radan, Meyerson and Croucher (2005), Sullivan (2005).

and Hock 2008), there is little doubt that agnostics and atheists increasingly find themselves in company of people of faith. In the 1990s, José Casanova already began to challenge the long-familiar view that modernization had resulted in the secularization of state politics and the privatization of religion. He called attention to the observation that, in the 1980s, "religion throughout the world was in the forefront of various forms of public collective action, agonic as well as discursive, often on both sides of every contested issue, itself being both the subject and the object of contestation and debate" (1994: 66, see also Juergensmeyer 1994). Since its introduction, Casanova's thesis has not only been affirmed and substantiated by the work of other scholars (see for example, Herbert 2003); it seems that the process of what he calls the "deprivatization of modern religion" has even accelerated in the decade following the publication of his book.

The present volume, while taking these two transfigurations as a point of departure, does not attempt to find a peremptory explanation for why they occur or how they are generally connected to each other. Instead, the chapters of this volume examine empirical case studies from various parts of the world (Bolivia, Cameroon, Cuba, Germany, India, Indonesia, Palestine, Morocco, the United Kingdom, the United States and Zambia) in order to elucidate how certain striking instances of these *trans*figurations are *con*figured towards each other.

This intellectual endeavour implies, first, taking notice of the fact that practices and discourses in legal and religious realms are ever-changing and to be seen in relation to sociocultural contextualities. Secondly, it also means bearing in mind that the ideas about the phenomenological existence of "legal" and "religious" realms developed over time and now confront us with copious conceptual biographies and trajectories of diffusion as well as the realization that they are *not* historically endogenous in many of the societies we study.[2]

When taking "the legal" and "the religious" as conceptual metaphors that can help us towards organizing our analytical perspective, however – as is a salient approach in the present volume – these two realms can be said to have in common that they are contested arenas of social interaction, each of which makes available to social actors specific registers for conducting debates, creating evidentialities and plausibilities, and steadying or interrogating relations of power. In addition, to our understanding, both realms have in common that they relate, in one form or the other, to wider problems of "order", both in the symbolic and ideational senses of the word and in the sense of the systematic – usually peaceable, though not power-free – arrangement of social affairs (see also K. von Benda-Beckmann and Pirie 2007).

We therefore suggest that an analytical focus on the intentness on "order" in the two realms can enhance our understanding of how – in present-day post-

2 For a historical discussion of the concept of "religion", see Saler (1987, 2000) and de Vries (2008). For a discussion of the concept of "law" in legal anthropology, see F. von Benda-Beckmann (2002). With F. von Benda-Beckmann we advocate a broad concept of "law" that takes the existence of situated pluralities of normative repertoires into account.

postmodern realities – said "legal"/"religious" transfigurations are configured towards each other. This is to say that, in this book, we proceed on the assumption that there is a homomorphy between "legal" and "religious" realms because each of them operates within dichotomies such as "legality"/"illegality", "natural"/"supernatural", "morality"/"immorality" and "order"/"disorder". At the same time, the asymmetric objectives pursued in each of the two realms – for example, the eradication of "immorality" or transmutation of "disorder" into all-encompassing "order" – in the final analysis turn out to be practical impossibilities because of the fact that the elements of a given dichotomy are necessarily *co*produced with each other. This means, for instance, that there is in fact no (positively valued) notion of "morality" absent the co-presence of a (negatively valued) notion of "immorality" or that, as Emile Durkheim pointed out a long time ago, in order "to say that certain things are supernatural, it is necessary to have the sentiment that a natural order of things exists" (1912: 36, see also Saler 1977, Klass 1995: 25–33). Because of such "pas de deux in which norm and transgression, regulation and exception, redefine each other" (Comaroff and Comaroff 2006: 5), the dichotomies inherent within "legal" and "religious" realms can be said to constitute *simultaneities* ("dis/order", "il/legality", "im/morality", "super/natural") which present themselves like figure-ground phenomena: Whatever element of a given dichotomy you concentrate on, the other element inevitably continues to loom in the background. Therefore, speaking on a more abstract level, one can suggest that the dichotomies in "legal" and "religious" realms are both unified *and* fragmented, stabile *and* fragile, structured *and* processual. In other words, what often appear to be static dichotomies usually are in fact uneasy ambiguities.

Further, we argue in the present volume that contemporary legal/religious transfigurations involve *permutations*, meaning that elements of "legal" and "religious" acts of ordering are at times repositioned within each realm and from one realm to the other. These permutations of order in part result from the fact that, in ethnographic settings like those examined in this volume, "legal" and "religious" realms are relational to – and in certain cases even constitutive of – each other. And they result in categoric transpositions and new social positionalities through which, among other things, "the legal" and "the religious" are blended into each other.

Sovereignties, Rifts, Blurrings

It goes without saying that any attempt to determine how transfigurations in "religious" and "legal" realms are empirically configured towards each other requires thorough consideration of what is meant by "the religious" and "the legal". And yet, when trying to increase the conceptual depth of focus in this regard, it quickly becomes evident that these two notions elude single-layered descriptions.

For one thing, in line with modernist perspectives, "the religious" and "the legal" are often said to be bound within separate institutions – the term "institution" used here in the sense of (more or less formally) organized realms of sociality, each centring on a special dimension of life and regulating discourses and practices within it. As a prominent mode of self-description and a hard standard by which modernity measures and valuates its ("non-modern") Other, such a perspective tends to stress the functional differentiation of institutions and the idea that institutions are related to each other in systematic ways.

In early social science and its offshoots in the present, this modernist separation of "the religious" from "the legal" has repeatedly been contrasted with what has long been reckoned to be a characteristic feature of *non*-modern societies, namely:

> a state which occurs in the history of all the families of mankind, the state at which a rule of law is not yet discriminated from a rule of religion. The members of such a society consider that the transgression of a religious ordinance should be punished by civil penalties, and that the violation of a civil duty exposes the delinquent to divine correction. (Maine 1863: 23)

According to legal historian Henry Sumner Maine, it was only with the ancient Romans that, in the evolution of Western societies, "the legal obligation and the religious duty have ceased to be blended" (1863: 193).

The modernist rift between "religion" and "law" has also been connected to deliberations on "rationality" and "legitimate power" as, for example, prominently formulated in the work of sociologist Max Weber who distinguished traditional and charismatic forms of authority from "rule by virtue of 'legality' [which is exerted] by virtue of the belief in the validity of legal statutes and practical 'competence' based on rational rules" (2004: 34).

In addition, in some sociological approaches (for example Luhmann 1977, Wilson 1982, Olson 2000, Bruce 2002), modernist perspectives are based on the assumption that the process of modernization undermines "religion" so that the latter loses its previously dominant role over other subsystems of society, such as "economy", "politics" and "law". It has been argued that this (alleged) decline of "religion" is adjunct to modern state-building and to an increased differentiation between the public and private spheres, and that it historically culminates in "secularization" – that is, in:

> a social condition manifest in (a) the declining importance of religion for the operation of non-religious roles and institutions such as those of the state and the economy; (b) a decline in the social standing of religious roles and institutions; and (c) a decline in the extent to which people engage in religious practices, display beliefs of a religious kind, and conduct other aspects of their lives in a manner informed by such beliefs. (Bruce 2002: 3)[3]

---

3 For a detailed analysis of the various ways in which "religion" interacts with processes of modernization, see Pollack and Olson 2008.

Taken together, in this view, functional differentiation and the process of secularization transformed a pre-modern *a*symmetrical configuration, in which "the religious realm" encompassed all other realms (including "law"), into a modern symmetrical configuration, in which "the religious realm" is contained in its role as a functional subsystem and is thus positioned – at least in principle and when seen from the perspective of other realms – on the same level as all others.

We posit that this symmetry is generally reached only in principle as histories of modernity are rife with social conflicts over the relationship between the realms. In these histories, periods of balanced complementarity alternate with periods characterized by the endeavours of social actors to make one realm prevail over others – for example, "the economic" over "the political" or "the legal" over "the religious". Moreover, as Bruno Latour (1993) has argued in a different thematic context, histories of modernity are characterized by efforts to "purify" modernist categorical distinctions which are, nonetheless, in fact constantly being challenged and blurred.

Such hybridization is reflected in the existence of internal subdivisions within these realms, for example, when a religious community distinguishes between "spiritual" and "juridical" affairs. But what is more, hybridization also emerges when categorical differentiations of realms are axiomatically rebutted, leading to transfigurations like those invoked in the opening sections of this introductory chapter. To be sure, such permutations do not merely constitute a contemporary materialization. In addressing the history of Christianity in sub-Saharan Africa, for example, Karen Fields has convincingly argued that the frantic reaction of colonial administrators in Northern Rhodesia (now Zambia) to the chiliasm of indigenous members of the Watchtower movement was due to the fact that "the colonial structure had a ready-made space for the God of the Watchtower millennium, because quieter but *kindred gods were cemented into its very foundation*, and because the propagation of belief helped maintain it erect" (1985: 22–3; emphasis added).

In the latter case and other comparable cases that can be found throughout history and across the globe, the hybridization of realms leads to an amalgamation of religious, legal, and political dimensions, a process that is possible because – as we suggest – these realms all have not only something to do with "order", but also with questions of *sovereignty*. As is well known, there are several different approaches to the latter notion.[4] And yet, in the abstract, the concept of "sovereignty" as used in relation to both sources and forms of power, as well as structural operations of law and religion, always insinuates the idea of the existence of a "beyond", that is, of a principled absoluteness which is set apart, posited as axiomatic (*Setzung*), and used as an abstract reference point when engaging in the concrete pragmatics of social discourse and practice.

---

4 For a study on concepts of (state) sovereignty in contemporary contexts and the question of how these concepts are related to the constitution of order, see especially Jacobsen, Sampford and Thakur (2008). For a discussion of how sovereignties are challenged in transnational contexts, see for example Bickerton, Cunliffe and Gourevitch (2007).

When seen in this light, the concept of "sovereignty" bears resemblance, in important aspects, to another notion that has long figured prominently in the anthropology and sociology of religion and in recent times has been employed fruitfully in discussions by legal scholars: "the sacred" in the sense of "things set aside" (Durkheim 1965: 62). In the introduction to their co-edited volume entitled *Law and the Sacred*, Martha Umphrey, Austin Sarat and Lawrence Douglas point out that "it seems that the specter of the sacred always haunts the law" (2007: 1). But they also caution that the idea of an irreconcilability of "the sacred" and "the law" is a historical product that should not prevent us from taking account of the fact that "the sacred" constitutes a *foundation* for the law in at least three domains of modern legality. This includes "theories concerning the moment of founding, interpretations of the status of constitutional texts as 'sacred', and assertions about the status of law more generally as a kind of 'civil religion'" (ibid.: 10). In examining these domains, the introduction to *Law and the Sacred* lays particular emphasis on the ambiguities inherent in "the sacred" by associating it with anthropological and psychoanalytic concepts of taboo, sacred impurity, desire, and fear. According to the authors, this allows us to apprehend a tension in modern law that "concerns less the existence of the sacred in law than the proper relation one ought to exhibit toward the law as it is expressed in sacred moments, objects, or regimes of meaning" (ibid.: 10).

The present volume carries this discussion further by, among other things, turning the spotlight on processes in (and in relation to) "religious" and "legal" realms that concern sovereign acts of *naming*, *classifying*, and *creating symbolic, ideational and social orders*. In pursuing such study, three premises are essential. First, "sovereignty" is a claim to singularity that, in empirical terms, usually comes in the plural. Second, and related to the first point, empirical sovereignties are controversial and contested (see also Hansen and Stepputat 2005). Third, in the context of modern statehood, "the religious" and "the legal" not only make available specific forms of and strategies for claiming "sovereignty" and creating orders, they themselves are the object of acts of classification and order-making by social actors who use them as a means of labelling dimensions of phenomenological reality and constituting power. As mentioned above, both "religion" and "law" therefore represent subjects *and* objects in the dual process of "classifying/ordering" and "being classified/ordered".

It is in the spirit of the latter view that the present volume begins with the observation that, as part of the transfigurations mentioned in the opening section of this chapter, the modernist notion of a clear categorical distinction between "the religious" and "the legal" realms has increasingly been challenged in recent decades. At present, what can be witnessed worldwide is a struggle between actors of different type and scale, some of whom blur religious/legal boundaries, while others commit themselves to sustaining or reintroducing these categorical distinctions.

Broadly speaking, this struggle is about the ontological foundation of sovereignty, the moral grounding of communal life, and the principles, means, and ends of social regulation. More particularly, it is suggested in the present volume that this struggle involves contradictory processes. On the one hand, both "religion" and "law" permit claims of ultimate validity with reference to (what are asserted to be) self-contained authoritative premises. On the other, in post-postmodernity, such claims are increasingly embedded in socio-political settings which relativize self-containedness and consequently make it necessary for social actors to legitimize their claims by specifying the relationship between "religion" and "law". Thus, the religious/legal capacity for social ordering inevitably hinges on and runs parallel to categorical ordering.

At the same time, it is clear that transnational processes have led to increased pluralization and have augmented the interconnectedness of "religious" and "legal" realms – in social, institutional, and categorical terms. In this context, modernist rationales of differentiating between "religion" and "law" and the agencies subscribing to them, including many state agencies worldwide, appear to be undermined by expanding systems of referentiality, while their discourses and practices of religious/legal dissociation nonetheless have to be taken into account by actors and agencies who blur the boundaries between realms.

Given this background, the contributions to this volume inquire into historical and contemporary instances in which the distinction between "religious" and "legal" realms is in dispute. They ask how the relationship between the two realms is conceptualized, negotiated, and enacted in particular socio-political settings, and explore how these processes are influenced by various (state and non-state) agencies of local, translocal and transnational scope. In doing so, and in focusing on the permutations of order between religious and legal normativities, an attempt is made to find new views on the existence and nature of – and to steer clear of the affirmative reiteration of – long-familiar dichotomies, such as the view of "religious law" and "legal religion" as a one-dimensional dichotomy in which religion is conceptualized as legitimating "law" while law is conceptualized as regulating "religion". Further, in contrast to many other scholarly accounts of the relationship between "religion" and "law",[5] this volume presents a symmetrical perspective which places the two realms on a par with each other and privileges neither realm over the other.

---

5 There is a wide range of academic literature that deals with the divide between "law" and "religion" and examines the relationship between these two realms from various angles, focusing especially on "religious law", the constitutional guarantees of the free exercise of religious practice, the relationship between "religion" and state legislation, and the role of "religion" in transnational law and within the human rights context. See for example Sadurski (1992), Bradney (1993), Watson (1996), Ahdar (2000), Feldman (2000), Huxley (2002).

De Jure: Religion

"While we should be knowledgeable about words," Benson Saler cautions in his classic review article on the Latin roots of the term "religion", "we must also struggle against a facile surrender to their authority, an authority that all too often turns out to be unstable or evanescent when probed" (1987: 398). It is perhaps this conjunction of authority and instability – in the sense that, over the centuries, much of its social force had to do with controversies over its becoming or its unbecoming – which lends "religion" such remarkable presence and performativity in the world. For instance, while itself not being part of the originative Divine *logos* as rendered in the Mosaic creation story, the word "religion" later came to be used in iterative speech acts through which humans created, in retrospect, that which they said had created them, but also pejoratively as the evolutionists' synonym for what they reckoned to be creationist "self-deceit".

Such performativity involves definitional work, be it in the form of descriptive, ostensive, prescriptive, real or nominal definitions. However, it is important to note that defining "religion" in a non-circular way is necessarily premised on the existence of an outside of "religion", that is, on the coexistence of a "shifting web of concepts making up the secular" (Asad 2003: 23). And yet, in the case of "religion", the distinction between the *definiendum* (the word that is defined) and the *definiens* (the word that defines) is often precarious and paradoxical, for example, when people who identify with a given *definiendum* of "religion" claim that this *definiendum* essentially encompasses its own *definiens*. For them, "religion" has to be accounted for in its own terms and can neither be understood nor even identified from vantage points outside of "religious" perspectives.[6] Yet since, as mentioned, the existence of "the religious" is premised on the existence of "the secular", the above view continually comes into conflict with those who claim that "secular law", not "religion", should be the superordinate *definiens par excellence*. And this is why the divergence in perspective has time and again – inside and outside of academia, parliaments, mosques and churches – culminated in endeavours to specify the relationship between "law" and "religion".

Of the different ways that this relationship has been delineated in the social sciences, two will be mentioned here. One such way has been to associate specific religions with specific generalized characteristics. For instance, while Christianity has often been described as being a *faith-based* religion (Ruel 1982; see also Kirsch 2004), and Chinese popular religion as being concerned less with orthodoxy than with *orthopraxy* (Watson and Rawski 1988, Watson 1993, 2007, see also Sutton 2007), Judaism and Islam have frequently been interpreted as *legalistic* religions. In an early and influential study on the history of jurisprudence, for example, James Bryce argued that "In Islam, Law is Religion and Religion is Law, because both have the same source and an equal authority, being both contained in the same divine revelation" (1901: II, 218).

---

6 On the category of "religion", see for example McCutcheon (1995).

Another way of determining the relationship between "law" and "religion" has been to consider these two notions in the abstract and to assume that each of them has its own principles and logic. In a book by a prominent proponent of this approach, for example, Harold J. Berman looks at "religion and law in the broadest possible terms – religion as man's sense of the holy, law as man's sense of the just" and suggests "that in all societies, though in widely varying ways, law draws on the sense of the holy partly in order to commit people emotionally to the sense of the just" (1993: 19; see also Berman 1974). On similar lines, the volume *Christianity and Law*, edited by John Witte and Frank Alexander, "is predicated on the assumptions that religion gives law its spirit and inspires its adherence to ritual and justice [while] Law gives religion its structure and encourages its devotion to order and organization" (Witte 2008: 1). Broadly speaking, in this approach, "religion" and "law" are, first, conceived as ideal types and categorically separated in order to, secondly, argue that they are empirically interdependent dimensions.

But of course, as Michel Foucault (1981: 92–102) has persuasively argued, with regard to other thematic contexts, classifying entities and making categorical distinctions always involves power. Seen in this light, the question of what, in a specific context, counts as "law" and what is reckoned to be "religion" is entangled in a power/knowledge nexus that – in constraining and enabling ways – configures people's perspectives on the world. It is in this sense that the relationship between "law" and "religion" is and always has been a *political* issue: relevant to a given polity, and involving authority and power.

Now, as regards societies in the contemporary world, the definition of "religion" that is particularly efficacious is that which is marked out and made authoritative by the legal apparatus of the state. This efficacy, however, does not mean that the definitional process is without contradiction since, as Charles Whelan has observed with regard to US constitutionalism: "The constitutional separation of church and state, and of government and religion, has one somewhat paradoxical result: government must get into the business of defining the nature and functions of religion and churches" (1979: 33).

Speaking to the issues raised above, in his contribution to the present volume, Anthony Good takes the statutes concerning "persecution for reasons of religion" in the *UN Convention Relating to the Status of Refugees* of 1951 as a starting point for his examination of legal precedents from the United Kingdom and the United States which define what legally counts as "religion" in these two countries. Demonstrating, among other things, that ostensible reference to a deity has long been an essential criterion for a belief or practice to legally rate as "religious", Good criticizes the courts' often essentializing and prejudiced understandings of "religion" and advocates the use of anthropologically informed polythetic definitions based on the Wittgensteinian notion of "family resemblances".

While Good's focus on asylum claims allows us to see how the legal definitions of "religion" enable or, in many cases, prevent the protection of refugees from persecution in their home country and their legal-political integration in the receiving country, René Kuppe's chapter looks at the conceptualization of "religion" in legal conflicts between Native American religionists and state agencies in the United States. The legal cases examined in his chapter are similar in that they concern the protection of Native American sacred spaces (such as burial sites) from being involved in development projects which restrict access to these sites or desacralize them by opening them up to the wider public. Kuppe argues that the courts' rulings in these cases violated basic principles of US religious freedom law and discriminated against the indigenous plaintiffs. This was due to the fact that the courts misunderstood Native American religions and implicitly subscribed to ethnocentric Judeo-Christian perspectives according to which, in Kuppe's words, "a religion is *not* endangered by the desecration of sacred places because ... believers can simply continue to practice their religion a few miles away from the respective places".

Both Kuppe and Good point to the fact that courts have on occasion based their jurisdictions and definitions of what constitutes "religion" on expert opinions from the social sciences. Stephan Palmié's contribution to the present volume supports and elaborates this insight by examining in an historical perspective how legal practitioners, social scientists, and state agencies in Cuba have joined forces in articulating and implementing normative visions of "national modernity" by constructing images of an irrational "African religious Other". Palmié traces the changing perceptions of Afro-Cuban wizardry (*brujería*) and explores legal and scientific attempts in early Cuban modernity to eradicate *brujería* as well as more contemporary efforts to celebrate it as an important cultural-religious expression of Cuban national heritage which is seen to be "a powerful antidote against the ideological poison emerging from Hollywood and other sites of global capitalist cultural production". This historical process involves, among other things, the symbolic transformation of confiscated "instruments of *brujería*" from forensic evidence employed in the legal persecution of those accused of *brujería* to scientific objects of knowledge on "religion" that are classified and displayed in museum showcases.

Contested Orders: States and Religious Movements

The question of how a specific definition of "religion" is made legally and politically authoritative by state agencies is connected to broader issues concerning the general relationship between states and "religion". For example, assuming the state's point of view and taking "affiliation" and "tolerance" as criteria in his qualitative analysis of Israeli perceptions of Israel as a liberal-democratic and Jewish state, Steven Mazie has recently identified five ideal-typical models of "state-religion" interrelations, namely: "(1) separation of church and state (unaffiliated/highly tolerant); (2) institutionalized religious pluralism (loosely affiliated/tolerant); (3) anti-religious (unaffiliated/intolerant); (4) theocratic (strongly affiliated/intolerant); and (5) established religion (affiliated/tolerant)" (2006: 6). In each of these types of relationship, the (relative) integration or (relative) separation of "state" and "religion" is established and maintained through legal regulations as well as through more or less secularized political theologies.

On the other hand, assuming the point of view of religious movements and focusing on people's quest for salvation, Bryan Wilson's now classic typology (1973: 22–6) distinguishes between seven types of religious "responses to the world": the "conversionist" response strives for the religious transformation of the self, leading to a new orientation to the world; the "revolutionist" response supposes that the secular world needs to be radically overturned and then restored with the help of divine forces; the "introversionist" response begins with the assumption that salvation is only possible through withdrawal from the world; the "manipulationist" response is based on the idea that salvation "is possible in the world and evil might be overcome if men learn the right means, improved techniques, to deal with their problems" (ibid.: 24); the "thaumaturgical" response is mainly concerned with the religious practitioner's personal relief from evil; the "reformist" response seeks religiously informed amendments of the secular world; and finally, the "utopian" response aims at the (peaceful) reconstruction of the world according to divine principles.

When applying these two typologies to the ethnographic case studies as discussed in the chapters in this volume, it is noteworthy, first, that the chapters exemplify a wide range of different "state-religion" interrelations, ranging from the attempt by religious institutions to be separate from the secular world, as in the case of the Old Colony Mennonites examined by Lorenzo Cañás Bottos, to the endeavours by African migrants in Germany to attain citizenship in the country of immigration via participation in Pentecostal churches, as demonstrated in the chapter by Nina Glick Schiller. Secondly, using Wilson's typology to probe into the legal dimension of "state-religion" interrelations, it becomes evident in the present volume that, of the various religious forms of "responding" to the world, it is the "manipulationist" response – more particularly, the manipulation of *judicalized* ways of ordering – that is playing an increasingly important role in how religious practitioners relate to secular domains. In these cases, law becomes a resource for micro- and macropolitical manoeuvring that is employed, in various ways and to different ends, by both non-religious and religious actors. It lends itself to being employed this way because, as Jean and John L. Comaroff have pointed out, "the language of the law affords an ostensibly neutral medium for people of difference – different cultural worlds, different social endowments, different material circumstances, differently constructed identities – to make claims on each other and the polity, to enter into contractual relations, to transact unlike values, and to deal with their conflicts" (2000: 329). On the side of religious institutions and movements, this judicial manoeuvring not only engages "law" as a secular means to religious salvation and as a technique to power, but also transfigures political theology into what has been called "theo-legality" and "legal theology" (J.L. Comaroff 2006: 5). Instead of "religion" being used to legitimate "law", "law" is used here to legitimate "religion", leading, in many cases, to the state-authorized accreditation of religious identities as well as the legal inscription and canonization of religious values.

However, as the chapter by Anindita Chakrabarti in the present volume makes clear, members of religious movements have not only used state law in order to protect themselves from non-religious forces, but also to solve conflicts *within* the movements themselves. Chakrabarti demonstrates how libel and succession disputes in the Svadhyaya movement in contemporary India came with a series of court cases over the access to and the closing of temples that were filed by different sections of the movement and involved judgments on the question of whether this reformed Hindu movement constitutes "religion" or not. In some of these judgments, the question of who has the right to act as a claimant in the name of "religion" was made contingent upon the respective person's legitimacy in feeling offended in his or her "religious sentiments". Therefore, since "libel could be filed only by the aggrieved persons and *not* by others on their behalf", the display or attribution of "religious sentiments" to some extent determined a person's legal capacity in state courts. Taken together, Chakrabarti describes a dialectic process in which "religion articulates and justifies itself in the legal-bureaucratic language of the state, while the state legitimizes itself as secular by intervening and arbitrating on the question of 'religion'".

In marked contrast to this example of what Chakrabarti calls a "judicial religion", the chapter by Lorenzo Cañás Bottos deals with the strategies employed by a religious community when trying to avoid judicial manoeuvring. Retracing the history of transnational movements of Old Colony Mennonites, Cañás Bottos shows how the Mennonites' striving for separation from the world was repeatedly linked to them being granted politico-legal privileges by state authorities, in return for which they were expected to contribute to projects of internal colonization, such as in the case of late eighteenth- and early nineteenth-century Russia. He argues with regard to present-day Mennonite colonies in Latin America that Mennonite colonies are an instance of "embedded sovereignty" where "the exception" and "the rule" are mutually constitutive in political and religious spheres. However, being "the exception" within the states they settle makes it difficult for Mennonite leaders to deal with *internal* exceptions, that is, with the legal question of what to do with what they consider to be religiously subversive acts by members of the colony. Given this background, Cañás Bottos demonstrates that excommunication is usually circumvented while the (alleged) dissenters are isolated and spatially externalized, thus making sure that they will either conform to the dominant religious discourses and practices or leave "voluntarily".

Nina Glick Schiller's chapter demonstrates that universalist claims by religions like Christianity can be strategically invoked by migrants who seek both incorporation into transnational religious networks *and* local incorporation into the citizenry of the country of immigration. Her comparative inquiry into Pentecostal congregations in small-scale cities in Germany and the United States starts off from the observation that these communities, although established and run by immigrants, do not define membership in ethnic terms. Instead, what is promoted in these communities is a supra-ethnic and supra-national religious identity which – in some sense not despite but *because* of its transnationalist logic – is considered by migrants to be a means of influencing the legal status of one's residence in the new country. Thus, using a universalistic Christian charter in order to insert themselves into local socialities and to claim legal rights to citizenship, migrant members of one of the churches even had specific prayers for passports.

Permutations on the Transnational Scale

As became clear above, permutations of order are not necessarily contained within states but in many cases transcend what Liisa Malkki has aptly termed "the national order of things" (1995). In acting on a global scale, present-day religious movements align their repertoires of normativities in various ways (Lucas and Robbins 2004, Juergensmeyer 2005, Eisenstadt 2007) with processes of transnational legal standardization. In doing so, some grassroots and top-down movements (Rudolph and Piscatori 1997) have transmogrified into rights-claiming movements – a process that, in the case of top-down movements, sometimes involves endeavours to legally institutionalize faith-based values by inserting them into discourses and practices of restorative, reconciliatory, and transitional justice (for example Hadley 2001, Chapman and Spong 2003, Tierney 2006).

It is this reconfiguration of "religion" and "law" in the context of transnationalism that is addressed in the chapters of the third section of the present volume. Claims to "religious" and/or "legal" sovereignty – and acts of contestation against them – are often embedded in trans-scalar arrangements, as Bertram Turner argues with regard to interactions between international development cooperation and Islamic activism in Morocco, Thomas G. Kirsch establishes with reference to the transnational diffusion of church constitutions to Zambia, and which Michaela Pelican demonstrates with a view to the influence of global human rights discourses on interpretations of witchcraft in Cameroon (Tsing 2000, Herod and Wright 2002).

Exploring how registers of ordering are diffused transnationally not only allows us to shed light on global-local entanglements but also on how scalar processes are connected to permutations within and between registers of ordering. What is noteworthy here is the fact that, in many cases, controversies about claims to "religious" and/or "legal" sovereignty differ according to the particular contextuality and the scalar range of validity of a given claim. In other words, claims and counterclaims to sovereignty are made and assessed in terms of their respective positionality within transnational arenas and local fields: What appears improper and illegitimate in one scalar configuration appears proper and legitimate in another.

Furthermore, in such scalar configurations with their peculiar waverings between homogenization and diversification, what is meant by "the legal" and "the religious" is dynamic and unmistakably equivocal. This ambiguity notwithstanding, both realms are often enacted in the form of claims to universal truth that currently reverberate in the remotest areas of the globe (see, for example,

F. and K. von Benda-Beckmann 2007) and at times compete with each other in a mutually exclusivist way. The latter point indicates that projects aiming at globally standardized notions of justice and lawfulness are in part chimeral, in part utopian. In addition, as a recent volume edited by Mark Juergensmeyer (2005) illustrates, local reactions to competing claims to universal truth take a variety of forms, ranging from resistance to accommodation. If people decide to resist, the idealistic vision of justice on a worldwide scale is undermined. Nevertheless, some scholars, among them William Sullivan and Will Kymlicka (2007), have expressed "tempered optimism" that a unified global system of ethics is possible.[7]

But it is not only that *religious* movements have transfigured into *rights*-claiming movements. By the same token, but with different effects, it also emerged in recent decades that self-proclaimed secular institutions progressively came under the influence of transnational faith-based perspectives, promises of salvation, and political visions of a God-given empire.[8] Social actors and agencies within transnational spheres – such as trans-state migrants and development agencies – thus became embroiled in conflicts over religious/legal sovereignty. In the process, globally circulating templates play an important role in allocating these actors and agencies specific positions in localized "religious" and/or "legal" realms. What is more, such acts of interpellation have increasingly come to be influenced by discursive transmutations that turn articles of *law* into something like articles of *faith* (see also Berman 1993, 2005: 80, 82f.). These transmutations from "the legal" to "the religious" run parallel to the juridification of politics mentioned above (compare Comaroff and Comaroff 2006) and in this way contribute to developments which have lately been discussed with regard to the globalization of ethics (Kymlicka 2007: 10).

Meanwhile, in recent debates about the prospects, conditions and modalities of "global order" and "global civil society", the relation between "the legal" and "the religious" has been a point of repeated contention and has been approached from a variety of perspectives. John Esposito and Michael Watson (2000), for example, argue that "religion" is more an *object* of processes of global ordering than it is a constitutive element of these processes. Shmuel Eisenstadt (2007), on the other hand, emphasizes that current transformations of order on the global scale do not entail a "clash of civilizations" but one of *domains* – a point of view with which the present volume engages by questioning the idea of bound domains. And Hanne Petersen argues that "it is amongst non-state parts of world society and in local societies that we should look for emerging practices and norms which combine secular and religious traditions in a new way" (2007: 220) – a perspective that is of importance for several chapters in this volume.

7 It appears that, among these different fields of contestation, the UN Declaration of Human Rights is among the most prominent (see also Barzilai 2007).

8 See, for instance, Belshaw and Caldrisi (2002) and Marshall and van Saanen (2007) on the cooperation between the World Bank and faith-based organizations (FBOs).

The chapters of the third section of this volume deal with some important dimensions of these transnational permutations of order. Michaela Pelican explores how state and non-state agencies in contemporary Cameroon react to witchcraft and accusations of witchcraft. In line with anthropological studies that understand the preoccupation with the occult in present-day Africa not as a simple reiteration of "traditional" witchcraft beliefs and practices but as a creative response to the challenge of global modernities, Pelican broadens the analysis of customary and state legal approaches to witchcraft by investigating how faith-based organizations frame accusations of witchcraft in terms of rights discourses emerging in the global arena. She discusses how, during a recent anti-witchcraft conference in northwest Cameroon, Christian activists spoke out against the violent and unlawful prosecution of suspected witches, demanding that the containment of witchcraft should follow human rights standards. The contrast between this approach and those described by early ethnographic studies of witchcraft and witchcraft containment in sub-Saharan Africa – for example, in Evans-Pritchard's *Witchcraft, Oracles and Magic among the Azande* (1937) – could hardly be larger.

The chapter by Thomas G. Kirsch addresses the transnational diffusion of models of canonized legality in the form of Christian church constitutions. Discussing the distinction between "the letter of the law" and "the spirit of the law" in the history of ideas and pointing to the far-ranging historical trajectory of the constitutional law of a Pentecostal-charismatic church in present-day rural Zambia, Kirsch explores how members of the church relate their constitution to other recognized sources of written and orally transmitted religious laws, namely the Bible and the Holy Spirit. He argues that the Holy Spirit is considered there to be a force that enables religious practitioners to discover systematic unity in religious-legal diversity. Thus, by accommodating the rational-legal attributes of the constitution to the church's Pentecostal-charismatic premises, reading this constitution aims at identifying – literally speaking – "the spirit of the law".

While the previous two chapters focus on trans-scalar configurations of "the religious" and "the legal" with regard to issues of social morality (Pelican) and religious constitutionalism (Kirsch), the chapter by Bertram Turner explores how globally circulating moral-religious discourses are connected to the expansion of economic neoliberalism. According to Turner, people in rural Morocco increasingly see themselves to be confronted with moralizing messages as propagated by transnational Islamic movements and international faith-based organizations, but also by non-religious development agencies that subscribe to a salvation-oriented concept of development. However, since the local economy and the regulation of access to natural resources have long been based on religious parameters, these new moral-religious discourses have had adverse effects on local exploitation of resources, leading not only to an increased economic vulnerability but also to changes in how the normative order of local modes of production is negotiated.

Registers of Argumentation and the Negotiation of Order

We have suggested above that "law" and "religion" are both subjects and objects in the dual process of "classifying/ordering" and "being classified/ordered" and that, through this process, relations of power can be stabilized or else be called into question. The fourth, and final, section of the present volume builds on this understanding and examines, with a view to ethnographic case studies from Indonesia and Palestine, how social actors make *self-authorizing* reference to "legal" and/or "religious" sovereignties, and in so doing, strategically draw on discursive intersections between religious and legal registers of argumentation when negotiating order.

This analytical focus on discursiveness and the use of different registers of argumentation by social actors marks a break with previous approaches in the social sciences that emphasize the institutionally bound nature of "law" and "religion". By taking this approach we try to show consideration for processes in the present-day world that entail a convergence between, on the one hand, the neoliberal privatization and informalization of judicature (Farrow 2008) and, on the other hand, the emancipation of religion from institutionalized settings through an increased emphasis on personal spirituality (Heffner 1998, Davie et al. 2003, Berman 2005, Flanagan and Jupp 2007). These processes open up new spaces for social agency whereby individual discursive practices (compare Day 2008) are brought to bear in public spheres (Herbert 2003), endowing "law" and "religion" with social power beyond formal institutions.

As the broad academic literature on multiculturalism and cultural diversity (for example Laden and Owen 2007, Mehdi et al. 2007, Tierney 2007) as well as the chapters by Jacqueline Vel, Franz and Keebet von Benda-Beckmann and Nahda Shehada in this volume attest, the aforementioned negotiation of order often involves the blending of "religious" and "legal" realms when the construction of social identities and categories of social differentiation, such as gender, is concerned (K. von Benda-Beckmann 2001). Of course, attitudes of custodians of the divide between "the religious" and "the legal" are characterized by an aversion against the contamination of "pure dogma", be it "secular legal", or "religious". At the same time, however, tensions, disjunctions and incompatibilities between different scales of judiciary, sociality, and polity – whether national, regional, or local – allow for politicized manoeuvrings between wide-ranging official doctrines of "law" and "religion" on the one hand, and various local repertoires of normativity on the other. This is made possible by the existence of complex histories of plurality which provide social actors and agencies with a multitude of cultural registers and allow them – dependent on context, situation, and strategy – to either merge or separate "legal" and "religious" strands of argumentation.

This socio-political manoeuvring is particularly pronounced in processes involving the formation, performance and politics of identity. As has been widely documented in recent decades, "legal" and "religious" registers are (again?) playing an increasingly important role in disambiguating multiple identities and demarcating boundaries and permeabilities within and between different forms of group membership. In this process, the paradigm of modernist political self-identification, "national identity", becomes challenged by social groupings which self-identify as religious-normative communities, and in so doing, factor out other criteria of group identity such as ethnic membership, territorial belonging, and civic relationality to the state.

What is more, the politics of identity is often affected by tensions between different normativities, for instance, when egalitarian notions of humanity are confronted with faith-based and normative ideologies that emphasize social stratification. In this way, religious ideas of "chosen people" (Smith 2007) or divinely sanctioned gender differences not only shape the social construction of people's identity, but also play a crucial role in the constitution of order in the familial and private spheres of life. The latter point also makes clear that the negotiation of identity via "religious" and/or "legal" registers frequently takes the form of a struggle between different registers of identification which serve as powerful discursive tools when the allocation of rights and duties and the regulation of access to resources are up for debate among different individual or collective claimants.

As Jacqueline Vel demonstrates in her contribution to the present volume, politicians have to take such configurations into account when standing for elections. Her chapter sets out with a discussion of how democratization and political decentralization in Indonesia since the late 1990s have resulted in the inclusion of religious elements into regional politics and legislation, leading to situations where aspirants to political offices take a strategic recourse to "religion" as a means of legitimizing their claim to leadership. Vel thus shows that, while the rules for holding elections are set by and legitimized through Indonesian state law, the symbolic enactments during election campaigns through which candidates seek legitimacy towards the electorate take recourse to religious registers derived from, for example, Christianity and local religiosities. In this way, politicians skilfully hybridize different registers of ordering, with some of these registers having operational functions and others playing a representational role.

Often, such political dynamics take place in contexts that are characterized by the existence of parallel legal institutions, such as religious courts, state courts and other, local decision-making agencies. These institutions may be specialized, and claim jurisdiction over different fields of social "transgression" and "deviance"; in other cases they may compete with one another and present themselves as options for forum-shoppers in pluralist legal fields (K. von Benda-Beckmann 1981). In addition, these institutions are usually based on different forms of legitimation and empowerment which, in turn, influences how they are, in practical terms, brought into relationship with each other. With this in mind, in their contribution to this volume, Franz and Keebet Benda-Beckmann examine inheritance disputes in Indonesia to investigate how power relations are negotiated between different sets of institutions and how social actors make strategic use of the different options and registers provided by them. Their chapter thus highlights the entangled relationship between "religion", "traditional law", and state agencies in the Indonesian context and shows that one and the same actor may argue and act differently according to circumstances, and in so doing, advocate either that "law" and "religion" should be categorically differentiated, or that they should be set in a hierarchical order, or otherwise that they are not separable at all.

Strategies of negotiating and manoeuvring between different legal/religious orders are also explored by Nahda Shehada in the final chapter of the present volume. Examining Islamic family law as practiced in contemporary Palestine, Shehada shows how women communicate their interests in state-controlled *shari'a* courts and how some judges support them in doing so by strategically shifting between formal and informal means of legal settlement. Her chapter combines an analysis of written legal sources with an ethnographic case study in order to explore disjunctions between the codified legal framework and the situated logic of judicial reasoning. This reasoning, Shehada argues, is characterized by a high degree of "indeterminacy, ambiguity, [and] uncertainty in the interplay of codified law, social customs, and the multi-referential framework of judges". Judges are thus at times confronted with the dilemma that an application of codified law appears "unjust" when seen from the perspective of the moral principles of the *shari'a*. Shehada demonstrates that judges resolve this dilemma by refraining from making written records of their interventions, relying solely on orality instead. In this way, law takes on a volatility similar to that of religious revelations.

Prologue to Conclusions

If, in this introduction, we have touched on several topics of "religion" and "law", and in so doing, have explored scalar arrangements, stressed that normativity is a social practice, spoken about the plurality of claims to sovereign singularity, and addressed the simultaneity of "ordering" and "being ordered", we have also wavered between realist and nominalist accounts of the two realms: religion/"religion" and law/"law". This is no coincidence. As an object of discourse and practice, "religion" and "law" is discussed, classified, and enacted in a variety of ways. As a subject of discourse and practice, religion and law provide registers and ways of talking, classifying, and acting. This book is an attempt to capture the unstable simultaneity of these moments and the movements between them, and to have a look at how the two realms – at times and in various ways – blend into each other, dislodging internal unity, and dichotomous juxtapositions.

References

Adogame, A. 2002. Traversing Local–Global Religious Terrain: African New Religious Movements in Europe. *Zeitschrift für Religionswissenschaft*, 10, 33–49.

Adogame, A., Gerloff, R. and Hock, K. (eds) 2008. *Christianity in Africa and the Africa Diaspora: The Appropriation of a Scattered Heritage*. London: Continuum.

Ahdar, R.J. (ed.) 2000. *Law and Religion*. Aldershot: Ashgate.

Asad, T. 2003. *Formations of the Secular: Christianity, Islam, Modernity*. Stanford: Stanford University Press.

Barzilai, G. (ed.) 2007. *Law and Religion*. Aldershot: Ashgate.

Bellamy, R. 2007. *Political Constitutionalism. A Republican Defence of the Constitutionality of Democracy*. Cambridge: Cambridge University Press.

Belshaw, D. and Caldrisi, R. (eds) 2002. *Faith in Development: Partnership between the World Bank and the Churches of Africa*. Oxford: Regnum Books and World Bank Publications.

Benda-Beckmann, F. von. 2002. Who's Afraid of Legal Pluralism? *Journal of Legal Pluralism*, 47, 37–82.

Benda-Beckmann, F. von and Benda-Beckmann, K. von 2007. Transnationalisation of Law, Globalisation and Legal Pluralism: A Legal Anthropological Perspective, in *Law Reform in Asia since the Crisis*, edited by C. Antons and V. Gessner. Oxford and Portland, OR: Hart, 53–80.

Benda-Beckmann, K. von. 1981. Forum Shopping and Shopping Forums. *Journal of Legal Pluralism*, 19, 117–59.

Benda-Beckmann K. von. 2001. Transnational Dimensions of Legal Pluralism, in *Begegnung und Konflikt – eine kulturanthropologische Bestandsaufnahme*, edited by W. Fikentscher. München: H.C. Beck, 33–48.

Benda-Beckmann K. von and Pirie, F. (eds) 2007. *Order and Disorder: Anthropological Perspectives*. New York: Berghahn Books.

Berman, H.J. 1974. *The Institution of Law and Religion*. London: SCM Press.

Berman, H.J. 1993. *Faith and Order: The Reconciliation of Law and Religion*. Atlanta: The Scholars Press.

Berman, H.J. 2005. Faith and Law in a Multicultural World, in *Religion in Global Civil Society*, edited by M. Juergensmeyer. Oxford: Oxford University Press, 69–89.

Bickerton, C., Cunliffe, P. and Gourevitch, A. (eds) 2007. *Politics without Sovereignty: A Critique of Contemporary International Relations*. London: University College London Press.

Borowik, I. (ed.) 2006. *Religions, Churches and Religiosity in Post-Communist Europe*. Kraków: Nomos.

Bradney, A.G.D. 1993. *Religions, Rights and Laws*. Leicester: Leicester University Press.

Bruce, S. 2002. *God is Dead: Secularization in the West*. Oxford: Blackwell Publishers.

Bryce, J. 1901. *Studies in History and Jurisprudence*. 2 vols. Oxford. Clarendon Press.

Casanova, J. 1994. *Public Religions in the Modern World*. Chicago: University of Chicago Press.

Chapman, G. and Spong, B. (eds) 2003. *Religion and Reconciliation in South Africa: Voices of Religious Leaders*. Philadelphia: Templeton Foundation Press.
Comaroff, J. and Comaroff, J.L. 2000. Millennial Capitalism: First Thoughts on a Second Coming. *Public Culture*, 12(2), 291–343.
Comaroff, J. and Comaroff, J.L. 2005. *Ethnicity, Inc.: On Indigeneity and its Interpellations*. Keynote lecture. Forthcoming 2009. *Ethnicity Inc*. Chicago: University of Chicago Press.
Comaroff, J. and Comaroff, J.L. (eds) 2006. *Law and Disorder in the Postcolony*. Chicago: University of Chicago Press.
Comaroff, J.L. 2006. *Reflections on the Anthropology of Law, Governance, and Sovereignty in a Brave Neo World*. Keynote lecture at the conference "Law and Governance", Max Planck Institute for Social Anthropology, Halle/Saale, Germany.
Davie, G, Heelas, P. and Woodhead, L. (eds) 2003. *Predicting Religion: Christian, Secular and Alternative Futures*. Aldershot: Ashgate.
Day, A. (ed.) 2008. *Religion and the Individual: Belief, Practice, Identity*. Aldershot: Ashgate.
Dembour, M.-B. and Kelly, T. (eds) 2007. *Paths to International Justice: Social and Legal Perspectives*. Cambridge: Cambridge University Press.
Durkheim, E. 1912. *Les formes elémentaires de la vie religieuse. Le système totémique en Australie*. Paris: Alcan.
Durkheim, E. 1965. *The Elementary Forms of Religious Life*. New York: The Free Press.
Eisenstadt, S. 2007. The Resurgence of Religious Movements in Processes of Globalization – Beyond the End of History or the Clash of Civilizations, in *Democracy and Human Rights in Multicultural Societies*, edited by M. Koenig and P. de Guchteneire. Aldershot: Ashgate, 239–50.
Esposito, J.L. and Watson, M. (eds) 2000. *Religion and Global Order*. Cardiff: University of Wales Press.
Evans-Pritchard, E.E. 1937. *Witchcraft, Oracles and Magic among the Azande*. Oxford: Oxford University Press.
Farrow, T.C.W. 2008. *Public Justice, Private Dispute Resolution and Democracy. Comparative Research in Law and Political Economy (CLPE)*. Research Paper No. 18.
Feldman, S.M. (ed.) 2000. *Law and Religion: A Critical Anthology*. New York: New York University Press.
Fields, K.E. 1985. *Revival and Rebellion in Colonial Central Africa*. Princeton: Princeton University Press.
Fink, C. 2001. *Living Silence: Burma under Military Rule*. London: Zed Books.
Flanagan, K. and Jupp, P.C. (eds) 2007. *A Sociology of Spirituality*. Aldershot: Ashgate.
Foucault, M. 1981. *The History of Sexuality*, vol. I. Harmondsworth: Penguin.

Goodale, M. and Merry, S.M. (eds) 2007. *The Practice of Human Rights: Tracking Law between the Global and the Local*. Cambridge: Cambridge University Press.

Hadley, M. (ed.) 2001. *The Spiritual Roots of Restorative Justice*. New York: New York University Press.

Hann, C. (ed.) 2006. *The Postsocialist Religious Question: Faith and Power in Central Asia and East-Central Europe*. Münster: Lit-Verlag.

Hansen, T.B. and Stepputat, F. (eds) 2005. *Sovereign Bodies: Citizens, Migrants, and States in the Postcolonial World*. Princeton: Princeton University Press.

Heffner, R.W. 1998. Multiple Modernities: Christianity, Islam, and Hinduism in a Globalizing Age. *Annual Review of Anthropology*, 27, 83–104.

Herbert, D. 2003. *Religion and Civil Society: Rethinking Public Religion in the Contemporary World*. Aldershot: Ashgate.

Herod, A. and Wright, M. (eds) 2002. *Geographies of Power. Placing Scale*. Malden, MA: Blackwell Publishers.

Houtman, G. 1999. *Mental Culture in Burmese Crisis Politics: Aung San Suu Kyi and the National League for Democracy*. Tokyo: ILCAA.

Huxley, A. (ed.) 2002. *Religion, Law and Tradition: Comparative Studies in Religious Law*. London: RoutledgeCurzon.

Jacobsen, T., Sampford, C.J.G. and Thakur, R.C. (eds) 2008. *Re-envisioning Sovereignty: The End of Westphalia?* Aldershot: Ashgate.

Jordt, I. 2007. *Burma's Mass Lay Meditation Movement: Buddhism and the Cultural Construction of Power*. Athens: Ohio University Press.

Juergensmeyer, M. 1994. *The New Cold War? Religious Nationalism Confronts the Secular State*. Berkeley: University of California Press.

Juergensmeyer, M. (ed.) 2005. *Religion in Global Civil Society*. Oxford: Oxford University Press.

Kirsch, T.G. 2004. Restaging the Will to Believe. Religious Pluralism, Anti-syncretism, and the Problem of Belief. *American Anthropologist*, 106 (4), 699–711.

Klass, M. 1995. *Ordered Universes: Approaches to the Anthropology of Religion*. Boulder: Westview Press.

Kurasawa, F. 2007. *The Work of Global Justice: Human Rights as Practices*. Cambridge: Cambridge University Press.

Kymlicka, W. 2007. Introduction: The Globalizations of Ethics, in *The Globalization of Ethics*, edited by W.M. Sullivan and W. Kymlicka. Cambridge: Cambridge University Press, 1–16.

Laden A.S. and Owen, D. (eds) 2007. *Multiculturalism and Political Theory*. Cambridge: Cambridge University Press.

Latour, B. 1993. *We Have Never Been Modern*. Cambridge, MA: Harvard University Press.

Lucas, P.C. and Robbins, T. (eds) 2004. *New Religious Movements in the Twenty-First Century: Legal, Political, and Social Challenges in a Global Perspective*. New York: Routledge.

Luhmann, N. 1977. *Die Funktion der Religion*. Frankfurt am Main: Suhrkamp.
Maine, H.S. 1863. *Ancient Law*. London: John Murray.
Malkki, L.H. 1995. Refugees and Exile: From "Refugee Studies" to the National Order of Things. *Annual Review of Anthropology*, 24, 495–523.
Marshall, K. and van Saanen, M.B. 2007. *Development and Faith: Where Mind, Heart, and Soul Work Together*. Washington: World Bank Publications.
Mazie, S.V. 2006. *Israel's Higher Law: Religion and Liberal Democracy in the Jewish State*. Lanham: Lexington Books.
McCutcheon, R.T. 1995. The Category "Religion" in Recent Publications. A Critical Survey. *Numen*, 42(3), 284–309.
Mehdi, R., Petersen, H., Sand, E., Woodman, G.R. (eds) 2007. *Religion and Law in Multicultural Societies*. Copenhagen: DJØF Publishing.
Olsen, D.V.A. 2000. *The Secularization Debate*. Lanham: Rowman and Littlefield.
Petersen, H. 2007. Changing Traditions, Preserving Values? in *Religion and Law in Multicultural Societies*, edited by R. Mehdi, H. Petersen, E. Sand and G.R. Woodman. Copenhagen: DJØF Publishing, 217–36.
Politi, M. (ed.) 2008. *The International Criminal Court and National Jurisdictions*. Aldershot: Ashgate.
Pollack, D. and Olson, D.V.A. (eds) 2008. *The Role of Religion in Modern Societies*. New York: Routledge.
Radan, P., Meyerson, D. and Croucher, R.F. (eds) 2005. *Law and Religion: God, the State and the Common Law*. London: Routledge.
Rajagopal, B. 2003. *International Law from Below: Development, Social Movements and Third World Resistance*. Cambridge: Cambridge University Press.
Richmond, O.P. and Carey, H.F. (eds) 2005. *Subcontracting Peace: The Challenges of NGO Peacebuilding*. Aldershot: Ashgate.
Rubin, B. (ed.) 2007. *Political Islam: Critical Concepts in Islamic Studies*. 3 vols. London: Routledge.
Rudolph, S.H. and Piscatori, J. (eds) 1997. *Transnational Religion and Fading States*. Boulder, CO: Westview Press.
Ruel, M. 1982. Christians as Believers, in *Religious Organization and Religious Experience*, edited by J. Davis. London: Academic Press, 9–31.
Sadurski, W. (ed.) 1992. *Law and Religion*. New York: New York University Press.
Saler, B. 1977. Supernatural as a Western Category. *Ethos*, 5(1), 31–53.
Saler, B. 1987. *Religio* and the Definition of Religion. *Cultural Anthropology*, 2(3), 395–9.
Saler, B. 2000. *Conceptualizing Religion: Immanent Anthropologists, Transcendent Natives, and Unbounded Categories*. New York: Berghahn Books.
Santos, B. de Sousa and Rodriguez-Garavito, C.A. (eds) 2005. *Law and Globalization from Below: Towards a Cosmopolitan Legality*. Cambridge: Cambridge University Press.

Sarat, A., Douglas, L. and Umphrey, M.M. (eds) 2007. *Law and the Sacred.* Stanford: Stanford University Press.
Seidman, L.M. 2006. Critical Constitutionalism Now. *Fordham Law Review*, 75, 575–92.
Simon, B. 2003. *Afrikanische Kirchen in Deutschland.* Frankfurt am Main: Otto Lembeck.
Smith, A.D. 2007. *Chosen Peoples. Sacred Sources of National Identity*. Oxford: Oxford University Press.
Sullivan, W.F. 2005. *The Impossibility of Religious Freedom*. Princeton: Princeton University Press.
Sullivan, W.M. and Kymlicka, W. (eds) 2007. *The Globalization of Ethics*. Cambridge: Cambridge University Press.
Sutton, D.S. 2007. *Ritual; Cultural Standardization, and Orthopraxy in China: Reconsidering James L. Watson's Ideas*. Beverly Hills: Sage Publications.
Tierney, N. 2006. Religion, the Globalization of War, and Restorative Justice. *Buddhist-Christian Studies*, 26, 79–87.
Tierney, S. (ed.) 2007. *Accommodating Cultural Diversity*. Aldershot: Ashgate.
Tsing, A.L. 2000. The Global Situation. *Cultural Anthropology*, 15(3), 327–60.
Tyndale, W.R. (ed.) 2006. *Visions of Development: Faith-based Initiatives*. Aldershot: Ashgate.
Umphrey, M.M., Sarat, A. and Douglas, L. 2007. The Sacred in Law: An Introduction, in *Law and the Sacred*, edited by A. Sarat, L. Douglas and M.M. Umphrey. Stanford: Stanford University Press, 1–28.
de Vries, H. (ed.) 2008. *Religion: Beyond a Concept*. New York: Fordham University Press.
Waluchow, W.J. 2007. Constitutionalism, in *Stanford Encyclopedia of Philosophy*. Available at: http://plato.stanford.edu/entries/constitutionalism/#Bib [accessed: 3 November 2008].
Watson, A. 1996. *The State, Law and Religion: Pagan Rome*. Athens: University of Georgia Press.
Watson, J.L. 1993. Rites or Beliefs? The Construction of a Unified Culture in Late Imperial China, in *China's National Identity*, edited by S. Kim and D. Lowell. Ithaca: Cornell University Press, 80–113.
Watson, J.L. 2007. Orthopraxy Revisited. *Modern China*, 33(1), 154–8.
Watson, J.L. and Rawski, E.S. (eds) 1988. *Death Ritual in Late Imperial and Modern China*. Berkeley: University of California Press.
Weber, M. 2004. *The Vocation Lectures: Politics as a Vocation; Science as a Vocation*. Indianapolis: Hackett Publishing.
Whelan, C.M. 1979. Governmental Attempts to Define Church and Religion. *Annals of the American Academy of Political and Social Science*, 446, 32–51.
Wiktoriwicz, Q. (ed.) 2004. *Islamic Activism: A Social Movement Theory Approach*. Bloomington: Indiana University Press.
Wilson, B. 1973. *Magic and the Millenium*. London: Heinemann.

Wilson, B. 1982. *Religion in Sociological Perspective*. Oxford: Oxford University Press.

Witte, J. 2008. Introduction, in *Christianity and Law: An Introduction*, edited by J. Witte and F.S. Alexander. Cambridge: Cambridge University Press, 1–32.

Woodman, G.R. 2007. The Possibilities of Co-existence of Religious Laws with Other Laws, in *Religion and Law in Multicultural Societies*, edited by R. Mehdi, H. Petersen, E. Sand and G.R. Woodman. Copenhagen: DJØF Publishing, 7–22.

PART I
De Jure: Religion

Chapter 2
Persecution for Reasons of Religion under the 1951 Refugee Convention

Anthony Good

Article 1A(2) of the 1951 *UN Convention Relating to the Status of Refugees*, the key international instrument covering asylum, defines a "refugee" as someone who has a "well-founded fear of being persecuted *for reasons of race, religion, nationality, membership of a particular social group or political opinion*" [italics added]. This article has undergone extensive legal interpretation ever since, and although asylum decisions are framed by national legislation and local administrative procedures, this jurisprudence has a strong international dimension; for example, British courts regularly draw on legal precedents from other countries, especially those with shared common-law traditions.

This chapter focuses on the similarities and differences in legal understandings of "religion", and hence of religious persecution, in the United Kingdom and United States. After briefly setting out the scope of religious freedom under international law, it turns to the domestic law of both countries to see how religion has come to be defined legally. Not surprisingly, given the nature of its Constitution, the US courts have given far more attention to this issue, yet the greater sophistication which has resulted does not appear to carry over into asylum decision making, at least where Muslim claimants are concerned. In both countries there is evidence of reliance upon stereotypes, of the nature of religion generally, and of Islam in particular. Bearing in mind the great variety of religious forms which asylum decision makers are liable to encounter, the conclusion drawn is that they would benefit from greater awareness of anthropological and sociological understandings of religion, and particularly, it is suggested, from taking a polythetic rather than an essentialist approach to the question of definition.[1]

1 Fieldwork was supported by ESRC Research Grant no. R000223352. This chapter saw the light of day at the Max Planck Institute in Halle/Saale in 2005, and achieved its present form as the 2006 Elizabeth Colson Lecture at the Refugee Studies Centre, Oxford. My thanks to both institutions and both audiences.

Persecution "for Reasons of ... Religion"

Article 18 of the International Covenant on Civil and Political Rights (ICCPR) affirms freedom of thought, conscience and religion, and covers actual practices, not just personal faith. This is true of the Refugee Convention, too (Symes and Jorro 2003: 144). Paraphrasing the ICCPR, the *Handbook* of the UN High Commissioner for Refugees (UNHCR) emphasizes people's right to change their religion and "to manifest it in public or private, in teaching, practice, worship and observance" (1992: 71). It adds:

> 72. Persecution for 'reasons of religion' may assume various forms, e.g. prohibition of membership of a religious community, of worship in private or in public, of religious instruction, or serious measures of discrimination imposed on persons because they practice their religion or belong to a particular religious community.
>
> 73. Mere membership of a particular religious community will normally not be enough to substantiate a claim to refugee status. There may, however, be special circumstances where mere membership can be a sufficient ground.

Restrictions on certain forms of religious activity may or may not be persecutory; thus, a total ban on practising one's religion would probably be seen as persecution whereas the existence of laws against proselytization might not (Symes 2001: 155–7). Persecution resulting from abandoning one's religion or converting to another also falls within the Convention. The sincerity of conversion is one factor to be taken into account, but not the only one. Even if the court doubts its genuineness, the question still remains, how will any purported conversion be viewed by the authorities in the convert's home country? For example apostasy is an offence in some Muslim countries, as we shall see.

Legal Definitions of "Religion"

What constitutes "religion" for Convention purposes? Hathaway's influential interpretive commentary on asylum law proposes the following approach:

> First, individuals have the right to hold or not to hold any form of theistic, non-theistic or atheistic belief.
>
> ... Second, an individual's right to religion implies the ability to live in accordance with a chosen belief, including participation in or abstention from formal worship and other religious acts, expression of views, and the ordering of personal behaviour. (Hathaway 1991: 145–6)

While having the virtue of generality, this does not specify how religious beliefs differ from ethical beliefs of other kinds (and as we shall see, defining religion in terms of belief is problematic in any event). Nor does it have legal force; in fact "the term 'religion' remains undefined as a matter of international law" (Gunn 2003: 190), so refugee decision makers must seek whatever guidance they can find in their own domestic law, to which we now turn.

The United States of America

The US Supreme Court has had far more to say on the definition of religion than the British courts, largely because of the recurring need to rule on whether particular kinds of activities are protected by the First Amendment to the Constitution, which states: "Congress shall make no law respecting an establishment of religion, or prohibiting the free exercise thereof." Supreme Court deliberations over the past 150 years display a dialectic between *substantive* approaches to religion, focusing on the content of belief; and *functional* approaches, focusing on cultures, ideology, world view and cosmology (Hunter 1990: 58).

This process began with three cases involving Mormon polygamy. In *Reynolds* (1878), the Supreme Court upheld the lower court's rejection of Reynolds's argument that polygamy was his religious duty, protected under the "Free Exercise Clause" in the First Amendment. The Court pointed out that marriage was not only a religious sacrament, but fundamental to civil society also; polygamy had always been an offence at common law, and "odious among the northern and western nations of Europe". In view of its decision, the Court was not required to produce a precise definition of "religion", but it did point out that the term is undefined in the Constitution too, so the scope of the First Amendment can only be understood in light of general eighteenth-century American views. Although those were overwhelmingly theistic, influential advocates of religious freedom such as Thomas Jefferson had not confined their arguments to theists.

Yet twelve years later in *Davis* vs. *Beason*, after assessing polygamy in similar terms, the Court took a more narrowly theistic stance: "religion" has reference to one's views of his relations to his Creator, and to the obligations they impose of reverence for his being and character, and of obedience to his will.

It went on to distinguish clearly between beliefs on one hand and practices on the other. The First Amendment did not protect "acts inimical to the peace, good order and morals of society" even if some particular sect designated them as "religious". Bigamy was a crime, and to claim it as religious was an offence to the commonsense of "all civilized and Christian countries". In a third Mormon case that same year (*Late Corporation of the Church of Jesus Christ of Latter-Day Saints*), the Court went even further, denying that a practice as "abhorrent" and "barbarous" as polygamy could possibly be religious at all.

Such substantive approaches to defining religion held sway for more than half a century. One key case in the subsequent shift towards a more functional approach was *United States* vs. *Ballard* (1944). Ballard stood trial for fraud, having obtained money from followers on the basis of his claim to have healing powers derived from spiritual encounters with Jesus and others. The Supreme Court upheld the trial judge's instructions to the jury that it could decide on the sincerity of Ballard's professed beliefs, but not on their truth or falsity. Heresy trials, it ruled, would be an unconstitutional violation of religious freedom:

> The religious views espoused by respondents might seem incredible, if not preposterous, to most people. But if those doctrines are subject to trial before a jury charged with finding their truth or falsity, then the same can be done with the religious beliefs of any sect. … The First Amendment does not select any one group or any one type of religion for preferred treatment. It puts them all in that position.

The effect of *Ballard*, therefore, was to make the sincerity with which religious beliefs were held, rather than their credibility, the key criterion when assessing whether religious activities were protected under the First Amendment (Davis 2004). But while allowing that a wide range of religious beliefs might enjoy such protection, the *Ballard* decision remained theistic in its underlying assumptions.

Not so the 2nd Circuit Court of Appeal in *United States* vs. *Kauten* (1943), among the first of many key cases to consider claims under the *Selective Training and Service Act*, which exempted from active military service any person who, "by reason of religious training and belief, is conscientiously opposed to participation in war in any form". Kauten, however, was an atheist whose opposition to war emanated, as the lower court put it, "from personal philosophical conceptions arising out of his nature and temperament, and [was] to some extent, political". Having declared the impossibility of defining "religion" succinctly, the Court proceeded to do precisely that for "religious belief":

> Religious belief arises from a sense of the inadequacy of reason as a means of relating the individual to his fellow–men and to his universe – a sense common to men in the most primitive and in the most highly civilized societies. It accepts the aid of logic but refuses to be limited by it. It is a belief finding expression in a conscience which categorically requires the believer to disregard elementary self-interest and to accept martyrdom in preference to transgressing its tenets.[2]

Conscientious objection, the Court concluded, can be seen as "a response of the individual to an inward mentor, call it conscience or God, that is for many persons … the equivalent of what has always been thought a religious impulse". Somewhat paradoxically, therefore, Kauten's objections to induction were dismissed because they were too rational, displaying insufficient disregard for his own self-interest! However, although Kauten lost his appeal, the Court's decision seemed to broaden

2 It is hard to imagine a present-day US court speaking of "martyrdom" in such positive terms!

the scope of "religion" to encompass virtually any kind of belief so long as it was sincerely held and based upon faith rather than reason.[3]

The process described thus far has been characterized (Donovan and Anderson 2003: 127) as one in which an initial definition of religion as "enlightened theism" (*Reynolds*) was first "transformed into the psychological criterion of sincere belief" (*Ballard*), and then (*Kauten*) subjected to the "epistemological requirement" that it be based upon faith rather than reason. Alternatively, Davis (2004) sees *Kauten*'s importance as lying in the fact that it "was the first to offer a functional definition of religion", rather than the "narrow, substantive definitions" adopted previously.

This new approach was not universally accepted right away. In 1946 the 9th Circuit Court of Appeal rejected it in *Berman* vs. *United States*, a conscientious objector case involving a humanist, on the grounds that "without the concept of a deity" a belief could not be "religious" in the sense used in the statute. This narrower definition was naturally preferred by government because it limited the scope of conscientious objection, and the 1948 *Selective Service Act* adopted its terminology, stipulating that "religious training and belief" meant a "belief in a relation to a Supreme Being involving duties superior to those arising from any human relation, but [excluding] essentially political, sociological, or philosophical views, or a merely personal moral code" (Donovan and Anderson 2003: 127).

This position was, however, repeatedly challenged on the grounds that it violated the First Amendment. In *Torcaso* vs. *Watkins* the appellant had been refused appointment to state office in Maryland because he would not declare a belief in god. The Supreme Court found that this violated the Constitution, pointing out – on the authority of the *Encyclopedia Britannica* as well as case law – that "Among religions in this country which do not teach what would generally be considered a belief in the existence of God are Buddhism, Taoism, Ethical Culture, Secular Humanism and others".

That statement appeared only in a footnote, however, and the binding ruling on the matter came four years later in *United States* vs. *Seeger* (1965). In the words of the Supreme Court, Seeger "was conscientiously opposed to participation in war in any form", but "preferred to leave the question as to his belief in a Supreme Being open". Seeger denied, however, that he was lacking in faith, asserting that one could believe in "intellectual and moral integrity ... without belief in God, except in the remotest sense". The lower court found that although his belief was sincere and his conscientious objection claim was made in good faith, it was not based upon "belief in a relation to a Supreme Being" as required by the *Selective Service Act*. However, the Supreme Court unanimously disagreed:

---

3 Conscientious objection can form the basis of a valid asylum claim but mere political opposition to state policy is not sufficient. The claimant must show that "participation in military action [is] contrary to his genuine political, religious or moral convictions, or to valid reasons of conscience" (UNHCR 1992: §170–74). This clearly encompasses non-theistic beliefs too, but does not specify how far this process may be carried.

> Congress, in using the expression 'Supreme Being' rather than the designation 'God,' was [trying] to embrace all religions and to exclude essentially political, sociological, or philosophical views ... the test ... is whether a given belief that is sincere and meaningful occupies a place in the life of its possessor parallel to that filled by the orthodox belief in God of one who clearly qualifies for the exemption. Where such beliefs have parallel positions in the lives of their respective holders we cannot say that one is 'in a relation to a Supreme Being' and the other is not.

In other words, *any* sincerely-held belief that is "structurally equivalent to" a theistic belief in terms of the "mental space" it occupies in a person's world-view (Donovan and Anderson 2003: 128), can fulfil the same function as theistic belief in terms of qualifying for exemption from military service. This disingenuous assumption that the US Congress had intended to broaden the legal definition of "religion" – when in fact it had sought to do exactly the opposite so as to restrict the scope for military exemption – was probably adopted by the Court as the lesser of two evils, since the alternative would have been to find that Congress's amendment was unconstitutional (see Davis 2004).

Be that as it may, in *Welsh* vs. *United States*, three years later, the Supreme Court produced an even broader definition. Welsh denied that his views were religious, and agreed that they were partly based on his political opinions; he asserted, however, his belief that "human life is valuable in and of itself ... therefore I will not injure or kill another human being", a belief which he saw as "essential to every human relation". In the majority view, this was enough to exempt him from military service because "his beliefs function as a religion in his life". The *Act*, it said, exempts from military service: "All those whose consciences, spurred by deeply held moral, ethical, or religious beliefs, would give them no rest or peace if they allowed themselves to become a part of an instrument of war."

The result of this changing emphasis from substance to function, therefore, was that over 150 years successive Supreme Court decisions gradually extended the range of beliefs benefiting from First Amendment protection, from conventional theisms (initially by implication Christian, but later extended to include Judaism, Islam and Hinduism) to a range of sincerely-held moral and ethical world views and ideologies. *Seeger* and *Welsh* established what Davis (2004) terms the "parallel position" and "ultimate concern" rules: beliefs are "religious" in Constitutional terms if they (a) occupy the same place in a person's moral life as religion does for a believer, and (b) are based on "ultimate concerns" rather than "policy, pragmatism, or expediency" (*Welsh*).

However, this process went into partial reverse in *Wisconsin* vs. *Yoder* (1972), an appeal by members of an Amish community against conviction for failing to send children to school beyond eighth grade. The Supreme Court exempted Amish from school attendance, largely on the basis of evidence from anthropologist John

Hostetler.[4] But the Court also adopted a less liberal definition of religion, probably to avoid opening the door to other claims for exemption (Donovan and Anderson 2003: 101):

> Ordered liberty precludes allowing every person to make his own standards on matters of conduct in which society as a whole has important interests. Thus, if the Amish asserted their claims because of their subjective evaluation and rejection of the contemporary secular values accepted by the majority, much as Thoreau rejected the social values of his time and isolated himself at Walden Pond, their claims would not rest on a religious basis. Thoreau's choice was philosophical and personal rather than religious, and such belief does not rise to the demands of the Religion Clauses.

These comments seem to negate much of the reasoning in *Seeger* by requiring the involvement of a collectivity, not only in practising "religion" but even in holding the associated beliefs; by denigrating "subjectivity" as a characteristic of religious belief; and by requiring such beliefs, in some contexts at least, to be "accepted by the majority".

The United Kingdom

Compared with the United States, religion has been little problematized by British courts in any area of law.[5] What little *has* been said in recent decades appears far more naively theistic even than the late nineteenth-century US Supreme Court, and infinitely narrower in scope than the broad perspective already adopted by the Supreme Court in *Kauten* and *Seeger* (see also British Humanist Association 2004).

For example, one much-cited opinion is that of Lord Denning in the Court of Appeal (*ex parte Segerdal* 1970), dismissing the Church of Scientology's claim that its East Grinstead chapel was a place of religious worship under the *Places of Worship Registration Act 1855*. Lord Denning decided that "place of meeting for religious worship", as used in the *Act*, meant a place whose principal use is as:

---

4 This seems to be the only occasion on which anthropological evidence has been crucial to a Supreme Court decision. However, the Court does not report Hostetler's professional views on the definition of religion. His own Amish background has led some to question his objectivity (see Rosen 1977: 564).

5 Such is the paucity of legal sources, that legal discussions often cite Lord Ahmed's suggested definition of "religion", in a House of Lords debate: "that system of beliefs and activities centred round the worship of God which is derived in whole or in part from a book revealed by God to one of his messengers" (*Hansard*, HL, 28 October 1999, col. 457). This is in no way a binding legal definition; it is also, self-evidently, an Islamocentric one!

> a place where people come together as a congregation or assembly to do reverence to God. It need not be the God which the Christians worship ... but it must be reverence to a deity. There may be exceptions. For instance, Buddhist temples are properly described as places of meeting for religious worship. But, apart from exceptional cases of that kind, it seems to me the governing idea behind the words 'place of meeting for religious worship' is that it should be a place for the worship of God.

Despite the somewhat tokenistic acknowledgement of Buddhism, this is root and branch a theistic definition, as is re-emphasized when he characterizes Scientology as

> a philosophy ... rather than a religion. *Religious worship means reverence or veneration of God or of a supreme being.* I do not find any such reverence or veneration in the creed of this church ... There is considerable stress on the spirit of man ... but there is no belief in a spirit of God [my italics].

Another influential approach is that of Mr Justice Dillon, in an appeal by a learned society against refusal to grant it charitable status (*In re South Place Ethical Society*, 1980). The Society described its objectives as "study and dissemination of ethical principles and the cultivation of a rational religious sentiment", but Dillon concluded that although the Society's objectives *were* charitable, they were not religious. The word "religion" was "not ... used in its correct sense" by the Society. It aimed to cultivate a state of mind "founded in reason", whereas "two of the essential attributes of religion are ... faith in a god and worship of that god". He rejected, and even mocked, the reasoning in *Seeger*:

> it is natural that the court should desire not to discriminate between beliefs deeply and sincerely held, whether they are beliefs in a god or in the excellence of man or in ethical principles ... But I do not see that that warrants extending the meaning of the word 'religion' so as to embrace all other beliefs and philosophies. *Religion, as I see it, is concerned with man's relations with God, and ethics are concerned with man's relations with man. The two are not the same, and are not made the same by sincere inquiry into the question, what is God.* [...] The ground of the opinion of the Supreme Court in Seeger's case, that any belief occupying in the life of its possessor a place parallel to that occupied by belief in God in the minds of theists is religion, prompts the comment that parallels, by definition, never meet [my italics].

The most recent discussion in English law concerning the definition of religion was the House of Lords 2005 decision in *R on the application of Williamson and others*, where teachers and parents of children at Christian independent schools sought judicial review of the ban on corporal punishment in schools introduced by the *Education Act 1996*. The appellants believed that it was in line with Christian teaching to administer corporal punishment to misbehaving children, and argued that the *Act* infringed their right to educate their children in conformity to their religious and philosophical convictions, as guaranteed under the *European Convention for the Protection of Human Rights and Fundamental Freedoms* 1950.

The Lords unanimously reaffirmed the Court of Appeal's dismissal of their appeal, however. In his leading speech, Lord Nicholls was reluctant to formulate any formal definition, partly because it was not necessary in this instance, it being undisputed that Christianity *was* a religion, however that term were defined, and partly because

> it does not matter whether the claimants' beliefs regarding the corporal punishment of children are categorised as religious. Article 9 embraces freedom of thought, conscience and religion. The atheist, the agnostic, and the sceptic are as much entitled to freedom to hold and manifest their beliefs as the theist. These beliefs are placed on an equal footing for the purpose of this guaranteed freedom.

Similarly, article 2 of the First Protocol to the Convention refers to "religious and philosophical convictions". It therefore applies to "ethical convictions which are not religious but humanist", just as, he noted, the relevant legislation was found to do in *Seeger*. He added with apparent approval that

> The trend of authority (unsurprisingly in an age of increasingly multi-cultural societies and increasing respect for human rights) is towards a 'newer, more expansive, reading' of religion (Wilson and Deane JJ in the *Church of the New Faith* case ... commenting on a similar trend in United States jurisprudence).[6]

What emerges from this discussion is that English courts have devoted far less attention than their American counterparts to producing a legal definition of "religion", and on the few occasions when this question has arisen they have either resorted to a naive theism which the US Supreme Court had already transcended in *Reynolds* a century and a half ago, or have clung to the coat-tails of broader recent rulings in the US and Australia, while showing great reluctance to commit themselves either way.

The question is, do these striking differences in national jurisprudence have any impact on how asylum claims founded upon religious persecution are assessed in the two countries? As we shall see, it seems that they do not: irrespective of whether their higher courts have virtually ignored the question of defining "religion", as in the UK, or subjected that question to repeated, detailed analyses, as in the US, asylum decision makers have generally stuck resolutely to the assumptions of received "common sense".

---

6 The *Church of the New Faith* case, in the High Court of Australia, gives a particularly thorough discussion of the definition of religion (even quoting Clifford Geertz) but is beyond the scope of this chapter.

Religion-based Asylum Claims in the UK

British asylum courts have generally treated the nature of religion as self-evident. The most common contexts in which religion has formed the basis of asylum claims in the UK in recent years concern Ahmadis from Pakistan, regarded as heretics by many other Muslims; and Falun Gong members claiming persecution by the Chinese government.

About 3 per cent of Pakistanis are Ahmadis, members of a movement founded in the nineteenth century by Mirza Ghulam Ahmad. After Pakistan's Independence in 1947, prison sentences were specified for Ahmadis calling themselves Muslims. Penalties for blasphemy were increased until death was the sole penalty, albeit rarely carried out. Many Ahmadis have been charged and imprisoned under blasphemy laws: They suffer restrictions of religious freedom; are prohibited from holding gatherings and proselytizing; and are targeted by religious extremists. Passport applications pose a particular problem for them: Applicants must declare their religious affiliations, and if they claim to be Muslims they must sign a declaration saying that Mirza Ghulam Ahmad was an impostor and his followers are non-Muslims.

Under the UK's *Asylum and Immigration Act 1996*, Pakistan was on a "White List" of countries where, in the Secretary of State's view, there was "in general no serious risk of persecution". Six thousand Pakistani asylum applicants, including many Ahmadis, therefore had their claims certified, meaning that they had no right of appeal against any adverse decision by an Adjudicator. When several unsuccessful applicants sought judicial review of their certification, the High Court ruled that the inclusion of Pakistan on the White List was invalid, and in May 2002 the Court of Appeal, headed by the Master of the Rolls, upheld that decision (*SSHD* vs. *Asif Javed and others*).

Asif Javed was an Ahmadi. He had been expelled from school in Pakistan for explaining his beliefs to other pupils. He was attacked and severely injured by former pupils, but the police advised him to renounce his faith if he wished to avoid arrest and imprisonment. He was later accused of preaching; the police tried to arrest him, but he escaped. He was attacked and wounded by a man with a knife. He claimed asylum in the UK on grounds of persecution by non-state agents, but the Secretary of State decided his account was not credible. He produced a police report naming himself as a wanted person, but the Secretary of State claimed – wrongly, it later proved – that no such police station existed.

More to the present point, his claim was refused on the further ground that, although Ahmadis suffered discrimination, Pakistan's judiciary was independent and there was no systematic persecution of religious minorities. The *Country Assessment* produced by the Home Office's Country Information and Policy Unit (CIPU) argued that "Ahmadis are recognized as a minority religious group and rights are safeguarded under the constitution", and the official who compiled that *Assessment* asserted to the Court of Appeal that "Ahmadis are not persecuted per se", although "individual Ahmadis may suffer persecution, depending on their particular circumstances". However, the Court preferred the "bleaker picture" painted by the then-President of the Immigration Appeal Tribunal (as it was then called), Judge David Pearl, an authority on Islamic law (Pearl and Menski 1998). Citing a Canadian report that Ahmadis suffered from government-supported discrimination, Pearl had concluded (*Kaleem Ahmed*) that although not all Ahmadis could claim to suffer persecution in Convention terms, they "live in Pakistan as a religious minority who are likely to meet examples of intolerance, discrimination and sadly at times blatant persecution in their everyday lives".

The Falun Gong ("Wheel of Law") movement, founded in 1992 by Li Hongzhi, combines Buddhist ideas with physical and breathing exercises. Some members assert that it is not a religion, but a method of self-cultivation; they also deny any political agenda. It was nonetheless banned by the Chinese government in 1999, for "advocating malicious fallacies [which] put people's life at risk and wreaked havoc on the society".[7] Many followers were detained and forced to make public confessions, and state employees participating in Falun Gong activities were threatened with dismissal or demotion. A mass demonstration in Beijing in April 1999 ended peacefully, but later events were prevented, would-be participants detained, and virtually all Falun Gong activities declared illegal. Several hundred followers were sent to labour camps or psychiatric institutions, and tens of thousands were detained.

Falun Gong appeals often take far longer than other hearings – I attended one where examination-in-chief alone lasted an entire day – because legal representatives try to demonstrate that their clients' claims are genuine by putting them through oral theological examinations.[8] This is a common legal response to the difficulty of demonstrating that religious beliefs are genuine (Musalo 2002: 50–52), yet to reduce sincerity to doctrinal understanding is to forget that "deep knowledge of [doctrine] may be less important than the spiritual feelings that come from communion with fellow believers" (Gunn 2003: 201).

The British courts have accepted without question that the beliefs and practices of both Ahmadis and Falun Gong followers are religious in character, even though some of the latter deny this. Partly because issues of definition have rarely arisen, there is no key House of Lords precedent-setting decision of the kind represented by *Islam and Shah* in the instance of "particular social group".[9] Moreover, the approach of one key source in British case-law on religious persecution, the Court of Appeal's judgment in *Omoruyi* (2000), is deeply unsatisfactory from an anthropological perspective.

7 http://www.chinaembassycanada.org/eng/xw/xwgb/t38870.htm; accessed 20 August 2008.

8 These inquisitions are practical exams too, because appellants are usually asked to demonstrate their distinctive aerobic exercises.

9 In *Islam and Shah*, the Law Lords decided that "women in Pakistan" formed a "particular social group" (PSG) within the scope of the 1951 Refugee Convention, thereby clarifying that it was not a requirement for the existence of such a group that all its members should actually suffer persecution.

Mr Omoruyi was a Nigerian asylum applicant who claimed to fear the Ogboni cult. He stated that his father was a member and wanted him to join as the eldest son, but he refused because it was contrary to Christian teaching. When he refused to allow his father to be buried according to Ogboni rites, he was told that "the penalty for this is death". He described Ogboni as "a mafia organization involving criminal acts", and a "devil cult" whose rituals involved idol worship, animal sacrifice and drinking blood, and claimed that Ogboni used human organs to prepare "satanic concoctions", and practised "ritual killing of innocent people". He alleged that soon after his father's burial, cult members murdered his brother in mistake for him and removed various bodily organs; and that since he came to the UK his own baby son had been killed and mutilated.

Mrs Scott-Baker, the Adjudicator hearing Mr Omoruyi's appeal, accepted his story on the basis of supportive documentary evidence, even though she found it "so incredible". The Tribunal reversed her decision, however, because in its opinion "the cult as described by the appellant is not credible". It is unusual for tribunals to overturn credibility findings, and particularly surprising that they did so here because the Home Office's own country information provided partial corroboration. CIPU's *Nigeria Country Assessment* (October 2002: 6.88–90), citing a reputed anthropologist (Morton Williams 1960) among its sources, confirmed that Ogboni is a secret society, officially banned but powerful throughout Nigeria; that membership is usually acquired patrilineally; that it allegedly follows "satanic practices" such as animal sacrifice; and that members who break their oaths of secrecy are reputedly threatened with death.[10]

Nicholas Blake QC argued in the Court of Appeal that his client's fear arose out of his religion, because his Christian beliefs prevented him from allowing his father to be buried according to Ogboni custom. However, Lord Justice Simon Brown preferred the Home Office contention that his problems stemmed not from Christianity *per se* but from his refusal to comply with Ogboni demands; his asylum claim therefore failed for lack of a Convention reason. The Home Office did not directly question Ogboni's status as a religion, but Simon Brown himself did so in his judgment. After citing Hathaway's definition of religion (quoted above), he considered whether Ogboni was a "religion" for Convention purposes:

> There are, [Mr Blake] suggests, clear religious elements to their practices which merit such a characterization: the worship of idols, sacrifice of animals and the like. This argument I would utterly reject. The notion that a 'devil cult' practicing pagan rituals of the sort here described is in any true sense a religion I find deeply offensive … It seems to me rather that these rites and rituals of the Ogboni are merely the trappings of what can only realistically be recognized as an intrinsically criminal organization – akin perhaps to the voodoo element of the Ton-Ton Macoute in Papa Doc Duvalier's Haiti.

10 The publicity surrounding the similar asylum appeal by Brown Nosakhare spurred the Canadian Immigration and Refugee Board to produce a research paper on Nigerian cults (IRB 2000).

This view, explicitly based upon emotional prejudice, does not survive a moment's anthropological scrutiny, as we shall see.

Islam and Apostasy in American and British Asylum Courts

Despite the increasingly broad definitions of religion developed by the Supreme Court, American approaches to religion-based asylum claims are often just as reliant on prejudicial stereotype as the *Omoruyi* decision in the UK. Akram provides several striking examples of this in her critique of the treatment of Islam by American courts.

Asylum claims by Muslims seem particularly susceptible to the prejudices of American legal decision makers, particularly the orientalist assumption that there are fundamental differences between the psyches of "Arabs" or "Muslims" and those of westerners, and as a corollary, that all Muslims, be they Indonesians or Arabs, share the same mentality. Those who start from such premises, says Akram (2000: 8), "explain every facet of Eastern/Muslim societies in light of the Muslim religion – as if there were no other reality or influence on these societies but Islam, and as if there were no complexity or diversity in the philosophies or practices of Muslim societies". Such prejudices appear laughably simplistic when set out explicitly, but may have life-threatening implications for those to whom they are applied. Among the undesirable consequences of such stereotyping, over and above its general dehumanizing of Muslims by denying their individual agency, is a tendency to accept as universally applicable "repressive and extreme versions of Islamic interpretation, currently being manipulated by fundamentalist repressive regimes" (Akram 2000: 9). Persecution is therefore represented, not as the outcome of localized social practices or specific political regimes, but as the inevitable consequence of a monolithic, socially repressive Islam which, according to this essentialist Western view, is always and everywhere the same.

It is common for asylum claims in both the US and UK to turn on the issue of whether claimed Muslim apostates face persecution, even death, if returned to their native countries. In *Bastanipour* vs. *INS* (1992), for example, it was argued that if the claimant were deported to Iran "he may be summarily executed for having converted from Islam to Christianity, a capital offense under Islamic religious law". This claim was rejected by the Board of Immigration Appeals (BIA), however. Its opinion was sardonically summarized by the 7th Circuit Court of Appeal as follows:

> After reciting various facts or pseudo-facts bearing on the question, including that Bastanipour has never been baptized or formally joined a church … and that apostasy though a capital offense under Muslim religious law is not the subject of a specific prohibition in the Iranian penal code, the opinion concludes that Bastanipour 'has not established that he has in fact converted to Christianity' – and that anyway there is no hard evidence that Iran has executed anyone for

> converting to Christianity, except for a man who became a Christian minister … All things considered, the Board concluded, Bastanipour's fears are speculative – why, Iran might not even discover that he *is* a Christian.

Any danger to Bastanipour, reasoned the higher court, would depend upon the view taken of his behaviour in Iran. Whether or not he had been formally baptized into Christianity was therefore irrelevant, as was the sincerity of his conversion:

> The offense in Muslim religious law is apostasy – abandoning Islam for another religion. Thomas Patrick Hughes, 'Apostasy from Islam,' in Hughes, *A Dictionary of Islam* 16 (1895). That is what Bastanipour did. He renounced Islam for Christianity. He has not been baptized or joined a church but he has made clear … that he believes in Christianity rather than in Islam – and *that* is the apostasy, not compliance with formalities of affiliation. Whether Bastanipour believes the tenets of Christianity in his heart of hearts or … is acting opportunistically (though at great risk to himself) in the hope of staving off deportation would not, we imagine, matter to an Iranian religious judge.

The BIA had asserted, on US State Department advice, that the Iranian penal code made no mention of apostasy. This advice, noted the 7th Circuit, "may be erroneous":

> Nader Entessar, 'Criminal Law and the Legal System in Revolutionary Iran,' *8 Bost. Coll. Third World L.J.* 91, 97 (1988), states that the Iranian penal code codifies the prohibitions of Islamic religious law, expressly including the prohibition against apostasy. But, more important, the State Department went on to say that 'were [Bastanipour] to be charged before a Sharia (religious) court in Iran of the crime of apostasy, we believe that he could face very serious punishment if convicted, quite possibly death.' The important thing is not what is written in the penal code but the fact that in Iran people receive temporal punishment, including death, for violating the tenets of Islamic law; and apostasy from Islam is indeed a capital offense under that law.

In these extracts the 7th Circuit repeatedly refers to "Islamic law", while in other places it mentions "Iranian law",[11] but the distinction between them is never made clear, and in subsequent case-law, on which *Bastanipour* has been very influential, "the case is uniformly cited as standing for the proposition that the asylum claim was based on a well-founded fear of persecution for the crime of apostasy under Islamic law" (Akram 2000: 20).

It is true, says Akram that *Iranian* law provides the death sentence for apostasy, but the court was incorrect "in claiming that such punishment was mandated under Islamic

11 For example, "If Bastanipour has converted to Christianity he is guilty of a capital offense under Iranian law".

law" (Akram 2000: 20). She criticizes the court's reliance on a single text written almost a century earlier by a Western scholar, in forming its definition of apostasy:

> Nowhere in the case is there a citation to original authority, whether the Qur'anic verses or *hadith*, or to various schools of interpretation on this question. [...] The hundreds of Muslim jurists, writers and activists knowledgeable about the subject who fundamentally disagree with such a conclusion are thus summarily dismissed without mention, and *Bastanipour* further entrenches Orientalists' belief about the barbarism of Islam. (Akram 2000: 21)

The irony is that these essentializing misrepresentations won Mr Bastanipour his appeal, which is precisely what made them attractive to his legal representatives and to those representing claimants in allegedly similar circumstances. This strategy is not always successful, however. In *Elnager* vs. *INS* (1991), the fallacious argument that the Koran required punishment by death for apostasy was accepted by the court, yet Elnager lost his appeal because the court did not accept that he was in the danger that he claimed. First, his fear was of non-state agents, the Muslim Brotherhood, and there was no evidence before the court indicating that the Egyptian government was unable to control this group. Second, there was no evidence, apart from the testimonies of his immediate family, that individual religious converts had been persecuted. The court therefore accepted the BIA's conclusion that "the government of Egypt does not participate in the persecution of religious converts, and further, that it takes steps to control such persecution". In Akram's view (2000: 24), however, a more nuanced analysis, contrasting the formal legal position in Egypt with the practices of religious extremists, and stressing the state's very limited ability, in practice, to control grassroots activities, would have much strengthened Elnager's case.

Since Akram wrote, apostasy has also been subjected to detailed analysis by the UK asylum courts in *FS*, a "Country Guideline" (CG) case. CG cases are intended to help improve the consistency of the Asylum and Immigration Tribunal's decision making, by establishing "factual precedents" as regards recurring aspects of background evidence about countries of origin. The Court of Appeal thought that this "exotic" strategy could, in principle, be "benign and practical" (*'S' and Others*), but its assessment presupposed that tribunals would carry out comprehensive analyses of all available material. Some early CG decisions fell far short of this ideal, basing themselves entirely upon a single Home Office source. Following a pointed critique by the Immigration Advisory Service (Yeo 2005) their quality significantly improved, however, and *FS* comes from this later phase.

The appellant FS[12] initially fled Iran for political reasons, but during the processing of his asylum claim he became a baptized Christian. The court

12 During the course of this litigation the Tribunal adopted a policy of referring to applicants by initials rather than full names; I do so here even when the actual legal decisions used the full name.

accepted that his conversion was sincere. At first appeal the adjudicator dismissed his asylum claim but allowed his human rights appeal. At second appeal, when FS sought to overturn the refusal of asylum, the Tribunal agreed with the adjudicator's conclusion but substituted its own reasoning. It decided, in line with two earlier cases, that FS "who is not an evangelical or likely to proselytize, will be able to practice his new religion in Iran without running any real risk of persecution or ill-treatment either by the authorities or by individuals in that country".

However, there were other Tribunal cases, and some in overseas courts, where contrary conclusions had been reached. In *Sarkohaki* (2002), for example, the Tribunal had followed the US State Department report, which stated that "Apostasy, specifically conversion from Islam, may be punishable by death", while in *Ghodratzadeh* (2002) the Tribunal concluded: "It is not entirely clear whether the full rigour of the law against apostasy has been imposed [but] there is clearly a real risk that if the authorities discovered that a person was an apostate, he might find himself being persecuted." The Federal Court of Australia had accepted that "for an apostate, the risk of extreme punishment will always exist" (*Appellant A*, 2002). The other foreign authority was *Bastanipour*, discussed earlier, which found that the risks of apostasy depend upon the overall relationship between the appellant and their home state. (Bastanipour had a drugs conviction, which was felt likely to predispose Iran to view him adversely.)

While accepting that every case had to be decided on its own facts, Lord Justice Sedley was concerned that different tribunals seemed to be making different evaluations of the background evidence regarding apostasy in Iran. He felt that such inconsistent decision making was "inimical to justice", and the Court remitted FS's appeal for reconsideration. This second Tribunal allowed FS's asylum claim, concluding as follows:

> FS has a past adverse political profile … It is not one which of itself would cause any significant difficulties … There is a real risk, however, that this would be known to the authorities in conjunction with his conversion; and that it would lead them to target him for questioning and a higher level of harassment, more akin to that which might be experienced by a proselytiser or evangelist.

The Tribunal also sought to provide a definitive general assessment of the risks associated with apostasy in Iran. In terms of breadth, its analysis is clearly superior to any of its US counterparts. It cites well over fifty documentary sources, as well as evidence from experts and other witnesses. In discussing the evidence regarding apostasy, the determination considers the relevant CIPU *Country Report* and numerous other reports by the US State Department and the Canadian Refugee Board; reports from Belgian, Danish, Dutch, Australian, and UN bodies; church reports; and several reports by expert witnesses. This huge body of material is assessed in what seems a fair and balanced fashion.

In the present context, however, we are concerned with the Tribunal's underlying assumptions, as revealed by its choice of words and selection of sources, at least as much as with its explicit conclusions. It notes that "Iran is an Islamic Shi'ite state", or later, "an Islamic theocratic state". "The interests of the state and its religion," it goes on, "are inseparable. Conversion from Islam is against the law, punishable as apostasy, in theory by death." Iran recognizes Christians as a religious minority but discriminates against them in various ways. Proselytizing of Muslims is forbidden, but "recent Protestant or evangelical Churches [do] proselytize and admit converts from Islam". It quotes an assertion from the CIPU *Report* which makes precisely the kind of conflation of Iranian and Islamic law criticized by Akram (2000): "Apostasy, or conversion from Islam to another religion, is not acceptable in Islamic law."

What is most striking, however, is that insofar as the documents and reports cited are religious in character and origin, they all stem from Christian sources. None of the references cited in the determination represent the views of Muslim scholars *qua* Muslims. Despite the balance and thoroughness of its analysis, therefore, which far exceeds that of the American sources analysed by Akram (2000), the Tribunal's stance is in this respect every bit as riddled with orientalist presumptions.

Anthropological Definitions of Religion

The question of how to identify and define religion cross-culturally has of course engaged many anthropologists over the years, although with the notable exception of the above-mentioned *Church of the New Faith* case in Australia, the law shows little or no awareness of this. At least four distinct approaches to such definitions can be identified – and there is a fifth, associated with Max Weber (1963), which stresses soteriology and theodicy but eschews definition in favour of minute descriptions and elaborate typologies.[13]

Firstly, *theological definitions* are concerned with religion as a matter of "faith" or "belief", and so represent elaborations upon the Tylorian lowest common denominator, "belief in spiritual beings" (Tylor 1871 I: 424). Tylor deliberately chooses this form of words to avoid the ethnocentrism of defining religion as "belief in god", which implies monotheism on the Judeo-Christian model, or even "belief in gods", which is still too precise in implying the existence of supreme beings. Even so, his approach retained the underlying assumption that all religions focus on spiritual or supernatural beings of some kind. This is not universally true,

13 Donovan and Anderson (2003: 125–43) give an interesting account of how American legal definitions of religion developed, but their discussion of anthropological definitions is highly idiosyncratic. The discussion here does not claim completeness, either; for example, it fails to address the views of Fraser, Eliade, Lévi-Strauss and Cantwell Smith, among others.

with Theravada Buddhism an obvious counter-example (Gombrich 1971). As the Buddha became extinct when he achieved nirvana there is no practical utility in praying to him or expecting him to intervene in worldly events (which is not to say that Buddhists do not occasionally pray to the Buddha as a form of expressive action *in extremis*). Instead, Sri Lankan Buddhists worship Hindu gods to solve their practical problems, but famously insist that "gods have nothing to do with religion".

More subtle problems arise with the notion of "belief". Firstly, religion involves actions too; it prescribes or prohibits certain kinds of behaviour in daily life, as well as entailing activities on its own account, such as worship. More crucially, belief – or rather, affirmation of belief[14] – is not always as central as it is for Christians, Muslims or Jews. Hinduism, for example, has no creeds to identify and divide its adherents, and displays far less sectarian hostility than Christianity or Islam. It is not belief but behaviour that counts; if one behaves like a Hindu, then for most practical purposes one is seen as Hindu, as my own experiences in rural South India bear out.

Secondly, Durkheim's *sociological definition* characterizes religion as "a unified system of beliefs and practices relative to sacred things, that is to say, things set apart and forbidden – beliefs and practices which unite into one single moral community called a Church, all those who adhere to them" (1915: 47). This explicitly characterizes religions as matters of "doing", not just "believing". Moreover, "the distinctive trait of religious thought" (1915: 37) is the division of the world into two complementary yet opposed categories of phenomena: sacred and profane. Different religions define sacred things differently but access to these is always restricted somehow, and even the priests who approach them on behalf of ordinary worshippers must first purify themselves appropriately. He uses "Church" in a broad, generic sense, recognizing that religion is a social affair involving organized collectivities. Rather than assuming that all human groups – or all but one – had deluded themselves, Durkheim accounted for religious differences sociologically. People rightly sense external powers greater than themselves, constraining their behaviour. Their error lies in conceptualizing these as supernatural in character, whereas in fact the only power effective enough to influence everyone's behaviour, yet flexible enough to take different forms in different societies, is society itself, shaping individual behaviour through shared rules, morals, and languages. Society is not the way it is because god willed it so; quite the reverse, our idea of god depends on the nature of the society in which we live.

Thirdly, there are *cultural definitions*, the best known being Clifford Geertz's famous characterization of religion as a set of symbols providing both "a model

14 Membership of most Christian sects is validated by affirmation of a particular creed. Yet we can only infer people's true beliefs from the apparent sincerity of what they say and do. In practice, what is at issue is not their inner state while reciting a creed, but their willingness to do so publicly in convincing fashion.

of and a model for reality" (1966: 7–8). Religions, in other words, provide us with models of the ultimate structure and meaning of the life in the world, as well as models for how that life should be lived, in the form of ethical precepts and moral codes. Religion thereby helps make sense of, and organizes, human experience.

Fourthly, cross-cutting the differences among the other three approaches (Southwold (1978: 369)) advocates a *polythetic definition* of religion. This approach – which is my own preference, too – sees "religion" as a Wittgensteinian "odd-job" word (compare Needham 1975: 365) definable only in relation to its signification or use, not with reference to the alleged essence of the "thing" signified. The big advantage of polythetic definitions is their open-ended character. One should not assume that all the various manifestations to which the label "religion" has been or might be applied have one core attribute in common. Paraphrasing Southwold (1978: 370–71), any phenomenon we might wish pragmatically to label religious must have at least some of the following "family resemblances", and as my glosses below are meant to show, these incorporate important elements of all the other approaches, without prioritizing any of them:

- a concern with godlike beings and men's relations with them [cf. Tylor]
- a dichotomization of elements of the world into sacred and profane, and a central concern with the sacred [Durkheim]
- an orientation towards salvation rather than worldly existence [Weber]
- ritual practices [Durkheim]
- beliefs held on the basis of faith [Tylor; Durkheim]
- an ethical code, supported by such beliefs [Geertz]
- supernatural sanctions on infringements of that code
- a mythology
- a body of scriptures, or similarly exalted traditions
- a priesthood, or similar specialist religious elite [Durkheim]
- association with a moral community, a church [Durkheim]
- association with an ethnic or similar group [Durkheim]

In terms of *all* these anthropological standards suggested over the past century and a half, Ogboni (discussed above) is undoubtedly a religion. Whether it is an attractive religion is not for a pragmatic anthropological relativist to judge, but neither should that be a relevant consideration in legal decisions regarding the existence of persecution for a Refugee Convention reason. I do not know what Lord Justice Simon Brown's personal religious convictions may be, but they are made relevant – as they surely should not be in a judicial decision – by his sudden descent into emotional and ethnocentric prejudice.

Conclusions

Gunn rightly emphasizes the difficulty in producing an adequate substantive definition of religion, but one particular aspect of his argument seems misguided. He asserts that awareness of the work of social scientists would not solve judicial problems over defining "religion", because in contexts of religious discrimination, "the scholarly definitions do not describe what religion means to those who are discriminating and persecuting" (2003: 197). Rather oddly, he blames scholarly insistence on analytical rigour for the inconsistencies which he, Musalo (2002) and others have identified in asylum decision making concerning the Refugee Convention ground of "religion". I argue, on the other hand, that it is precisely the *lack* of such rigor among legal decision makers, their reliance on taken-for-granted, ethnocentric prejudices, which lies at the root of these problems.

In any asylum claim based upon persecution on grounds of religion, it must first be established against some agreed standard that the persecution experienced is indeed "religious" in character. In that context, awareness of scholarly definitions would at least preclude (for the applicants concerned, potentially fatal) judicial philistinisms such as that concerning the religious character of Ogboni. Second, an awareness of the culturally-contextualized, contested character of "religious" beliefs and practices permeates all current anthropological definitions whatever their differences otherwise. Again, this is precisely what is needed in asylum claims, yet in practice proves often to be lacking. Given the huge variety of religious beliefs and practices which asylum decision makers are liable to encounter, the correct legal application of the Refugee Convention, whatever that might be – and as an expert witness it is not my place to decide! – can only be strengthened by greater legal engagement with the anthropology of religion, and particularly, in my personal view, by the adoption of some kind of polythetic rather than essentialist definition.

Cases Cited

Appellant A vs. *Minister for Immigration and Multicultural Affairs* [2002] FCA 148

Bastanipour vs. *INS* 980 F.2d 1129 (7th Cir., 1992)

Berman vs. *United States*, 156 F.2d 377, 381 (9th Cir. 1946), 329 U.S. 795 (1946)

Church of the New Faith vs. *Comr of Pay-Roll Tax* (Victoria) [1983] 154 CLR 120

Davis vs. *Beason* 133 U.S. 333 (1890). 8

Elnager vs. *INS* 930 F.2d 784 (9th Cir., 1990)

FS: *SSHD* vs. *FS* [2002] UKIAT06086 [IAT, 16 January 2003]; *FS* vs. *SSHD* [2003] EWCACiv1562 [CA]; *SSHD* vs. *FS and others* [2004] UKIAT00303 Iran CG [IAT]

Ghodratzadeh vs. *SSHD* [2002]UKIAT01867, 10 June 2002
In re South Place Ethical Society: Barralet vs. *Attorney General* [1980] 3 All ER 918, [1980] 1 WLR 1565
Islam and Shah: *Islam* vs. *SSHD*; *R* vs. *IAT and another, ex parte Shah*, 25 March 1999, 1999 Imm AR 283, [1999] 2 All ER 545, [1999] 2 AC 629, [1999] 2 WLR 1015
Kaleem Ahmed vs. *SSHD*, 12774, 7 December 1995
Late Corporation of the Church of Jesus Christ of Latter-Day Saints et al. vs. *United States* 136 U.S. 1 (1890)
Omoruyi vs. *SSHD*, C/2000/0025, 12 October 2000, [2001] INLR 33 [2001] Imm AR 175
R vs. *Registrar General ex parte Segerdal* [1970] 3 All ER 886; [1970] 3 WLR 479
R (on the application of Williamson and others) vs. *Secretary of State for Education and Employment and others* [2005] UKHL 15; [2005] 2 All ER 1
Reynolds vs. *United States*, [1878] 98 U.S. 145
'S' and Others vs. *SSHD*, [2002]EWCACiv0539, 24 April 2002 [CA] [2002] INLR 416
SSHD vs. *Asif Javed, Zuifiqar Ali and Abid Ali*. C/2001/0291, 17 May 2002 [CA]
SSHD vs. *Sarkohaki* [2002]UKIAT05659m 6 December 2002
Torcaso vs. *Watkins*, 367 U.S. 488 (1961)
United States vs. *Ballard*, 322 U.S. 78 (1944)
United States vs. *Kauten*, 133 F.2d 703 (2d Cir. 1943)
United States vs. *Seeger*, 380 U.S. 163 (1965)
Welsh vs. *United States*, 398 U.S. 333 (1970)
Wisconsin vs. *Yoder*, 406 US 205 (1972), 15 May 1972

References

Akram, S.M. 2000. Orientalism revisited in asylum and refugee claims. *International Journal of Refugee Law*, 12, 7–40.

British Humanist Association. 2004. *The Draft Charities Bill. A Submission to the Parliamentary Joint Committee on the Bill from the British Humanist Association.* Available at: www.humanism.org.uk/site/cms/contentPrintArticle.asp?article=1853 [accessed: 4 August 2005].

CIPU (Country Information and Policy Unit). 2002. *Nigeria Country Assessment, October 2002*. London: Home Office.

Davis, D.H. 2004. *The Church of Scientology: In Pursuit of Legal Recognition.* Paper presented at the CESNUR 2004 International Conference on Religious Movements, Conflict, and Democracy: International Perspectives, Baylor University, Waco, Texas.

Donovan, J.M. and Anderson, H.E. III 2003. *Anthropology and Law*. New York and Oxford: Berghahn Books.

Durkheim, E. 1915. *The Elementary Forms of the Religious Life*. London: George Allen and Unwin.
Geertz, C. 1966. Religion as a cultural system, in *Anthropological Approaches to the Study of Religion*, edited by M. Banton. London: Tavistock, 1–46.
Gombrich, R. 1971. *Precept and Practice: Traditional Buddhism in the Rural Highlands of Ceylon*. Oxford: Clarendon.
Gunn, T.J. 2003. The complexity of religion and the definition of "religion" in international law. *Harvard Human Rights Journal*, 16, 189–215.
Hathaway, J. 1991. *The Law of Refugee Status*. London: Butterworths.
Hunter, J.D. 1990. Religious freedom and the challenge of modern pluralism, in *Articles of Faith, Articles of Peace: The Religious Liberty Clauses and the American Public Philosophy*, edited by J.D. Hunter and O. Guinness. Washington, DC: Brookings Institution, 54–73.
IRB (Immigration and Refugee Board, Canada). 2000. *Nigeria: State Protection Available to Potential Victims of Ritual Violence or Individuals Threatened by Cult Members*. Available at: www.cisr.gc.ca/en/researchpub/research/publications/index_ e.htm?id=24&cid=161 [accessed 27 March 2003].
Morton Williams, P. 1960. The Yoruba Ogboni cult in Oyo. *Africa*, 30, 362–74.
Musalo, K. 2002. *Claims for Protection Based on Religion or Belief: Analysis and Proposed Conclusions* (Legal and Protection Policy Research Series: doc. PPLA/2002/01). Geneva: UNHCR.
Needham, R. 1975. Polythetic classification: Convergence and consequences. *Man* (N.S.), 10, 349–69.
Pearl, D. and Menski, W. 1998. *Muslim Family Law*. London: Sweet and Maxwell.
Rosen, L. 1977. The anthropologist as expert witness. *American Anthropologist*, 79, 555–78.
Southwold, M. 1978. Buddhism and the definition of religion. *Man* (N.S.), 13, 362–79.
Symes, M. 2001. *Caselaw on the Refugee Convention: The United Kingdom's Interpretation in the Light of the International Authorities*. London: Refugee Legal Centre.
Symes, M. and Jorro, P.A. 2003. *Asylum Law and Practice*. London: LexisNexis.
Tylor, E.B. 1871. *Primitive Culture*. London: John Murray.
UNHCR (United Nations High Commissioner for Refugees). 1992. *Handbook on Procedures and Criteria for Determining Refugee Status*. Geneva: UNHCR.
Weber, M. 1963. *The Sociology of Religion*. Boston: Beacon Press.
Yeo, C. (ed.) 2005. *Country Guideline Cases: Benign and Practical?* London: Immigration Advisory Service.

Chapter 3
Religious Freedom Law and the Protection of Sacred Sites

René Kuppe

Modern religious freedom law in the Euro-American human rights tradition developed chiefly as a response to challenges raised by the religious beliefs and practices of adherents of Christian denominations. To a lesser degree, the Jewish and the Muslim religions have also had an impact on the shaping of modern religious freedom law. However, as a universal human right, religious freedom law should not only protect "old" established world religions, but also should protect the religious conscience and behaviour within the framework of other religious beliefs. This idea seems to be beyond any doubt and is expressed in the Universal Declaration of Human Rights which states that:

> Everybody has the right to freedom of thought, conscience and religion; this right includes freedom to change his religion or belief, and freedom, … in public or private, to manifest his religion or belief in teaching, practice, worship and observance. (Universal Declaration of Human Rights, Art. 18, 1948)

In accordance with the above, the constitutional human rights provisions of modern Western states do not limit their guarantees concerning freedom of religion to members of certain specific religious groups or communities.[1] For example, the first amendment of the Constitution of the United States provides that "Congress shall make no law respecting an establishment of religion, or prohibiting the free exercise thereof". In the terminology of American lawyers, the first part of this sentence is called the *Establishment Clause*, the second part the *Free Exercise Clause*. Based on the words of these clauses, most legal scholars argue that legislators and government authorities should not even discriminate against groups or individuals that hold views abhorrent to the (state) authorities; all religions are to be treated equally under religious freedom law standards based on modern international and national human rights standards.

---

1 Technically, it is feasible that religious freedom would be granted to believers of "conventional" religions alone, or only to adherents of some "officially recognized religions". However, the extension of religious freedom to all forms of religion is also a requirement of human rights law in general, which prohibits all forms of discrimination according to race, ethnic origin, or religion.

Nevertheless, the experience of the United States is a good example of how the application of the guarantees of the First Amendment to the United States Constitution to adherents of religions distinct from mainstream Judeo-Christian beliefs has been very discriminative.

I argue in this chapter that the discriminatory treatment of indigenous religions in the United States is the result of a culturally insensitive application of standard religious freedom law. In the following, I will first discuss the principles of US religious freedom law. Then, after explaining the importance of sacred sites for the traditional religions of American indigenous peoples, I will analyse United States case law in order to show that these standards have not been applied to the protection of the religious interests of believers of indigenous religions in the United States. I will show that this had to do with the fact that judges misunderstood and misconstructed important aspects of native American religions in the United States, and their site- and space-oriented worldviews in particular.

The Principles of US Religious Freedom Law

Generally speaking, rights are never guaranteed without any limits. Even fundamental rights have legitimate limits in order to allow the state to protect other important concurring interests. However, as we will see in the following, the judiciary of the United States has developed specific and rather strict standards in defining possible limits for the freedom of behaviour justified by religious beliefs.

Before the Supreme Court of the United States ruled on its first case involving a native American free exercise claim with regard to a sacred site, it had written several opinions which have subsequently served as a basis for a legal analysis procedure for indigenous religious freedom claims heard in lower courts. How did the Supreme Court, in fact, define limits in these legal documents that might be imposed on the religious freedom of individuals? In *Sherbert* vs. *Verner* (1963), the court determined that the state must have a "compelling interest" to justify any infringement of a First Amendment right. In the case, the court found that the State of South Carolina had no compelling interest that allowed for the denial of unemployment compensation to a Seventh-Day Adventist who was fired and could not find other work because she refused to work on Saturday, her day of Sabbath. The Court stated that "to condition the availability of benefits upon this cardinal principle of her religious faith effectively penalizes the free exercise of her constitutional liberties" (Fish 1988: 3). Justice Douglas, in his concurring opinion, pointed out that "the government cannot exact from me a surrender of one iota of my religious scruples" without a compelling state interest (375 US 398, 412).

In *Sherbert* vs. *Verner*, the Supreme Court followed a two-step analytic procedure – generally called a "test" by American constitutional lawyers – for analysing free-exercise claims: First, the claimant has to demonstrate that the state imposes (by practice, regulation, or law) a burden on the exercise of religion.

Second, the burden is justified only if it is necessary to advance a "compelling state interest" that outweighs the impaired religious rights (see also Cohen 1987: 773–4). Furthermore, the state has to demonstrate that no less restrictive means are available that might serve its interests without impairing the claimant's free exercise rights (375 US 398, 407). Legal scholars writing on American religious freedom law have called this approach the "Sherbert balancing test".

The factors that define a burden on religious practice and whether such a governmental burden is warranted were outlined in another case decided by the Supreme Court in 1972: In *Wisconsin* vs. *Yoder*, an Amish community would not allow their children to attend public school past the eighth grade, claiming that the education and circumstances surrounding the education provided by the government were influences contrary to Amish faith values. One threshold criterion outlined by the court in this case mandated that the actions for which a defendant seeks protection must be "rooted in religious belief". In other words, protected actions may not be based on philosophical choice, or on "a way of life … [however virtuous and admirable] if it is based on purely secular considerations" (406 US 205, 215). The court further considered whether the (burdened) practices in question were part of an "organized religion" shared by a group, not just a matter of personal choice, and whether the interference – namely, secondary schooling – was a real threat to the practice of the religion in community. In addition, the court asked if the burden imposed on the community's religion would, in the eyes of the members of the religious group, "endanger their own salvation and that of their children by complying with the law". In sum, using the threshold criteria, the court found that the compulsory school attendance law forces the Amish people to "either abandon [their] belief and be assimilated into society at large or be forced to migrate to some other and more tolerant region" (ibid.: 218). By stating that, in order to compel the school attendance of the respondents' children, "it must appear either that the State does not deny the free exercise of religious belief … or that there is a state interest of sufficient magnitude to override the interest claiming the interest under the free exercise clause" (see also Hardt 1989: 618), the Supreme Court applied (and further developed) the test developed in the case of *Sherbert* vs. *Verner*. In doing so, it balanced the free exercise of religion with the importance of the state's interest to impose a legitimate burden on exercise of religion.

Cases like *Sherbert* vs. *Verner* and *Wisconsin* vs. *Yoder* also evidence the Supreme Court's view that the protection of the free exercise of religion is not limited to the direct governmental regulation of religion because: "A regulation neutral on its face may, in its application, nonetheless offend the constitutional requirement for government neutrality if it unduly burdens the free exercise of religion" (*Wisconsin* vs. *Yoder*, 220). In this ruling, it is not relevant whether the burden on religion is intended by or merely the result of the state's regulation.

In US law, the Free Exercise Clause of the First Amendment is complemented by the Establishment Clause. However, the significance of the latter clause is hotly contested, especially in its relation to the Free Exercise Clause. The most important problem is to draw a line between the legitimate "accommodation" of religious practice (which seems to be a requirement of the Free Exercise Clause) and the impermissible "establishment" of religion (see Yablon 2004: 1648). Accommodation merely removes obstacles to the exercise of a religious conviction adopted for reasons independent of the government's actions, while establishment is understood as any state regulation or policy measure that creates incentives or sometimes even compulsions on citizens to adopt a religious practice or belief (ibid.).

A leading case in this context is *Lemon* vs. *Kurtzman* (1971), in which the Supreme Court set out a three-part Establishment Clause test, holding that, in order to pass the establishment scrutiny that must be applied by the courts, a governmental action or regulation must (a) have a secular purpose, (b) not have a primary effect that either advances or inhibits religion, and (c) not foster an "excessive entanglement with religion" (see *Lemon* vs. *Kurtzman*, 403 US 602, 612–13). Later, in cases like *County of Allegheny* vs. *ACLU*, 492 US 573 (1989), the Supreme Court modified its Establishment Clause doctrine, emphasizing that the "main evil" that the Establishment Clause should prevent is the endorsement of religion by the state. State actions should therefore neither have as their purpose or primary effect the endorsement of religion.

The Relevance of Undisturbed Sacred Sites to Indigenous Religions

Most native American cultures are connected to certain natural sites. Based on their world view, these places hold significant spiritual value for members of a given ethnic group. There are different types of sacred sites, some associated with the group's creation myths, some seen to be the homes of spiritual beings that are important for the group's welfare or destiny, and some with a sacred character that arises from the burial places situated there. Despite these differences, most of them share the fact that they are vital to the continued exercise of religion. Given this background, these sites maintain their significance today, and native Americans visit them to pray, to hold ceremonies, or to gain spiritual strength.

At present, however, the "Indian nations' ability to maintain their relationship with these sacred sites is threatened" (Carpenter 2003: 620). As a long-term consequence of the conquest of their lands, indigenous people have lost most of the decision-making power over their lands, and many of the lands where sacred places are situated are now either privately owned or are public lands managed by non-indigenous people. In many cases, moreover, the new owners of these places have been involved in land development projects that are inconsistent with their character as sacred sites.

Over the decades, the sacred sites have in fact faced many different kinds of threat. Not all development projects have changed or even destroyed their physical characteristics. But, according to indigenous beliefs, a serious threat to sacred sites is created when they are opened to the public, thus undermining their sacred character and spiritual power. In some cases, dam building projects have flooded sacred sites, preventing traditional believers from undisturbed access to the sites.

In view of such situations, indigenous believers have sought judicial remedies against the desecration of their lands: Considering the firm way US courts have protected religious freedom rights, outlined above, one expects that plaintiffs would stop developments threatening indigenous sacred sites and, by extension, indigenous religions. Yet, the record of these cases indicates that native Americans have failed to win judicial protection for their sacred sites. In these cases, the courts paid lip service to the standard model of religious freedom protection as it had been developed with a view to non-native cases by the courts of the United States. In the end, however, the application of this model did not prevent the native plaintiffs from losing their cases. In the next section of this chapter, I will outline the reasons for this to occur.

The Failure of Conventional Legal Standards of Religious Freedom to Protect Sacred Sites

In *Sequoyah* vs. *Tennessee Valley Authority* (1980), Cherokee Indians brought suit to obtain an injunction against the proposed impoundment of a flooded water reservoir, claiming that the land which would be flooded was their "sacred homeland". The government's plan was to result in the destruction of "sacred sites, medicine gathering sites, holy places and cemeteries". Yet, despite the fact that the waters, once released, did in fact completely submerge numerous sacred sites, especially important burial sites from the early nineteenth century, the Court of Appeals for the 6th Circuit held that the flooding was constitutional because plaintiffs failed to offer enough evidence to support the relevance of the flooded places for Cherokee religious life (620 F.2d 1159). One of the main reasons why the court dismissed the Cherokee claims had to do with the fact that it qualified the beliefs of the plaintiffs as having merely "secular character". According to the court, the Cherokee had not demonstrated a "constitutionally cognizable infringement of a First Amendment right". The First Amendment protects only the exercise of *religion*, not the exercise of traditional *cultural life*. Therefore, according to the court:

> The overwhelming concern [of the plaintiffs] appears to be related to the historical beginnings of the Cherokees and their development. It is damage to tribal and family folklore and traditions, more than particular religious observances, which appears to be at stake [but] these are no interests protected by the First Amendment [at stake]. (620 F.2d 1164)

The analysis of the Court did not thus even reach the first step of the balancing test advanced by the Supreme Court in *Sherbet* vs. *Verner* (1963) and *Wisconsin* vs. *Yoder* (1972). Government activities might have burdened "culture" and "tradition" but it did not, according to the court, burden "religious" belief or practice, and therefore "there is no need to balance the opposing interest of the parties or to determine whether the government's interest in proceeding with its plans … is 'compelling'". The court's finding that the practice associated with the flooded site was not rooted in religion was sufficient to dispose of the case.

In another case decided by the District Court of Utah in 1977, individual Navaho Indians (among them several medicine men) and three Navaho "chapters" (that is, local organizations of the Navaho nation) filed a complaint against the creation of a lake by the US government as part of a water storage project. The artificial lake covered natural rock formations, held by the claimants to be indigenous prayer spots. The water also flooded the base of "Rainbow Bridge", a large natural sandstone arch that is believed by the Navaho to be the physical incarnation of a god. Plaintiffs alleged that by flooding the arch, the government had destroyed the sacred character of the site and denied the Navaho access to their necessary prayer spots, thereby violating the Free Exercise Clause.

The District Court stated that plaintiffs claimed "that their religious interest involves the use of Rainbow Bridge … for religious ceremonies" (*Badoni* vs. *Higginson*, 455 F. Supp. 641, 647). However, the Court also stated that there had been an absence of religious ceremonies in recent times, and that the Navaho had explained that "[their] ceremonies are not periodic ceremonies [but] are performed when needed, and requested by an individual or family". According to the Court, the Navaho religion was missing core elements of an organized religion, because "the medicine men who allegedly conduct the religious rites involving Rainbow Bridge and the surrounding areas are not recognized by the Navaho Nation as such" (ibid.). In addition, the Court pointed out that the training of these medicine men (as legitimate religious functionaries) had not been organized tribally, and that "religious ceremonies [at Rainbow Bridge] had been attended only infrequently".

The District Court used these elements of Navaho religion to distinguish the case from *Wisconsin* vs. *Yoder* because the Navaho had failed "to demonstrate in any manner … a 'history of consistency' which would support their allegation of religious use of Rainbow Bridge in recent times" (ibid.: 646). In this way, taking the idea of "organized religion" as a criterion for its decision, the Court considered the religious interest of the plaintiffs in the flooded lands to be minimal. Furthermore, based on a second principle, the District Court also dismissed the claim because the Navaho lacked property interests in the flooded lands. This aspect was not conclusive, but an additional factor for the Court to consider in playing down the interest of the plaintiffs. Like the Circuit Court in *Sequoyah* vs. *Tennessee Valley Authority*, the District Court in *Badoni* vs. *Higginson* could dispose of the case without going into detail as to how religious interests were burdened, and balancing these with government interests.

In *Crow* vs. *Gullet* (1982), traditional chiefs of the Lakota (Sioux) and Tsistsistas (Cheyenne) nations complained about road construction and other construction works carried out by the State Park authorities of the State of South Dakota in Bear Butte State Park. Bear Butte is part of the Black Hills, an area with immense cultural and historical importance for the indigenous people of the Northern Great Plains. Indeed, Bear Butte is said to be the place where the "Lakota originally met with the great spirit". The Indian plaintiffs requested the Court to declare their right to "full, unrestricted and uninterrupted religious use" (*Crow* vs. *Gullet*, 541 F. Supp. 785, 788) of the mountains. According to the Indian plaintiffs, the state authorities had desecrated the sanctity and spiritual power of the ceremonial areas through the construction of access roads, parking lots, and a viewing platform. Therefore, they claimed, the defendants and the general public were violating their right to the free exercise of religious belief.

When analysing these claims, the Court failed to find a *coercive effect* of the restriction as it operates against the practice of the religion. A "coercive effect" had previously been defined by US courts either as a governmental regulation requiring actions violative of religious belief ("direct burden") or governmental benefits receivable only on renunciation of religious practice ("indirect burden").[2] By definition, anything else would not impermissibly "burden religion". In the eyes of the Court, the facts in *Crow* vs. *Gullet* simply did not fit into these categories, and did not therefore have any "prohibitory effect" on the exercise of the plaintiffs' religion (see also Andreason 1984: 325).

In summary, in *Crow* vs. *Gullet*, the Court concluded that the plaintiffs failed to show that the construction projects, against which an injunction had been sought, burdened any rights protected by the Free Exercise Clause. According to the Court, plaintiffs could not demonstrate that their "conduct" in the course of exercising their beliefs had been unduly restricted (ibid.: 541 F. Supp. 785, 790/91). The Court underlined its view of the requirements of religious freedom law in stating: "We conclude that the free exercise clause places a duty upon a state to keep from prohibiting religious acts, not to provide the means or environment for carrying them out". By finding that the religious behaviour of the plaintiffs had not been unduly restricted by governmental action, the Court did not have to advance to the second step of the balancing test: As the Court did not find any burden on plaintiff's religion, it was not necessary to examine the interest behind the activities of the State Park authorities.

Similarly, the United States Court of Appeals of the District of Columbia did not balance the indigenous religious freedom claim against a possible compelling governmental interest when Navaho and Hopi plaintiffs challenged the expansion of privately run ski facilities on the San Francisco Peaks. The Peaks are considered to be holy mountains by both the Navaho and Hopi people of the North American Southwest. The plaintiffs therefore argued that the proposed expansion of the "Snow Bowl" ski area violated their rights to religious freedom by diminishing the intrinsic sacredness of the area. The Court admitted the (religious) "indispensability" of the peaks to the practice of Navaho and Hopi

---

2 As described above, in *Sherbert* vs. *Verner*, a Seventh Day Adventist woman had been denied welfare benefits due to the observance of her religious beliefs. The state had placed a burden on her religion by forcing her to choose between the precepts of her religion and forfeiting benefits, and benefits that could be received by abandoning one such precept.

religions (*Wilson* vs. *Block*, 708 F.2d 735 [1983], 744). However, for the Court, "the evidence does not show the indispensability of the … small … permit area". Pointing out that the Forest Service, a state authority managing the Snow Bowl Area, had not denied the plaintiffs access to the Peaks, and had not interfered with their ceremonies and the collection of ceremonial objects, the Court concluded that the ski expansion project did not prevent indigenous people from engaging in their religious practices (ibid.: 745).

It was therefore logically consistent for the Court *not* to recognize a compelling government interest in the ski expansion project. Similar to the other cases, discussed above, the balancing test derived from *Sherbert* vs. *Verner* and *Wisconsin* vs. *Yoder*, which had been developed as a sharp sword for defending Christian sects, was converted into a dull knife when the Court was requested to analyse the (alleged) violation of the religious practices of the Navaho and Hopi peoples. Plaintiffs had contended that their burden was even greater than that in *Sherbert* vs. *Verner*, because the Seventh-Day Adventist woman could have continued her religious practice simply by choosing to forgo government unemployment benefits. The Court, however, declined to extend cases like *Sherbert* vs. *Verner* beyond their specific factual situation, and eventually dismissed the argument (see also Cohen 1987: 788).

In very few cases only, American courts reached the second step of the *Sherbert* vs. *Verner* and *Wisconsin* vs. *Yoder* balancing test. In *Badoni* vs. *Higginson* (1980), the Court of Appeals for the 10th Circuit rejected the basis of the Circuit Court's opinion (see above). The Circuit Court subsequently undertook the second step of the *Wisconsin* vs. *Yoder* balancing test. In doing so, however, it stated that the government had shown the importance of the Glen Canyon Reservoir, involving the flooding Navaho sacred sites, to be a *crucial part* of a multi-stage water storage and power generating project; and it recognized that "the storage capacity of the lake would be cut in half if the surface level were dropped to an elevation necessary to alleviate the infringements [as had been requested by the Navaho plaintiffs]" (638 F.2d 172, 177). It concluded that since the reservoir had to be maintained at the current level and no other action besides reducing the level could alleviate the infringements on the plaintiffs' religious practice, there was no less restrictive manner for the government to attain its interests.

Taken together, the Court decided that continuing a power, water, and recreation project was more important than a centrally important holy place of a long-standing native American religion (as the court itself recognized). The result of the balancing process was also perhaps influenced by the fact that the Court assumed the burden on the plaintiffs' religion to be minimal. After all, it was pointed out by the Court that access to the sacred site had *not* been curtailed – except for the fact that it was flooded: "the government here has not prohibited plaintiffs' religious exercise in the area of rainbow Bridge" (ibid.: 178).

In *Badoni* vs. *Higginson*, native Americans had not only filed a complaint against the flooding of their sacred rocks by an artificial lake. The new lake also provided convenient public access to the Rainbow Bridge Monument. Prior to the creation of the lake, the area had been a very remote region, rarely visited by strangers. After the lake's formation, boats licensed by the National Park Service – a government agency – brought tourists to the monument, and tourist facilities had been constructed by the Park Service. The native Americans complained that tourists brought to the site did not behave in a respectful and appreciative manner, and that they desecrated the sacred nature of the place by noisy conduct, littering and even defacement, so that it could no longer be appropriately used for prayers and ceremonies.

The Court responded to these claims by stating that "we do not believe plaintiffs have a constitutional right to have tourists visiting the bridge act 'in a respectful and appreciative manner'". According to the Court, the Indian plaintiffs sought government action "to exclude others from the Monument, at least for short periods, and to control tourist behavior" (ibid.). But this was considered by the Court as "affirmative action by the government ... in the name of the Free Exercise Clause". The control of tourist behaviour, as requested by the Indian plaintiffs, was accordingly qualified by the Court as a violation of the Establishment Clause, even though the Indian plaintiffs only requested the removal of obstacles to the exercise of their religion that had been created by a governmental agency. After all, the Park Service had encouraged tourists to visit the sacred monuments of the Navaho by facilitating boat excursions and constructing other facilities in a formerly isolated region.

Similarly, like the court in *Badoni* vs. *Higginson*, the United States District Court for the District of South Dakota warned in *Crow* vs. *Gullet* (541 F. Supp. 785, 794) that any "special treatment" or "special privileges" that might occur in favour of indigenous American believers might violate the Establishment Clause. For example, it stated that the Park Administration of Bear Butte had limited public access to trails and tourist platforms, while Indian religious practitioners could freely roam the area. Moreover, the general public could hike the Butte only during a 12-hour period of a day, while Indian religious practitioners could stay on it without time restrictions. The court recognized that these policies were justified because they took account of the value and importance of the Bear Butte for indigenous religion, but in doing so, "the government risks being hauled into court by those who claim that the same rights of the general public are being unduly burdened [by the state]" (ibid.: 794). The court in *Crow* vs. *Gullet* therefore not only failed to consider a deprivation of constitutional rights of the indigenous religious believers by not finding a coercive effect on their religion, but instead found that the government had probably done too much in favour of their religion.

Even worse, in a case decided in 1996, the Wyoming Federal District Court stated that the Climbing Management Plan issued by the National Park Service involving a ban on sports climbing on the Devils Tower National Monument during the month of June for the benefit of indigenous religious ceremonies was in violation of the Establishment Clause (*Bear Lodge Multiple Use Association* vs. *Babbit*, 2 F. Supp. 2d 1448). According to the Court, the Management Plan was a "subsidy of the Indian religion". While Devils Tower is famous as an important rock climbing area, it is also a sacred site for several indigenous ethnic groups. According to legend, seven sisters took refuge from a pursuing bear and finally ascended to heaven, thereby forming the stars of the Big Dipper. Only later, when the National Park Service revised the Management Plan and issued a voluntary climbing closure, the same court ruled that a *voluntary* ban on climbing for non-believers in indigenous religion does *not* violate the Establishment Clause (for details, see Bonham 2002).

Changing the Standards of Religious Freedom Law

So far, I have discussed numerous cases of First Amendment suits that have been filed by indigenous plaintiffs challenging the constitutionality of particular uses of sacred native sites. These cases have not reached the United States Supreme Court. Lower courts of the United States have evaluated these religious claims in different ways, but never have they found in their favour.

In *Lyng* vs. *NW Indian Cemetery Protective Association* (1988), the Supreme Court had, for the first time, a chance to determine how American religious freedom law should be applied in indigenous sacred site cases. In this particular case, members of three ethnic groups from Northern California challenged the decision of the United States Forest Service to build a road through part of a National Forest and to permit timber harvesting in that particular area. The indigenous people use a part of the forest, called "High Country", for religious purposes, such as the search for spiritual power (see Falk 1989: 518) and communication with pre-human spirits. Indigenous religious practitioners believe that people can attain a spiritual power at High Country that helps to stabilize the world and protect human beings. Spiritual use of this area thus depends on the religious practitioner's ability to achieve a specific inner state. However, physical disturbances – like noises in the vicinity of a road – can prevent believers from achieving the inner state necessary to communicate with the spirits (ibid.: 518–19).

The Forest Service commissioned Dorothea Theodoratus, an anthropologist, to undertake a study of the importance of High Country to the native people. Her study recommended that the Forest Service should use an alternative route for the road, because "[i]ntrusions on the sanctity" of the area were "potentially destructive of the very core of Northwest [indigenous] religious beliefs and practices" (Theodoratus Report, 420, cited after 565 F. Supp. 586, 594–5). Having subsequently modified the logging plan to protect specific sites, the Forest Service decided to build the disputed road, but Indian groups nonetheless sued to halt the Forest Service's plan, following which the latter institution agreed not to build the road until the case was resolved. The District Court for the Northern District of California subsequently held that the Forest Service plans violated the Free Exercise Clause and forbade road-building and logging in the High Country (565 F. Sup. 586 [1983]).

When the case finally reached the Supreme Court, many experts thought that there was a good chance that the indigenous groups who sued the state would win their case: The Theodoratus report had concluded that the preservation of the land was indispensable to the rituals of the tribes. Moreover, the road had not been built because plaintiffs had acted quickly enough to hold up construction pending the outcome of the lawsuit. Thus, public money had not yet been spent on the project, implying a weaker government interest, an aspect that could have influenced the outcome of the test in which the court was supposed to balance the religious interest of plaintiffs against the government's interest in road building.

However, *Lyng* vs. *NW Indian Cemetery Protective Association* in fact turned out to be a case in which the Supreme Court effectively decided against the application of the First Amendment to force federal agencies to protect Indian sacred sites (Yablon 2004: 1629) as the Court defined the case primarily as a dispute over property rather than one over religious freedom (ibid.). It understood the claim of the native Americans as a challenge to the federal government to use government (or "public") land (High Country was federal public land) according to its own plans (Carpenter 2003: 624–5).

How did the Court respond to the native Americans' request that the government manage the sacred lands in a way that would protect the "privacy" and "solitude" necessary for their religious practice? It responded by stating that "a law forbidding the Indian[s] from visiting the [sacred] area would raise a different set of constitutional questions. Whatever rights the Indians may have to use the area, however, those rights do not divest the Government of its right to use what is, after all, *its* land" (*Lyng* vs. *NW Indian Cemetery Protective Association*, 108 S. Ct. 1319 (1988), 1327; italics in original). The court, moreover, emphasized that "the government has taken numerous steps … to minimize the impact [of road construction]" (ibid.: 1328) and that the plaintiffs could not request the government to do more for their religious interests.

In this ruling, management of federally owned land was characterized by the Supreme Court as the government's conducting its "own internal affairs":

> The Free Exercise Clause simply cannot be understood to require the Government to conduct its own internal affairs in ways that comport with the religious beliefs of particular citizens. [The Clause] affords an individual protection from certain forms of governmental compulsion; it does not afford an individual a right to dictate the conduct of the Government's internal procedures. (ibid.: 1325)

The Court admitted that the proposed road and timber harvesting would have "severe adverse effects on the practice" of the traditional indigenous religions. However, it did not define these effects as "governmental compulsion". In addition, it strangely analogized the facts in *Lyng* vs. *NW Indian Cemetery Protective Association* with the facts in *Bowen* vs. *Roy* (1986), another native American case in which the Supreme Court addressed the right of an Abenaki father to object to the government's use of his minor daughter's Social Security Number in the public computer system. The father claimed that use of the number would "rob the spirit of his daughter" and violate his group's free exercise of religion (476 US 693, 696). The majority of judges in this case found that the government's use of the child's Social Security Number did *not* violate the free exercise of religion, the main argument of the Court being that the use of the number involved only (internal) governmental action, but required or prevented no action of the plaintiff.

In *Lyng* vs. *NW Indian Cemetery Protective Association*, the Supreme Court used this distinction to imply that road building and timber harvesting on governmentally owned lands was likewise only *internal action* on the part of the government. The Supreme Court thus held that the Free Exercise Clause did not require the government to present compelling justifications for internal procedures, even if these should have *incidental effects* on the exercise of religion. It recognized that the government's actions in this case could "virtually destroy the Indians' ability to practice their religions" (108 S. Ct. 1319, 1321). However, by subsuming the facts of *Lyng* vs. *NW Indian Cemetery Protective Association* under a new category of Free Exercise claims, it states that protection is only sought against the management of the government in the conduct of internal affairs. In brief, by deciding that the administration of public land was an "internal" government affair, the Supreme Court withdrew the management of sacred sites situated on public lands from Free Exercise protection. In fact, it even withdrew the destruction of a religion from strict Free Exercise review. The court held that this was no Free Exercise violation because the government was not coercing Indians into accepting religious beliefs.

Misunderstandings and Misconstructions of Indigenous Religions by US Courts

Justice William J. Brennan, in his dissenting opinion[3] to the above case, stated that the view of the majority was wrong as it was based on a problematic imposition of Western norms on indigenous religions. It is instructive to cite the key passages from Justice Brennan's statement:

> In marked contrast to traditional Western religions, the belief systems of native Americans do not rely on doctrines, creeds or dogmas. Established or universal truths – the mainstay of Western religion – play no part in Indian faith. Ceremonies are communal efforts undertaken for specific purposes in accordance with instructions handed down from generation to generation. Commentaries on or interpretations of the rituals themselves are deemed absolute violations of the

3 A dissenting opinion is an opinion of one or more judges expressing disagreement with the opinion held by the majority. Dissenting opinions do not create binding precedent, but can have persuasive authority, and are sometimes cited when arguing against the majority opinion.

> ceremonies, whose value lies not in their ability to explain the natural world or to enlighten individual believers but in their efficacy as protectors and enhancers of tribal existence. ... Where dogmas lie at the heart of western religions, native American faith is inextricably bound to the use of land. The site-specific nature of Indian religious practice derives from the native American perception that land is itself a sacred, living being. (108 S. Ct. 1319, 1331)

The words of Justice Brennan are an apt summary of some elements that distinguish indigenous American religions from conventional "Western" religions and Christianity in particular. The Judeo-Christian concept of a supreme and immortal deity can be divorced in many respects from specific spatial sites or modes of worship. Also, Judeo-Christian religious practice is bound by doctrine which is regarded to be the result of divine revelation. This revelation, in turn, is conceived of as a historical event, and the elements of the revealed truth have to be preserved for the spiritual salvation of present and future generations.

In contrast to this, worship among North American Indians does not focus on (historical) revelatory events, but on spiritual renewals through ceremonies and individual relationships with sacred places. For example, according to the testimony of the Assiniboine Chief John Snow, "If [a sacred] area is destroyed, marred, or polluted, my people say, the spirits will leave the area. If pollution continues not only animals, birds and plant life will disappear, but the spirits will also leave" (cited in Gordon 1985: 1449).

Generally speaking, therefore, the religious interests of indigenous people at stake have been misunderstood and misconstrued in the judicial cases discussed above, and the protection of the Free Exercise clause has therefore been denied to Indian plaintiffs (see also ibid.: 1448). This was indeed not only true for the Supreme Court decision in *Lyng* vs. *NW Indian Cemetery Protective Association*. A brief review of case law illustrates that a large part of the failure of indigenous American people to win sacred-site cases is rooted in the traditional Western ethnocentric background of religious freedom law.

In *Sequoyah* vs. *Tennessee Valley Authority*, for example, the judge who saw the beliefs of the plaintiffs to have merely "secular character" failed to understand the inseparable relations between the spheres of the "sacred" and the "profane" from an indigenous American perspective. When the Cherokee plaintiffs explained that the flooding of their ancient cemeteries led to a loss of their "tradition", they did not necessarily mean that the loss of tradition has no religious meaning. But the modern Euro-American legal system is characterized by the idea of a separation of "church" and "state", so that the Court imposed dividing lines on a non-Western culture where these lines do not exist.

On the other hand, the District Court in *Badoni* vs. *Higginson*, and the Circuit Courts in *Crow* vs. *Gullet* and in *Wilson* vs. *Block* found that no burden had been placed on indigenous religion by development projects that desecrated sacred lands or holy mountains because, as the courts maintained, the government did not regulate or prohibit the belief or practice of individual believers. The perceptions of the courts leading to these rulings have been influenced by Western-Christian notions of individual free will, which is considered to be the fundament of religious belief and must be respected and legally protected. But courts were reluctant to accept that native free exercise claims assert the right to control and prevent adverse impacts on *land*. It was not recognized sufficiently by the courts that indigenous Americans strive to maintain a natural order in the places that they worship and where they believe that spiritual forces exist. Indigenous American religions do not have the intention of remembering historically revealed truths, but place belief in spiritual powers that are effective in certain spatial areas. The desecration or destruction of the physical world thus impedes the effectiveness of these powers, and therefore undermines the religion and endangers the well-being of human and other beings.

In brief, from a Judeo-Christian perspective, a religion is *not* endangered by the desecration of sacred places because it is assumed that believers can simply continue to practice their religion a few miles away from the respective places. For indigenous believers, by contrast, the new use of the sacred land burdens their religion more than a mere prohibition of prayer on certain parts of the land.

In cases in which courts balanced the religious interests of indigenous plaintiffs against the interest of the state to impose a burden on the indigenous free exercise of religion, the results have been influenced by what appears to be a general leitmotif in Euro-American legal culture, namely the suppression of indigenous cultures in the name of white development and progress. The westward expansion of the American "frontier", the conquest by Euro-Americans of Western lands that were defined as pristine wilderness, has widely been seen as a "natural" historical process.

The theme of *victory through settlement over savages and wolves* (note that this idea was even promoted by George Washington; see also Bonham 2002: 199) is deeply rooted in Euro-American culture. In North America, moreover, indigenous peoples have not been deprived of their lands and intellectual resources by the application of force, but by an expropriation process based on *legal* principles that were developed and applied by the "courts of the conqueror". This also implies that competitive interests involving lands considered to be sacred by indigenous American groups fall into a legal explanatory framework in which land (and natural resources more generally) should be subject to rational and efficient development. Therefore, developmental interests do not need any further justification for outbalancing the interests of indigenous groups. Through the lens of this principle, the courts of the American mainstream society have trivialized indigenous religious interests in lands against economic interests such as the exploitation of oil, minerals, or even the expansion of recreation lakes or ski areas.

When courts warned that giving in to indigenous claims to protect sacred sites would constitute "special treatment" or "special privileges" that might violate the Establishment Clause (compare above, as an example, the District Court in *Crow* vs. *Gullet*), they misunderstood the function of the Establishment Clause and the non-dogmatic character of indigenous American religions: As mentioned above, a characteristic of traditional religions in the Americas is that their religious content is "site-related" and inseparably connected to the socio-cultural context. That is to say that the spiritual power of these religions functions only in the original setting. Members of these religions do not therefore intend to propagate their religion to non-believers; from their perspective, proselytism and missionary activities make no sense.

Yet, according to a liberal understanding of human rights, citizens can choose their religion without state interference. Thus, considering that the main purpose of the Establishment Clause is to ensure the freedom of citizens from government imposition of religion, the courts seem to have confused the forbidden *promotion or advancement* of religion with the legitimate *accommodation* of indigenous religions. The courts wrongly implied that any protection of the exercise of indigenous religion creates incentives for non-indigenous persons to adopt these religions, even if these are bound to their original locale and cultural context by their very nature.

Conclusions

Summing up, I have shown in this chapter that the application of religious freedom law in contemporary US courts is based on a strong cultural bias anchored in Western religion, in which the core value of religious freedom pays respect to individual adherence to religious beliefs and behavioural codes. Complying with such beliefs and codes – which are believed to have their (historical) origin in divine revelation – is fundamental to the individual's religious "salvation". According to this understanding, the worst that can happen to a religious believer is to receive pressure that is imposed to violate his religious rules. Conventional religious freedom law is thus based in the Christian religion, and is also rooted in Jewish and Muslim traditions. These religions share the idea that religious rules can (or even should) be revealed to anybody by the *word*. For this reason, in principle, they can be carried out by any human being who believes in the divine revelation – wherever he or she lives – and are not dependent on specific spatial and socio-cultural contexts.

This, however, differs strikingly from the views of indigenous religious believers; their religions are not traced to a revelatory founding event, and for them, "communal involvement in ceremonies and continual renewal of relationships with holy places are more important than the efforts to conform individual behavior to religious dogma" (Andreason 1984: 320).

US courts, however, have generally concluded that religious freedom constitutes a duty on the part of the state to refrain from prohibiting religious acts of believers, but not to guarantee the natural environment for carrying them out. As in the *Bear Butte* case, the courts began with the proposition that the integrity and undefiled appearance of the sacred site has nothing to do with the indigenous peoples' rights to practice their religion (see Pemberton 1985: 328).

Thus, while failing to recognize the indigenous groups' religious veneration for sacred land, American courts have not protected indigenous religions that do not separate land and spirit as Western religious traditions do. This has to do with the fact that, according to Western law, issues of religious freedom are a matter of prohibiting (or proscribing) the behaviour of human beings, but are not an issue of land management, resource administration, or public economic decision making. This view is also backed by the way in which conflicts of religious freedom are conceived by courts in America: Conventional religious freedom law allows for a burden to be placed the exercise of religion, but the burden has to be justified by a compelling state interest. In this manner, the procedure used to decide on conflicts concerning the protection of sacred sites follows the logic of conflicts between "private" religious interests and opposing interests of a state representing the "public".

As we have seen, however, the balancing process generally disfavours minority religions. It is difficult to convince the courts that the religious practices at stake outweigh the "public" interest if the believers are only a few people and if the "public" is defined as being the expression of the interests of "many". I therefore argue that a new framework for protecting the interests of indigenous believers at sacred sites should be developed in order to overcome the Western-religious cultural bias underlying conventional religious freedom law. I suggest that the protection of indigenous American religions can only be reached by widening the scope of religious freedom rights, as they are defined in national and international law, by making them consistent with indigenous people's rights.

References

Andreason, J.T. 1984. Indian Worship vs. Government Development: A new breed of religion cases. *Utah Law Review*, 2, 313–36.

Bonham, C.H. 2002. Devils tower, rainbow bridge and the uphill battle facing native American religion on public lands. *Law and Inequality*, 20: 157–202.

Carpenter, K.A. 2003. In the absence of title: Responding to federal ownership in sacred sites cases. *New England Law Review*, 39, 619–33.

Cohen, M.S. 1987. American Indian sacred religious sites and government development: A conventional analysis in an unconventional setting. *Michigan Law Review*, 85(4), 771–808.

Falk, D. 1989. *Lyng* vs. *Northwest Indian Cemetery Protective Association*: Bulldozing first amendment protection of Indian sacred lands. *Ecology Law Quarterly*, 16, 515–70.

Fish, N. 1988. *Free Exercise Rights, Sacred Sites, and Lyng*. Professor Nell Newton seminar class "American Indian Law", Law School, Catholic University of America, Washington D.C.

Gordon, S.B. 1985. Indian religious freedom and governmental development of public lands. *Yale Law Journal*, 94, 1447–71.

Hardt, S. 1989. The sacred public lands: Improper line drawing in the Supreme Court's free exercise analysis. *University of Colorado Law Review*, 60, 601–57.
Pemberton, R. 1985. "I saw that it was holy": The black hills and the concept of sacred land. *Law and Inequality*, 3, 287–342.
Yablon, M. 2004. Property rights and sacred sites: Federal regulatory responses to American Indian religious claims on public lands. *Yale Law Journal*, 113, 1623–62.

Chapter 4
The Cuban Republic and its Wizards

Stephan Palmié

In the aftermath of Giorgio Agamben's and Jacques Derrida's acclaimed disquisitions on the mystical foundations of the law and the political theologies at the heart of the sovereignty exercised by the secular nation state, it has become somewhat of a commonplace to assert that the conceptual separation between "the religious" and "the legal" is a fiction characteristic of, or even foundational to, modern forms of governance. In this chapter, it is not my aim to dispute such abstract claims concerning the contingent (rather than necessary) nature of such conceptual separations and their role in legitimizing contemporary statecraft. Rather than elaborate a metatheoretical position concerning religion and law as contested sovereignties, I intend to empirically specify how, over the course of the past century, social scientists, state agents, politicians and legal practitioners in a post-colonial Caribbean nation state deployed the construct of an irrational "African religious other" in seeking to implement and legitimize their (historically changing) visions of a national project and its appropriate normative order. My goal in this is less to foreground the violent nature of the conscription of elements of Cuba's African cultural heritage into such projects of self-consciously "modern" rational governance and normativity (though this will become obvious enough); rather, what I am interested in is a moment of "conjuring" evident, or so it seems to me, in the practices of Cuban social scientists, secular lawmakers and state agents concerned with domesticating – through persecution or co-optation – what they perceived as a moral order coexisting with, but largely beyond the control of aspirationally "modern", and notionally "scientific" forms of governance. As I hope to show in the following sketch of two episodes in a "long conversation" between the Cuban Republic and its African wizards ("*brujos*") and deities ("*orichas*"), what is at issue here is not an empirically fortuitous blurring of boundaries between sacred and secular normative orders (or, from another perspective, an equally contingent revelation of the fictitious nature of such boundaries). It is the operation of a fundamentally "hybrid"[1] dynamic that accrues from the historical interdependence and mutual articulation of both "African wizardry" and "Cuban national modernity".

1 In Bruno Latour's (1993) sense.

Human Sacrifice

In the course of a period of at least two decades of massive, often violent repression, beginning in late 1904, Cuban social science and Afro-Cuban religions came to enter into mutually constitutive relations. In November of that year, a 20-month-old female toddler named Zoila Díaz disappeared from her parents' homestead in a rural town south of Havana. Within days, three elderly Africans were arrested and charged with having assassinated and disembowelled the child. A theory about their motive emerged early on, and although it was never proven in court, led to the execution of Domingo Bocourt and his alleged accomplice, the creole Victor Molina. Being a "locally known" *brujo* or African wizard, Bocourt, so the reasoning went, had aimed to cure an African woman of a magical harm (*daño*) done to her by the whites in the period of slavery by application of the girl's blood. Selected to procure the victim, Molina, in turn, had killed the girl, and extracted not only the blood, but various organs from her body which he intended to fashion into charms to be sold commercially.[2]

The story is as fascinating in its dramatization of themes pertaining to the abuse of dehumanized bodies for economic purposes – a key feature of slavery if there ever was one – as it is obscene in its political implications and concrete results. Neither was it an isolated case. Between 1904 and the early 1920s some two dozen incidents involving the death or disappearance of children were publicly interpreted as *brujería*-related crimes, and repeatedly elicited not just vociferous bursts of public outrage, but mob violence, and attempted or consummated lynchings of presumed black *brujos*. In public discourse, the term "brujería" came to flourish as a highly inclusive category, metonymically condensing a variety of practices by means of a superimposed metaphorical scheme in which Afro-Cuban cultural otherness and the violent murder of children interacted to form a novel complex that exhibited stunningly expansive tendencies. "Brujería" proliferated – if in the form of a growing ubiquity of signs perceivable as symptoms of its presence, or created in the course of measures to eradicate it. Particularly in the aftermath of the so-called "race war" of 1912 – the violent military campaign to smash the *Partido Independiente de Color*[3] – Havana's urban police increased raids on Afro-Cuban cult groups in attempt to stem what was felt to be a rising tide of African witchcraft complementing black political unrest in a dangerous manner. The copious evidence of African-looking ritual paraphernalia thus produced seemed to indicate a sinister process insidiously unfolding behind closed doors or under cover of darkness.

By the time of the second US occupation (1906–1909), the American forces could not help but face up to the problem. In the wake of the so-called "niña Luisa" case in Alacranes (Province of Matanzas) in 1908, the commanding officer of the American occupation forces in Matanzas saw fit to report to his superiors the

2 This and the following section draw on the material presented in Palmié (2002: 201–59).

3 On which see Helg (1995).

results of his confidential investigations in the beliefs and practices "responsible for most, if not all, of the child-murders that so frequently occur in Cuba". "One of their beliefs" Colonel O.J. Sweet concluded "is that the blood of a child is a sure cure for some diseases. The higher and nobler the birth of the child, the greater and surer the efficacy of its blood" (US National Archives Record group 199, Prov. Govt. Cuba, Conf. Corr. 1906–1909, case file 248). What particularly perplexed Cuban observers was that none of these practices seemed to be traceable to the colonial period. Instead, if Cuba appeared to be in the throes of an epidemic of ritual crime, such atrocities were entirely contemporaneous with – indeed, as Bronfman (2004: 39) writes, constituted an "inherent but inexplicable" feature of – Cuban republican modernity. As a commentator in *El Día* put the matter in 1918, "Until after the triumph of the revolution blacks raised white children without eating or abusing them". Now that national independence had been achieved and Afro-Cubans endowed with full citizenship rights, they "have begun to drink the blood of white children" (cited in Bronfman 2004: 39).

As the latter quote indicates, it is of course not difficult to see to what interests the construct of *brujería* spoke. As Helg (1995) argues, the concept of *brujería* and the techniques of repression it suggested well served a new Cuban elite bent on avoiding to have to address the problem of persisting racial inequality under a nominally colour blind constitution. Similarly, Chávez Álvarez (1991) suggests that the niña Zoila case dramatizes, in symbolic form, the turn from the "violent mechanism of slavery" to the "violence of racial discrimination" vital to the political-economic order characterizing the US-sponsored first Cuban republic. In his view, *brujería* focused, and thereby rendered more effective, general strategies of racializing social inequality.

Helg and Chávez are certainly right in situating the case within its larger political – and political economic – context, including, not incidentally, the role of US interference in the economic and political affairs of the Caribbean region. Sharing important structural features with the North American obsession of the sexual defilement of white women by black men, the image of the disembowelled body of white female children sacrificed to African deities for the sake of healing illiterate ex-slaves invoked not only a symbolical inversion of the projected future of the Cuban nation – suggesting the ravage of white republican progeny as an atonement for the clinging evil of a slaveholding past. It also constituted a "national" embarrassment in respect to Cuba's accreditation as a civilized state.

Ever since the 1820s, Cuban critics of slavery had branded Spain's policy of building up its last prosperous colony by condoning the illegal import of Africans instead of white metropolitan labourers. Now, it seemed, the Cuban Republic laboured under the lasting heritage of a misguided colonial development scheme, and its unintended social, cultural, and – most painfully for contemporary nationalist thinkers – biological results. The very presence of an African and African-descended population within the social and political space defined by the new Cuban state posed a vexing ideological problem. As in many other Latin America nations, the reception of European scientific racism and positivistic social thought by local intellectuals and the political elite since the late nineteenth century had created an obsessive awareness not only of the existence of an African population, but of the "racially mixed" status of the better part of the national population – an awareness that appeared to call for attempts, on the part of self-consciously modernists to rid Cuba of its racial stigma by discursive and/or physical means.

Here, then, was a second arena in which the niña Zoila case, and its successors came to perform cultural work. No doubt, the early twentieth-century "witch-hunts" served the overt political purpose of discrediting Cuba's black electorate and justifying the manner in which landless rural Afro-Cubans were shuttled back into coercive labour regimes different from slavery only in the formal legitimatory structure undergirding their exploitation. But to say as much is to stop short of the larger analytical task of relating concrete technologies of repression to the ideological templates that not only inform them, but within which instances of repression, in turn, come to function as cultural performances reproductive of situated projections of identity and moral community. As I shall argue in the following, the concept of *brujería* acquired its tremendous power as a device for constructing overtly racialized notions of Cuban national self-hood precisely at a moment when Cuban versions of European science came into their own. The conjuncture was not fortuitous. The vision of social progress and scientific control of human affairs that animated Cuban intellectual life in the early republican period was deeply imbricated in the construct of an atavistic other whose very body – indeed, its anatomy and visceral structure – would serve as the theatre within which apprentices of an international sorcery would perform their cures of the Cuban national organism.

One of the obvious problems that self-consciously modernizing witch hunters (as well a enforcement agents and prosecutors) in early Republican Cuba encountered was that *brujería* was legal intractable. Indeed, a critical defect of the old Spanish criminal code – still in force in the early republican period – was that it failed to provide for legal measures to be directed against the evil Cubans now found themselves facing. While the Spanish colonial government had outlawed the male secret society *abakuá* since 1876 as a seditious and criminal organization, rendering its ceremonies acts of "unlawful association", no such legal grounds existed for the persecution of practitioners of other Afro-Cuban religions at the time of Zoila Díaz's death (Palmié 2002: 225–33). Moreover, the Cuban constitution explicitly guaranteed freedom of religion and peaceful association for legal ends, thus, among other things prolonging the lease of life of many of the old *cabildos de nación* – legally inscribed voluntary associations of Africans and their descendants organized along the lines of New World constructions of African ethnic identity. Although Cuban witch hunters went as far as trying to resurrect Spanish slave law to construct people engaged in African-derived practices into incriminable subjects, they fared particularly badly in cases where the victims of police raids were civic associations, and – to the dismay of the officers in charge – could usually produce written permissions of the municipal government to stage "festivities according to the African custom". In more than one sense, the rule of law – and a curiously hybrid of Spanish penal legislation and Republican constitutional guarantees, at that – was key to the inability of republican persecutors to achieve their goals of eradicating the "African savagery" in their midst. Inscribed within one and the same legal framework, Afro-Cuban cult groups and the executive organs of the Cuban state were technically constitutive of each other. The "Africanity" of the one not only mirrored the "Westernness" of the other. They were deeply implicated in each other.

Writing in 1921, Fernando Ortiz seems to have recognized this strange collusion between the modern state and its African deities. "The governmental aim [...] of transforming the cabildos into modern associations failed completely", he lamented, arguing that while the socially positive functions of the cabildos had been repressed, a "savage animistic fetishism under a Catholic advocation" now subsisted under reglementations

> adapted to the demands of legal formalism. And the authorities were satisfied. How much better would have been a contrary outcome! How much better would it be if we today had mutualist cabildos and public dances with African drums, and not temples of brujería, of clandestine or tolerated nature! (Ortiz 1921: 30)

By then, Ortiz was already on his way to a fundamental revaluation of Afro-Cuban culture as a vital part of Cuban national culture. Still, it was he who initially put the legally intractable phantom of *brujería* on the map of a regime of knowledge geared towards constituting the odious racial and cultural other as an object of scientific elimination.

Captured by Science

By the time Ortiz first entered the debate on *brujería* with his bestselling monograph *Los negros brujos* in 1906, he had become closely associated with the "nouva scuola penale" of Cesare Lombroso. Lombroso positivistic theories of delinquent behaviour as a function of physiologically determined (and anatomically detectable) moral "atavism" – that is individual regression to biologically "older", animalic psychological states conflicting with the stage of moral evolution of the delinquent's social milieu – had strongly impacted not only European, but Latin American thought on the scientific rationalization of social control. This new criminological idiom – allowing for the establishment of a correlation between delinquency and physiology on the one hand, and an evolutionary scheme of collective "moral progress" on the other – paved the way to a conceptual refiguration of long-standing elite constructions of black deviance into scientifically circumscribable indices of "Africanity". For many a Latin American modernist, this was an appealing solution. It was not through massive physical repression, but through the scientific policing of the population and through the transposition of conceptions of deviance and crime into an idiom of physiological or psychic abnormality that irruptions of "Africanity" into the public sphere would become knowable as "racial atavisms", and, therefore, subjectable to rigorous measures of social hygiene. Particularly in the Cuban case the metaphor of hygiene – with its implications of scientifically enforced cleanliness, and transparency – provided a powerful rhetorical tool for the objectification of *brujería* as a noxious agent, a social pathogen. This solution was especially compelling, because the successful eradication of yellow fever through the sanitation campaigns conducted by the American occupational forces between 1900 and 1902 had been based on the Cuban physician Carlos Finlay's earlier discovery of its vectors, and could, thus, be claimed as a triumph of Cuban science. Hence the scientistic savagery of Ortiz's early vision of a medical-criminological regime based upon positive knowledge:

> The first [measure] in the defensive struggle against the *brujería* has to be to finish off the *brujos*, to isolate them from their faithful like those afflicted with yellow fever, for *brujería* is by its nature contagious, and while these [i.e. the *brujos*] enjoy more or less compete liberty to continue their parasitism, it will subsist, and will attempt to maintain those who sustain it in the intellectual passivity necessary for that they continue to support it even happily. Once those swindlers are gone, their feasts, dances and savage rites ended, their temples destroyed, their impotent deities confiscated, all the tentacles of the *brujería* which chain its believers to the barbaric bottom of our society cut, then, free of hindrances, they will be able to alleviate their still not de-Africanized minds of the weight of confused superstitions, and rise to successive zones of culture. (Ortiz 1973: 242)

The complex intertextuality between physiological and moral discourses, and the enormous semantic productivity of the metaphoric linkages between ethnography and epidemiology, sanitation and punishment, science and domination Ortiz established in *Los negros brujos* immediately impacted a wide discursive field. Ortiz's positivistic regime of knowledge production initially foisted itself not "empirical" data, but on secondary recensions of "atavistic bodies", "African customs", and Afro-Cuban practices which he had merely culled from newspaper reports while still in Spain, and fused into the authoritative product of a truly "Cuban" contribution to the world of science. Nevertheless, as the public reception of *Los negros brujos* shows, once removed from the genre of "reportage" to that of "science", the veracity of the "data" so produced, and the questionable referential functions of the theories built upon them turned into a non-issue; a certainty on which other forms of discourse began to build, and which was soon fed back into those genres from which it had, originally, taken off. In an ingenious comparison between the texts of a verdict rendered upon the alleged authors – meanwhile lynched (or fusilladed in flight, if you will) – of the 1919 killing of "la niña Cecilia" in Matanzas, Chávez Álvarez (1991) has shown in detail how the very wording of the incriminatory document indicates beyond doubt the wholesale transfer of entire passages from *Los negros brujos* to a legal text ostensibly describing a crime that took place 14 years after the book's first publication.

More obviously yet, Ortiz's diagnostic and therapeutic suggestions amply fed back into the journalistic discourse from which they had taken their initial departure. In the context of the so-called "niño Cornelio" case of 1913 Havana's *Diario de a Marina* reprinted a letter to the editor of the periodical *El Día*. Signed x.x., it suggested the following measures against *brujería*:

- perpetual deportation for all those who are justifiably considered to be *brujos*, regardless of sex or race
- males and females are to be confined separately in different localities so as to render impossible their coming near each other
- the localities to be designated for their deportation could be the keys or islets which surround our island, or any other territory bought by the state for this purpose, and in these places the vigilance necessary to avoid the escape of the confined will be enacted
- in these banishment territories arable land will be distributed among the confined, who will there be at liberty to, and have access to the means of, work

> In summary: What is needed is to organize colonies of *brujos* and *brujas*, absolutely, and definitively closed off to the outside, while giving them freedom within the territory they inhabit, and the means to subsist by labour, but impeding them from escape and reproduction.

Another commentator in *El Día* offered rather more severe variations on a theme by Ortiz. As in the animal kingdom there existed the threefold distinction between "tame", "tamed" and "wild" beasts, he suggested, so humanity divided itself among the "civilized", "civilizable" and "refractory". If, in both cases, the third category universally merited extirpation, Cubans would do well to face up to the example given by the nation whose civilizing efforts it had benefited from so much in the past.

> The Americans, insuperable people in as far as practical sense is concerned, have given to us a good object lesson and grand proof in respect to that problem occupying us now. It is known that [the US] is the most tolerant country of the world, the great 'country of tolerance' par excellence: there all sects – however excitable they may be, are respected. Well then, the so-called 'Moros of Mindanao and Jolo' (in the Philippines) were, are, an equivalent to the Cuban *brujos*: in their barbarous practices, in as far as they eat children, cut the throat and mutilate Christian maidens, with which they attain the heavenly reign (of their heavens, that is). And what did the Americans do? Well, they publicly, officially, and without unnecessary qualms, gave the order to exterminate them. And General Wood [well known to Cubans as the head commander during the second occupation], obediently and happily 'dimished them' (as the Mexicans say) with gusto. And at this very moment, under the present American administration, we just read the following (fresh off the press) what the *New York Herald* of the 22

> of the past month of June tells us in respect to those Philippine equivalents to the *brujos*: 'As the government of President Wilson is convinced that the troglodyte crimes of the "Moros of Jolo" and the septentrional part of Mindanao represent a formidable threat for the civilized natives and resident Americans, as well as that any solution given to the Philippine problem has nothing to do with the extirpation of a savagism "immune to Christian teachings", it has been decided in Washington [that it is necessary] to "destroy which one cannot regulate"'. (*El Día* 7/4/13)

The author added that even "illustrious anthropologists" nowadays sustained that practitioners of *brujería* did not constitute a "race", but a "species". The trajectory of reduction Ortiz had suggested in commending "the progressive immunization against the microbe of brujería" (1973: 248) had run its full biotic course: In a metaphoric progression running across diverse fields of inquiry, the *brujo* had evolved from microbiotic to simian incarnations, from feral to indomitable stages, and from republican civic status to that of a product of nature – a different species, noxious, parasitic and irredeemable. And it is surely not accidental that the verb "*lynchar*" entered Cuban Spanish as an American loanword at just that time, and in precisely this context.

Hence the task of "criminal anthropology": to penetrate beneath the surface of criminal appearances, and develop a regime of knowledge capable to rendering the *brujo* transparent to the gaze of science in order to forestall cruder, and politically more costly forms of violence. Perhaps the most symptomatic figure in all this was Israel Castellanos, at the time professor of criminology at the University of Madrid. In his prize-winning memoir *La brujería y el náñiguismo desde el punto de vista medico-legal* Castellanos (1916) declared the *brujo*'s body the theatre in which the nascent science of Cuban criminology would perform its most significant feats. Emulating the taxonomic and procedural regime of an anatomy of the criminal body, Castellanos dissects the *brujo*'s physiology in search of typologically salient features – few as they surprisingly turn out to be: the "simian cleavages" of his brain, the smallness of his ears, the asymmetrical implantation of his eyes, the tendency to cover his small – by "racial standards" – lower jaw with a beard, his longevity. Castellanos's pompous memoir, in fact, reads like an awkward attempt to prove the physiological normalcy of the handful of convicted *brujos* who did not escape the calipers of Cuban amateur anthropometrists. Of course, for Castellanos, this somewhat embarrassing fact indicated nothing less than that he was on the right track. For the semiotics of the *brujo*'s body apparently involved a cunning attempt at biotic simulation. The *brujo*'s body was as polymorphous as the civic status of Cuba's African or African-descended population remained polysemic under the Republican regime. And both were in need of "fixing".

This bizarre exercise in conjuring up a textual simulacrum of the physiologically invisible *brujo* was not a mere aberration, a quirk of scientistic opportunism. Not only the prize Castellanos's memoir won from Havana's Academía de Ciencias, but the very heuristics and methodology upon which it was based bespoke the working of a much more widely dispersed regime of knowledge, a form of semiosis that – in re-inscribing relations of dominance and inequality upon human bodies in the form of relations between civilization and savagery – constantly strove to materialize its object, only to annihilate it. Visualizing the *brujo* was the first step. Sanitary measures would follow. As a site of both lynch-justice, and criminological science, the *brujo*'s body was little else than a scenario within which a variety of discourses, afloat in early republican Cuba found or created their reified referents.

Castellanos's efforts to "make science" from the stuff of black Cuban bodies bear a striking resemblance to the semiotics of police investigations in the aftermath of raids productive of "instruments of *brujería*". Not surprisingly, officers barging into tenement buildings or private homes often found themselves faced not only with a multitude of people engaged in activities of unclear portent, but with a profusion of objects of even stranger aspect (Bronfman 2004). Carted off by the police in vast quantities, duly catalogued, and usually included in legal files and press reports in the form of long descriptive lists, such objects came to perform a double function in the making of *brujería*. On the one hand, the catalogues of items confiscated by the police precisely because of their strange appearance and ostensibly nonintelligible function reveal a peculiarly "archaeological" mechanism of interpretation that assigned "ritual" value to what, in fact, were simply ill-understood heaps of de-contextualized objects. Though such lists undoubtedly contain what must have been perceived by the victims of the raid as ritual objects, the main purpose was not to understand their meaning, but to create evidence of something which had no meaning – and, indeed, could have none – in the eyes of their original owners/manipulators: *brujería*. We might call this the enunciatory function of such loot. Yet these sadly jumbled remains of sacred objects and assemblages, reassembled according to a bizarre new logic together with unrelated mundane articles at the hand of cataloguing police clerks underwrote the reification of *brujería* in yet another way. For on the other hand, they objectified not just the presumed existence of the referent of *brujería*, but served as palpable signs for the effectiveness of the reconnaissance strategies with which law-enforcement and scholarly agencies pursued what otherwise seemed to elude them. Not accidentally, many of these objects wound up in the newly founded Anthropological Museum of the University of Havana, where they underwent yet another set of semantic transformations circling around the idea of *brujería* at the able cataloguing hands of Dr Luis Montané, a former disciple of Broca. Then and there, they assumed their second function as signs not of *brujería*, but of the productivity of a science they served to constitute.

Here we might note a rather intriguing parallelism of practices. Part of the catalogues of crimes laid at the doorstep of Cuba's *brujos* was the desecration of graves to obtain human body parts. To this day, bones or dirt from the graves of specific persons do, indeed, play a significant part in the rites of *palo monte* and other traditions known collectively as *reglas de congo*. Such remnants of the dead serve to animate complex objects – known in Cuba today as *ngangas* or *prendas*

– by installing the spirit of the dead in a relationship determined by the object's owner's power to "feed" and manipulate it for his or her ends. Possession over the remains of a person, to this day, represent the key to access the power of his or her spirit. It is a relation surrounded by sinister images of slavery, wage labour and dependence. But just as modern day *paleros* constitute their priestly competence on the domination of one or more *muertos* [spirits of the dead], so did the science practised by Castellanos and his colleagues in the Museo de Antropología constitute itself on the grounds of the bodily remains of dead *brujos*. As Castellanos (1916: 22) himself opined, the fact that the brains of the garroted authors of the Zoila crime (sacrificed as they had been to the fetish of modern republican statehood) wound up – along with innumerable other objects – in the hands of the illustrious Dr Montané was a sign of auspicious portent regarding the future of Cuban science. As contemporary priests of *palo monte* might say, the Museo Antropológico had turned into a giant *nganga*, animated by the enslaved remains of the powerful dead.

A Hundred Years of Solitude

In late November 1994 I picked up a copy of the newspaper *Juventud Rebelde* somewhere on the streets of Havana. It carried a notice pertaining to the upcoming festivities for Santa Bárbara on 4 December – a popular occasion for rituals in honour of *Changó*, a deity associated with the day of this saint. Reflecting the current party line on Afro-Cuban religions, the author was at pains to point out that the legends of white children abducted on that day, and sacrificed by black wizards to African idols not just referred to a *thing* of the past. Rather, he argued, they harkened back to a previous stage of Cuban society when ideologies of racial otherness still effectively served to mystify the fundamental class antagonism alienating the Cuban nation from a realization of its common Latin-African cultural heritage. The implication was that the spectre of African *brujería* had always been an epiphenomenon of capitalism – an ideological phantasm dividing the Cuban working class along racial lines, and securing imperialist domination. Hence its obsolescence in a society where socialism had eradicated the class antagonisms it had served to mystify, and so realigned social thought with material reality.

If so, however, why disabuse a socialist readership – fully 35 years after the triumph of the Revolution – of the notion that frightful things might happen on the night of 4 December? Should it not have been evident to the readers of *Juventud Rebelde* that the drums echoing throughout the poorer and notably blacker "barrios" of Havana that evening were testimony to the revolutionary working class's righteous celebration of the culture of what Castro called "un país latinoafricano", not incidentally, on the eve of Cuba's entry into the Angolan war? "If, under capitalism, the bourgeoisie declared the values created by the dominant classes [to be the] cultural patrimony", the Moscow-trained anthropologist Guanche (1983: 475) had written in 1983, "under socialism it is necessary to valorize the creations of the old dominated classes and, with the proletariate in power, to consider as cultural patrimony the totality, positive or identificatory of what is Cuban, in the material and spiritual traditions of the [national] culture". As sociologists Argüelles Mederos and Hodge Limonta (1991: 143) phrased the official consensus obtaining in the early 1990s,

> for the practitioners of these cults, the Revolution has meant not only social liberation, but also a certain revalorization of their cults through the consequent policy of the Party and Revolutionary Government, and the granting of importance to the preservation of the cultural values to which the syncretic cults associate themselves in [respect to] the music, dance or instruments which enrich Cuban folklore.

If so, again, why even point out, in so many words, that there was nothing sinister about such ceremonies, and that phenotypically white children need not be locked up at home after dark? For Alejandro, a graduate student, and recent convert to Pentecostalism who never failed to strike up a conversation in English with me whenever we ran into each other on the street, matters were rather more straightforward. "Why", he asked me, fully aware of the focus of my research, "do you keep going to these witchcraft parties [meaning Afro-Cuban religious ceremonies]? They kill people, you know."[4]

To be sure, neither Alejandro's disapproval of Cuba's African cultural heritage, nor such academic paeans to the revolution's policies of cultural revalorization would have been thinkable only ten years earlier. Up until the late 1980s, the Cuban revolutionary state's declared politics of scientific atheism would certainly not have allowed Alejandro to openly express his views of the dangers posed by "witchcraft parties" in a manner that implied his own belief in the diabolic nature of such rites. More significantly, perhaps, they would also have forced those Cuban ethnographers still active after the demise of the short-lived Instituto de Etnología y Folklor (1961–73) to argue that their task consisted in "salvaging" remnants of Cuba's pre-revolutionary popular religious heritage before its aesthetic or otherwise edifying manifestations melted away, along with its mystifications, under the glaring sun of socialist rationalism. While no longer proposing that it was the goal of practitioners of Afro-Cuban religions to insure that "in the midst of the revolutionary process there persist in our fatherland a horrible and mysterious chunk of fifteenth century equatorial Africa", as a contributor to *El Militante Comunista* had written at the heighday of the "revolutionary offensive" of 1968 (Anonymous 1968: 45), in 1983 Jesús Guanche (1983: 65) argued that it was Cuban anthropology's responsibility to "demystify" and creatively assimilate those aspects of Afro-Cuban religious culture worth "conserving in the form of positive values created by the popular traditional culture, as a testimony to the

4 Wirtz (2004: 429) reports the continued vitality of similar rumours for Santiago de Cuba.

periods our people has lived through from the origin of national sentiment to its consolidation as a socialist nation". For as his colleague Rogelio Martínez Furé (1979: 267) had proposed only four years earlier, the

> development of a country's folklore can be stimulated in an intelligent and scientific manner. So-called negative folklore (superstitions, taboos without scientific basis, idealistic concepts about supernatural forces that govern men's lives, practices of curanderismo, coprolag[n]ia, xenophobia, etc.) can be gradually eliminated, while enriching and employing positive folklore (everything that aids the harmonic development of society, that contributes to the reinforcement the links of solidarity among men, that exalts the traditions of struggle against the forces of oppression, as well as humorous folklore, empirically beneficial pharmacopoeia, and all artistic forms that flourished around popular religious conceptions, but which possess cultural value independent of their idealistic content, of which they can be purged so as to give them a new, revolutionary social function.[5]

Little more than 30 years after Martínez Furé published this master recipe for getting rid of Afro-Cuban wizardry – this time not through the physical elimination of its proponents, but through strategic secularization and patrimonialization of their religious practices – the tides had turned again. Limitations of space will not allow me here to even begin to speculate about the effects the so-called "special period in times of peace" announced upon the disintegration of Cuba's economic ties to the Soviet bloc in 1991 may have had upon the relations between the Cuban state and its black wizards.[6] Still, Argüelles and Hodge's monograph *Los llamados cultos sincréticos y el espiritismo*, published the same year, amply demonstrated that Marx's dictum that social being determines social consciousness was now boomeranging back towards those Cuban ideologues once prepared to escort

5 Similar programmatics can be found in Navarro (1998 [1978]) and López Valdés (1985: 3f.). One of the most interesting examples is that of Mirta Aguirre's "prologue" to Loudes López's unpublished "Estudio de un babalao" – a 1975 report on the conversion of a former babalao (priest of the ifá oracle) named Gabriel Pasos to socialism conceived as a form of therapy – where Aguirre notes the following: "The direct attention given to Gabriel Pasos by the [members of the] Party nucleus of [his] work centre came to play a very important role in this period of de-fanaticization. These *compañeros* worked patiently and systematically with Gabriel, discussing his anxieties, doubts and even personal problems, aiming to provide him with a collective solution. This ideological work of the *compañeros* with the ex-babalao has had – and continues to have – positive results. Although we cannot affirm that he has ceased to believe, he is on his way to doing so, for his incorporation into revolutionary tasks is improving day by day" (cited in Menéndez 2002: 42f).

6 See Argyriadis (1999), Hagedorn (2001), Ayorinde (2004) and Wirtz (2004) for such speculations. Hearn's (2004) brief ethnographic study of the interface between the state and practitioners of Afro-Cuban religions in the context of urban community development programs in Havana remains a notable and highly welcome exception.

Afro-Cuban deities to the graveyard of collective representation that history had come to pass by. Conceding that even "under the conditions of socialism there exist subjective and objective factors that permit the reproduction of religious practices and beliefs in some sectors of the population" (Argüelles and Hodge 1991: 10), they eventually admit that the puzzling "increase of the membership of these religious groups" may be due to the influx of "persons who feel the 'need' of expressing religious beliefs with a mythical-magical-superstitious conception of the world without this necessarily implying their distancing themselves from the revolutionary process" (Argüelles and Hodge 1991: 217). Their careful wording notwithstanding, the question now had become this: can a revolutionary engaged in building a socialist society afford to entertain beliefs of a mythical–magical–superstitious character? Can a "militante comunista" feel a need to express religious belief? The answer given by the IVth Congress of the Cuban Communist Party in the same year that Argüelles and Hodge's book appeared in print was an ambiguous, but nonetheless legally binding yes. And so it came to pass that the Cuban state once more entered into a mutually constitutive relation with its "African wizards" – some of whom, by then, turned out not only to be socially white, but to have occupied politically responsible positions for quite some time (Argyriadis 1999: 274).

It may well still be too early to judge the lasting effects of such incorporative legal gestures, coming as they did in the continuing absence of an effective body of civil legislation regulating religious practice (something that had not existed in Cuba since the US Military Government had forced Cuba to separate Church and State in the first republican constitution of 1902). Yet what clearly compounds the situation is that whatever policies the Cuban state nowadays decides to pursue in regards to Afro-Cuban religious practices, their object is no longer confined to the island's jurisdiction, but flourishes in a score of countries in the Americas, as well as – documentably – Spain, Italy, Germany, the Netherlands, and France. What is more, Afro-Cuban religious debate nowadays no longer takes place within the confines of localized cult groups which the state can recognize at will. It has taken on virtual dimensions to a degree where a random Google search for "Santeria" can pull up 2,750,000 sites, while even such more specific terms as "Lucumí", "Regla de Ocha", or "Oricha" will generate 183,000, 44,800, and 136,000 hits respectively.[7]

The issue is thus not just that a mere 11 years after the publication of Argüelles and Hodge's still somewhat perplexed conclusions, researchers affiliated with the same Center for Psychological and Sociological Research (CIPS) would have issued policy recommendations including for example "the gradual substitution of narrow, dogmatic, prejudiced, unilateral and anti-dialectical conceptions of the so-

7 Searches performed 8 March 2008. I have tried to control (to a certain degree) for Spanish spelling so as to rule out sites originating in Nigeria and the Anglophone Americas. To just give an example, while the Hispanophone "oricha" produced only 136,000 hits, the Anglophone "orisha" generated 409,000.

called 'scientific atheism' with dialectical, open, flexible and logical ones", "more frequent references to religion in the media", or "increase of human and material resources for religious organizations" (Roa and Castañeda Mache 2002). Nor is it that Martínez Furé nowadays sports luxurious African clothes and regales his audiences at public events with Afro-Cuban liturgical chants that – as the ritual necklaces he wears indicate – may *or may not* hold merely folkloric significance to him. What is at stake here is not even the exquisite historical irony that the founding member and director of Santiago de Cuba's *Casa del Caribe*, Joel James Figarola would see fit to pronounce that in the "most profound sense", the "Cuban nation constitutes – in its history, in its reality, and in its perspective – a great and exceptional *nganga*" (James Figuerola 2006: 27): a power-object, in other words, that allows contemporary Cubans to conjure with, and harness the force of the dead (that is in James's sense, their own history) to the building of their own futures, although the real, rather than metaphorical presence of such objects in any Cuban citizen's home might have constituted a crime less than 50 years ago, and a potential index of anti-social tendencies as late as the beginning of the last decade of the twentieth century. Rather, what really is at issue here is that socialist Cuba has begun to openly capitalize on the presence of its African deities as a country-factor advantage – not only in the literal economistic sense which has already seeded popular speech with neologisms such as "santurismo" or "diplosanteros", but also in regard to what, at first glance, appears a truly mind-boggling rhetorical, but possibly also ideological, *volte-face*.

The latter moment found its most visible expression in the staging of the 8th Global Orisha Congress in Havana's "palácio de las convenciones" in July of 2003 that had been organized under the auspices of the Asociación Cultural Yorubá – a state-backed association of practitioners of Afro-Cuban religion based in a beautifully restored nineteenth century palace facing Havana's American-built capitol. Presided over by the US-based Nigerian babalawo and cultural entrepreneur Wande Abimbola, this event united some 700 priestly delegates from about ten different countries in deliberation about the future of their partly shared faiths and practices as a "world religion". But it also featured a rousing speech by Cuba's minister of culture, Abel Prieto, who reminded the audience that their traditional African religiosity was not only entirely compatible with socialist modernity, but that it represented a powerful antidote against the ideological poison emerging from Hollywood and other sites of global capitalist cultural production. Apparently including the several dozen US-based delegates in his definition of "tercermundistas", Prieto concluded that would behoove "all of us" to stave off such dangers by heeding the call of those African deities which, as he chose not to mention, had once been launched on the path towards their current global dissemination by the Cuban revolution itself. For had it not been for the post-1959 exodus from that island, which spread Afro-Cuban religious practices across much of the Western world, chances are that the event at which Prieto uttered such momentous words might never have taken place (compare Frigerio 2004, Argyriadis 2005, Palmié 2005).

But Prieto's glib instrumentalization of Afro-Cuban religion as emblematic of what Cuba's "multiracial, but monoethnic" and "culturally hybrid" (Martínez-Echazábal 1998, Argyriadis 2005) socialist nation could contribute to the making of a novel post-Cold War internationalism was not merely rhetorical window-dressing. Uttered almost exactly a century after the niña Zoila case, his speech was also an exercise in what Povinelli (2002) in an Australian context calls the "cunning of recognition". As Carlos Martí, head of the Union of Cuban Writers and Artists put it, the Asociación Cultural Yorubá, although "there still exist few institutional linkages, has added its name to the call we have made for a global antifascist front" (Castañeda 2003). By the same token, however, these linkages to the state – resulting as they do for members of the Asociación in tangible benefits, such as permits to stage ceremonies, access to sacrificial animals, hard currency, or foreign travel – have rendered the Asociación rather more an agent of a state-controlled projection of Afro-Cuban religion and its role within a socialist legal culture, than a corporate actor in its own right. For although the Global Orisha Congress certainly united a large number of Havana's luminaries in Afro-Cuban religion, it excluded at least two groupings who have, since the mid-1990s not only boycotted the Asociación Cultural Yorubá's *letras del año* (yearly divinatory predictions for Cuba and the world[8]), but consistently issued dissenting versions on the internet (compare Argyriadis and Capone 2004, Routon 2006). I do not want to enter here into the lively debate about whether the Asociación's predictions merely add divine ratification to what is policy anyway, a debate that – it should be mentioned – resulted in a political skirmish spanning the Florida Straights when Miami-based *oriaté* (ritual specialist) and high-profile Santero-politician Ernesto Pichardo[9] accused the Asociación Cultural Yorubá of being a "foreign subversive organization" whose US members and contacts ought to be put under surveillance by the US Department of Homeland Security and investigated by the US Treasury Department's Office of Foreign Assets Control for illicit transactions with Cuba (Pichardo and Forbes 2006, Routon 2006). But it needs to be noted that since Cuban law prohibits two or more legally inscribed bodies to execute the same functions, the recognition of the Asociación Cultural Yorubá legally pre-empts all further claims from its rivals. On the other hand, to phrase the matter as a question of co-optation (or transformist hegemony, if you will) may be to miss the point that such incorporative moves on the part of the Cuban state – even in the absence of legally well-defined "institutional linkages" – constitute cultural performances in their own right. No less than the technologies of repression

8 The divination ceremonies determining the *letra del año* appear to go back to at least the early twentieth century, though it is not clear if the tradition was ever monolithic and its pronouncements uncontested among Cuba's *babalaos*. Since 2001, the Asociación Cultural Yorubá has been circulating its version both in print (distributed free of charge in the streets of Havana), and over its government sponsored website www.cubayoruba.cult.cu.

9 In 1993, Pichardo won a US Supreme Court case legalizing animal sacrifice for members of his Church of the Lukumí Babalú Ayé (compare Palmié 1996).

unleashed against practitioners of Afro-Cuban religion in the name of scientific modernity a hundred years ago, the socialist state's courting Cuba's African deities for their legitimatory powers, both at home and abroad, deeply implicates it in the "religious irrationalities" it was only too recently willing to eradicate. In fact, only slightly overstating the case we might say that what nowadays increasingly looks like a localized case of a survival of "socialist tradition" in the midst of global neo-liberalism is now being absorbed into a rapidly internationalizing Afro-Cuban religious modernity far more "rationalized" in Max Weber's sense, than anything the Revolution could nowadays muster, ideologically.

Conclusion: Remembrance of Hybrids Past

Even that, however, is not the bottom line. For since the cultural programme of the 8th Orisha congress did not include a visit to the sprawling Calixto García hospital complex, few of the delegates might have suspected that the socialist modernity into which Prieto strategically inserted their beliefs and practices included the Museo de la Cátedra de Medicina Legal de la Universidad de la Habana, where the section "criminal ethnography", still houses, among an amazing jumble of objects, ritual and secular, the skulls of "African wizards" – garroted in far too insufficient numbers, as Israel Castellanos once complained, to allow for proper scientific analysis. Of course, as the Cuban museologist Luis Alberto Pedroso (2002: 138) has recently argued, the tables have turned insofar as the exhibits at the Museo de la Cátedra de Medicina Legal are now in themselves worthy of preservation as an illustration "of a museographical concept of which no other examples are left". The structural inversion could not be more perfect. For now those sorry objects – and artifacts – of a brutal ideology of scientific progress and modernity have become the data for a version of Cuban science that, in aiming to transcend that past, repeats it by other means. Reposing there for close to a hundred years of solitude, perhaps these skulls are best thought of as silent witnesses to precisely the kind of indigenous Caribbean modernity a republic enchanted by science could then not countenance – and arguably has yet to come to terms with today. If the Cuban nation indeed is the great *nganga* some of the engineers of its newly mystically enhanced socialist internationalism make it out to be, then one ought to do well to remember whose mortal remains animate and give power to the histories and futures it purports to bring into being. And the Museo de la Cátedra de Medicina Legal would seem the logical place to start searching for the pasts in which such futures would necessarily have to be implicated. What such excavations – and I mean this in a literal rather than Foucaldian sense – could bring to light might not exactly be grist for the mill of metaphysical pronouncements on the mystical violence involved in the institution of The Law. But pursuing such a course of investigation might tell us a good deal about how exactly a particular regime of governance and legality managed to obscure its – historically specific – origins in practical and symbolic violence. Pedroso's efforts notwithstanding, that has not happened yet.

References

Anonymous. 1968. La sociedad secreta abakuá. *Militante Comunista*, August 1968.
Argüelles M., Hodge Limonta, A. and Hodge Limonta, I. 1991. *Los llamados cultos sincréticos y el espiritismo*. La Habana: Editorial Academía.
Argyriadis, K. 1999. *La Religion à la Havane*. Paris: Editions des Archives Contemporaines.
Argyriadis, K. 2005. Religión de indígenas, religion de científicos: Construcción de la cubanidad y santería. *Desacatos*, 17, 85–106.
Argyriadis, K. and Capone, S. 2004. Cubanía et santería: Les enjeux politiques de la transnationalisation religieuse (La Havana–Miami). *Civilisations*, 51, 81–138.
Ayorinde, C. 2004. *Afro-Cuban Religiosity, Revolution, and National Identity*. Gainesville: University of Florida Press.
Bronfman, A. 2004. *Measures of Equality: Social Science, Citizenship and Race in Cuba, 1902–1940*. Chapel Hill: University of North Carolina Press.
Castañeda, M. 2003. 8vo congreso mundial tradición y cultura Orisha: Intensos debates académicos sobre aspectos culturales y religiosos. *Granma Internacional*, 23 July 2003.
Castellanos, I. 1916. *La brujería y el ñáñiguismo en Cuba desde el punto de vista medico-legal*. La Habana: Lloredo y Companía.
Chávez Álvarez, E. 1991. *El Crímen de la Niña Cecilia*. La Habana: Editorial Ciencias Sociales.
Figarola, J.J. 2006. *Cuba: La gran nganga*. Santiago de Cuba: Ediciones Caserón.
Frigerio, A. 2004. Re-Africanization in secondary religious diasporas: Constructing a world religion. *Civilisations*, 51, 39–60.
Guanche, J. 1983. *Procesos etnoculturales de Cuba*. La Habana: Editorial Letras Cubanas.
Hagedorn, K. 2001. *Divine Utterances: The Performance of Afro-Cuban Santería*. Washington: Smithsonian.
Hearn, A. 2004. Afro-Cuban religions and social welfare: Consequences of commercial development in Havana. *Human Organization*, 63, 78–87.
Helg, A. 1995. *Our Rightful Share: The Afro-Cuban Struggle for Equality, 1886–1912*. Chapel Hill: University of North Carolina Press.
Latour, B. 1993. *We Have Never Been Modern*. Cambridge: Harvard University Press.
López Valdés, R. 1985. *Componentes africanos en el etnos Cubano*. La Habana: Editorial Ciencias Sociales.
Martínez Echazábal, L. 1998. Mestizaje and the discourse of national/cultural identity in Latin America, 1845–1959. *Latin American Research Review*, 25, 21–42.

Martínez Furé, R. 1979. *Diálogos imaginários.* La Habana: Editorial Arte y Literatura.

Menéndez, L. 2002. *Rodar el coco: proceso de cambio en la santería.* La Habana: Editorial Ciencias Sociales.

Navarro, D. 1998 [1978]. El folklor y unos cuantos peligros, in *Estudios afrocubanos: selección de lecturas I*, edited by L. Menéndez. La Habana: Editorial Felix Varela, 295–326.

Ortiz, F. 1921. Los cabildos afrocubanos. *Revista Bimestre Cubana*, 16, 5–39.

Ortiz, F. 1973 [1906]. *Los negros brujos.* Miami: Ediciones Universal.

Palmié, S. 1996. Which center, whose margin? Notes towards an archaeology of U.S. Supreme Court Case 91-948, 1993, in *Inside and outside the Law*, edited by O. Harris. London: Routledge, 184–209.

Palmié, S. 2002. *Wizards and Scientists: Explorations in Afro-Cuban Modernity and Tradition.* Durham: Duke University Press.

Palmié, S. 2005. The cultural work of Yoruba globalization, in *Christianity and Social Change in Africa*, edited by T. Falola. Durham: Carolina Academic Press, 43–83.

Pedroso, L.-A. 2002. Las exposiciones de "cultos afrocubanos" y la necesidad de su reconceptualización. *Catauro*, 3, 126–41.

Pichardo, E. and Forbes, K.B. 2006. *Blasfemia: An Investigative Report on Fidel Castro's Intelligence Gathering Religious Front Group.* Washington, DC: Concejo de Latinos Unidos.

Povinelli, E. 2002. *The Cunning of Recognition.* Durham: Duke University Press.

Roa, A. del Rey and Mache, Y.M. 2002. El revivamiento religioso en Cuba. *Temas*, 31: 93–100.

Routon, K. 2006. The Cuban "Ministry of Orula" or the transnational politics of prophecy. *Anthropology News*, December 2006, 6–7.

Wirtz, K. 2004. Santería in Cuban national consciousness: A religious case of the double moral. *Journal of Latin American Anthropology*, 9, 409–38.

PART II
Contested Orders: States and Religious Movements

Chapter 5
Judicious Succession and Judicial Religion: Internal Conflict and Legal Dispute in a Religious Reform Movement in India

Anindita Chakrabarti

> Today almost for everything we have to approach government, in temple disputes, charity disputes, in disputes between brothers and in disputes between a husband and a wife.
>
> (Athavale 1976: 33)

> When we began Svadhyaya, there was no question of inheritance because there was nothing to inherit.
>
> (Former senior Svadhyayī, July 2004, Mumbai)

Introduction

This chapter explores the unfolding of a succession dispute in a contemporary religious movement in India. The question of succession, which – as it turned out – could not be resolved by the members of the movement themselves, was brought before the court of law by evoking the concept of "religious rights".[1] Through an analysis of the succession dispute, I explore the complex relationship between religion and the state in the context of secular democracy.

In India, the secularism debate has been framed around "circumscribing" the role of religion in the matters of the modern state (Smith 1963) or alternately the impossibility of such separation in the South Asian context (Madan 1987). While the conventional view that secularism is based on the ideology of the separation between state and religion has been challenged in recent scholarship,[2] there is

1 I would like to thank Tulsi Patel, J.P.S. Uberoi, and the participants of the workshop on "The Legitimate and the Supernatural: Law and Religion in a Complex World" at the Max Planck Institute for Social Anthropology, Halle/Saale for their comments and suggestions on an earlier version of the article. In the paper, apart from the leaders of the movement, I have used pseudonyms to protect the identity of the informants.

2 Going beyond the framework of the "separation of religion from politics", Gurpreet Mahajan has brought a new dimension to the debate by recognizing the neglected link between secularism and citizenship rights (Mahajan 2003).

paucity of ethnographic work on the relation between the two. The following examination of a succession dispute in the Svadhyaya movement shows that whereas the legislative role of the modern democratic state influences the internal development of religious bodies, it is by intervening and mediating in "matters of religion" that the state is deemed as secular. Thus, the relationship between the "modern" state and "traditional" religion is not that of a confrontation over the question of legitimacy or authority, but one marked by a complex process of negotiations.

The Indian Constitution regards "freedom of religion" as a fundamental right, but it also categorically distinguishes between the freedom of religious groups to manage their own affairs in "matters of religion" and these groups' rights and duties in owning and administering property, which have to follow state law.[3] In other words, "religious freedom" in this context does not mean exemption from state intervention in the material aspects of spiritual life. But while adjudicating on these "*non*-religious" aspects of religious life, the judiciary needs to decide which aspects constitute "matters of religion" and which do not. Against this background, I describe in this chapter how an internal conflict within a religious movement throws up questions for the judiciary that can only be resolved by defining and deciding what "religion" is.

Even though state intervention in succession disputes within religious groups has had a long history in India, what is unique about the modern court system is that it frames questions of religious dispute as a matter of "religious liberty/rights" and fulfils a legislative role which was absent in the pre-colonial context. There are records of religious sects seeking intervention of the Mughal royal court, in the pre-British period, when their succession dispute could not be resolved by the members themselves. For example, when a major split had taken place among the Bohra Muslim community in 1588 over the struggle for leadership between Shaykh Sulayman b. Hasan and Daud b. Qutubshah, it was taken to and fought in the royal courts during the reigns of the Mughal emperors Akbar (1542–1605) and his son Jehangir (1569–1627). But the very intervention of the Mughal court in the internal dispute of the sect brought it to the attention of the royal power and it was later persecuted as a heretic sect by Emperor Aurangzeb (1618–1707) (Lokhandwalla 1971: 389). In this context, the aim of the court was not to defend "religious rights" or to define "religion", but instead to mediate an internal conflict or to uphold the state-sponsored religious orthodoxy. In view of this, it becomes evident that scholars, who argue that the distinction between "modern" and "traditional" law is not as sharp as it has been generally regarded, miss the

3 Article 26 of the Indian Constitution, which addresses the fundamental right of Indian citizens to freely manage religious affairs states: "Subject to public order, morality and health, every religious denomination or any section thereof shall have the right (a) to establish and maintain institutions for religious and charitable purposes; (b) to manage its own affairs in matters of religion; (c) to own and acquire movable and immovable property; and (d) to administer such property in accordance with law."

point that the modern legal system (unlike its traditional counterpart) protects the "rights" of members of religious groups, intervening into "religious matters" in order to uphold non-discrimination and equal liberty for all citizens.[4]

As concerns India, the relation between law and religious movements/sects has not generated much scholarly discussion.[5] At the very outset, I would like to draw attention to the fact that the juridical issues at stake in the context of religious movements are quite different from those involved in the context of well-established temple institutions.[6] Religious movements emerge with messages of salvation and reform, and it is in these movements that the kaleidoscopic nature of the religious pluralism in India becomes evident to the observer. Moreover, reform movements begin with a new interpretation of texts and rituals by charismatic leaders, and then – over time – develop their own textual, ritual, and organizational "traditions". Therefore, as the case of the Svadhyaya movement illustrates, adjudication on questions of "religion" can *not* be based either on textual (*śastric*) or on customary (*laukik*) sources. In other words, in approaching questions of "religion" via a search for authoritative traditions, state courts invariably fail to appreciate the fact that charismatic movements emerge *in opposition* to traditional authority.

Another aspect that is crucial to my concerns here is the fact that, for a religious movement to be successful beyond the first generation, the question of the transference of power within the movement needs to be resolved.[7] Succession in a religious movement is a moment of transference of *spiritual* as well as *material*

---

4 According to Christopher Fuller, the difference between traditional and modern law is overstated. Focusing on a selection of Supreme Court cases, Fuller has argued that since the court very often decides on the basis of authoritative texts, using a classical Hindu mode of reasoning, the contrast between modern and traditional law becomes but a matter of degree (Fuller 1988: 247).

5 The emergence of religious movements/bodies that question the established church and subsequently develop into sects has been well studied within the context of Christianity (See Weber 1922, 1930; Troeltsch 1956). Sects as protest groups, based on charismatic authority, are seen as questioning not only dominant religious authorities but also the ethics and practices of the larger society. However, the sectarian aspect of Hinduism has been both understudied and undertheorized even as the presence of sects did not escape the attention of sociologists who had primarily considered caste and not sect as the most important aspect of Hinduism (Dumont 1970).

6 The disputes in South Indian temples have been the focus of in-depth ethnographic work and much of the discourse on the topic of law and religion has been shaped by the nature of the issues that have been seminal to these disputes (Appadurai 1981, Shankari 1982, Presler 1987).

7 Bryan Wilson has noted that, since the sect provides a total reference group for the individual within which a person's status is re-evaluated and sanctified, leadership roles are very often important features of sect organizations. Therefore, it is not surprising that disagreements over power and status constitute a principal cause of schism and disruption in sects (Wilson 1966: 211).

assets from one generation to the next, and there are several ways that this can be done. In the case of the Svadhyaya movement at the end of the twentieth century, the question of succession was supposed to be resolved by the founder-leader of the movement, Pandurang Shastri Athavale (addressed as Dadaji by his followers) in consultation with a group of senior leaders in the movement. But when Dadaji declared his adopted daughter to be the future leader, this appeared unacceptable to a number of senior leaders.[8] An internal conflict ensued and was soon brought before the court of law. And as I show below, the legislative role of the court became clear as the dispute changed from revolving around issues of "temple entry" into a conflict over the question of whether the Svadhyaya movement was a "religion" or not.

I begin with a brief description of religious reform that Dadaji preached as well as the material and organizational aspects of the Svadhyaya movement. Then I discuss how the internal conflict over the judicious selection of a successor evolved into a labyrinth of court cases, bringing to fore the multivocal nature of judicial decisions in questions of "religion" in contemporary India.

The Svadhyaya Movement: Reinventing a Religious Tradition

The Svadhyaya movement was founded by Pandurang Shastri Athavale (1920–2003), a Maharashtrian Brahman who believed that Hinduism needed to be reformed if Hindu society was to develop and change. From 1942 onwards he drew a small but committed group of followers who came to listen to his religious exegesis (*pravacans*) on the Vedas, Upaṇiṣads and the Bhagavad-Gīta (Gīta, in short), held in downtown Mumbai in three vernacular languages. Dadaji's teachings are based on the soteriological premise that one's own salvation is dependant on the salvation of others in society. For Dadaji, it was the world-renouncing Hindu soteriology that had led to the decline of the Hindu society.[9] He urged Svadhyayīs to combine the two aspects of Hinduism, namely renunciation (*sannyās*) and non-renunciation (*gṛhasth*), in their lives. To be a Svadhyayaī is to believe that the "self" could be reformed only by reforming the "other". This other-directedness takes place on the basis of the correct understanding of the idea of devotion (*bhakti*) which is always an "inner-worldly" phenomenon.

Thus, Svadhyayīs perform *bhakti* by participating in a number of *prayogs* "projects" that symbolize the "inner-worldly" nature of Svadhyaya religiosity. These *prayogs*, which literally means "experiments", can be described as

8 Analysing succession to high office, Jack Goody has pointed out that the purpose behind the pre-mortem selection of a successor is clearly legitimacy when succession rules allow for uncertainty (Goody 1966: 8).

9 Louis Dumont had pointed out that the structure of Hinduism is such that the developments of renunciation, with all their riches, are contained after all within narrow limits, which they were unable to go beyond. The renouncer, an individual-outside-society is linked to it but at the same time is impotent against it (Dumont 1970).

multifarious developmental activities initiated with a view to the needs of the communities. Dadaji explained to his disciples that offering one's professional efficiency (*nipuṇatā*) to God is an apt way to serve him; it is described as *srama bhakti* "labour as devotion". A portion of the income thus generated is distributed among the needy of the community or the village as *prasād*, the "grace of God".

Organizationally, Svadhyaya is based not on full-time cadres, but on volunteers who believe that extending themselves to others, especially the disadvantaged in society, is their religious duty. The movement began with a unique process of religious journeys, called *bhaktipherī*, that are regularly undertaken by Svadhyayīs to develop relations with people and convey to them the message of Svadhyaya.[10] *Bhaktipherī*, that is, the process of changing the self by going to others, is spontaneously carried on by the Svadhyayīs and does not require any legal-bureaucratic structure.

Reinterpreting the concept of a "temple" has been an important part of Dadaji's theological innovation. In his exegesis, Dadaji repeatedly explained that the temple was an institution that upheld equality and equity. The idea behind offering money to temples is the redistribution of wealth in society and it is not meant for constructing ostentatious buildings.[11] But quite ironically, it was around the issue of "temple entry" that the first court case was filed against the Svadhyaya movement.

Taken together, in the Svadhyaya movement, the concept of "temple" is evoked to carry out a range of congregational activities. There are only two consecrated Svadhyaya temples located on the premises of two educational institutions – the Tatvajnana Vidyapith at Thane and the temple at Bhavnirjhar in Ahmedabad – whereby the temple situated at Tatvajnana Vidyapith is regarded as the most sacred of all Svadhyaya sites. The deities at these two temples are represented as stone idols of Krishna, Shiva, Parvati and Ganesh; the deity Surya is represented in the form of sun light. This type of worship known as *pancayatana* is supposed to have been started by Adi Shankaracharya, and is a form of worship that is associated with the *smārta* tradition (Renou 1962): A simple daily *pūjā* is offered at this temple by the resident Brahman or by the students of the temple.[12]

---

10 Though most of the followers belong to different parts of Gujarat, Svadhyaya originally began in Mumbai. The connection between the genesis of Svadhyaya in downtown Mumbai and its spread in Gujarat is easy to understand when we consider the presence of Gujarati communities in the business life of Mumbai city.

11 Such an innovative view of the temple can be found in other reform sects as well. Shree Narayana Guru, the founder of the Shree Narayana Paripalana Yogam (SNDP) religious sect in Kerala, had consecrated mirrors in SNDP temples which signified the unity between the finite and the infinite souls.

12 A similar form of worship was approved by Sahajanand Svami, the founder of the Svaminarayan sect, as a part of private ritual in which Krishna remained the main deity.

Apart from these two temples, the other "temples" in Svadhyaya are unconventional, and they are integrally related to the theology of Svadhyaya reform. *Loknath Amritalayam*, the Svadhyaya "temples" that are constructed in the villages, fall into this category. "Temples" of the *Loknath Amritalayam* type are built in a village when 80 per cent of the villagers have become Svadhyayīs. They have no priests, and married Svadhyayī couples from the village perform a daily prayer ceremony in front of the deity with lamps. However, unlike the Tatvajnana Vidyapith and Bhavnirjhar temples, at "temples" of the *Loknath Amritalayam* type, no consecration (*prān.pratiṣṭhā*) ceremony is performed; instead a simple ceremony called *bhāv pratiṣṭhā* – where the consecrated idols are kept only as photographs – takes place. According to the senior leaders of the movement, this was one of Dadaji's innovations. Likewise, in tribal villages, another unique type of "temple" – called *gharmandir* – exists. In this type of "temple", the images of Krishna, Shiva, Parvati and Ganesh travel from one home to another, whereby each of the visited homes becomes a "temple" for that period of time. Unlike a consecrated temple, in this case, it is the congregation that creates a sacred space at a particular point of time. Therefore, though the disciples consider these to be sacred sites they are *not* temples from a legal point of view.[13]

In India, religious institutions come under the Charitable and Religious Trusts Act and acquire the status of a legal entity as soon as they emerge. All Svadhyaya trusts have been registered under the Bombay Public Charitable Act of 1950 – an act which regulates the administration of public, religious and charitable trusts in the state of Bombay. I was told that when Dadaji began his Svadhyaya work, the activities did not require much financial commitment. During the initial years, the camps and other programmes were conducted in a spontaneous manner. I was told that when someone used to offer money to Dadaji, he would refuse to take it. But later, when he organized a Svadhyaya camp, he would ask the same person to bear some of the financial responsibility towards the expenses of the camp. Such an arrangement made it possible for him to carry on with Svadhyaya work without a formal financial or administrative structure. Camps and other programmes were organized by raising funds directly from the Svadhyayīs. Over the years, however, with the success of Svadhyaya at the grassroots level, the local programmes and centres began to rely on the resources of local activists. As a result, the trusts began to accumulate an increasing amount of money.

The structure of the Svadhyaya trusts is such that the Tatvajnana Vidyapith trust, which, in 1956, was the first trust to be set up in the Svadhyaya movement as an educational trust, controls all other trusts. At the time of the registration of the Tatvajnana Vidyapith trust, the goals of the movement were explicitly educational. They were:

13 The *Loknath Amritalayams* are registered under the Atreyabhavpujan Trust.

- Promotion and propagation of comparative and critical study of philosophy, sociology, culture and religion and with special emphasis on ancient Aryan philosophy, sociology, culture and religion as propounded in the Vedas and Vedic literature and Smriti texts, Darshans and Puranas.
- Upliftment of society based on ancient Aryan culture, that is, Vedic view of life.
- Making adequate provision for the study and teaching of and establishing, conducting and managing institutes of philosophy, sociology, culture and religion by establishing and managing a residential college with free lodging and boarding and other facilities for the purpose of the said studying and teaching.
- Publishing books, journals and periodicals in any language for the purpose mentioned in sub-clause … hereof.
- Awarding scholarship for research work, appointing persons to spread the objects of the trust in the world, at large.
- Carrying on any other activity incidental or germane to the aforesaid objects. (Source: Trust Deeds 1956)

Though education was stated as the main objective of the Svadhyaya movement, it has generally been a rather low-key project. At the same time, by connecting the countryside with the metropolitan cities, bringing together upper and "backward" castes, men and women in its agenda of reforming Hinduism by reaching out to "others", especially the underprivileged, Svadhyaya has emerged as a grassroots movement in contemporary Gujarat.

But the transference of these "riches of non-renunciation" from one generation to the next has proved to be a difficult issue to resolve. A charismatic movement has, by definition, no fixed tradition or precedent to fall back on, and a bitter succession dispute broke out during the last years of Dadaji's life. Despite quite a few attempts at mediating the rift between the conflicting groups, the succession dispute very soon turned into a legal dispute that gained momentum with the question of "temple entry".

Dispute over Selecting a "Suitable Successor"

Those who worked with Dadaji recall that he was involved in virtually all facets of Svadhyaya work, be it kitchen management or financial matters. Dadaji's decisions were not questioned, and Svadhyayīs believed that he had a divine vision (*divyā dṛṣti*) regarding the future.

Yet, from the early 1990s onwards, once Dadaji turned seventy, he along with the senior leaders from Mumbai began to prepare a constitution for future Svadhyaya work. It was called the *Amnaya* and charted out the structure of leadership in the Svadhyaya movement. The draft of the *Amnaya* was finalized in 1998–1999. In this draft, it was decided that there would be a system in which 20–25 people would be selected from all over India, who would then – together with Didi, Dadaji's adopted daughter (his brother's biological daughter) – manage the *sanghāt*, that is, a system of regional divisions through which Svadhyaya organizational and administrative work are carried out.[14] The senior leaders pointed out to me that this system was functional between 1991 and 2000. But, even during that period of time, the highest administrative committee was not in fact functional as Dadaji's permission was necessary for all the work undertaken.

Since her childhood, Didi had a prominent presence in the Svadhyaya movement. But at the same time, it was understood that she was not Dadaji's spiritual successor, and he would not select her to sit on the *vyāspīth* – the seat from which he delivered his exegesis. Nobody doubted her superb organizational skills and formidable energy, but at the same time she was not generally seen as someone who was endowed with the knowledge and spirit of the sacred scriptures (*Ved vicār*). People thought it possible that, after Dadaji's death, there would be a collective leadership in which the work would be divided in such a way that separate groups and trusts would look after different aspects of the Svadhyaya work.

In February 2000, while in the United States, however, Dadaji sent a letter stating that he had indeed chosen Didi as his successor. Until then, the senior leaders had been in charge of all the work under Dadaji's leadership. In June 2000, about 100 to 150 Svadhyaya leaders were invited to the Tatvajnana Vidyapith. At that gathering, Dadaji repeated his declaration that Didi was to succeed him since she had all the necessary qualities to lead the Svadhyaya movement. The senior Svadhyayīs told me that they were shocked to hear Dadaji's declaration because he had always spoken against the hereditary leadership practised within *sampradāys*, "sects". But they did not voice their opinion at that time.

Six months later, Aśīti Vandanā, a function celebrating Dadaji's eightieth birthday, was held. But, as it turned out, this served just as much to solemnize Didi's position as the future leader of the Svadhyaya movement, as it did to celebrate Dadaji's birthday. The tension between the senior and the younger leaders was palpable even as the preparation for the Aśīti Vandanā was underway. The senior leaders were not given any important responsibilities, and, in the end, they were visibly marginalized at the function.

It was soon after Aśīti Vandanā, in January 2001, that the tension within the movement became public through a physical scuffle at the Pāṭhśālā,[15] when Didi's opponents were physically threatened by her supporters who had taken offence at the criticism levelled at Didi by dissident Svadhyayīs. The immediate cause of this incident was the discontent that had ensued in the movement upon the discovery of a set of love letters allegedly written by Didi and her lover, Ashokbhai, a

14 Effectively, the leaders were from Mumbai and Gujarat.

15 The Pathshala refers to a hall in downtown Mumbai where Dadaji used to deliver his sermons. Though it is a part of a large building rented from a temple trust, the Pathshala is a sacred site for the disciples.

Svadhyayī volunteering at Nirmal Niketan, the Svadhyaya headquarters in Mumbai. Nimeshbhai Shah, an important trustee who "discovered" these letters, along with a few other dissident Svadhyayīs, began mobilizing the Svadhyayīs against Didi. On learning of this "conspiracy" against Didi, Svadhyayī members who belonged to the fishing communities decided to round up these men. On that fateful day, Nimeshbhai was attacked by the members of the fishing community at the Pathshala. At the time of this attack, a few senior leaders came to his rescue but they were attacked as well, and all of them ran to the Lakshminarayan temple in the vicinity for safety.

After this shocking incident, the conflicting groups felt that mediation was necessary and Dadaji appointed a committee consisting of 17 Svadhyaya leaders to look into the contentious issues and suggest a suitable course of action. In the end, the committee recommended that Didi should consult the committee before taking or executing any decision. It also sought to curb Didi's freedom of movement in view of the alleged love affair.[16]

These recommendations were unacceptable to Dadaji who declared that the "love letters" were part of a conspiracy to defile Didi's reputation. He travelled to different places in Gujarat, explaining to the Svadhyayīs that the senior leaders of the movement were opposed to Didi because they themselves were after power and money and were therefore indulging in a malicious "character assassination" of his daughter. During this period, a number of attempts were also made by a few intellectuals, who, although not Svadhyayīs themselves, were close both to Dadaji and the senior leaders, to reconcile the difference between the conflicting groups. However, these negotiations did not yield any result, and the antagonism between the two conflicting groups intensified.

It is noteworthy in this context that, even after the physical scuffle at the Pāṭhśālā, the conflict remained an internal matter and even well guarded from the Svadhyayīs who were not linked with the administrative structure. A few dissident Svadhyayīs from Mumbai who wanted to mobilize the Svadhyayīs against Didi were, on occasion, physically attacked when they went to the villages. But the conflict in the Svadhyaya movement became a public issue when, on 19 June 2002, an eminent Svadhyayī trustee in Ahmadabad and a former Chief Justice of the Gujarat High Court, B.J. Diwan, published an open letter in the *Gujarat Samachar*, a popular Gujarati daily, announcing his resignation from one of the most important Svadhyaya trusts, the Jnana Vistarak Sangh. Following this, in July 2002, the dissident groups from Mumbai and Ahmadabad called a meeting at the Bhavnirjhar temple complex in Ahmadabad. A large number of Didi's supporters, however, also arrived at this meeting, leading to a scuffle.

Fearing that the dissident leaders would influence the disciples through their access to the Bhavnirjhar temple, the temple was closed to the public in September

16 In the course of time, as the conflict intensified, the letters were published in regional-language newspapers. The Svadhyaya leadership maintained that they were fabricated.

2002. The security of the temple was the reason stated for this action since the Akshardham temple in Ahmadabad, a temple belonging to the Svaminarayan sect, had previously been attacked by armed militants. While the Akshardham temple was briefly closed, the Bhavnirjhar temple was never reopened to the public for regular visits. Devotees were able to visit the temple only on Sundays when Dadaji's video cassettes were played. One month later, the first court case was filed by dissenting Svadhyayīs against one of the Svadhyaya trusts on the ground of "temple entry". The internal dispute was thus brought to the court in a dispute between the devotees' *right* to enter the temple and the temple authority's decision to keep it closed.

Court Cases in Svadhyaya: The Making of a Judicial Religion

In India, the question of caste has often been the cynosure of academic attention with regard to the question of temple entry.[17] Thus, while the issue of temple entry has time and again revolved around the problem of upper castes debarring "ritually impure" castes from entering temples, it is often overlooked that prohibiting one group of devotees from entering the temple, as a matter of control over it, has a long history in the context of Hindu sectarian disputes. For example, in the battle of succession among the followers of Vallabhacarya, one of his disciples, Krishnadas, had barred Vitthalnath, Vallabhacarya's son, from entering the main temple for a period of six months in 1549–1550 (Barz 1992: 52).

In the case of the Svadhyaya movement, the court cases began with the closure of Bhavnirjhar, one of the most important Svadhyaya temples. The question that was raised in this context was whether the Bhavnirjhar temple was a place of worship (as claimed by the dissenting group) or just a prayer hall of the school also situated on the same premises (as claimed by the defendants). In the court case that was filed by a section of Svadhyayīs against the Tatvajnana Vidyapith trust, it was claimed that the temple should be opened for the complainants since they were devotees who had been visiting the temple since 1988.[18] The complainants argued that the temple was established by Pandurang Shastri Athavale for the devotees in Ahmadabad, who had contributed money for its construction. Moreover, they indicated, the 69 acres of land, where the Bhavnirjhar stood, enjoyed tax exemption as a temple.

In defence, the Tatvajnana Vidyapith trustees signed an affidavit stating that the Bhavnirjhar was *not* a temple for the general public, but that it was a prayer hall for students of a Svadhyaya school that was also situated on the Bhavnirjhar

17 Scholars have often regarded caste as the focal point of the controversy on the question of temple entry, an issue integrally related to the question of religious freedom in India (See B.K. Mukherjea 1952: 389).

18 This case was *Pankajbhai Trivedi and two others* vs. *Tatwajnan Vidyapeeth, a Public Charitable Trust (2002).*

premises.[19] In addition, they argued that none of the traditional rituals that are performed at temples were performed at the Bhavnirjhar temple since the idols in the temple had not been consecrated. The defendants also stated that, according to the Bombay Public Trust Act, complaints regarding temple entry could be lodged only after obtaining the permission of the Charity Commissioner which was not done in this case. However, the Joint Civil Judge (Ahmedabad) finally dismissed the case on the technical ground that, since the Tatvajnana Vidyapith trust that controlled the Bhavnirjhar institution was registered in Maharashtra, the suit should have been filed in Maharashtra.[20]

While the controversies over the temple remained unresolved, the tension between Didi's supporters and the leaders who opposed her mounted. And it was at this moment that an anonymous booklet entitled *Ashubh* appeared, which was circulated in order to raise awareness of the internal dispute in the Svadhyaya movement. The booklet contained all the complaints and affidavits regarding the Bhavnirjhar court case. It had a photograph of the Svadhyaya deity Lord Yogeshvar (Krishna) on the cover page with the subtitle: "*Is this the death of the Bhavnirjhar temple?*"

With the publication of the booklet, the lawsuit on temple entry turned into a lawsuit of "religion". Many Svadhyayīs took offence to the subtitle, and a lawsuit was filed submitting that this statement had hurt their religious sentiments. In that lawsuit, Sections 295A and/or 505(1)(c) of the Indian Penal Code (IPC) were to be applied.[21] Within a brief period of time, the number of lawsuits regarding *Ashubh* rose, filed in different courts of Gujarat. In most of these cases, the main allegation was that the religious sentiments (*dhārmic lagṇi*) and beliefs (*mānyātā*) of the Svadhyayīs had been hurt (*dubhayel*) by writing the word *Ashubh*, meaning "inauspicious", in relation to Yogeshvar's image.[22] It was also pointed out that to use the word "death" in discussing a temple was a sin. Upholding the "principle of secularism", the petitions stated that by publishing this booklet and distributing it to the public, the accused were hatching a criminal conspiracy (*gunahīt kāvatru*)

---

19 It should be mentioned here that the Bhavnīrjhar institution does not have a separate trust but is maintained by the Tatvajnana Vidyapith trust.

20 By order dated 20 September 2003, Section 51 of Bombay Public Trust Act.

21 Sections 295A and 505(1)(c) of the IPC deal with the following offences: (1) 295A–Deliberate and malicious acts, intended to outrage religious feelings of any class by insulting its religion or religious beliefs. Whoever, with deliberate and malicious intention of outraging the religious feelings of any class of citizens of India, by words, either spoken or written, or by signs or by visible representations or otherwise, insults or attempts to insult the religion or the religious beliefs of that class, shall be punished with imprisonment of either description for a term which may extend to three years, or with fine, or with both. (2) 505–Statements conducting to public mischief. (1) Whoever makes, publishes or circulates any statement, rumor or report, (c) with intent to incite, or which is likely to incite, any class or community of persons to commit any offence against any other class or community; shall be punished with imprisonment which may extend to three years, or with fine, or with both.

22 The Svadhyayīs, however, translated the word *Ashubh* as "sin".

to malign the pious (*sāttvik*) philosophy (*vicār*) of Pandurang Shastri Athavale. In addition, the complainants evoked the Contempt of Court Act (1952) since the booklet apparently attempted to influence the ongoing Bhavnirjhar temple case.

But, according to Section 196 of the Code of Criminal Procedure, complaints under Sections 295 and 505 could be filed only after obtaining the sanction of the state or central government, which these complainants had not done. Therefore, when the defendants approached the Gujarat High Court at Ahmedabad to quash the complaints, an interim stay was granted by the High Court.

The accused Svadhyaya leaders filed an affidavit with the Ahmedabad High Court which had three central points. First, it argued that the aforementioned sections of the IPC applied only if two *different* religious sects or creeds were concerned. Yet, in this particular case, as it was claimed, the question of different religions, sects, or creeds did *not* arise because both parties – the complainants and the accused – were members of the Svadhyaya movement: Just because the accused differed in their views on the administration of the trusts of the Svadhyaya Parivar and the manner in which the work was executed, did not entail their adherence to another "class of religion". According to the signatories of the petition, therefore, Section 295(a) had been wrongly evoked.

Second, it was pointed out in the petition that the Svadhyaya Parivar itself was not a separate religion, sect, or creed since the Svadhyaya movement had no rituals, fixed prayers, binding beliefs, or oaths. In brief, it did not place any conditions on the undertaking of different activities or the enforcement of any discipline, whether by dint of birth or otherwise. Svadhyayīs worship any god, and there was no material fact to prove that the Svadhyaya Parivar was a religious body because *svadhyaya* was a Vedic word applicable to anyone engaged in the "study of the self". Therefore, there could not be a Svadhyaya *sect*.

Third, the affidavit drew attention to the fact that the Svadhyaya Parivar exists in the form of several public charitable trusts, and that their activities are confined to charitable objectives as mentioned in said trusts. Therefore, it was argued, that the word *dhārmic* – as invoked in the complaint – did not fall within the purview of the sections quoted. And finally, the petition called attention to the temple entry lawsuit, in which the Svadhyaya trustees – while closing down the Bhavnirjhar temple – had themselves said that it was *not* a temple, but only a prayer hall for students. This supported the submission of the defendants that Svadhyaya was not a religion.

While the appearance of the *Ashubh* booklet in October 2002 turned the case of the temple entry into a case in which a community's religious sentiments had (allegedly) been hurt, another booklet entitled *Jagrut Parivar* appeared in 2004. This booklet contained a number of extremely critical pieces about the Svadhyaya movement, compiled from articles that had been downloaded and translated from an Internet website. In the booklet, thirty dissident Svadhyayīs were named as donors and well-wishers.

Similar to what had happened with the *Ashubh* booklet, in the course of 2004, about 20 complaints against *Jagrut Parivar* were lodged with the police in different towns of Gujarat.[23] The complainants submitted that the printer and publisher of the booklet had been responsible for defamatory literature against Pandurang Shastri Athavale and the religious activities of the Svadhyaya Parivar. They were therefore accused of offending the religious sentiments of the Svadhyaya Parivar as well as of generating disputes and fear among people. The First Information Report (FIR) lodged with the police urged that the offences should come under Sections 295(a), 505(1)(c), 120(b), and 114 of the IPC.

Those accused, in turn, claimed that they did not know anything about the booklet and had received it by post. In an affidavit, they stated that Didi was acting against the letter and spirit of the trust deeds and that, therefore, the senior leaders had distanced themselves from the Svadhyaya Parivar. Their affidavit drew attention to the fact that this had all been reported by the media to a wider public, and that a number of cases of assault by Didi's followers had been filed. They claimed that it was Didi who had instigated the Svadhyayīs to file these complaints.

In their reply affidavit, the complainants alleged that the accused were interested in taking over the management of the Svadhyaya Parivar trusts. Having failed to do so, it was claimed, the accused had made the false allegations mentioned above, whereby Didi's name was drawn into these cases, tarnishing her image and reputation in society. Thus, they were attempting to cause severe damage to the religious harmony and society at large, especially in Gujarat, where communal relations were already strained.

Finally, the defendants filed a rejoinder affidavit in which they made an appeal to quash the complaints, and argued (as in the *Ashubh* case) that the offences do not evoke Sections 295(a) and 505(1)(c) of the IPC because the Svadhyaya Parivar is *neither a religion nor a sect.*

Summing up, in this section I have discussed how an internal dispute in the Svadhyaya movement, which was brought to court in a case concerned with disciples' right to enter the premises of a temple, turned into a controversy over the question of "religion" in the course of time. As we will see, the judgments from the Ahmedabad High Court on these cases came within a period of two years, taking two different approaches in the question of the religious dispute. The following section discusses how the judiciary itself varies in its adjudication on the question of "the religious", thus illustrating the multivocal nature of judicial reasoning.

Polyphony of Judicial Reasoning: What Defines a Sect?

It appears that, on the whole, the judicial discourse on the *Jagrut Parivar* booklet focused on the task of deciding whether the Svadhyaya Parivar is a religion or not

23 The defendants had all the complaints transferred to the Ahmadabad High Court. They feared that if they went to the smaller towns of Gujarat, they would be physically assaulted.

by delving into the definition of "religion", whereas the case of the *Ashubh* booklet addressed the issue of libel and succession disputes within a religious group. These different judgments affirm the view that, in contemporary India, Hindu religious and charitable endowment law is essentially a judge-made law.

The judgment on the *Jagrut Parivar* case focused on the question of "religion" and ruled that the Svadhyaya Parivar was indeed a religious sect.[24] The judgment stated that though the petitioners and respondents belonged to the same group, that is Svadhyaya Parivar, it was possible to evoke Sections 295(a) and 505(1)(c) of the IPC, since it was not necessary that the person whose feelings had been hurt must belong to a specific religion. According to the judge, it is sufficient that he or she belongs to a particular class of religion whose religious beliefs have been offended. At the same time, in order to decide whether the Svadhyaya Parivar is a religion/sect or not, the court had to decide on a definition of "religion". Acknowledging the fact that it was difficult to define a phenomenon as complex as "religion", the judgment relied on a couple of Supreme Court judgments. The precedents cited were the case of *S.P. Mittal* vs. *Union of India and others* (AIR 1983 Supreme Court) and the case of *Commissioner, Hindu Religious Endowment, Madras* vs. *Shirur Mutt* (AIR 1954 Supreme Court).

In the first of the above cases, the question confronting the Supreme Court was whether Aurobindoism was a religion or not.[25] Interestingly, the *Jagrut Parivar* verdict was based on the minority view held by a single judge that Aurobindoism was a religion. The authority cited in this context was a brief text on Sri Aurobindo in the *Encyclopaedia Britannica*:

> The *Encyclopaedia Britannica* refers to Aurobindo again under the head 'Idealism' and says: 'Aurobindo reinterpreting the Indian Idealistic heritage in the light of his own Western education, rejected the *maya* doctrine of illusion, replacing it with the concept of evolution. Arguing that the "illumination of individuals will lead to the emergency (sic) of a divine community". Aurobindo founded the influential Pondicherry Ashram, a religious and philosophical community, and headed it until his death.'

The other precedent referred to in the *Jagrut Parivar* case was the judgment on the well-known Shirur Mutt case, from which the definition of "religion" was cited:

> Religion is a matter of faith with individuals or communities and it is not necessarily theistic. There are well-known religions in India like Buddhism and Jainism which do not believe in God or in any Intelligent First Cause. A religion

24 Order dated 16 August 2004 for SCR. A. 666/2004, Gujarat High Court, Ahmedabad.

25 The case was brought about due to law and order problems in Auroville, the community created by Sri Aurobindo and his disciples as well as mismanagement of funds by the Aurobindo Society (see Minor 2000 for an account of this dispute).

> undoubtedly has its basis in a system of beliefs or doctrines which are regarded by those who profess that religion as conducive to their spiritual well being, but it will not be correct to say that religion is nothing else but a doctrine or belief. A religion may not only lay down a code of ethical rules for its followers to accept, it might prescribe rituals and observances, ceremonies and modes of worship which are regarded as integral parts of religion and these forms and observances might extend even to matters of food and dress. (AIR 1954 Supreme Court 282)

Based on these two precedents, it was decided by the court that the activities of the Svadhyaya Parivar were religious in nature and that it was a sect of Hinduism.

The court therefore ruled that Sections 295(a) and 505(1)(c) of the IPC could be evoked in this case. And since the FIRs were lodged at different police stations of Gujarat, it was also decided that – in order to avoid contradictory outcomes – the FIRs should be investigated by the centralized state agency. An order was given to conduct an investigation by the Crime Investigation Department (CID) in Gandhinagar. And eventually, after two years of investigation, the CID declared, in its August 2006 report, that all accused in the *Jagrut Parivar* case had been found not guilty.

Interestingly, the judgment on the *Ashubh* booklet case evoked a completely different context for adjudicating on the question of "religion".[26] It did not delve into the definition of "religion" but looked into the allegation of offending religious sentiment by insulting a religious place, namely Bhavnirjhar. It moreover took up the issue of defamation, but unlike the previous case, did not address definitional issues. Instead, the judgment went into the details of the succession dispute which constituted the backdrop for the allegations made in these complaints: It described the rift in Svadhyaya leadership, and how the civil suits concerning temple entry were filed by a section of the dissident leaders. Angered by their action, a number of criminal cases were filed, not by the persons implicated in the civil suits, but by Svadhyayī disciples. The judgment stated that after going through the details of the complaints, the court came to the decision that the criminal complaints were filed in order to thwart the civil proceedings initiated against the Svadhyaya leaders who were in charge of the management and administration of the trust properties.

In its rulings, the judgment drew attention to two aspects of the case: First, it ruled that libel could be filed only by the aggrieved persons and *not* by others on their behalf. No allegation was made against the Svadhyaya Parivar as a whole in the booklet, and therefore complaints filed by Svadhyayīs were considered untenable. Second, as far as the question of "religion" was concerned, it pointed out that while the court had earlier adjudicated that the Svadhyaya Parivar was a religion, in the Bhavnirjhar case the trustees themselves had argued that the Bhavnirjhar temple was just a prayer hall, that is, that it was *not* propagating any

---

26 The case was decided on 9 March 2006 by Justice K.A. Puj in the High Court of Gujarat, Ahmedabad.

"religion". Therefore, the judgment ruled that no offence related to "religion" had been committed by the petitioners. The court quashed the complaints exercising its power under Section 482 of the Criminal Procedure Code.[27] These contrapuntal judgments illustrate some of the complexities in the relation between the legal and the religious institutions in a secular democratic nation-state.

The complex nature of the enactment of the modern Hindu law of religious and charitable endowment has repeatedly been noted by scholars studying temple disputes (Appadurai 1981, Shankari 1982). It has been pointed out in this context that – unlike the king, whose powers *vis-à-vis* the temples were administrative and judicial but not legislative – the modern Indian state has all three powers. But the state exercises these powers through three different branches (legislative, judiciary and executive) which are very often at odds with each other. The case of the Svadhyaya succession dispute shows that the judiciary was itself divided in its verdict in the two cases that raised similar complaints.

Given this background, in the concluding section of my chapter, I argue that the Svadhyaya case study shows that the interaction between judiciary and religious organizations not only influences the developmental cycle of religious movements; it also illustrates how the secular credentials of the state are based on its intervention in the question of "religion". As the internal succession dispute turned into a judicial dispute, the "principle of secularism" was evoked by the appellants who expected the judiciary to protect their "religious rights".

Conclusions

Max Weber pointed out that the charisma of the disciples/staff comes to the fore in the context of succession when *charismatically qualified* administrative staff designates the person who is endowed with charisma (Weber 1947: 365). But in the context of the succession dispute discussed above, the senior leaders, who were the "charismatically qualified" disciples/staff and had so far controlled the movement, did not get a chance to express their opinion on the appointment of the successor. The senior leaders expected a more collective leadership structure and could not accept Dadaji's decision to appoint Didi as the highest authority. As long as succession was a matter internal to the movement, the legal-bureaucratic aspects of the religious body were kept away from the public gaze. But when the internal dispute could not be resolved by its members, the judiciary became the crucial arbitrator in the dispute and had to decide what "religion" was and whether Svadhyaya constituted a "religious group" or not.

---

27 Around the same time, in a tragic turn of events, the leader of the dissident Svadhyayīs, who had been heading the court cases in Ahmedabad, was murdered and a few Svadhyayīs were arrested in connection with his murder. Family members of the deceased Svadhyayī who live in the United States are unwilling to pursue a court case in Ahmedabad; the case is currently being tried by a public prosecutor.

In this chapter I have drawn attention to the problem of legally acknowledging the question of religious pluralism. It has been argued by the Supreme Court that "what constitutes the essential part of a religion is primarily to be ascertained with reference to the doctrines of that religion itself" (*Shirur mutt* case, 1954). But this legal position does not take into consideration the multivocal nature of religion. In other words, it does not recognize the fact that there could be more than one view or interpretation within a particular religion/religious group *vis-à-vis what* constitutes the essential part of a religion. And when such a debate takes place, the court takes it upon itself to decide what is essential and integral to a religion.

The Svadhyaya succession dispute shows that the religious body itself was divided when it came to deciding the "essential" aspects of religious belief and practice. The Svadhyayīs held at least two different perspectives with regard to the transference of charismatic authority within the movement. Disagreements were also seen *vis-à-vis* the importance given to certain ritual practices. For example, in the "temple entry" case, the dissenting Svadhyayīs had contested in their petition that *darśan* – the blessed exchange of glance between the deity and devotee – was an important aspect of being a Svadhyayī and that they needed to visit the Bhavnirjhar temple for performing the same. Whereas the Svadhyaya leadership argued that no such ritual took place at Bhavnirjhar since it was not a temple but just a prayer hall built for the students of a Svadhyaya school situated on the same premises. The Svadhyaya case shows that the "doctrines" of a particular religion are open to multiple interpretation by the practitioners themselves.

Moreover, as the internal dispute reached the court of law, Svadhyaya was forced to disown the innovations it had brought about in order to reform Hinduism. While arguing in the affidavit that Bhavnirjhar was not a temple, the Svadhyaya leaders cited a number of customary practices as proof of a real temple and pointed out that those rituals were not performed at Bhavnirjhar, although Dadaji had otherwise dismissed these customary ritual practices as superfluous aspects of a temple. Therefore, it could be said that in the context of the legal battle, what Svadhyaya propounded as the judicious interpretation of "religion" was sacrificed for a judicial definition of "religion".

At the same time, the dispute also highlighted the problem faced by the court in deciding what constitutes an "essential part of religion" when both classical textual and customary sanctions are absent. In deciding whether an organization was "religious" in nature or not, the court based its judgment on the *Encyclopaedia Britannica* and on a very selective interpretation of a Supreme Court judgment. This shows how the definition of "religion" relies heavily on what the judges consider as authoritative sources. In the process of arriving at a judicial definition of "religion", the court overlooked the tense relation between the practices of charismatic religious movements and the "classical" and "customary" aspects of traditional religion.

Studying the relation between law and religion by analysing a Supreme Court case, Marc Galanter has pointed out that the nature of judicial intervention in religion illustrates that in secular democracies, religion is not merely a datum for constitutional law; it is, in part, the product of that law (Galanter 1971: 479). By capturing the ethnographic details of the unfolding of a succession dispute within a religious movement, the present chapter has tried to contribute to a better understanding of this complex process. I have shown how the transference of charisma in a religious reform movement became an occasion for the Indian state to intervene and adjudicate in accordance with the concept of "citizen rights" and also to uphold the concept of secularism. The Svadhyaya case study thus clearly affirms the view that the concept of secularism has been erroneously framed within popular as well as academic debate on the possibility and desirability of the separation of religion from politics/state. The case study presented in this chapter makes it clear that, within the secular democratic regime, religion articulates and justifies itself in the legal-bureaucratic language of the state, while the state legitimizes itself as secular by intervening and arbitrating on the question of "religion". Thus, in this context, the relationship between religion and the state is best appreciated as one of complex mediation – negotiated and articulated through the modern legal system.

Rerferences

Appadurai, A. 1981. *Worship and Conflict under Colonial Rule: A South Indian Case*. Cambridge: Cambridge University Press.

Athavale, P.V. 1976. *Valmiki Ramayan*. Mumbai: Sat Vicar Darshan Trust.

Barz, R. 1992 [1976]. *The Bhakti Sect of Vallabhacary*. New Delhi: Munshiram Manoharlal Publishers.

Dumont, L. 1970. *Homo Hierarchicus: The Caste System and its Implications*. Oxford: Oxford University Press.

Fuller, C.J. 1988. Hinduism and scriptural authority in modern Indian law. *Comparative Studies in Society and History*, 30(2), 225–48.

Galanter, M. 1971. Hinduism, secularism and the Indian judiciary. *Philosohpy East and West*, 21(4), 467–87.

Goody, J. (ed.) 1966. *Succession to High Office*. Cambridge: Cambridge University Press.

Lokhandwalla S.T. 1971. Islamic law and Ismaili communities (Khojas and Bohras), in *India and Contemporary Islam: Proceedings of a Seminar*, edited by S.T. Lokhandwalla. Simla: Indian Institute of Advanced Study, 379–97.

Madan, T.N. 1987. Secularism in its place. *The Journal of Asian Studies*, 46(4), 747–59.

Mahajan, G. 2003. Secularism, in *The Oxford India Companion to Sociology and Social Anthropology*, edited by V. Das. New Delhi: Oxford University Press, 908–34.

Minor, R.K. 2000. Routinized charisma: The case of Aurobindo and Auroville, in *Religion and Public Culture: Encounters and Identities in Modern South India*, edited by K.E. Yandell and J.P. John. Richmond, Surrey: Curzon Press, 130–47.

Mukherjea B.K. 1952. *The Hindu Law of Religious and Charitable Trusts*. Kolkata: Eastern Law House.
Presler, F.A. 1987. *Religion under Bureaucracy: Policy and Administration for Hindu Temples in South India*. Cambridge: Cambridge University Press.
Renou, L. 1962 [1951]. *The Nature of Hinduism*. New York: Walker and Company.
Shankari, U. 1982. *Sociology of Religion: A Temple in Tamilnadu*. Unpublished PhD Dissertation, Department of Sociology, Delhi University.
Smith, D.E. 1963. *India as a Secular State*. Princeton, NJ: Princeton University Press.
Troeltsch, E. 1956 [1912]. *The Social Teaching of the Christian Churches*. London: George Allen and Unwin.
Weber, M. 1922. *The Sociology of Religion*. Boston: Beacon Press.
Weber, M. 1930. *The Protestant Ethics and the Spirit of Capitalism*. Translated by T. Parsons. London: Routledge.
Weber, M. 1947. *The Theory of Social and Economic Organization*. New York: Oxford University Press.
Wilson, B.R. 1966. *Religion in Secular Society*. Middlesex: Penguin Books.

Chapter 6
Order and Dissent Among Old Colony Mennonites: A Regime of Embedded Sovereignty

Lorenzo Cañás Bottos

Introduction

Using the example of the Old Colony Mennonites, this chapter presents an ethnographically grounded discussion on the interface between political and religious practices of "the exception" and "sovereignty". The Mennonites are a religious group with roots in sixteenth-century Friesland. After fleeing the religious persecution that followed the reformation in sixteenth-century Holy Roman Empire to Prussia, they later migrated to Ukraine (1780s), Canada (1870s), Mexico (1920s), Bolivia (1970s), and Argentina (1980s).[1] In all these instances, the Mennonites negotiated "states of exception" as preconditions for their immigration into the territories where they settled, and left them in order to avoid the imposition of public schooling and military service.

This chapter proposes the concept of "embedded sovereignty" to understand the complexities of the relationship between: (a) states and Mennonite authorities; (b) states and Mennonite believers as citizens; (c) Mennonite authorities and Mennonite believers. In this context, "embedded" refers to two aspects. On the one hand, it refers to the "spatial" configuration of the various grounding bases of the different institutions claiming sovereignty, thus producing a nesting effect like Russian dolls, and inviting one to empirically examine how this nesting is negotiated and maintained, and to investigate the conflicts that it generates. On the other hand, it refers to how different spheres (in this case the political and the religious) interact with each other in the process of legitimation and the practice of sovereignty, bringing into question how political and religious agents misinterpret, mirror, and misrepresent themselves and each other in these processes.

Giorgio Agamben's resurrection of *homo sacer* and his revitalization of Carl Schmitt's notion of sovereignty (Agamben 1998, 2005, Schmitt 2005) has been the flashpoint of a recent explosion of analyses of contemporary political events. This production has focused chiefly on extreme cases of politics of exception and biopolitics, such as concentration camps (Feuchtwang 2006, Gregory 2006),

1 The dates mentioned refer to the immigration to the preceding polity.

prisons (Rhodes 2005), the treatment of migrants, asylum seekers and refugees (Prem Kumar and Grundy-Warr 2004, Turner 2005, Feldman 2007), and post 9/11 US policy (Chappell 2006). Having become the norm in governmentality, the exception has also become the privileged cipher (together with the other by-product of sovereignty, *homo sacer*) that enables the sovereign to be identified. But the analysis of sovereignty carries a risk similar to that of thinking the state; as Pierre Bourdieu (1998: 33) puts it, "of taking over (or being taken over by) a thought of the state, of applying to the state categories of thought produced and guaranteed by the state". Therefore, in order not to be taken over by the sovereign, we need to think the sovereign from the outside. Indeed, the question of "the one" who decides on the exception as the crucial test of sovereignty (Schmitt 2005) can be seen as a direct expression of the thought of the state in its attempts at establishing itself as the holder of the "monopoly of the universal" (Bourdieu 1998: 59). Therefore, to stop the analysis at the point of identification of the sovereign runs the risk of contributing to the recognition (and consolidation of) the success of the state in attaining the monopolies it claims.

One of the strengths of anthropological analysis is its use of unfamiliar cases to help us rethink our naturalized world and categories. This means that from an anthropological perspective, both state-based juridical, political, and philosophical concepts – such as *homo sacer*, sovereignty, citizenship, nationality and the exception – as well as the jurists, genealogists, and scribes that produce them are to be taken as expressions of a particular emic perspective – despite their (implicit and explicit) discursive claims to universality and normativity. Hence, the anthropological studies of statecraft have been insistent on the problematization of the relationship between sovereignty and citizenship, depicting the nuances and layers that characterize it (Buur 2005, Hansen 2005, Jensen 2005, Turner 2005, Hansen 2006, Kelly and Shah 2006, Rodgers 2006). In this direction of analysis, the Old Colony Mennonites provide three further characteristics that make them into an interesting example in the examination of practices of sovereignty.

First, if, as Carl Schmitt (2005) argued, all political concepts are secularized theological concepts, then the exploration of the political sphere within a religiously defined polity like the Old Colony Mennonites is a privileged locus of observation. The Mennonites can be seen to be an exception among narratives of secularization, within which Schmitt's argument is located: Narratives of modernity consider the disenchantment of the world to be the outcome of processes of structural and functional differentiation that lead to the privatization and decline of religion. In these narratives, the expansion of rationalization and science is accompanied by the expansion of "the natural" over "the supernatural" while the latter becomes a residual category. Religion, therefore, once captured by modernity as one amongst other domains in the process of differentiation, becomes re-defined through the reference to "the supernatural" or contained within the domain of ethics (Latour 1993, Bruce 1996, Durkheim 2001).

In this context, religious formations that refuse to play the part assigned them by narratives of modernity are either perceived as an oasis of morality and ethics, havens from the exacerbated consumerism and individualism produced by modernity, or are portrayed as fundamentalists, irrational obscurantist fanatics pitched towards the elimination of modernity and the instauration of the rule of God on earth. In either case, they have become exceptions (for how the Amish have been portrayed by the media see Weaver-Zercher 2001, for a critique of representations of Mennonites see Cañás Bottos 2005: Chap. 4, Cañás Bottos 2006, Cañás Bottos 2008a: 4–9).

Second, the Mennonites' historical relationship with nation-states has been characterized by a cyclical negotiation of privileges for obtaining "states of exception", and emigration when those privileges were lost. This willingness on the part of the Mennonites for a state of exception provides a crucial contrast to cases where "the exception" is seen solely in its negative effects on the subjects (for an analysis of the Venezuelan 1999 *Tragedia* where the state of exception was also willed by the subjects of the sovereign, see Fassin and Vasquez 2005).

Third, the coextension of social and religious domains in Old Colony Mennonite settlements has compelled their religiously defined authorities to act as secular ones. Therefore, while in practice the religious authorities adopted political functions, they concealed and rejected this fact discursively through their promotion of values such as pacifism and separation from the state. This chapter shows how the Mennonites constructed a regime of sovereignty embedded within their negotiated state of exception. This allows for questioning the quest for the ultimate "One" that decides on the exception. Thus, through the concept of "embedded sovereignty" we can bring to the fore the multiple layers and practices involved in sovereignty.

The application of secularized theological concepts (Schmitt 2005) to a case like that of the Mennonites, who seemingly have remained separate from the process of secularization (or at least who discursively claim to have done so) requires several acts of translation and transformation. The meaning of religion, the exception, and the political sphere differ in secularized and non-secularized contexts. Whereas the concept of sovereignty codifies all social processes under the category of "the political"; within the Old Colony Mennonites, "the religious" is the master trope that subsumes them all. Therefore, to translate *bios* and *zoē* (Agamben 1998) in culturally sensitive ways we have to ask what the crucial distinction is that they are marking and that the figure of *homo sacer* carries.

If we are to translate these passages into the Christian religious tradition, we have to focus on the decision on damnation/salvation. It is the decision on eternal life that marks the Christian sovereign. This decision however, lies in the cosmic future, to be applied by the deity. In the meantime the appropriate means of achieving this decision while on earth has been delegated by the deity to the leadership of the church on earth. Within the religious sphere of the Old Colony Mennonites, the decision on the exception takes the form of a combination of baptism and excommunication, and not the miracle as Schmitt (2005) argues. An excommunicant in a religious community is like a citizen without rights: bare life (Agamben 1998).

The first part of this chapter outlines the processes of the historical formation and maintenance of the Old Colony Mennonites' moral and social order in their attempts to build a church of believers separate from the world. This will depict their quest to become exceptions as well as the process by which the political was absorbed by the religious structure. I then focus on the contemporary organization of Old Colony Mennonites in late-twentieth-century Argentina and Bolivia. This chapter finishes with two cases of conflict that illustrate the strategies by which colony authorities attempted to suppress and exclude dissent and heresy, thus constituting examples of the practice of embedded sovereigns. I argue that in order to assure their own continuity as internal sovereigns, they resorted not only to the usage of an institutionalized exception like excommunication, but to the avoidance of due process.

Negotiating and Becoming "the Exception"[2]

The Mennonites owe their name to Menno Simons (1496–1561), a Dutch reformer whose main theological tenets were the baptism of adults, separation from the world, the separation of church and state, universal priesthood, and pacifism. They are part of a wider Christian movement known as "Anabaptism" (due to their practice of rebaptizing adults who had been baptized during childhood in the Catholic Church). In sixteenth-century Europe, the Mennonites formed a dispersed movement, with followers coming from a wide variety of backgrounds. They were persecuted by mainstream Protestant groups and Catholics alike. In an imperial mandate issued as a consequence of the Diet of Speyer (1529), Charles V decreed that "every Anabaptist and rebaptized man and woman of the age of reason shall be condemned and brought from natural life into death by fire, sword, and the like, according to the person, without proceeding by the inquisition of the spiritual judges" (Bossert quoted by Williams 2000: 238).

As a consequence of their persecution by both Catholics and Protestants, the Mennonites fled the Holy Roman Empire for Prussia, where they were tolerated due to their economic contributions stemming from their expertise in agriculture in swampy areas and in the construction of dikes and canals (Williams 2000: 609, Urry 2006: 35ff). However, the rise of the Hohenzollern aristocracy and their militaristic policies were not received well by the pacifist Mennonites. In 1789, although they managed to negotiate the exemption of military duties in exchange for additional payments, they also suffered restrictions in land acquisition and various other measures, which they considered as threats to their religion (Urry

2 For the formative period during the reformation, George Huntston Williams's The Radical Reformation (1962) is the best point of departure. For the "Russian" and "Canadian" periods see Urry (1978, 1989, 2006). For Canada and Mexico see Redekop (1969) and Sawatzky (1971). For a more detailed historical reconstruction, as well as a critique of sources used, see Cañás Bottos (2005, 2008 a).

2006: 52). This made them receptive to an offer made by Georg van Trappe, a colonizing agent under the orders of Grigori Potemkin who, in turn, was in charge of the territories in the Ukraine recently conquered by Catherine the Great. As part of a wider colonization plan designed to populate and consolidate suzerainty over these territories, the Mennonites were offered a series of privileges to lure them to the Ukraine (the actual document that contains them is usually referred to as the *Privilegium*). They were offered, among other things, religious freedom, tax exemptions, and land. In exchange, they were required to settle in unpopulated areas, and not to try to convert other Christians – although they were free to Christianize Muslims.

In accepting these offers, the Mennonites became agents of the Russian state for the incorporation of the territories. They transformed an indistinct nomadic space into one that the state could read, understand, measure, simplify and tax (see also Deleuze and Guattari 1987, Scott 1998). For this, the Mennonites provided the Russian state with a grid as a settling pattern, the epitome of state readability.[3] In brief, through the Mennonites, the Russian state effectively "captured" the territory (Deleuze and Guattari 1987: 440). On a symbolic level, the Mennonites' acceptance of the *Privilegium* can be interpreted as recognition of the legitimacy of the Czarina as the sovereign over the territories where they settled. Oblivious to these material and symbolic contributions to the consolidation of the sovereign, the Mennonites seized this opportunity to attempt to bring about a "separation from the world" and the founding of the "community of true believers". The *Privilegium*'s imposition to settle in unpopulated areas made them form exclusive colonies that were almost isolated from the rest of the population and which transformed the meaning of "separation from the world" from a *spiritual* to a *geographical* one. On the other hand, through the creation of a differentiated legal regime, the *Privilegium* created a space of exception which provided the conditions for the rooting of an embedded sovereign who would rule within this sphere. Under these conditions, the Mennonites grew through extended reproduction, and through the reception of new migratory waves. While they created several new colonies, they also suffered several internal schisms.

During the reign of Alexander I, in an attempt to normalize the political administration of local governments, the Mennonites were forced to accept a new politico-administrative structure in 1801 which can still be found in the colonies today: a *Schult* (major) for each linear village of a colony, and a *Fäaschta* for each colony, in charge of coordinating the *Schult* and linking with the external state authorities. In addition, each colony also has a *Leardeenst*, a collective body formed by various *Prädjasch* (preachers, sing. *Prädja*), one *Dia'koon* (Deacon) and one *Eltesta* (literally "the Eldest" but which today Mennonites translate into Spanish as *Obispo* –"Bishop").

---

3 This layout is very similar to the one used in Hutu refugee camps in Tanzania (Malkki 1995) and in "high modernist" planning (Scott 1998).

By 1871, as part of Alexander II's empire-wide reforms, the Mennonites' *Privilegium* was revoked and their status changed from "foreign colonists" to "settler proprietors".[4] The reforms involved the limitation of land division upon inheritance (leaving a great number of landless Mennonites), the introduction of Russian in schools, and were soon followed by compulsory military conscription.

In its attempts at Russifying the immigrants through schooling (and lifting the state of exception that granted them different privileges), the Russian state attempted to include them in the "body of the nation", which had become one of the three pillars of sovereignty as expressed in the imperial motto "Autocracy, Orthodoxy, and National Character" coined by Count Sergey Uvarov. By changing the principles of legitimation, the absolutist state was transformed into a nation-state (Hobsbawm 1992: 80, 84) and set for itself the task of the construction of "the people" that would provide its very legitimation (Morgan 1988). In this way, the *bios* of the subject was now threatened to be "captured" through schooling in order to inculcate a particular type of *zoē* that would internalize its inculcator as sovereign.

Whereas some Mennonites agreed with these changes, others felt they could not accept them, and after failed negotiations with Russian state representatives, broke their communion with those who remained and migrated to Canada. In the early 1870s they had negotiated a *Privilegium* with the Canadian government. They were offered land, and similar conditions to those lost in Russia. Territorial consolidation through agricultural settlement was also part of the agenda behind the invitation: Canada wished to attain effective occupation of the area close to the recently established border with the US. The Mennonites therefore settled on two tracts of land in Manitoba, one of which was literally on the border with the US. As in the Ukraine, the Mennonites obtained a state of exception in exchange for their contribution to the territorialization of the state.

The voluntary acceptance of the public schooling system and of the Canadian village administrative structure together with the modernization of singing among some Mennonite congregations led to a schism which gave rise to the Old Colony Mennonites. Later, within the context of the First World War, the School Attendance Act of 1916 was passed in the Manitoba legislature and English was made the sole language of education in the province. The Mennonites failed in negotiations to maintain their own schooling system. Again, some accepted the imposition while others considered international migration as a viable course of action.

In February 1921, a Mennonite delegation met with the president of Mexico, Álvaro Obregón, and obtained a *Privilegium* that granted them, among other things, schooling autonomy and exemption from military service. The Mennonites established a number of colonies in the states of Chihuahua and Durango. And as they grew in number they formed new colonies in the states of Zacatecas, Campeche, and Tamaulipas. Some years later, the fear of an imposed military service, economic changes, and an internal schism due to the adoption of modern

4 For a detailed discussion on the use of land in Russia, see Longhofer (1993: 399).

pick-up trucks and electricity, prompted further migratory movements to British Honduras (1958), Bolivia (1960s), Argentina (1986) and Paraguay (where there was already an important presence of Mennonites from Russia who had escaped the Stalinist regime in the 1930s).

After the disastrous Chaco War (1932–1935) against Paraguay, the Bolivian government implemented a population policy of the Oriente (mostly within the department of Santa Cruz de la Sierra). In addition to internal migration from the Andean region, it also incorporated Japanese colonists from Okinawa, and Russian Old Believers, who built four and three agricultural settlements respectively. In this context, the Mennonites again obtained a "state of exception" thorough a presidential decree which exempted them from military service, taxes, the import duty for agricultural machinery, and public schooling. By 2000, when I conducted my fieldwork in Bolivia, there were forty Bolivian colonies with a total population of approximately 40,000 people.

In Argentina, on the other hand, Mennonites from Mexico and Bolivia established La Nueva Esperanza in 1986, in the Province of La Pampa. They did not manage to obtain a written *Privilegium* at the moment of their immigration, but government officials promised them that they would not be coerced into military service and that they could retain their schooling system. However, within fifteen years of their arrival, the provincial and national governments started to put pressure on them to adopt the state approved curricula. Although the state initially intended to incorporate all children of schooling age who were resident in the colony into the official schooling system, following negotiations it was agreed that, following the principle of *ius solis*, only those born in Argentina would be subject to the schooling policy (and this was reduced to the teaching of Spanish). The Mennonites, in turn, claimed jurisdiction over these children through the principle of *ius sanguinis*.

These conflicts reveal that the *bios* of individuals is at stake in the dispute between the state and the *Leardeenst*. It reflects a veritable battle over the capture of the *bios* for its transformation into a particular *zoē*, a transformation either via baptism with the aim of transforming the *bios* into a Christian *zoē*, or via the national schooling system into a national *zoē*. This transformation would also indicate the primary (or rather ultimate) loyalty to be demanded from the individual: either to be willing to die bearing witness to Jesus as saviour, or for its national equivalent as best expressed in Horace's principle *dulce et decorum est pro patria mori* ["It is sweet and appropriate to die for the fatherland"]. Both cases involve a process of internalization and legitimation of a particular sovereign's powers over life and death.

This imposition by the Argentine state in the late 1990s resulted in a migratory movement back to Bolivia by those most unwilling to comply, although so far it has resulted neither in the breaking of communion with emigrants nor in a schism (but such an outcome is not unlikely in the near future). It is now time to examine how this internally embedded sovereign operates within its own semi-autonomous space.

The Internal Exception

The Mennonites say that life on earth should be led according to the Scriptures. Within the colonies, rules and regulations, prescriptions and prohibitions are all supposed to be based on the Bible, or to follow Biblical principles and values. In addition, a number of other sources are used as guidelines, including Menno Simons's writings (Simons 1983), a *Catechism and Confession of Faith*, a Hymnal, and the *Martyrs' Mirror* (Braght 1982).

Besides this corpus of unchanging and widely available texts, the Old Colony Mennonites also use the *Ordninj*, a text maintained by members of the *Leardeenst* and read once a year during the worship service. The agreement between different colonies on a common *Ordninj* allows them to recognize each other as equals and binds them across localities and international borders, therefore forming a trans-statal community (Cañás Bottos 2008b). In this way, membership in a particular colony enables the individual to transfer to another one if he or she chooses to move.

The *Ordninj* contains a set of rules that regulate a broad range of aspects of everyday life, including details about attire and personal grooming, but also prohibitions on the ownership of televisions and cars, and the installation of electricity in homes. These prescriptions and prohibitions are, in everyday life, transformed into visible marks of group boundaries and membership. When Mennonites explained to me why certain things were forbidden, compulsory, or desirable, the verbal reference used in most cases was the Spanish expression "*la religion*" (the religion). This simple speech act, which identifies "the religion" with its codification, evidences the success in establishing the legitimacy of the *Ordninj*.

In his analysis of the genesis of the state, Pierre Bourdieu (1998) shows, on the one hand, how the state contributes to the modern structural differentiation of domains, generating a different type of capital in each one of them. On the other hand, the state also strives to attain a monopoly over each and every type of capital as well as of the rates of exchange between them, claiming the "monopoly of the universal" (1998: 59) and hence, the subsumption of all spheres to the political. The *Leardeenst*, by contrast, claims the monopoly of the universal by hindering and externalizing the process of differentiation of domains. In the eyes of the Old Colony Mennonites "religion" is a "total social fact" in which the moral, legal, political, and economical threads have not been disentangled, but subsumed to the authority of the *Leardeenst*. Although they do have specialists (such as the *Schult*, *Fäaschta*, cheese factory administrators, "doctors", an internal insurance system, singers) the *Eltesta* retains the last word on *every domain* (for an analysis of the dilemmas and contradictions in this situation see Cañás Bottos 2008a: Chapter 4).

The *Leardeenst*'s main duty is to maintain the social and moral order in the colonies. This is achieved through regimes of socialization – for example, by overseeing and controlling the school curricula and weekly worship services – and social control – through, for instance, the threat and usage of excommunication.

Through baptism, a member is incorporated into "the body of Christ on earth", and this sacrament thus becomes the basic prerequisite for being saved in the afterlife. However, changes in social context have meant that the social consequences of baptism have changed over time: In sixteenth-century Europe, baptism in the Roman Catholic Church was compulsory; therefore, the incorporation of a new member in a dissenting Anabaptist congregation (such as the Mennonites) would have required a new baptism which, in turn, would have been liable to persecution. Within the contemporary Old Colony, baptism is, in practice, compulsory. Nowadays, baptism is required for acquiring full adulthood rights within the colony, most importantly to be able to marry and to be able to own land, and the crucial question is thus not whether one should be baptized or not, but instead the *timing* of such an event. In short, baptism has been routinized and transformed into a ritual that marks the member's coming of age.

Whereas in an unbaptized state he or she is answerable to his or her parents, after baptism, he or she is accountable to the wider community. Baptism accordingly transfers the *bios* from the sphere of the domestic to that of the *Leardeenst*. Now, in order to make a youngster a suitable candidate for baptism, he or she needs to have gone through the Mennonite schooling process, in which, using the Bible, they are taught how to read and write, and must memorize the questions and answers set forth in their catechism. Just as states use the schooling system to inculcate the basic presuppositions of the national self-image and to transform children into citizens appropriate for a particular polity, Mennonite schools inculcate a worldview designed to transform children into adults, while this entails the generation of Mennonites as future citizens of heaven, and not of earthly polities.

Losing control of schooling would mean that the Mennonites would lose the process by which individuals come to "voluntarily" accept baptism and submit to the Old Colony as the sovereign (in a similar way that love for one's country and flag is instilled through schooling in most nation-states).

The "opposite" of baptism, representing the *Leardeenst*'s main tool for obtaining compliance is the *Kjoakjebaum* (excommunication, but also referred to as *Ausschluss* ("exclusion") or *ban*). Following Matthew 18: 15–19, a number of intermediary steps need to be taken before excommunication is carried out: On the discovering of a breach of conduct, a *Prädja* or two visit the culprit to indicate the offence and request an explanation, repentance, and, if applicable, the abandonment of the reproachable behaviour or object. If this fails, the offender is summoned to the *Donnadach* (the bi-weekly meeting of the *Leardeenst*) where he would be admonished by the full *Leardeenst*. If this is not sufficient, the offender's case is raised again during a worship service, in front of the full congregation. Repentance and compliance is requested once again, and if the answer does not satisfy the *Leardeenst*, the *Kjoakjebaum* is decreed.

Again, we need to point out differences between contemporary Old Colony Mennonites and those in the days of Menno Simons. Whereas during sixteenth-century Europe converted members would be considered a persecuted religious minority, among contemporary Old Colony Mennonites, the limits of the social unit, within which the greatest part of social interaction occurs, are coterminous with and subject to the limits set by the church authorities. This means that whereas in the days of Menno Simons, the religious authorities' power was confined to the spiritual sphere, in the contemporary Old Colony the exertion of power by colony authorities (especially through the use of excommunication) has very concrete and practical implications that can range from internal social ostracism and, sometimes, even the loss of the means of subsistence.

Excommunication, however, has its limits due to its anchoring in "the exception": If used in a generalized fashion, the *Leardeenst* would create the conditions for yet another space of exception in which an embedded sovereign could root itself, as in practice, excommunication implies a prohibition on members in good standing of socializing with the apostate. Since the apostates are already excluded, no further action can be taken against them, and nothing prevents them from maintaining social relationships amongst themselves. The generalization of the exception can therefore leave the sovereign without its subjects. Faced with this scenario, an exception has to be made to the application of the exception. This is, in broad lines, what happened in the two cases of conflict analysed in the following pages, where excommunication – although it should have been implemented – was avoided by the *Leardeenst*.

Case 1: Benjamin

Benjamin was born in 1970 in Colonia Norte, and one year later moved with his parents to Capulín colony (both in Mexico). In 1986 they left Capulín in order to join La Nueva Esperanza, in Argentina, where Benjamin was baptized and later married. In conversation with me, Benjamin did not consider his baptism to have made much of a change in his life as he claimed that he continued to smoke, drink, and only thought in terms of making money. The "great change", as Benjamin himself called it, came in 1998 and was a result of meeting Sergio, an Argentine religious seeker who at some point (unsuccessfully) tried to be incorporated in the colonies. Sergio and his wife did, however, succeed in building a network of Mennonite supporters, but in doing so, triggered several conflicts within the colonies.

According to Benjamin, the first time he had invited Sergio to their home, he emphasized the missionary message of the Bible, Menno Simons's active position in the spreading of the Gospel, and reflected on stories from the *Martyrs' Mirror* (Braght 1982). Then, Sergio gave his testimony, a practice which is not performed among Mennonites.[5] From that day onwards, Benjamin considered Sergio to be "brother in Christ", and he started to read the Bible, Menno Simons's works, and the *Martyrs' Mirror*. Benjamin claimed that he discovered, during this process of reading and discussing with Sergio, that he had previously believed in things which were either wrong or of no importance: He had believed, for example, that the Mennonites were Israelites, and that the only way of being a Christian was to live in a colony.

5 For an analysis of "witnessing" and its efficacy, see Harding (1987).

These reflections are an expression of Benjamin's changing perceptions of the definition of "Christianity" and "community" – perceptions that differed increasingly from those held in the Old Colony: He proposed an individualized, internal, and affective relationship with Christ by being his witness to the world, and by living in a community tied by common faith and spiritual kinship as opposed to one that was based on common descent and custom, that was externalized and ritualized, and that strove to separate itself from the world. Through this alternative definition of the *Corpus Christianum*, he challenged the legitimacy of the *Leardeenst*'s monopoly in the matter of salvation and damnation. Sergio sent some of his treatises to Benjamin, who recalled upon receiving them: "He showed, in these letter, the errors that the Mennonites were making, and there was not a single word in those letters that was not backed up by a verse in the New Testament, or by resorting to other books such as Menno Simons's works or the *Martyrs' Mirror*."

Benjamin translated *The Church of God*, one of Sergio's essays, and made photocopies of it for distribution within the colony "in order to awaken faith in Christ". When a copy reached the *Eltesta*, he summoned Benjamin and ordered him to retrieve all copies. Benjamin, in turn, refused to do so until it was proven to him that the essays were wrong. Benjamin and some of his supporters were expecting the *Eltesta* to produce a Bible-based refutation of *The Church of God.* However, the *Eltesta*'s reply was harsh and rather disappointing for them; he said: "There is nothing wrong with it, but we do not need a *Weltmensch* [worldly man, the categorical opposite to being a Christian] to teach us on these topics. We already have those books in our houses, that is enough." Benjamin attempted to defend his newly found spiritual brother, but the *Eltesta*'s answer remained in the same tone: "We do not need to discuss this." Benjamin had not been summoned for a discussion of either Sergio's religiosity or his biblical hermeneutics; he had been summoned to obey. During this conversation Benjamin was explicitly "forbidden to open the Bible with non-Mennonites". The *Eltesta* could therefore be seen to be using his office-based authority to close down avenues for the emergence of dissenting biblical interpretations that were threatening to undermine the current social order.

When moving between Mennonite colonies, it is necessary to obtain a letter of transference from the *Eltesta*, which serves as proof that the respective person is a member "in good standing" and which recommends the person's acceptance in another colony. However, when Benjamin – in the year 1999, just after the conflict with the *Eltesta*, outlined above – left La Nueva Esperanza for Pinondi (in Bolivia), he did not have such a letter. Without proof of his good standing and without having been excommunicated, he was neither in nor out, but betwixt and between, in a truly liminal position (Turner 1995). Upon arrival in Pinondi, he was nevertheless accepted temporarily and required to produce the letter of transference within a specified period of time. Thus, in refusing Benjamin his letter, the *Eltesta* of La Nueva Esperanza not only avoided the process of excommunication himself, but by providing his peers with a ready made reason for non-acceptance freed them from having to resort to this process should they need to discipline or get rid of Benjamin.

In Pinondi, Benjamin was appointed as a teacher, but this, as I later came to know, was *not* due to his degree of literacy or scriptural abilities, nor was it an indication that he was trusted: For a couple of months, Benjamin and I had been trying to organize a joint trip to visit Sergio. Eventually Benjamin told me that he was ready to go and mentioned that the following weekend was his last chance to visit Sergio because the school term would start the following week. We arranged that I would take the train from Santa Cruz to Yacuiba, and he would join me at Charagua Station. However, when I met him at the station, he told me he could not come with me and said: "Mennonites can go wherever they want, but there is a small plot of land in Tarija that has been forbidden to me."

This remark made me realize what was really going on: As a teacher, he received land, housing, and a salary. Thus, because he was living in a house that was property of the colony, he was not really free to receive visitors; this concerned especially those who would have required staying overnight. The teaching schedule, with classes both in the morning and in the afternoon, meant that there was little spare time to receive and make visits. And since he had to teach six days a week, he was virtually confined to the colony. In addition, having to teach from the Scriptures meant that other members of the colony could check for any deviations from the established interpretations by asking their children what they were being taught by Benjamin.

In short, his appointment as teacher was something akin to house arrest, and the control was both physical and ideological. In this way, internal ostracism and an intensification of social control was added to his precarious membership status. In the end, the *Leardeenst* succeeded through these measures of isolation and ideological asphyxiation. Not only in controlling the spread of Sergio's ideas, but also in obtaining compliance from Benjamin, who eventually lost touch with Sergio, and the rest of the members of their network.

Case 2: Bernard

Let us now turn to Bernard, where the conflict resulted in the externalization of the dissenter, that is, without resort to excommunication or expulsion, he was progressively pushed to the edges of the Old Colony, resulting in him leaving "voluntarily". Bernard and his family were living in Swift Current colony, in Bolivia's department of Santa Cruz, in a house provided him with his job as an attendant of the colony-owned store. He was born in a colony in Mexico, and came to Bolivia at a late point. As he told me, while preparing for his baptism, he came across a "Confession of Faith" in the Centro Menno in the Mexican town of Nuevo Casas Grandes.[6] In the text, the "washing of the feet" and what he called "the search for the lost souls" attracted his attention. Upon consulting with his

6 The "Centro Menno" is the name given to local centres run by the Mennonite Central Committee, which is formed by non-colony Mennonites in Canada and the US, primarily for missionary efforts.

father, he received a chiding reply: "Why are you looking for writings from the outside? We should read the New Testament, the *Gesangbuch* [hymnal], and that is enough." However, Bernard continued to read any book that he came across, but keeping his doubts to himself in order to avoid any further reprimands.

In 1998, between Christmas and New Year's Eve – that is, at a time when Mennonites refrain from working and have plenty of time to visit each other – Sergio appeared in the Swift Current colony and Bernard invited him to his house:

> I realised that he was a person of faith, of a very strong faith in Jesus Christ; he was very religious. He told me about the Martyrs' Mirror, of things I knew and of things I was about to know. I realized that he had a good understanding of these things so I liked it …

When Sergio went to live in his own settlement in the department of Tarija he spoke about Bernard to the former Amish who were his neighbours. They, in turn, decided to pay Bernard a visit on one of their trips to Santa Cruz, as did a group of Russian Christian (Old Believer) colonists who also befriended Sergio. Those visits were shortly followed by two *Prädjasch* telling Bernard to stop receiving people. Recalling the event, Bernard told me:

> So I told them that 'according to the Holy Scriptures I am obliged to accept any visits'. I don't know how to say this to you exactly, but by accepting visitors, some have received angels in their homes, without knowing they were angels. But they did not want to hear. I told them 'treat me with love, and convince me, through the Holy Scripture, that I am going on the wrong path and I will immediately stop doing it, but otherwise, I cannot tell my brothers not to come.' But where I cannot be convinced by the Holy Scriptures, and by love, I think I should follow God instead of men. Well, they refused to refer to the Bible. They did not even mention a single word. They just said: 'We have come to warn you not to do it anymore.' That was it, they were gone.

Things were getting out of hand: Bernard continued to incorporate people into his spiritual kinship family, while the *Leardeenst* tried to stop it before it spread. And it did so in the same fashion that it did in reacting to Benjamin's case: No defense, discussion, or negotiation was allowed. Bernard's protest and attempt to induce a discussion "Bible in hand" was dismissed. The party was sent to relay orders, not to discuss them.

Then, in December 1999, Bernard received notice that from the beginning of the new year his services would no longer be needed in the store and that he had one month to find another place to live as he would have to vacate the house by the end of January. In brief, the matter was settled as a simple laying-off of an employee. Unable to pay the inflated land prices in the Swift Current colony, Bernard had to move to a newly established colony in the south of Bolivia. There,

Bernard was again kept under control, his visitors having to report to one of the *Prädjasch* to ask for permission before staying at his house. When I was there, the *Prädja* instructed me in no uncertain terms to let Bernard know that if he wanted to change the lifestyle of the colony, he should leave it for good. Sergio sent me a letter in May 2007 informing me Bernard had left the colony and joined him.

Taken together, control of the spread of ideas seems to have been the prime objective on the part of the different colony authorities regarding the handling of internal dissent. They therefore directly admonished against receiving visitors, attempted to restrict the circulation of certain printed materials, and prohibited members to engage in Bible-based discussions with outsiders. Then, having failed in the control of the circulation of the materials that carried these ideas, the *Leardeenst* focused on the people who espoused them. In doing this, however, they circumvented the excommunication process but, instead, engaged in isolating and externalizing dissenters. In the final instance, this meant to (slowly and steadily) push them towards the margins of the Old Colony, leaving it up to them to either comply or leave.

Conclusion

In this chapter, I have shown how the relationship between Old Colony Mennonites and different nation-states has been characterized by the use of "exceptional" treatment, through the negotiation of privileges in exchange for their contribution to the territorial consolidation of sovereignty. In this configuration, the constitution of exclusive settlements transformed the Mennonite ideal of a "separation from the world" from a spiritual metaphor into a socio-spatial order. As the recipients of privileges from states, they created a "space of exception". In turn, this "space of exception" allowed for the creation of a domain in which the colony authorities formed a regime of "embedded sovereignty". In this way, Old Colony Mennonites contest (symbolically and in practice, but not in an overt and discursive way) claims to sovereignty by nation-states by claiming an "exception" within which they establish a domain of sovereignty and over which they reserve the right to decide on "the exception". In this regime of embedded sovereignty the *Leardeenst* absorbs "the political" under the guise of "the religious", while at the same time claiming its exclusion. "Religion" here becomes the cloak of acceptability of this embedded sovereign. To those outside the Old Colony, this self-definition in religious terms contributes to defuse possible threats to the host states by hiding the political sphere. To those inside the Old Colony, the *Leardeenst* needs to centre itself within the religious sphere without appearing too "political" in order to maintain legitimacy.

I have also shown how the relationship between these two sovereigns is far from unproblematic, especially when it comes to the control of the institutions through which bare life is transformed either into a citizen or a Christian and through which fundamental categories for understanding the world and one's ultimate loyalty are instilled. The social construction of the structures upon which the exceptions can take effect thus precedes the decision for an exception. Hence beginning by the decision on the exception naturalizes the process by which the exception itself becomes possible and legitimate.

The circumvention of excommunication shows, on the one hand, the implicit recognition by the *Leardeenst* of its limits as a tool for social control, and the dangers of the normalization of the exception. The procedure of excommunication would have contributed to the dissemination of the dissenters' ideas by providing them with a public forum in which they could be voiced. Indeed, both Bernard and Benjamin were eager to enter into a public discussion, Bible in hand, in order to defend their ideas and to carry out what they saw as their duty in paying witness to their faith. Had they succeed in spreading their message, it would have created a context for the mass excommunication of dissenters. This, in turn, would have created yet another space of exception within which another embedded sovereign could have taken root. Hence the avoidance of the process of excommunication was a means of protecting the *Leardeenst* as an embedded sovereign.

Acknowledgements

The author acknowledges the CVCP, Fundación Antorchas and the University of Manchester for funding the research. Final drafting was done under Estonian Science Foundation grants SF0130033s07 and ETF7360.

References

Agamben, G. 1998. *Homo Sacer: Sovereign Power and Bare Life*. Stanford: Stanford University Press.

Agamben, G. 2005. *State of Exception*. Chicago: University of Chicago Press.

Bourdieu, P. 1998. *Practical Reason: On the Theory of Action*. Stanford: Stanford University Press.

Braght, T.J.V. 1982. *The Bloody Theater or Martyrs' Mirror of the Defenseless Christians*. Scottdale: Herald Press.

Bruce, S. 1996. *Religion in the Modern World: From Cathedrals to Cults*. Oxford: Oxford University Press.

Buur, L. 2005. The sovereign outsourced: Local justice and violence in Port Elizabeth, in *Sovereign Bodies: Citizens, Migrants, and States in the Postcolonial World*, edited by T.B. Hansen and F. Stepputat. Princeton, NJ: Princeton University Press, 192–217.

Cañás Bottos, L. 2005. *Christenvolk: Historia y Etnografía de una Colonia Menonita*. Buenos Aires: Antropofagia.

Cañás Bottos, L. 2006. Old Colony Mennonites in South America: Refractions of the "Other". *Cambridge Anthropology*, 26(1), 1–23.

Cañás Bottos, L. 2008a. *Old Colony Mennonites in Argentina and Bolivia: Nation Making, Religious Conflict and Imagination of the Future*, Leiden, Boston: Brill Academic Publishers.

Cañás Bottos, L. 2008b. Transformations of Old Colony Mennonites: The making of a trans-statal community. *Global Networks: A Journal of Transnational Affairs*, 8(2), 214–31.

Chappell, B. 2006. Rehearsals of the sovereign: States of exception and threat governmentality. *Cultural Dynamics*, 18(3), 313–34.

Deleuze, G. and Guattari, F. 1987. *A Thousand Plateaus: Capitalism and Schizophrenia*. Minneapolis: University of Minnesota Press.

Durkheim, E. 2001. *The Elementary Forms of Religious Life*. Oxford: Oxford University Press.

Fassin, D. and Vasquez, P. 2005. Humanitarian exception as the rule: The political theology of the 1999 *Tragedia* in Venezuela. *American Ethnologist*, 32(3), 389–405.

Feldman, I. 2007. Difficult distinctions: Refugee law, humanitarian practice, and political identification in Gaza. *Cultural Anthropology*, 22(1), 129–69.

Feuchtwang, S. 2006. Images of sub-humanity and their realization. *Critique of Anthropology*, 26(3), 259–78.

Gregory, D. 2006. The black flag: Guantánamo bay and the space of exception. *Geografiska Annaler Series B*, 88(4), 405–27.

Hansen, T.B. 2005. Sovereigns beyond the state: On legality and authority, in *Sovereign Bodies: Citizens, Migrants, and States in the Postcolonial World*, edited by T.B. Hansen and F. Stepputat, Princeton, NJ: Princeton University Press, 169–91.

Hansen, T.B. 2006. Performers of sovereignty: On the privatization of security in urban South Africa. *Critique of Anthropology*, 26(3), 279–95.

Harding, S.F. 1987. Convicted by the Holy Spirit – the rhetoric of fundamental Baptist conversion. *American Ethnologist*, 14(1), 167–81.

Hobsbawm, E.J. 1992. *Nations and Nationalism since 1780. Programme, Myth, Reality*. 2nd Edition. Cambridge: Cambridge University Press.

Jensen, S. 2005. Above the law: Practices of sovereignty in Surrey Estate, Cape Town, in *Sovereign Bodies: Citizens, Migrants, and States in the Postcolonial World*, edited by T.B. Hansen and F. Stepputat, Princeton, NJ: Princeton University Press, 218–38.

Kelly, T. and Shah, A. 2006. Introduction – a double-edged sword: Protection and state violence. *Critique of Anthropology*, 26(3), 251–7.

Latour, B. 1993. *We Have Never Been Modern*. Cambridge: Harvard University Press.

Longhofer, J. 1993. Specifying the commons: Mennonites, intensive agriculture, and landlessness in nineteenth-century Russia. *Ethnohistory*, 40(3), 384–409.

Malkki, L.H. 1995. *Purity and Exile: Violence, Memory, and National Cosmology among Hutu Refugees in Tanzania*. Chicago: University of Chicago Press.

Morgan, E.S. 1988. *Inventing the People: The Rise of Popular Sovereignty in England and America*. New York: Norton.

Prem Kumar, R. and Grundy-Warr, C. 2004. The irregular migrant as homo sacer: Migration and detention in Australia, Malaysia, and Thailand. *International Migration*, 42(1), 33–64.

Redekop, C.W. 1969. *The Old Colony Mennonites. Dilemmas of Ethnic Minority Life*. Baltimore: Johns Hopkins University Press.

Rhodes, L.A. 2005. Changing the subject: conversation in supermax. *Cultural Anthropology*, 20(3), 388–411.

Rodgers, D. 2006. The state as a gang: Conceptualizing the governmentality of violence in contemporary Nicaragua. *Critique of Anthropology*, 26(3), 315–30.

Sawatzky, H.L. 1971. *They Sought a Country: Mennonite Colonization in Mexico*. Berkeley: University of California Press.

Schmitt, C. 2005. *Political Theology: Four Chapters on the Concept of Sovereignty*. Chicago: University of Chicago Press.

Scott, J.C. 1998. *Seeing like a State: How Certain Schemes to Improve the Human Condition Have Failed*. New Haven: Yale University Press.

Simons, M. 1983. *The Complete Works*. Aylmer: Pathway.

Turner, S. 2005. Suspended spaces – contesting sovereignties in a refugee camp, in *Sovereign Bodies: Citizens, Migrants, and States in the Postcolonial World*, edited by T.B. Hansen and F. Stepputat, Princeton, NJ: Princeton University Press, 313–32.

Turner, V.W. 1995. *The Ritual Process: Structure and Anti-Structure*. New York: Aldine de Gruyter.

Urry, J. 1978. *The Closed and the Open: Social and Religious Change amongst the Mennonites in Russia (1789–1889)*. PhD Thesis, Oxford, University of Oxford.

Urry, J. 1989. *None but Saints: The Transformation of Mennonite Life in Russia, 1789–1889*. Winnipeg: Hyperion Press.

Urry, J. 2006. *Mennonites, Politics, and Peoplehood: Europe – Russia – Canada 1525 to 1980*. Winnipeg: University of Manitoba Press.

Weaver-Zercher, D. 2001. *The Amish in the American Imagination*. Baltimore: Johns Hopkins University Press.

Williams, G.H. 2000 [1962]. *The Radical Reformation*. 3rd Edition, revised and expanded. Kirksville: Truman State University Press.

Chapter 7

There is no Power Except for God: Locality, Global Christianity and Immigrant Transnational Incorporation

Nina Glick Schiller

Despite the German December chill, Ruby[1] was dressed in summery beige clothing, from her hat down to her high-heeled beige short boots with very pointed toes. In her posture, as well as her carefully styled outfit, she exuded a sense of confidence and determination as she strode up to the front of the assembled congregation. As usual, the final portion of the Sunday service of the Miracle Healing Church God's Gospel Church was devoted to testimonial. This particular service had strayed beyond the scheduled 13:00 closing time and members of the congregation seemed restless. However, soon as she began to testify, she held the attention of the congregation.

> I have found a German man who wants to marry me. The problem is the paper. I have been told that I have to send to Nigeria for a paper. But there has been a two-month strike of public workers there, and no one is filling out any papers … I went to speak to the lady in that office [in charge of papers] about the strike.[2] The woman refused to listen and said that the marriage could not happen without the paper… I told the lady that I believed in God and I did not need that paper. She said, 'Who is this God?' I said, 'He is all I need and not you or your paper' and I left.
>
> I went back to my man and said, 'I have had enough of you. You don't believe in God. And when I pray, you say, "Who is this God you are always talking to? I don't see anyone there and I can't talk to someone who is not there." And when

1 I use pseudonyms for all local religious organizations, their leaders, and members to protect the confidentiality of respondents, in keeping with the informed consent agreement under which the research was conducted. Public figures within Christian networks and place names are not changed. For this reason, quotations from pastors and organizational documents and websites are not referenced.

2 Throughout her narrative Ruby spoke in general terms about the bureaucratic process, using terms like "a certain paper and that office, … some of you will know what I mean". She did not seem to want to name names. I am not sure why. She was referring to the *Ausländerbehörde*, known in English as the foreign office. I discuss the powers of the *Ausländerbehörde* below.

> I pray and want you to say "Amen", you say "nein" [German for "no"]. And so I am packing because I will not marry you unless you believe in God. The reason why we have no paper to get married is because of you, because you don't believe in God'. And my man said, 'Ruby, don't leave me.'
>
> So I got him a German Bible but he still did not believe. But now he seems to be changing. If I wake up and don't pray, he reminds me, 'Ruby, you forgot to pray.' … Finally, praise the Lord, he began to pray. So I am here today to talk about how God changed the heart of the man. And now he must begin to come to church because I am sure when he comes to church, the paper will come and we will be married. Because I know that there is no power except for God.

I begin this chapter with a vignette that reflects on the understanding of God and power that is embraced by Christian migrants in two small-scale cities, one in Germany and one in the United States. It is an understanding that reflects migrant strategies of local and transnational incorporation that have often been bypassed in discussions of immigrant religion. Emphasizing the universal power of God, the migrants with whom I worked legitimated their rights to belong to a locality by situating their religious identity and practices within transnational networks and Christianity's claim to globality. In this chapter I examine use of religion as a *non-ethnic* form of migrant local and transnational incorporation. I argue that the ethnic approach to migration studies has tended to keep migration scholars from examining the way in which migrants may embrace a global religion and its transnational networks as a charter for settlement and a claim to rights in a new land. Religion provides migrants with a simultaneously local and transnational mode of incorporation that may configure them not as ethnics but as citizens of both their locality of settlement and of the world. By universalistic I mean a belief system that claims to apply to all people, governments, places and times. I suggest that the universalistic claims of global religions can in certain cases facilitate the local and transnational incorporation of migrants.

Please note that I see non-ethnically organized religious practices and identities as just one of multiple pathways of migrant incorporation. In other cases, it is through the structure and solace of ethnically organized institutions that migrants may find a way of settling, maintaining transnational social fields, and sometimes accessing more universalistic identities and incorporations (van der Veer 2001, Levitt 2003). My chapter comes with another caveat: Islam as well as Christianity makes claims that God knows no nationality, and that the basis of government should be divine law. Currently there is increased research and police surveillance of Islamic transnational networks and concern in both Europe and the United States that Islamic theology and the mosques, which teach universalistic Islam, place migrants in opposition to the states in which they have settled (Allievi and Nielson 2003, Eckert 2005). At this juncture, it is useful to highlight that Christianity also teaches a universalism that places the word of God as interpreted through religious doctrine about the law of any state.[3] I have decided to use the term fundamentalist for those churches that believe that the Bible should be interpreted literally and applied to everyday life; maintain that God's law must be the foundation of all states and politics; and assert that the basic dividing line among the peoples of the world is not that of nations but between those who are on the side of Jesus and all others who stand with the devil.[4] I have adopted the term to facilitate drawing parallels between those practitioners of Islam, Christianity and Judaism who ground their politics on a literal and exclusive interpretation of their religious texts. Currently – unlike the reception of Muslim migrants – Christian migrants find acceptance within their states of settlement when they embrace a universalistic Christianity. These Christians are accorded this acceptance, despite the fact that, as do some Muslims, they believe that God's laws supersede state authority.

Theories of Mirant Religious and Ethnic Affiliation

The study of immigrant religion has a long history within US migration studies. Initially assimilationist theorists and historians of different immigrant nationalities emphasized the role of religious institutions in the settlement of newcomers (Park and Miller 1921, Schermerhorn 1949, Gordon 1964, Handlin 1972).[5]

Beginning in the 1960s, scholars of migration focused their attention on ethnicity and identity politics. They explored ethnogenesis and the construction of ethnic groups first within the new land of settlement and then, beginning in the 1990s,

3 In the past, Catholic migrants to the US were denounced as disloyal because of their allegiance to church doctrine (Hirschman 2004).

4 There is a considerable debate among scholars of Christianity about the meaning of the term fundamentalist and its applicability to various strands of Christian belief and practice. Some scholars of Christianity prefer to use the term fundamentalism within theological history to categorize a coterie of churches that share some elements of particular kind of asceticism and religious practice with Pentecostalism but have a distinctive twentieth-century identity (see for example Robbins 2004: 122). The Christians I am describing might also be called Pentecostal but the term Pentecostal encompasses a variety of different doctrines that produce different relations to the state, to political action, and to materialism (Gifford 1991, Hunt 2000). Some Pentecostalists insist on separating what they consider the kingdoms of God and man; others are increasingly politically engaged (Austin-Broos 1997). While the churches I describe here have connections to Pentecostal networks or organizations, the pastors and members of the churches rarely use the word.

5 In US history, struggles emerged between different nationalities of immigrants to control church institutions such as the long term contestation between Irish and Italian immigrants for leadership of Catholic parishes and dioceses (Tomasi 1975, Bodnar 1985). Members of various ethic groups fought fiercely among themselves to establish different doctrines within the local churches that they built (Dolan 1975, Buczek 1976).

transnationally (Glazer and Moynihan 1963, Glick Schiller 1977, Sollors 1989, Pessar 1995, Lessinger 1996). More recently, along with global trends away from secularism, migration studies have once again found religion, and the topic has produced a new and vibrant scholarship wherever there are significant migrations.

However, there remains an often unexamined separation between the scholarship that describes migrants as members of ethnic groups or diasporic populations and the discussion of global religions such as Christianity. This is because, reflecting an ingrained methodological nationalism, many migration scholars and scholars of immigrant religion tend to see migrants as primarily identified by their nationality or ethnicity. R. Stephen Warner for example, one of the scholars who revived an interest in migrant religion in the United States, focused on "what new ethnic and immigrant groups are doing together religiously and what manner of religious institutions they were developing *of, by, and for themselves*" (1998: 9). Those scholars who assume that migrants' religion is shaped by their cultural background leave no conceptual space in which to analyse the implications of migrants' non-ethnic religious institutions and identities. Yet in some cases Christianity's claims to universalism are not only central to migrants' local and transnational incorporation.

Even when migration scholars moved to study migrants' transnational religious ties, they often stayed within the ethnic or pan-ethnic group as a mode of analysis (Adogame 2002, Chafetz and Ebaugh 2002). Cecilia Menjívar's excellent discussion of "Religious Institutions and Transnationalism" is a case in point. She reminds us that

> immigrant churches have always played an important role linking the immigrant's communities of origin and the new communities they enter. … What needs to be investigated is how religious institutions respond to the efforts of today's immigrants to sustain ties with their homelands and the challenges and opportunities that increasing trends of globalization pose. (1999: 593)

Here Menjívar highlights immigrant churches that link homeland and new land. Yet, Menjívar's own data reveals a more globe spanning Christian identity among some of her respondents. Salvadorians in Emmanuel's Temple, one of the evangelical churches Menjívar studied in Washington DC, don't pray *only* with Salvadorians or emphasize an ethnic-based identity.

Emmanuel's Temple was only half Salvadoran and included Guatemalans, Dominicans and Haitians (whose national language is not Spanish). The leader of the church, Pastor Mario, united people around a Christian identity. He stated that God "doesn't recognize nationalities … Our new identity is simply being Christian." Menjívar notes that "Behind the altar are two flags, the US flag and what the pastor called the Christian flag". Pastor Mario stressed that "the moment you become a Christian, this is your flag, this is what you owe allegiance to. Your country becomes the Christian world" (Menjívar 1999: 606).

Peggy Levitt (2003: 855) takes a somewhat different analytical approach in her work on transnational religion, although she continues to approach migrants through ethnic or national categories, referring to the "Brazilian, Dominican and Irish communities of the Boston metropolitan area". Focusing on the organizational levels of migrant religious practice from the individual to the nation of a "transnational religious field" Levitt (2003: 864) notes that some of her informants such as a Pastor she interviewed insisted that there are "ways of being in the world that have nothing to do with whether you are Brazilian or whether you are from the US but whether you have faith in Christ. … We live in a world where Christ is king, not George Bush or Frenando Calor".

Both Menjívar's and Levitt's ethnography challenge scholars to further research and theorize the use of global Christian identities as a pathway of migrant local and transnational incorporation.

Until very recently, those scholars who have looked at universalistic Christian identities and organizations have tended to argue that these religious beliefs lead to political quietism (Robbins 2004). However, it has become increasingly clear that many evangelizing Christian groups bring their universalistic stand in local and national politics, taking stands on political issues and providing funds and voting to support political leaders who promise to "put God in command". Their clearly stated goals are to convert the entire world and so end all other religions. In other words, they cast all other sets of beliefs as "religions" and maintain that what they believe is *not* "religion" but the Truth (Gifford 1991).

Recognizing the political claims of members of this movement, Vásquez and Marquardt (2003) in their book *Globalizing the Sacred* argue that in a globalized economy where local identities are at risk, Pentecostal and other churches with transnational religious networks offer migrants and non-migrants alike alternative systems of meaning. They ask the following set of questions about migrant participation in transborder fundamentalist networks: If migrants are not ethno-nationalists in their religious practice, but instead espouse of a global Christian identity, is the nation-state irrelevant in an analysis of their identities and practices? Should we abandon the term "transnational" when analysing Christian networks and speak only of the global Christian "cosmopolitans"?

This chapter responds to these questions by rejecting the dichotomy Vásquez and Marquardt pose between a global Christian identity and loyalty to a nation-state and its localities. I argue that migrants who participate in a universalistic fundamentalist Christianity wield their faith as a biblical charter that entitles them to simultaneous membership in the locality in which they are settling, the nation-state they have entered, and the transnational networks connecting them to other Christians. The Christian universalism of these migrants allows them to breach native-migrant divides by identifying migrants as social citizens who contribute to their new home (Glick Schiller 2005b; 2008a). At the same time, the universalism of fundamentalist Christian migrants, while globe-spanning and transnational, is not cosmopolitanism. Cosmopolitanism can be defined as "openness to otherness" or "openness to human commonality on the basis of difference" (Beck 2000, van der Veer 2001, Glick Schiller 2008b). Even as it unites Christian migrants with natives the universalism of migrant fundamentalism divides Christians from all others (Gifford 1991).

To illustrate my argument, in this chapter I shall examine migrants' participation in born-again Christianity in two small cities, namely Manchester (New Hampshire, United States) and Halle an der Saale (Sachsen-Anhalt, Germany). Research in several churches and church organizations in these cities was conducted between 2001 and 2005.[6] Much of research on immigrant religion has been conducted in cities that are either considered global, such as New York, Paris or London, or gateways – Berlin, Chicago, Manchester (UK), Marseilles – that serve as historic entry points of migrant settlement. Manchester, US, and Halle/Saale, Germany were chosen because they are small-scale cities, that is to say they are competitively at a disadvantage in the global competition for financial and cultural capital. The term small-scale refers not to size but to the relative positioning of the cities within global hierarchies of power (Glick Schiller, Çaglar and Guldbrandsen 2006, Glick Schiller and Çalgar 2009).

I have argued elsewhere that small-scale cities are useful for studying migrants' local and transnational pathways of incorporation because the modes of incorporation may well differ from global and gateway cities, ethnic pathways may be less significant or lacking, and non-ethnic pathways may be more prevalent (Glick Schiller, Çaglar and Guldbrandsen 2006, Glick Schiller and Çaglar 2009).

Halle an der Saale is an eastern German city which, broadly speaking, has experienced the permanent settlement of migrants only since the reunification of Germany in 1990.[7] I include in the category migrant the handful of naturalized citizens, persons with rights to permanent residents in Germany (through refugee status or intermarriage), students, many of whom were looking for ways to remain in Germany, and asylum seekers. When legal status matters for the analysis, I will specify. Most of these migrants were actually members of the European Union – Italians and Greeks for example – who were accepted without contestation. It was the migrants from numerous African countries, Vietnamese, Kurds and Russians (many of whom are actually legally not considered foreigners but ethnic Germans) who some natives saw as bringing a culturally uncomfortable strangeness

6 In the research in Halle and Manchester I worked with Thad Guldbrandsen, Ayse Çaglar, Evangelos Karagiannis, and several research assistants including Peter Buchannan and Bettina Klein. In 2003, Evangelos Karagiannis contributed to the ethnography in Halle, working primarily with a French-speaking congregation described below. I am indebted to him for his contributions. See also Karagiannis and Glick Schiller (2006, 2008 forthcoming).

7 In point of fact, various periods in the city's history were marked by in-migrations. After World War II, there were large scale population movements including the resettlement of "ethnic Germans" whose ancestors had lived for generations in what is now Poland. The reasons why these migrants were not officially seen as foreigners and their actual reception by inhabitants of the city are beyond the scope of this chapter.

to the city and taking social benefits that are needed by the native population. Foreigners numbered only about 4 per cent of the 230,000 people of the city in 2000 (Commission on Foreigners 2000, Brinkhoff 2004).[8] The unemployment rate among natives was over 20 per cent. Very few migrants from outside the EU, whether or not they had permanent resident status, were able to obtain regular employment unless they began their own businesses.

Manchester had a similar number of people in its metropolitan area (207,000) and about the same percentage of new migrants (Manchester Economic Development Office 2004). Most of the new migration occurred since the 1980s, although there was a Hispanic settlement of growing proportions that began in the 1950s and there was also an aging European and French Canadian foreign-born population, most of whom arrived before World War II. In Manchester recent migrants held a variety of legal statuses including naturalized citizen, legal permanent residence, refugee or student (most of whom wished to stay), and persons with irregular status who had crossed the border illegally or overstayed their visas.[9] Newcomers, who have come from various African countries, Vietnam, the former Yugoslavia, and throughout Latin America, found work in small factories. The unemployment rate was about 4 per cent; employment was available but even migrants with postgraduate educations at New Hampshire universities could only find unskilled work.

While there are significant differences in the migrants' economic insertion in the two cities, the political and economic leadership of both cities have greeted newcomers with a welcome that was shaped by the similarities of these cities positioning within national and global flows of economic and cultural capital at the time of the research. On the one hand, the political and economic leadership understood that in the increasing competition between cities for investment capital – both national and foreign – and for tourists, it was important for a city to be seen as "ethnically diverse", "cosmopolitan" and "welcoming". From this perspective, migrants were officially welcome and invited to participate in various public rituals to mark the multicultural nature of the city. On the other hand, both cities had minimal degrees of economic or political power or cultural prominence. Because of this, they had access to little tax revenue or other sources of funding to provide public services, and both provided very little in the way of resources and programmes to facilitate the incorporation of foreigners.[10] In point of fact, both cities provide few opportunities for social or economic advancement for migrants or natives.

---

8 This number did not include "ethnic Germans" or students.

9 Permanent resident status was obtained through marriage, family reunion, employment, or the US Diversity lottery. Permanent residents can apply for citizenship, although the process is increasingly expensive and onerous. Refugees have a right to apply for this "green card" status after a year of residence in the US.

10 In 2001–2003, I interviewed city leaders and local bureaucrats in both locations.

Global Christian Fundamentalism and Migrant Incorporation

In 2001, when I first began research with a congregation of migrants in Halle and heard Ruby testify, the church she was attending conformed to the image of an "ethnic church" that dominates the migration literature. After all, at the time, most of the forty or so members of the Miracle Healing Church were Nigerian asylum seekers, as was the pastor. Similarly, a second migrant church in the city, *L'Esprit du Seigneur*, was made up primarily of Congolese. However, neither of the churches was organized on the basis of a shared ethnic identity nor did they seek to preserve an ethnic identity among migrants as they settled in Germany. Moreover, although they maintained transnational links, neither church served as the base of a transnational network that linked migrants to their homeland. In Manchester, I found a large religious organization, the Resurrection Crusade, whose founder was a Nigerian migrant. While this organization, which was composed of a network of local churches, was well incorporated into a transnational social field, it was not organized around the ethnic or homeland identities of its migrant members.

As I began to explore the relationship between universalistic Christian identities and local claims and actions of migrants, I realized that rather than classifying migrant religious organizations and practices as aspects of ethnic communities, it was important to develop a mode of analysis that could situate the religious organizations to which migrants belong within the study of religion. I suggest analyzing migrant religious organizations in terms of the following categories:

1. religious belief system
2. religious practices
3. cultural identities
4. organizational and individual networks

These categories allowed me to identify aspects of the religious activities I was observing that were not products of ethnic cultures or transnational ties to homelands but were part of a globally circulating religious discourse and set of practices. In this chapter I can provide neither a full ethnography of the religious organizations in which I worked nor fully address the ongoing transformations of fundamentalist Christianity. However, by deploying these categories I hope to contribute to larger comparative projects. Approached in categories useful to the study of religion but highlighting the experience of migration, settlement and transnational connection, the study of the migrant religion can bridge the divide between migration studies and religious studies.

The two churches I describe in Halle were very different from each other, although both were begun by immigrants. Most of the members of *L'Esprit du Seigneur* were asylum seekers and quite poor. The Congolese pastor, Mpenza, and his wife had been granted refugee status with permanent residency but only a few others had a right to permanent residence. Unable to obtain asylum, many members fled to the greater anonymity of western Germany or other parts of the EU, making the membership of the congregation fluid during much of our study. Numbering at most 30 members, the congregation, although mostly Congolese and Angolan included a few German women. Only a few of the African members spoke passable German. Services were in French and Lingalla. The Sunday donations were small and the congregation could not afford its own space for worship.[11]

In contrast, by 2005 the Miracle Healing Church was more successful in recruiting both migrant and white German members resulting in approximately 150 people who regularly attended prayer services. Increasing numbers of its migrant members had permanent legal status, primarily through marrying Germans. About 15 per cent of the membership was non-African, mostly German, from Halle neighbouring towns and cities and this included women and men who served as part of the leadership of the church. In 2004, the congregation had a sufficient income from the tithes and donations from its congregants to rent and renovate its own building, where it held Sunday services, meetings, counselling, "Friday miracle healing services", child care during Sunday services, Bible study, and German classes. Many members could speak some German, Pastor Joshua could speak fluent German and the use of both languages in all prayer services facilitated the migrant members in their learning German. Speaking German was said to be essential, not only so that the migrants could settle properly in Germany but also so that they could "bring God's word to the city".

A Nigerian refugee, Heaven's Gift, founded the Resurrection Crusade, a prayer network of local primarily white American churches in Manchester (US). The purpose of the Crusade was to win the city for God. From the beginning, several of the core activists were migrants from different regions of the world. Within a few years the organization had its own office, a network of approximately 15 churches, and activities that included healing conferences of several hundred people and prayer breakfasts held in the city centre and attended by local politicians. The churches in the network of churches were predominantly white with a scattering of migrants from Africa, the Middle East, Asia, Latin America and the Caribbean. Only one was primarily composed of migrants, and this church stressed its Christian identity rather than the Hispanic background of its congregants.

All three religious organizations in which I worked drew on elements of theology, religious practice and identity politics that can be found in global fundamentalist Christianity (Gifford 1991). They used fundamentalist Christian theology as a universal charter through which to claim rights to settle in the country of immigration and to maintain transnational connections. This charter is articulated through their religious practices, which they identify as "true Christianity". Thus, claiming community among born-again Christians, they become part of broader religious institutions and networks within their new locality and nation, as well as globally. Comparing the organizations in terms of the four categories I sketched above illustrates the synergy between their global claims to the local and national

11 By 2005 the congregation began to be increasingly composed of women whose relationships to German men yielded rights to remain in Halle.

and their transnational networks, which connected them through evangelizing activities to Christians around the world. This comparison also illustrates that the universalist claims and evangelical mission of all three organizations facilitated their local as well as transnational incorporation through a dividing line that separated them from all non-believers, whatever their cultural backgrounds.

Religious Belief System

As had Ruby, in the testimony that opens this chapter, other members of the two churches in Halle and the Resurrection Crusade churches in Manchester spoke often about power. When I first attended the Miracle Healing Church in Halle in 2001, the members sang almost incessantly that "there is power in the blood of the Lord". The pastor at the time, and Pastor Joseph who succeeded him, insisted that "there is no power except for God". This view was summarized by Pastor Mpenza of the church, *L'Esprit du Seigneur*, in a sermon he gave about the power of the Word. Quoting Matthew 21,18ff, he said:

> We must believe in the power of the Word. God has the final say. God is the answer to your problems. Why do you have problems? The problem is your faith, the lack of faith. I know what I am speaking about. God remained the same. You cannot fire a God. God dominates everything.

Heaven's Gift, the Nigerian pastor who began the Resurrection Crusade Ministry in Manchester, also stressed that power and authority were in the hands of God not man. Heaven's Gift did this at the diverse settings at which he spoke: at prayer meetings, church breakfasts, prayer conferences and special training meetings held for "prayer intercessors", those members of the congregation felt to be spiritually strong enough to engage in "spiritual warfare" with demonic spirits.

In all three cases migrants link this power to the ability of God to decree who has *rights to specific territory*. In such issues, it is God rather than earthly political powers that have jurisdiction. Therefore for believers, the term "land" is a floating signifier that can refer to specific cities, political units such as US, Nigerian or German states, or nation-states. In their narratives, territory matters. God is always local in his globality.

Pastor Joseph from the Miracle Healing Church in Halle stressed: "This city belongs to God. He is going to take over the city. He is going to move in this city." He could also speak of "God taking command of Germany". Heaven's Gift formed a network of churches in the greater Manchester region and spoke of God coming to Manchester or New Hampshire. Thus, when launching its second Manchester Prayer and Leadership Conference with the theme "Breaking the Fallow Ground", the goal of the Crusade's network of churches was "to win Manchester for God". As Heaven's Gift expanded his US Christian network, he visited other US cities and prayed both for God to take leadership in that city and for America to "once again arise spiritually".

Non-migrant fundamentalist ministers in both Manchester and Halle also focused on God's dominion over territory when they shared the pulpit with migrant pastors. At a prayer breakfast hosted by the Resurrection Crusade, one such pastor quoted from the book of Joshua (6: 16), saying: "Shout; for the Lord hath given you the city." This was said after the Mayor of Manchester had addressed those assembled. Members of the Crusade interpreted the presence of the Mayor to mean that it was God, *not* the Mayor, who was in charge of the city.

In all three religious organizations, migrants interpreted this "gift of the city" as their charter to settle in the respective country but they did not ignore the power of the state that made borders difficult to transverse and has made it difficult for them to migrate and settle. However, whatever politicians might say, in the eyes of Pastor Mpenza, pastor of God's Gospel Church, the message of the Bible was clear: "Every place whereon the soles of your feet shall tread shall be yours" (Deuteronomy 11: 24). For him, God promised true Christians the right to the city and to Germany: "For ye shall pass over Jordan to go in to possess the land which the Lord your God giveth you, and ye shall possess it, and dwell therein" (Deuteronomy 11: 31). Pastor Joshua of the Miracle Healing Church made the same claim.

The asylum seekers in Halle, who were the most powerless of the migrants, and faced the likelihood that they would be denied residency and forcibly deported, found sustenance in the idea that they had a God-given right to live in Germany. They saw in biblical texts legitimization for their view that God does not recognizes "frontiers and barriers", and that they have the right to live in their new country.[12] It is noteworthy in this context that, in the first few years of the Miracle Healing Church in Halle, there were specific prayers for passports. Saul, an asylum seeker who was appealing his deportation order and who sometimes substituted for the pastor, led these prayers and explicitly linked them to a God-given right to Germany. He specifically legitimated the African presence in Germany, saying: "The land of Germany is not just for the Germans. The land belongs to God and everyone on earth is a visitor. If God is the father and it is his land, than Germany is the fatherland to everyone, including Africans. We all have rights to this land."

Similarly, Ruby's testimony reflected her strong belief that her ability to become incorporated in Germany rested in God's hands. In her eyes, the pathway that would allow her to become incorporated in her new country was marriage to a German man. However, this required action on the part of two states: Nigerian officials had to provide documentation of her identity and to certify that she was currently unmarried. The German state, on the other hand, had to recognize and accept her Nigerian documents and allow her to marry Markus.

This access to Germany, that Ruby expected God to give her, was considered by church members to be part of a broader covenant that God made with Christian migrants, a covenant that is central to the mission of the Resurrection Crusade Ministry in Manchester and has become more clearly articulated by the two

12 See ter Haar (1995: 26) for a similar finding elsewhere in Europe.

churches in Halle over time. At its core there was a concept of reciprocity at work: God gives the land to all those who will win it for God. Accordingly, in Halle, the two migrant pastors claimed that God has sent them and other migrants to win over Halle: "It is not by accident that I am in this place", was a phrase I heard often. In this logic, the right to claim the land is linked to the responsibility of all church members, migrants and non-migrants alike to bring "the good word" to the locality and country of immigration. While this responsibility was shared by all Christians, it had a particular resonance with the migrants because it casts them in the role of missionaries sent to a place to bring the word of God. Although increasingly the leading members of the Miracle Healing Church in Halle won rights to permanent residency (primarily though marriage to Germans), they found that despite their altered legal status they were still treated by many local people as stigmatized outsiders. In this context, the members of the congregation therefore stressed forcefully that they are in Germany not as foreigners but as *messengers of God.*

Religious Practices

To bring Jesus to greater numbers of people, members of both churches in Halle and the members of the religious network of churches in Manchester stressed conversion through direct personal experience of the "ever living God". A person became "born again" through accepting Jesus into her life and establishing a personal relationship with Jesus. Consequently, while Christians were expected to live moral lives, as compared to many other Pentecostal congregations that defined themselves as born again, there was relatively infrequent discussion of drinking, sexual promiscuity, homosexuality, or abortion. Instead pastors and members focused on discussing and reporting miracles.

Over time in all three organizations, healing miracles and the expulsion of demonic spirits "in the name of Jesus" became an important form of evangelism. While for several years Pastor Mpenza, the Congolese pastor of the struggling French and Lingalla-speaking congregation had preferred private sessions, by 2005 he performed acts of miraculous healing as part of the routine of Sunday worship, although his practice of healing was relatively low key. Calling worshippers up to the front of the room, the pastor placed his hand on their heads, first shouted to all "evil spirits" to be gone and then declared that "all ties were now broken with these spirits the name of Jesus". In the instances of healing I observed in this church, the sufferers did not go into trance but just quietly returned to their seats.

The situation was much more dramatic in the healing sessions held by Miracle Healing Church in Halle and in some of the congregations and in the healing conferences organized by the Resurrection Crusade network. Those who came forward to be healed either individually or in a line of sufferers, which faced the pastor, fell backwards into a trance when the pastor touched their foreheads. After the pastor and assistants prayed over those lying at their feet, the believers would usually slowly sit up, look dazed, and walk back to their seats. However sometimes the person in trance moved or shouted or did not rapidly wake up. Then a more intensive "deliverance" session would be held with loud shouting by the pastor who commanded all evil spirits and demonic influences to be gone. His male and female assistants, who in Manchester were known as "prayer warriors", sometimes added their shouts, while the entire congregation extended their right hands towards the sufferer in prayer.

In both the Miracle Healing Church and the healing conferences of the Resurrection Crusade, some of the persons being healed of demonic spirits, who were said to bring cancer, HIV, back pains, blindness, and "women's problems", and some of the assistants were white Christians who were native to the city or country. At the healing conferences of the Resurrection Crusade, some of the visiting pastors conducting the healing and deliverance sessions were white Americans. In Halle, when Pastor Joshua first initiated rituals of exorcism at the Miracle Healing Church, he called out loudly that all covenants made by ancestors should be broken. With increasing numbers of Germans in his ministry, he changed his frame of reference to more universal ills, such as "the spirit of sugar diabetes" and "the spirit of high blood pressure".

Miracles were closely linked to evangelic practices to foster conversion. Therefore the pastors insisted that it was incumbent on believers to testify about "their" miracles. Publicly testifying about the presence of Jesus was seen as presenting evidence necessary in order to win over others to the decision to become born again. Testimony was regularly included in the worship of the Miracle Healing Church and the Resurrection Crusade churches I have attended, and sometimes in the *L'Esprit du Seigneur*. In Manchester and Halle, testimony ranged from how Jesus had provided solutions to life's dilemmas including a lack of money, unemployment, interpersonal relations, and physical. As the Miracle Healing Church grew to have a steady core of Germans, increasingly the testimony from both Africans and Germans described miraculous cures.

Ruby's testimony, which began the chapter, was somewhat more elaborate than many but followed a pattern: Those testifying first described an impasse they had reached – an illness that medical science could not explain or cure, for example. The impasse was framed as a test of faith and faith was rewarded by the believer, against all odds, receiving her "miracle". Pastor Joshua preached that "Anytime a man praises God there are miracles". Donations to the church were defined as a form of prayer to be answered by miraculous prosperity so that money given would come back one-hundred fold. As people danced up to the front of the church to drop their donations into a large basket, the congregation sang: "He is a miracle working God."

Together with two missionary organizations – one led by an Egyptian-German and the other by US Mennonites – Pastor Joshua organized a healing conference in a hockey rink in Halle in 2005. The poster read "Come and Experience the Miracle, Nothing is Impossible". Two-thirds of the 250 people who attended some of the activities over the course of five days were German. Many of them came forward to be healed, following the procedures I just described. Those who went into trance were urged to perform their testimony. For example, people who had said that they were crippled by back problems, multiple sclerosis, and stroke were commanded to climb the steep steps of the arena. They did to the cheers of those assembled.

Cultural Identities

Despite the fact that as part of their religious practice, the pastors and members in these religious organizations stress their Christian identity, there were some differences in the way the three organizations represented themselves when evangelizing. When asked about whether his congregation was Congolese, Pastor Mpenza replied:

> No, no. It isn't a Congolese church. This is not the origin of the Word of God. I have told you about my origin. I have come from Congo where I met my Lord, where I worked for the Lord. And now I am here, in Germany, where I had the feeling that the inhabitants were in need of the same message. So I've clearly said that this church is not a Congolese church. I've clearly said it is a church of Jesus.

However, despite his disclaimers, the initial mode of evangelization adopted by Pastor Mpenza's church required him to accept some identification as an *African* church. This identification was not, as is often claimed in the literature on immigrant religion, a defensive stance of community enclosure. Rather members of this congregation have decided that it is through African religious music that they could bring the people of Halle, both migrants and non-migrants, to God. The identification of the *L'Esprit du Seigneur* emerged in the context of a dialogic process in which the church members wanted to evangelize the city and there were local resources and support networks available for these efforts if the church represented itself as African. The church had a choir, and members of the congregation also formed gospel choirs, which participated in multicultural public concerts and events in the city that featured "foreigners" and/or "Africans". As a result, members of this church, despite the limited German of its members, developed local networks and participated in the life of the city. However, the Pastor insisted the church members participated in these events in the name of Jesus.

In 2003, Pastor Mpenza agreed to speak at a ceremony honouring Wilhelm Amo, an eighteenth-century resident of Halle, who was the first African to study and teach in Germany. While the *L'Espirit* choir sang and Pastor Mpenza prayed, the vice mayor laid a wreath at Amo's statue. The city and university representatives used the occasion to claim Halle's roots as a multicultural city. Pastor Mpenza replied by speaking of the "living presence of Jesus in the city".

The Miracle Healing Church, by contrast, generally did not participate in public displays of "African identity". Instead, Pastor Joshua, working with missionary organizations in Halle, began a series of healing prayer sessions in nearby cities. Most of these sessions attracted primarily Germans and all were bi-lingual; each was videotaped and sold, so that evidence of the healing could be popularized. In all these activities, the *Christian* identity of the Miracle Healing Church and its pastor was primary. At the same time, a subtext of the evangelizing message was that Pastor Joshua – as an *African* – brought with him a religiosity that made the healing miracles possible. However, this aspect of the pastor's identity was never explicitly stated.

In Manchester, the African identity of Heaven's Gift and the several African pastors, most of them Nigerian, who visited regularly was sometimes acknowledged. Occasionally, the white Texas preacher Eddie Smith, whose Christian network extended into Nigeria where he had evangelized together with Heaven Gift's father, made reference to the outpouring of Christian faith he had witnessed there. However, it was because of their spiritual powers as *Christians* that Pastor Heaven's Gift and the other immigrants were accepted into the fundamentalist churches. In the 2003 programme of the Manchester Prayer and Leadership conference, for example, the endorsement of Pastor Heaven's Gift's leadership was described by the minister of one of the largest of the attending churches as follows: "A great passion … refined in the fires of persecution and hardship have fashioned a brother with a mission and a message for Manchester, New Hampshire, and New England. The message? A call for holiness, a commitment to prayer, and a quest for revelation knowledge of the Master." And he continues: "The Resurrection Crusade explicitly states that it is dedicated to prayer with great intentions of *bringing Christians together beyond denomination and race* for His healing power of prayer" (Glick Schiller field notes).

Organizational and Individual Networks

The ethnographic description provided so far of the three religious organizations contains a frequent reference to the networks of the migrants in all three organizations. In both Halle and Manchester migrants were embedded in networks that stretched into the life of the city and beyond it. Visiting pastors, who circulated through these networks, situated each organization and its migrant members in a set of ongoing and deepening local, national and transnational relationships. The various pastors earned respect by raising the money to host conferences and large prayer meetings that feature visiting pastors who arrive to heal, counsel, preach and convert. Through these meetings, members of the churches, who do not travel, come to know the respective pastors, eating with them, hosting them, providing personal testimony, and praying with them.

However, there were significant differences in the degree to which the political and the religious overlap in Halle and Manchester reflected dramatic differences in the place of fundamentalist Christianity in Germany and the United States. While, in both cities, some migrants claim a place for themselves in the city through their participation in fundamentalist Christianity, it also has to be noted that fundamentalist religion played a very different role in the life of the general population in Halle and in Manchester. In Germany most Germans saw the kind of religious practice described here as distant from the German political life. In contrast, in the United States fundamentalist religious practice was part of mainstream politics, both within the city of Manchester and on the level of national political life.

Moreover, while in Germany, mainstream Christian churches were seen as legitimate and were supported by taxes, religion was not part of the daily life in Halle, which was a part of the former East Germany (German Democratic Republic). Most people did not see themselves as Christians. In addition, although Halle has about eleven fundamentalist religious organizations, including the two described in this chapter, and although they were members of an officially recognized German umbrella organization, these churches were seen as culturally strange by those Hallensians who belonged to the tax-supported churches. In Manchester, churches – big and small – are everywhere, most people claim to believe in God and fundamentalist Christianity has become part of the mainstream of religious life. Some of the more mainstream denominations such as Congregational have become part of the prayer network developed by Heaven's Gift.

As we have seen, Pastor Mpenza, despite his lack of fluency in German, was part of networks that made him a featured speaker in public rituals in Halle. While occasions such as the wreath laying ceremony gave him occasions to evangelize and claim Halle for God, there was a sharp separation between the Christian globality of the pastor and the political identities of members of the pastor's networks who did not share his fundamentalist Christian identity. On the other hand, the Christian universalism of the pastors in Germany gave them local, national, and transnational links that brought them far beyond the bounds of their ancestral nationality. Both congregations had worked with a white German Pentecostal church in the city of Magdeburg (Sachsen-Anhalt, Germany) to become formal members of a German Pentecostal organization, the *Bund freikirchlicher Pfingstgemeinden*. In June 2003, several members of the Miracle Healing Church attended a pan-European Pentecostal conference in Berlin that was called to organize a European-wide organization of Pentecostal Churches. Both congregations participated in transnational fundamentalist networks that brought them a range of visiting preachers.

In addition to the US Mennonites who helped build the Healing Conference, the Miracle Healing Church had ties with African preachers of various nationalities as well as an Indian pastor who is part of a global Pentecostal network. This pastor has visited Halle more than once, and had convinced the church to support his missionary work in India by sending funds on a regular basis. Moreover, through another global Christian ministry from the United States, the church sent funds to Christianize Israel. By the end of 2005, Pastor Joshua was launched into the international circuit of pastors, participating in a massive prayer meeting in South Korea and travelling with a delegation of German pastors to India.

In a similar vein, although his church was considerably smaller and with fewer resources at its disposal, the Congolese Pastor Mpenza had ties to other churches in Belgium, France, Congo and Chad. His personal networks of family and friendship gave him ties to pastors of other churches, which brought visiting preachers to his congregations. The networks of the pastor were part of a social field that was travelled by other church members as they sought to obtain legal papers, goods to trade and send to their homeland, and information about the possibilities of incorporating in several different countries in Europe.

In Manchester, on the other hand, the Resurrection Crusade Ministry became significant enough that the Republican Governor of New Hampshire and the Democratic Mayor of Manchester have attended their prayer breakfasts. Pastor Heaven's Gift and the migrants who were active in the Crusade and its member congregations became part of a network of fundamentalist Christian churches that stretches globally. Because this network was part of a transnational social field that extended into the Bush White house, there was a continuing US nationalist aspect to the politics of many of these networks. At one point Pastor Joshua led a prayer meeting in a public park on the US National Day of Prayer that endorsed the US war in Iraq and global extension of American military power, which was defined as doing the work of God (for a further development of this theme, see Glick Schiller 2005a).

In all three religious organizations studied, pastors do have homeland ties but they have interpreted these ties within a universalist understanding of Christianity. For example, Heaven's Gift, an Ogoni by birth, claimed refugee status in the United States on the basis of the Nigerian government's efforts to suppress the Ogoni movement against Shell Oil. He had studied theology in Nigeria and been ordained a minister as had his father before him. For several years, from a base in a refugee camp, Heaven's Gift had worked with a US missionary church, establishing a series of new churches. This experience convinced him "of the importance of uniting people in prayer rather than beginning competing congregations". He began this project while still in Nigeria and continued it in Manchester. His network of churches included a home church in Port Harcourt, Nigeria, but that church was defined as part of a broader Christian missionary project. As US fundamentalist prayer networks developed a renewed interest in missionary and development work in Africa, Heaven's Gift added a set of US-based churches designed as "partners" to his New Hampshire prayer network and began to speak of bringing clean water as well as God to various localities in Africa including "Ogoniland".

Analysis and Conclusion

To date, because migrant religion has been defined as ethnic or diasporic, scholars have tended to emphasize aspects of cultural difference. I argue that we need to develop an analytical framework that situates the study of migrant religion within the broader field of religious studies. Examining non-ethnic congregations and religious networks founded by migrants but open to all Christians contributes to such a development. We need more research on the transnational ties of migrants that are *not* only linked to homelands or are linked to homelands in projects that place localities with a global Christian project and identity. At the same time that the study of such congregations and networks can contribute to a global study of contemporary Christian practices, beliefs, and claims, it can also contribute to our understanding between the various ways that Christian migrants settle locally and reshape localities. The global claims of Christianity allow migrants to settle in a locality and contribute to its religious life.

The next step of this comparative project would be to not only examine the ways in which migrants claim local and national belonging through their universal Christian identity and networks but also to trace the variations that arise from migrant settlement in localities that are differentially positioned within national and global networks. Those scholars who step out of a methodological nationalist orientation by situating migrants within global religious networks tend to ignore the significance of different places of settlement in shaping the local and transnational variation in migrant religious beliefs, practices, and social networks. Even Peter van der Veer (2001: 14) who draws attention to locality focuses on only one type of domain, the global city. He notes that

> locality is produced by global forces and the global city is a very real domain in which cosmopolitanism as a pattern of inclusion and exclusion in the public sphere emerges. Especially, transnational movements which help migrants to cope with the conditions of migration and labour flexibility, such as the Tablighi Jama'at in Islam and the Visva Hindu Parishad in Hinduism, do not simply build religious enclaves, safe havens of the self, but are creatively developing new religious understandings of their predicament, entailing an encounter with the multiplicity of Others on their own terms. It is impossible to simply call these movements closed, confined and confining, provincial as against cosmopolitan.

From the vantage point of the religious organizations in two small-scale cities, it is possible to endorse van der Veer's call to privilege locality in the study of transnational religious connections and yet critique his facile references to cosmopolitanism and his inability to see beyond the global city. Van der Veer's statement leaves unexplored questions of whether or how migrants use religious networks in cities that are not considered as hubs within the global economy but which are still restructured in relationship to global flows of capital, ideas, and people.

Fundamentalist Christianity engages migrants in local identities and transnational networks wherever they settle. However, localities of settlement differ greatly in the opportunity structures and possibilities for migrants to form local social ties and deploy transnational networks. Systematic comparative work is required before we assume that the forms of religious incorporation such as those organized on the basis of ethnicity and nationality described for global or gateway cities apply to migrant religious incorporations everywhere. Reading the ethnographic data provided by Menjívar (1999) and Levitt (2003) without an ethnic lens, I found some evidence that even in global and gateway cities, some Christian migrants stress universalistic identities as a key to local and national incorporation.

However in small-scale cities such as Halle and Manchester non-ethnic Christian identities that allow migrants to legitimate their presence as carriers of the word of God may prove to play a greater role in migrant incorporation. Only future comparative work can make this clear.

However, the ethnographic insights provided in this chapter can speak to the question of whether fundamentalist Christian universalism, which does not claim the exclusivity of a national and ethnic identity, contributes to those forces that offer humanity a global vision. The religious organizations and networks I have described were indeed open to all who approached them as religious seekers. All the pastors denounced racism and white Germans and Americans accepted the leadership of black pastors. These religious organizations did not celebrate cultural difference nor did they dwell on variations in cultural practices except for those that were seen linked to demonic spirits rather than to God. While some churches in Manchester signalled the unity of all Christians and the "disciplining" of all nations through displaying panoply of national flags, they did not divide believers by nationality. In fact, by accepting the claims of migrants, including asylum seekers, that God had granted them the right to the city and to their new country of settlement, they challenged the dominant citizenship regime of Germany and the United States. They acknowledged the "social citizenship" of all their members, whatever their legal status (Glick Schiller 2005b, 2008a). As do indigenous people who appeal to universal charters of human rights or environmentalists who assert global claims to protect rain forests *vis-à-vis* the sovereignty of a particular nation-state, members of a religion may appeal to the universalistic discourse of the religion and its transnational institutions to assert national and local rights (Brecher et al. 2000).

In this sense adopting a universalistic Christian fundamentalism can be seen as an act of resistance against a regime of nation-states that increasing seeks to exclude those who are classified as foreigners. However, this stance does not denounce nationalism or a world of nation-states. Instead it supports the efforts of migrants to claim territorial rights, both in their city and country of settlement. These claims are made and supported on the basis of an alternative theory of power, one that makes God rather than man the ultimate authority in each nation-state. However, the members of all three religious organizations were neither open to difference in beliefs and practices of non-Christians nor able to embrace others on the basis of a common human condition. Members of the religious organizations and their networks described in this chapter should not be considered cosmopolitan (Glick Schiller 2008b). We lose important political and conceptual distinctions if we conflate Christian anti-racism and a positive stance towards immigration with cosmopolitanism. Whatever its merits, Christian universality is not a form of human openness.

References

Adogame, A. 2002. Traversing local-global religious terrain: African new religious movements in Europe. *Zeitschrift für Religionswissenschaft*, 10, 33–49.
Allievi, S. and Nielsen, J.S. (eds) 2003. *Muslim Networks and Transnational Communities in and across Europe*. Leiden: Brill.
Austin-Broos, D.J. 1997. *Jamaica Genesis: Religion and the Politics of Moral Order*. Chicago: University of Chicago Press.
Beck, U. 2000. The cosmopolitan perspective: Sociology of the second age of modernity. *British Journal of Sociology*, 51(1), 79–105.
Bodnar, J. 1985. *The Transplanted: A History of Immigrants in Urban America*. Bloomington, IN: Indiana University Press.
Brecher, J., Costello, T. and Smith, B. 2000. *Globalization from Below: The Power of Solidarity*. Boston: South End Press.
Brinkhoff, T. 2004. *City Population, Germany*. [Online]. Available at: http://www.citypo pulation.de/Deutschland.html [accessed 10 October 2005].
Buczek, D. 1976. Polish American priests and the American Catholic hierarchy: A view from the 1920s. *Polish American Studies*, 33, 34–43.
Chafetz, J. and Ebaugh, H.R. 2002. The variety of transnational religious networks, in *Religion across Borders: Transnational Immigrant Networks*, edited by H.R. Ebaugh and J. Chafetz. Walnut Creek, CA: Alta Mira Press, 165–91.
Commission on Foreigners. 2000. Facts and Figures on the Situation of Foreigners in the Federal Republic of Germany. Berlin.
Dolan, J. 1975. *The Immigrant Church: New York's Irish and German Catholics*. Baltimore: Johns Hopkins University Press.
Eckert, J. 2005. *Introduction to the Social Life of Anti-Terrorism Laws*. Paper to the Conference: The Social Life of Anti-Terrorism Laws, Max Planck Institute for Social Anthropology, Halle (Saale), Germany, 26–27 May 2005.
Gifford, P. 1991. Christian fundamentalism and development. *Review of African Political Economy*, 18(52), 9–20.
Glazer, N. and Moynihan, D. 1963. *Beyond the Melting Pot; the Negroes, Puerto Ricans, Jews, Irish, and Italians of New York City*. Cambridge: MIT Press.
Glick Schiller, N. 1977. Ethnic groups are made not born, in *Ethnic Encounters: Identities and Contexts*, edited by G. Hicks and P. Leis. North Scituate, MA: Duxbury Press, 23–35.
Glick Schiller, N. 2005a. Transnational social fields and imperialism: Bring a theory of power to transnational studies. *Anthropological Theory*, 5(4), 439–61.
Glick Schiller, N. 2005b. Transborder citizenship: Legal pluralism within a transnational social field, in *Mobile People, Mobile Law: Expanding Legal Relations in a Contracting World*, edited by Franz von Benda-Beckmann, Keebet von Benda-Beckmann and Anne Griffiths. Aldershot: Ashgate, 27–50.

Glick Schiller, N. 2008a. "And ye shall possess it, and dwell therein": Social citizenship, global Christianity, and non-ethic immigrant incorporation, in *Citizenship, Political Engagement, and Belonging. Immigrants in Europe and the United States*, edited by D. Reed-Danahay and C. Bretell. New Brunswick: Rutgers University Press, 203–25.

Glick Schiller, N. 2008b. What Can a Transnational Perspective on Migration Contribute to Debates on Modern Citizenship, Religion, and Cosmopolitanism? Paper to Seminar on Reflexive Modernization, Institute for Sociology, Munich, 5 November 2008.

Glick Schiller, N. and Çaglar, A. 2009 forthcoming. Towards a comparative theory of locality in migration studies: Migrant incorporation and city scale. *Journal of Ethnic and Migration Studies*.

Glick Schiller, N., Çaglar, A. and Guldbrandsen, T.C. 2006. Beyond the ethnic lens: Locality, globality, and born-again incorporation. *American Ethnologist*, 33(4), 612–33.

Gordon, M. 1964. *Assimilation in American Life: The Role of Race, Religion and National Origins*. New York: Oxford University Press.

Handlin, O. 1972. *Boston's Immigrants, 1790–1865: A Study in Acculturation. Boston*: Athenaeum.

Hirschman, C. 2004. The role of religion in the origin and adaptation of immigrant groups in the United States. *International Migration Review*, Fall (38), 1206–33.

Hunt, S. 2000. Dramatising the "health and wealth gospel": Belief and practice of a neo-Pentecostal "faith" ministry. *Journal of Beliefs and Values*, 21(1), 73–86.

Karagiannis, E. and Glick Schiller, N. 2006. Contesting claims to the land: Pentecostalism as a challenge to migration theory and policy. *Sociologus*, 56(2), 137–71.

Karagiannis, E. and Glick Schiller, N. 2008 forthcoming. "… the land which the LORD your God giveth you". Two churches founded by African migrants in Oststadt, Germany, in *Christianity in Africa and the African Diaspora: The Appropriation of a Scattered Heritage*, edited by A. Adogame, R. Gerloff and K. Hock. London: Continuum International.

Lessinger, J. 1996. *From the Ganges to the Hudson: Indian Immigrants in New York City*. Boston: Allyn and Bacon.

Levitt, P. 2003. "You know, Abraham was really the first immigrant": Religion and transnational migration. *International Migration Review*, Fall (37), 847–73.

Manchester Economic Development Office 2004. *Fingertip Facts: Manchester, NH*. [Online]. Available at: http://www.manchesternh.gov/CityGov/MED/files/5364A383B67 44050AB6D967047A4600B.pdf [accessed 10 September 2005].

Menjívar, C. 1999. Religious institutions and transnationalism: A case study of Catholic and Evangelical Salvadoran immigrants. *International Journal of Politics, Culture, and Society*, 12(4), 589–612.

Park, R. and Miller, H.A. 1921. *Old World Traits Transplanted.* New York: Harper.

Pessar, P. 1995. *A Visa for a Dream: Dominicans in the United States*. Boston: Allyn and Bacon.

Robbins, J. 2004. The globalization of Pentecostal and charismatic Christianity. *Annual Review of Anthropology*, 33, 117–43.

Schermerhorn, R.A. 1949. *These our People: Minorities in American Culture*. New York: D.C. Heath.

Sollors, W. (ed.) 1989. *The Invention of Ethnicity*. New York: Oxford University Press.

Ter Haar, G. 1995. Strangers in the Promised Land: Africans in Europe. *Exchange*, 1(24), 1–33.

Tomasi, S. 1975. *Piety and Power: The Role of Italian Parishes in the New York Metropolitan Area, 1880–1930*. New York: Center for Migration Studies.

Vásquez, M.A. and Marquardt, M.F. 2003. *Globalizing the Sacred: Religion across the Americas*. New Brunswick, NJ: Rutgers University Press.

van der Veer, P. 2001. *Transnational Religion***.** Paper given to the conference on Transnational Migration: Comparative Perspectives. Princeton University, 30 June–1 July 2001. WPTC-01-18 [accessed 20 September 2008].

Warner, R.S. and Wittner, J. (eds) 1998. Introduction: immigration and religious communities in the United States, in *Gatherings in Diaspora: Religious Communities and the New Immigration*, edited by R.S. Warner and J. Wittner. Philadelphia, PA: Temple University Press, 3–36.

PART III
Permutations on the Transnational Scale

Chapter 8
Customary, State and Human Rights Approaches to Containing Witchcraft in Cameroon

Michaela Pelican

Introduction

This chapter examines the relationship between "law" and "religion" by focusing on state and non-state reactions to (perceived) acts and discourses of witchcraft in Cameroon. In recent years local actors have explored a variety of strategies in containing witchcraft, including customary and state legal approaches as well as violent encounters and mediation via non-governmental associations.[1]

The study is situated in northwest Cameroon, also known as the Western Grassfields. This area is characterized by centralized chiefdoms in which the containment of witchcraft is considered the responsibility of so-called traditional authorities. In the 1990s, however, in the context of Cameroon's political liberalization and growing social insecurity, customary methods of witchcraft containment weakened in their efficacy. Conversely, the local population engaged in violent witch-hunts which triggered state intervention and responses from non-governmental organizations.

In my contribution I focus on an anti-witchcraft conference held in 1999 in northwest Cameroon. The event was organized by Christian human rights activists who demanded the fair treatment of individuals suspected of occult aggression. Moreover, they encouraged customary and state legal institutions not to compete but collaborate in the containment of witchcraft. The anti-witchcraft conference exemplifies the interconnectedness of transnational legal arenas and local fields, and illustrates the ways in which witchcraft accusations have been framed in terms of globally circulating notions of human rights.

---

1 Research leading to this chapter was conducted in 2000–2002 with the support of the Max Planck Institute for Social Anthropology, Halle/Saale, Germany. For a more comprehensive analysis of the dynamics of changing political and legal strategies in northwest Cameroon see Pelican (2006).

Anthropological Perspectives on Witchcraft

Over the past 15 years, the theme of witchcraft, or more generally the occult, has experienced resurgence in anthropology (for example Comaroff and Comaroff 1993, 2001a, Geschiere 1997, Bond and Ciekawy 2001, Clough and Mitchell 2001, Moore and Sanders 2001a, Niehaus et al. 2001, Kapferer 2003, Meyer and Pels 2003, West and Sanders 2003, Ellis and ter Haar 2004, Stewart and Strathern 2004, Wendl 2004, Ashforth 2005, Kiernan 2006, Ranger 2007). Many authors have recognized a significant increase of occult activities in Africa and other parts of the world. They agree that contemporary discourses on the occult are no simple reiteration of traditional witchcraft beliefs and practices, but constitute new responses to new challenges. Already in 1937, in his analysis of witchcraft beliefs among the Azande, Evans-Pritchard stated, "new situations demand new magic" (1937: 513). The "new situations", Africans and the rest of the world are facing, are characterized by the expansion of the global market and the advent of "millennial capitalism" (Comaroff and Comaroff 1999a, 2001b). The "new magic" of this era is innately modern (Geschiere 1997, Moore and Sanders 2001b). It entails novel ways of making sense, and of deploying "a world in which the *possibility* of rapid enrichment, of amassing a fortune by largely invisible methods, is always palpably present" (Comaroff and Comaroff 1999a: 293).

African notions of witchcraft are rooted in an epistemological framework that differs from the Anglo-European worldview informed by Cartesian rationality (Nyamnjoh 2001). For most Africans the world is composed of both a visible and invisible realm. The latter is the sphere of ancestors, spirits, witches[2] and other supernatural beings whose deeds may well impact on the visible world.[3] Thus for many Africans, witchcraft is not something one can choose or refuse to believe in, but it is part of social reality. While witchcraft may be seen as a component of African belief systems or religion, it also plays into the social and political realm. Witchcraft accusations may function as mechanisms of social sanctioning, as pointed out by anthropologists of the Manchester School (for example Douglas 1970, Gluckman 1973 [1966]: 81–108) who tended to view witchcraft as the antithesis of social order. However, in many parts of Africa knowledge of the occult is not seen as exclusively negative, but as an indispensable source of power (Rowlands 1987, Bongmba 1998). Hence the intention of local institutions concerned with the containment of witchcraft is not to eradicate the occult, but to domesticate and use it to the benefit of society.

Concurrently with the recent rise of witchcraft discourses, the demand for effective methods of containing occult aggression has increased. The widespread idea that older ways of protecting oneself are no longer fully effective has led to the

2 The term "witch" is here used to denote both genders, as in most African societies women as well as men may be suspected of practicing occult activities.

3 In his analysis of the recent but widespread phenomenon of child-witches in the Congolese capital Kinshasa de Boek (2004, 2005) addresses the question of what may happen when the invisible world takes over or pushes aside the visible.

emergence of new forms of witchcraft containment, some of which have shocking consequences on their own (Geschiere 1997: 21). For example, self-proclaimed witch-finders, who judge their suspects merely on the grounds of rumours, have proliferated (Auslander 1993). In consequence, the issue of occult aggression has become a two-fold problem, including both the abuse *by and of* alleged witches.

This chapter deals with the multiple responses to the perceived rise of occult activities in the late 1990s in Cameroon. The regional focus is on the Western Grassfields, an area characterized by a multitude of independent polities. Here the containment of witchcraft is mainly in the hands of the so-called "traditional" authorities, meaning the local chief and his counsellors. In addition, "modern" agents, such as the state and non-governmental organizations, claim alternative solutions to the two-fold witchcraft problem.[4] Yet the position held by government and NGO agents differs significantly from the population's concern. While Grassfields villagers and traditional authorities are preoccupied with eradicating the sources of occult aggression and disciplining witches, government and NGO workers aim at controlling acts of self-justice and restoring public order.

Containing Occult Aggression

Various authors writing on occult activities in Cameroon have differentiated between southern Cameroon and the Grassfields regarding locally established methods of containing witchcraft (for example Fisiy and Geschiere 1991, Geschiere 1996, 1997, Geschiere and Nyamnjoh 1998). The peoples of the southern and coastal areas are relatively segmentary; chieftaincy structures have only been introduced in the colonial period. Here the containment of occult activities is mainly in the hands of ritual specialists, so-called "witch-doctors", and occasionally witchcraft cases are tried in court (Geschiere 1997: 169–97). Conversely, the Western Grassfields are characterized by centralized chiefdoms in which the containment of occult aggression is entrusted to the local chief and his counsellors.[5] Over the past two decades, however, the efficacy of customary methods of witchcraft containment has been doubted, and individuals have resorted to alternative strategies, such as violent witch-hunts which, in consequence, have triggered the response of state authorities, and church and human rights activists.

4 The terms "traditional" and "modern" are here used as a heuristic device to reflect emic distinctions between customary and state or non-governmental institutions. To simplify the reading of the text I relinquish the use of inverted commas. Tradition and its Pidgin English equivalent *country-fashion* are commonly used by Anglophone Cameroonians to denote practices inherited from previous generations which are still relevant in everyday life and therefore variable and adaptable to contemporary situations.

5 It has to be noted here that Grassfields chiefdoms differ in their extent of centralization; in consequence, Grassfields chiefs do not enjoy the same degree of respect and authority in all areas.

Traditional Methods of Witchcraft Containment

In the Grassfields local authorities are generally perceived as the main institution to regulate instances of occult aggression. While the royal counsellors are said to possess occult powers, enabling them to identify witches, the chief is thought to remain outside of the realm of the occult, and thus holds the final moral authority of handling witchcraft cases in the interest of the local community (Geschiere 1996: 316–20, Goheen 1996: 141–8).

The persecution of suspected witches is a complex procedure that involves a number of steps. At first, it is the victim's relatives who investigate the act of assumed occult aggression with the help of a diviner. Consequently, they confront the suspects identified by the diviner with the accusation of witchcraft. The latter are generally encouraged to confess their deeds so that their occult powers should be tamed by a ritual specialist, which enables their social reintegration. If this procedure fails, the case is reported to the chief and his counsellors who regularly hold court, trying cases of both (alleged) occult and secular transgression. Here again, suspects are first encouraged to confess their deeds. Alternatively, they may be compelled to undergo a poison (*sasswood*) ordeal to disprove the witchcraft accusation. Poison ordeals are performed by drinking a toxic substance prepared with the bark of the *sasswood* tree (*Erythraphleum quineense*).[6] Notorious witches are socially sanctioned or ousted from the community. The success of the penalty depends on the consent and cooperation of the culprit's family and on communal backing. In pre-colonial times, recalcitrant witches occasionally were abducted into slavery or executed. Nowadays, these penalties are no longer feasible as they conflict with state law.

In the view of many Grassfielders, the efficacy of traditional methods of witchcraft containment has weakened over the past two decades. Grassfields chiefs have been suspected of being co-opted by witches, in particular by members of the external elite (Goheen 1996: 161, Fisiy and Goheen 1998). Furthermore, the veracity of the *sasswood* ordeal has been questioned. While most Grassfielders still believe in the power of *sasswood* as an intelligent substance that is able to distinguish lies from truth and punishes only culprits, there are doubts if *sasswood* could not be tricked, for example by vomiting intentionally, or by drinking oil so that the poison should not enter the blood system. Concurrently, accidental deaths of suspected witches as a result of the *sasswood* ordeal have occurred and are generally frowned upon, as the aim of the ordeal is not to kill the culprits, but to make them confess their deeds and to be purified and re-socialized. Finally, Grassfielders are increasingly concerned about the lack of solidarity among family and community members, which constitutes a vital precondition for the efficacy of social sanctions against witches. Thus, with

6 *Sasswood* ordeals were common in many parts of the Western Grassfields. As Geschiere and Nyamnjoh (1998: 78) point out, they were banished in the colonial period but resurfaced in the 1990s.

growing doubts in traditional procedures of containing occult aggression, the demand for alternative methods has increased.

State Legal Containment of Occult Aggression

One of the main alternatives to traditional procedures of witchcraft containment is the state legal prosecution of alleged witches. The Cameroonian government claims the responsibility to control any transgression of state law, including secular and occult aggression. In the view of state representatives, witchcraft is a socially negative force that impedes progress and development in the rural areas and thus has to be eliminated. In the mid-1980s, for example, the Cameroonian government commissioned a team of researchers from the Institute of Human Studies in Yaoundé to investigate the extent to which local witchcraft beliefs affected the success of development programmes, and to find solutions to this problem.[7]

The sincerity of the government's attempts to gain control over occult aggression has been doubted, as the economic and political power of state agents themselves may also be attributed to occult means. In addition, individual politicians and elite members have endorsed the dissemination of witchcraft rumours via the press and public discourse as a way of supporting the fragile basis of their authority (Fisiy and Rowlands 1990: 82–3). Moreover, many Cameroonians are convinced that the state is more inclined to protect alleged witches against false accusations than to assist the victims of witchcraft assaults.

The ways in which witchcraft has been dealt with in the political and legal domain have changed significantly since the advent of colonialism. Different regimes followed different approaches, ranging from the denial of its existence to the manipulation of witchcraft rumours for political purposes. During the colonial period, there was no scope for legal prosecution of occult activities (Fisiy and Rowlands 1990: 67–9). While the British refused to acknowledge the existence of witchcraft, the French focused on the fraudulent dealings of ritual specialists (so-called witch-doctors).[8] Colonial judges were perceived as allies of witches who were regularly set free for lack of substantive proof. Only after independence did the Cameroonian government acknowledge the existence of witchcraft. With the introduction of section 251 of the Cameroonian Penal Code in 1967 acts of witchcraft as well as anti-witchcraft became punishable:

---

7 Among the researchers was Cyprian Fisiy, a Cameroonian legal anthropologist, who was charged with the examination of the Cameroonian legislation in respect to witchcraft offences (Fisiy and Geschiere 2001). My explanations of state legal prosecution of witchcraft are largely based on his work (Fisiy 1990, 1998, Fisiy and Geschiere 1990, 1996, 2001, Fisiy and Rowlands 1990).

8 Cameroon has a triple colonial legacy. Initially administered by the Germans, it was split in 1919 and placed under the mandate of the French and British colonial powers. Contemporary northwest and southwest Cameroon were part of the British mandate area.

> Whoever commits any act of witchcraft, magic or divination liable to disturb public order or tranquillity, or to harm another in his person, property or substance, whether by the taking of a reward or otherwise, shall be punished with imprisonment for from two to ten years, and with a fine of from five thousand to one hundred thousand francs. (Section 251, Penal Code of 1967)[9]

As Fisiy and Geschiere (1990, 2001: 230–35) argue, section 251 was introduced as an extension of state control over local communities, since any alternative source of power, not mediated by state institutions, was seen as potentially dangerous. This interpretation has to be seen against the background of the autocratic regime of the former President Ahidjo, which nurtured a socio-political climate of distrust and vigilance. Consequently, the population largely refrained from legal prosecution of witchcraft, as they perceived state institutions as a threat rather than an aid to orderly life (Rowlands and Warnier 1988: 127). It is only in the 1980s that the legal prosecution of witchcraft cases increased, most prominently in eastern and southern Cameroon (Geschiere and Fisiy 1994, Geschiere 1997: 169–97). This development has been interpreted as a long-term effect of labour migration and urbanization; that is with the expansion of social networks in the urban context, the control of deviant behaviour by traditional institutions has become more difficult and recourse to state authorities more immediate (Fisiy and Rowlands 1990: 70).

Moreover, section 251 does not provide the court with clear guidelines, but leaves ample room for the judge's discretion. As Fisiy and Geschiere (1990, 1996, 2001) point out, most often the proof of witchcraft assaults is based on the defendant's confession or on witch-doctors' testimonies. Both measures distort the meaning of confession as understood in the traditional context, where it is seen as the initial step to neutralizing maleficent powers and to witches' subsequent re-socialization. Conversely, in contemporary jurisprudence, confession leads to imprisonment and social alienation (Fisiy 1990). Furthermore, the most dangerous secrets are said to be taught in jail where witches meet up with criminals from all over the country (Geschiere 1997: 196). Detention, hence, is deemed to increase rather than contain the menace of witchcraft. In addition, witch-doctors' partaking in the verification of witchcraft accusations casts doubt on the court's impartiality. Witch-doctors are perceived as part of the occult world and thus lack credibility and moral authority (Fisiy and Geschiere 1990: 146–7, Geschiere 1997: 196–7).

Against the background of these discrepancies and misgivings, it is understandable that for many Cameroonians state legal prosecution constitutes no valid alternative to traditional methods of witchcraft containment. Even among state agents, opinions about the effective containment of occult aggression differ. This will be illustrated by the following discussion of the divergent approaches of two consecutive administrators.

---

9 Cited in Fisiy and Geschiere (2001: 234).

'Traditional' versus 'Modern' Attempts in Containing Witchcraft in Misaje[10]

The Divisional Officer (DO) serving at the time of my arrival in Misaje was a man from Nso, one of the major chiefdoms of the Western Grassfields. His proclaimed objectives included the resolution of inter-chiefdom disputes, cattle theft and farmer-herder problems, while the containment of witchcraft figured only secondarily.

Two years later, his successor who originated from southwest Cameroon, took over and proclaimed an end to occult aggression in his area of jurisdiction. In his view, witchcraft constituted a serious obstacle to rural development and had to be counteracted effectively. He deemed the methods pursued by local Grassfields authorities as inefficient and contrary to state law and modern values. When in 2002 two elderly women accused of witchcraft died as a result of undergoing the *sasswood* ordeal, he issued a prefectorial order banning poison ordeals in the Misaje Sub-Division.

The different positions held by the two consecutive Divisional Officers are best understood by taking into account their regional backgrounds. The previous DO belonged to one of the largest and most influential chiefdoms in the Western Grassfields, where the containment of occult aggression lies exclusively in the hands of the chief and his counsellors. His indifference towards witchcraft, thus, can be read as entrenched in his experience and conviction that witchcraft cases are best handled by traditional authorities. By contrast, the successive DO's focus on the eradication of witchcraft is arguably rooted in his south-western background. In the popular media as well as in anthropological reports (for example Ardener 1970, Geschiere 2001) southern Cameroon features as an area where witchcraft rumours are most prevalent. Due to the absence of efficient local institutions, occult aggression is experienced as a predicament that threatens to dissolve the society from within and requires external mechanisms of resolution (Fisiy and Geschiere 1990, 1996, Fisiy 1998).

Against this background the successive DO's focus on the eradication of witchcraft is understandable, as well as his conviction that traditional methods were inadequate. However, his radical attempt of banning the poison ordeal and replacing it by legal prosecution did not elicit the desired response from the population. Witchcraft accusations were still reported to the palace, and *sasswood* ordeals continued to take place. Even the Mayor of Misaje, who was supposed to serve as a leading example for his community, ignored the DO's prefectorial order, since he considered the *sasswood* ordeal the most effective method of defending himself against witchcraft attacks. Unfortunately, the Mayor died about a year after the ordeal and most villagers were convinced that he was killed by his relatives' witchcraft.

10 Misaje is the primary fieldsite of my research. It is a small town with about 7,000 inhabitants and is located at the northern fringes of the Western Grassfields. It is the headquarters of the Misaje Sub-Division which is part of the Donga-Mantung Division (Pelican 2006: 38–68).

Taking into account the population's disappointment with traditional and legal methods of containing occult aggression, it is not surprising to hear of acts of self-justice and violence against suspected witches. In northwest Cameroon, such incidents occurred mainly in the 1990s and triggered a reaction not only from traditional and state authorities, but also from Christian and human rights activists.

Civil Society Perspectives on Witchcraft Containment

In the course of Cameroon's democratization in the 1990s, global discourses on human, minority and cultural rights gained prominence (Pelican 2006). As a result, a vast number of non-governmental organizations with a focus on human rights emerged. Some of these associations originated from a religious background and combined Christian doctrine with a human rights perspective. Their main concern has been the decline of moral and social values and the inviolability of human beings in the face of witchcraft and its violent ramifications.

Initiatives of Christian Human Rights Organizations

In the following I will present the case study of a conference entitled "Battling witchcraft in our society" that was organized by three Christian human rights NGOs in 1999 and held in Nkambe, the headquarters of the Donga-Mantung Division in northwest Cameroon.[11] The three Christian human rights NGOs were ACAT, EYPIC and the Peace and Justice Committee of the Kumbo Diocese. ACAT (Action by Christians for the Abolition of Torture) is an ecumenical human rights NGO, represented in various parts of Cameroon and other countries. It bases its goals on article 5 of the UN Declaration of Human Rights that focuses on the abolition of torture and all forms of cruel, inhuman or degrading treatment. The north-western branch of ACAT was founded in 1993 and its projects include public education and prison work. EYPIC (Ecumenical Youth Peace Initiative Committee) is also an ecumenical human rights NGO, based in northwest Cameroon. Its activities are concentrated on conflict mediation between local communities. The third organization, the Peace and Justice Committee of the Kumbo Diocese, is part of the Catholic Church in Donga-Mantung. Members of the three associations (that is educated elites and local Christian churchgoers) shared their understanding of the Church as a religious and secular institution with the social responsibility of educating its members on the inviolability of human beings, as proclaimed by the Christian faith. They saw it as their duty to bring to public attention the atrocities that had been committed against individuals suspected of witchcraft in the Donga-Mantung Division.

11 The following account is based on three reports by Akuma and Kwai (1999) and Akuma (2000, 2001), documenting the progress of the joint "witchcraft-programme" of the three NGOs. My thanks go to Joseph Akuma who made these documents available to me.

According to the ACAT statistics of 1999, six individuals had been executed by enraged mobs during the previous two years. The most severe cases occurred in Binshua village where a group of youths had been installed as an anti-witchcraft force by the local chief and had set up its own laws and procedures of prosecuting suspected witches.[12] Victims were threatened, beaten or confined under house arrest, some banished from the village, and others publicly executed. Confronted with a large, vicious mob, neither government nor traditional authorities intervened. As argued by the conference organizers, the general increase in violence and lawlessness in the recent years was linked to the country's political transition of the 1990s. As a consequence, many communities put up their own vigilante groups to protect villagers and their property against both physical and occult assaults. These village defence groups, however, had the propensity of turning into a socially destructive force, such as in the case of the Binshua anti-witchcraft force.[13]

The conference was attended by approximately 700 participants.[14] These included the traditional authorities of more than 60 polities in Donga-Mantung, representatives of the administration, the judiciary and the forces of law and order (gendarmerie, police and army), church and human rights activists, and the local population. The aims of the organizers were to educate the general public on the adverse effects of illegal sanctions against suspected witches, and to promote dialogue and cooperation between the various institutions of witchcraft containment. For this purpose they invited resource persons to present Christian and human rights perspectives and to clarify customary and state legal procedures of witchcraft containment.

Organizers and speakers generally acknowledged the existence of witchcraft and interpreted it as a feature of social relations that flourished in the context of poverty, disease and ignorance. Speakers presenting a Christian and human rights perspective argued against the maltreatment of suspected witches. They appealed for forgiveness, neighbourliness, love and reconciliation as values promoted in the Bible. Furthermore, they emphasized the inviolability of human beings who were modelled after the image of God. Resource persons clarifying the state legal approach to witchcraft explained that, although section 251 of the Penal Code does not define witchcraft, it provides sanctions for both those who practised witchcraft and those who illegally punish suspected witches. As they explained, unlawful punishment includes defamation, forceful displacement, physical harm and

12 A similar case has been described by Auslander (1993) for Zambia. Comaroff and Comaroff (1999b) draw a clear link between the formation of youths squads preoccupied with witch-finding and the rise of unemployment in South Africa.

13 Similar incidents had happened in the Donga-Mantung area in the 1930s with the emergence of the Maka cult as an anti-witchcraft movement (thanks to David Zeitlyn for this information).

14 The conference was funded by international organizations, namely Helvetas and the Swiss Catholic Leten fund (Akuma and Kwai 1999).

depredation of property. Although these measures are part of traditional methods of witchcraft containment, they have to be prosecuted under state law.

Various contributors expressed criticism on existing methods of witchcraft containment. They criticized local Grassfields authorities for encouraging mob action and imposing sanctions that conflicted with state law and human rights. Moreover, they considered the state legal approach not specific enough in defining witchcraft, and thus unable to efficiently deal with its manifestations. Finally, they also laid blame on the administration for failing to eradicate the factors that promoted witchcraft, namely poverty, illness, rural-to-urban migration and lack of development.

As possible strategies to resolve the two-fold witchcraft problem, the conference organizers proposed that traditional and state institutions of witchcraft containment should collaborate more closely. Since the authority of local chiefs and their counsellors was highly respected among Grassfielders, the organizers advised the chiefs to alert their subjects to the adverse effects of mob-action and violence against suspected witches, and to encourage legal prosecution. Moreover, they proposed educational visits to selected polities in order to assist the chiefs in this duty.

The efforts of the conference organizers to provide solutions to the two-fold witchcraft problem were received with positive response by most conference participants. As part of the assessment procedure, selected conference attendants were asked to fill in a questionnaire handed out at the end of the meeting. When asked for their opinion regarding mob-action against suspected witches, 29 out of 35 respondents denied its validity, while the remaining six respondents were either supportive or ambivalent. Concerning their assessment of different methods of witchcraft containment, ten respondents preferred traditional methods, eight favoured legal procedures and three proposed joint efforts. Finally, participants were asked to identify the weaknesses of the conference. Two major criticisms emerged; the first concerned the priority given to state representatives over local Grassfields authorities. Secondly, conference participants expressed their disappointment with the organizers' focus on assaults against suspected witches rather than the protection of potential victims of occult aggression.

As a result of the conference, 62 chiefs of Donga-Mantung came together a week later in an official meeting and resolved to educate their subjects on the Penal Code section 251 on witchcraft prosecution. Furthermore, the Binshua anti-witchcraft force was dissolved and violent action against suspected witches reduced. In the subsequent two years, members of ACAT and EYPIC held educational meetings in 15 chiefdoms in Donga-Mantung which were attended by a total of approximately 7,000 people. The majority of attendants were local chiefs, notables and ritual specialists, but also members of the general public. The chiefs generally promised to educate their subjects on the negative effects of mob-action, and to abolish the poison ordeal and the exiling and killing of alleged witches. They decreed that witchcraft accusations should first and foremost be resolved within the family. Only complicated cases should be reported to the traditional authorities. If no resolution was achieved, the case should be handed over to state legal prosecution. The chiefs also recommended that the divisional administration should encourage members of the external elite to return home and partake in rural development.

Despite the resolutions adopted by most chiefs, the poison ordeal and the exiling of recalcitrant witches continued to be practiced. A particular example occurred in Misaje in 2002 when (as mentioned above) two elderly women died as a result of undergoing the *sasswood* ordeal. Ironically, during the visit of ACAT representatives in 1999 the chief and his counsellors had publicly refuted the use of *sasswood* in witchcraft trials.

Containing Occult and Physical Aggression: Non-state versus State Approaches

As the preceding elaborations have shown, the issue of containing occult aggression is a serious one that has triggered differing and competing responses by traditional authorities, state agents, non-governmental organizations and the general population.

The approach of Christian human rights activists to witchcraft and its containment corresponds closely to the state legal approach. Both are concerned with public order and the physical ramifications of witchcraft. Conversely, members of the local public and their traditional authorities are more interested in effective methods of containing occult aggression than in protecting the human rights of suspected witches. Nonetheless, the identification, punishment and reintegration of witches remain the prerogative of customary institutions. Moreover, Christian human rights activists and state agents look to traditional authorities to implement their strategies of containing witchcraft and securing public order. We may thus infer that, while witchcraft and its containment has remained a field of contention, traditional methods are most trusted by the local public and are tacitly tolerated by state agents, as long as they do not cause further deaths or social disruption.

Conclusion

In concluding the chapter I will highlight the interconnectedness of transnational legal arenas, national political contexts and local fields by pointing at the role of civil society institutions and their mediation between different moral orders.

The current relevance of civil society institutions in Cameroon and elsewhere has to be seen against the background of global trends in development policies and legal discourses. For example, the international donor community significantly contributed to Cameroon's embarkation on the democratization process (Konings 1996, Takougang and Krieger 1998: 103). Furthermore, many development agencies have been collaborating with local non-governmental organizations with the aim of strengthening civil society institutions as an alternative to the "weak African state".[15] Several of these non-governmental organizations have been invoking globally circulating notions of human, minority and cultural rights, thus drawing on transnational legal arenas to make their case.[16] As concerns the non-governmental organizations involved in the containment of witchcraft in northwest Cameroon, we may mention that besides evoking global notions of human rights they also refer to Christian values, thus drawing on religious as well as legal moral orders.

Moreover, in order to assess the impact of the Christian human rights NGOs and other civil society institutions, it is necessary to situate their action in the context of the national political developments of the 1990s. The moral authority of state institutions has been questioned, as state agents have been implicated in violent acts against the general public during the early phase of Cameroon's democratization (Krieger 1994, Konings 2002). In addition, there have been ongoing allegations of their involvement in banditry and corruption. The resulting legal vacuum has been filled by non-governmental organizations, many with a focus on human rights. Yet as the above case study has shown, the aim of the Christian human rights organizations is not to take over the responsibilities of the state and provide new solutions, but to restore the functionality of existing customary and state legal institutions.

Finally, to understand the implications of the NGOs' involvement in the containment of witchcraft, it is important to take into account local variations of political organization among Grassfields chiefdoms – a fact that Fisiy and Geschiere have largely ignored in their comparative work on southern and northwest Cameroon (Fisiy and Geschiere 1991, 1996, Geschiere 1997, 2001). The polities in Donga-Mantung, unlike those in the core areas of the Grassfields, are characterized by relatively loose hierarchical structures. Many occupy an intermediary position between segmentary and hierarchical societies, and their chiefs' competence in handling cases of occult aggression is limited. In this context there is considerable political space for civil society institutions to intervene. Furthermore, the principal leaders of non-governmental organizations are mainly members of the educated elite. Their endorsement of traditional authorities, both with regard to containing occult aggression and governing the local public, gives them the opportunity to partake in local power structures as advisors to their chiefs.[17]

---

15 I here portray the perspective of the international development establishment. Anthropologists have questioned the state-civil society opposition and the generalized perception of African states as weak states (for example Ferguson 2006: 89–112).

16 Several anthropologists have pointed at the ambiguous sides of this evocation of global rights discourses (see for example Kuper 2003, Li 2000 as regards the concept of "indigenous peoples").

17 A similar argument has been put forward by Fisiy and Goheen (1998) and Goheen (1996: 141–62) regarding the elites' involvement in local politics, legitimated by the attribution of traditional titles.

We may end this chapter by stating that the issue of witchcraft and its containment challenges clear categorical distinctions between the religious and the legal realm, as witchcraft itself is part of both African belief systems and social order. Furthermore, debates about the containment of occult and physical aggression draw on a variety of moral orders, including customary rule, state legal regulation, Christian values and notions of human rights, thus integrating local and global as well as religious and legal discourses.

Acknowledgements

Earlier versions of this chapter were presented at the workshop 'The Legitimate and the Supernatural: Law and religion in a complex world' at the Max Planck Institute for Social Anthropology in Halle/Saale, 25–27 August 2005, as well as at the AEGIS conference in Leiden, 11–14 July 2007. I would like to thank Gerhard Anders, David Gellner, Billy MacKinnon, David Zeitlyn and the editors of this volume for their valuable comments.

References

Akuma, J. 2000. *Project Report of ACAT Bamenda on the Execution of its Annual Action Plan for the Year 2000.* Bamenda: unpublished report.

Akuma, J. 2001. *The Role of the Government and Non-governmental Organisations against Violence*. Bamenda: unpublished report.

Akuma, J. and Kwai, J. 1999. *Battling Witchcraft in our Society. Project Report on Witchcraft Conference Organized by ACAT, EYPIC and Kumbo Diocese on the 6th of April 1999 at Donga Mantung Division, Republic of Cameroon.* Bamenda: unpublished report.

Ardener, E. 1970. Witchcraft, economics and the continuity of belief, in Witchcraft, Confessions and Accusations, edited by M. Douglas. London et al.: Tavistock Publications, 141–60.

Ashforth, A. 2005. *Witchcraft, Violence and Democracy in South Africa*. Chicago: University of Chicago Press.

Auslander, M. 1993. *"Open the Wombs!" The Symbolic Politics of Modern Ngoni Witchfinding, in Modernity and its Malcontents. Ritual and Power in Postcolonial Africa*, edited by J. Comaroff and J.L. Comaroff. Chicago: University of Chicago Press, 167–92.

Bond, G. and Ciekawy, D. (eds) 2001. *Witchcraft Dialogues: Anthropological and Philosophical Exchanges*. Athens, OH: Ohio University Press.

Bongmba, E.K. 1998. Toward a hermeneutic of Wimbum Tfu. *African Studies Review*, 41(3), 165–91.

Clough, P. and Mitchell, J.P. (eds) 2001. *Powers of Good and Evil: Moralities, Commodities and Popular Belief.* New York and London: Berghahn Books.

Comaroff, J. and Comaroff, J.L. (eds) 1993. *Modernity and its Malcontents. Ritual and Power in Postcolonial Africa*. Chicago and London: University of Chicago Press.
Comaroff, J. and Comaroff, J.L. 1999a. Occult economies and the violence of abstraction: Notes from the South African postcolony. *American Ethnologist*, 26(2), 279–303.
Comaroff, J. and Comaroff, J.L. 1999b. *Cultural Policing in Postcolonial South Africa*. Working Paper of the American Bar Foundation, University of Chicago.
Comaroff, J. and Comaroff, J.L. (eds) 2001a. *Millennial Capitalism and the Culture of Neoliberalism*. Durham and London: Duke University Press.
Comaroff, J. and Comaroff, J.L. 2001b. Millennial capitalism: First thoughts on a second coming, in *Millennial Capitalism and the Culture of Neoliberalism*, edited by J. Comaroff and J.L. Comaroff. Durham and London: Duke University Press, 1–56.
de Boeck, F. 2004. On being Shege in Kinshasa: Children, the occult and the street, in *Reinventing Order in the Congo. How People Respond to State Failure in Kinshasa*, edited by T. Trefon. London: Zed Books, 155–73.
de Boeck, F. 2005. The divine seed. Children, gift and witchcraft in the Democratic Republic of Congo, in *Makers and Breakers: Children and Youth in Postcolonial Africa*, edited by A. Honwana and F. de Boeck. Oxford: James Currey, 188–214.
Douglas, M. (ed.) 1970. *Witchcraft Confessions and Accusation*. London et al.: Tavistock Publications.
Ellis, S. and ter Haar, G. 2004. *Worlds of Power: Religious Thought and Political Practice in Africa*. London: C. Hurst.
Evans-Pritchard, E.E. 1937. *Witchcraft, Oracles and Magic among the Azande of the Anglo-Egyptian Sudan*. Oxford: Clarendon Press.
Ferguson, J. 2006. *Global Shadows: Africa in the Neoliberal World Order*. Durham and London: Duke University Press.
Fisiy, C.F. 1990. Le monopole juridictionnel de l'état et le règlement des affaires de sorcellerie au Cameroun. *Politique Africaine*, 40, 60–71.
Fisiy, C.F. 1998. Containing occult practices: Witchcraft trials in Cameroon. *African Studies Review*, 41(3), 143–63.
Fisiy, C.F. and Geschiere, P. 1990. Judges and witches, or how is the state to deal with witchcraft? Examples from southeastern Cameroon. *Cahiers d'Etudes Africaines*, 118, 135–56.
Fisiy, C.F. and Geschiere, P. 1991. Sorcery, witchcraft and accumulation. Regional variations in South and West Cameroon. *Critique of Anthropology*, 11(3), 251–78.
Fisiy, C.F. and Geschiere, P. 1996. Witchcraft, violence and identity: different trajectories in postcolonial Cameroon, in *Postcolonial Identities in Africa*, edited by R. Werbner and T. Ranger. London and New Jersey: Zed Books, 193–221.

Fisiy, C.F. and Geschiere, P. 2001. Witchcraft, development and paranoia in Cameroon: Interactions between popular, academic and state discourse, in *Magical Interpretations. Material Realities: Modernity, Witchcraft and the Occult in Postcolonial Africa*, edited by H. Moore and T. Sanders. London and New York: Routledge, 226–46.
Fisiy, C.F. and Goheen, M. 1998. Power and the quest for recognition: Neo-traditional titles among the new elite in Nso', Cameroon. *Africa*, 68(3), 383–402.
Fisiy, C.F. and Rowlands, M. 1990. Sorcery and law in modern Cameroon. *Culture and History*, 6, 63–84.
Geschiere, P. 1996. Chiefs and the problem of witchcraft. *Journal of Legal Pluralism*, 37–8, 307–27.
Geschiere, P. 1997. *The Modernity of Witchcraft: Politics and the Occult in Postcolonial Africa*. Charlottesville and London: University Press of Virginia.
Geschiere, P. 2001. Witchcraft and new forms of wealth: Regional variations in South and West Cameroon, in *Powers of Good and Evil*, edited by P. Clough and J.P. Mitchell. New York and Oxford: Berghahn Books, 43–76.
Geschiere, P. and Fisiy, C. 1994. Domesticating personal violence: Witchcraft, courts and confessions in Cameroon. *Africa*, 64(3), 323–41.
Geschiere, P. and Nyamjoh, F. 1998. Witchcraft as an issue in the "politics of belonging": Democratisation and urban migrants' involvement with the home village. *African Studies Review*, 41(3), 69–91.
Gluckman, M. 1973 [1966]. *Custom and Conflict in Africa*. Oxford: Blackwell.
Goheen, M. 1996. *Men Own the Fields, Women Own the Crops. Gender and Power in the Cameroon Grassfields*. Madison and London: The University of Wisconsin Press.
Kapferer, B. (ed.) 2003. *Beyond Rationalism: Rethinking Magic, Witchcraft and Sorcery*. New York: Berghahn Books.
Kiernan, J. (ed.) 2006. *The Power of the Occult in Modern Africa: Continuity and Innovation in the Renewal of African Cosmologies*. Berlin: Lit-Verlag.
Konings, P. 1996. The post-colonial state and economic and political reforms in Cameroon, in *Liberalisation in the Developing World; Institutional and Economic Changes in Latin America, Africa and Asia*, edited by A.F. Jilberto and A. Mommon. London and New York: Routledge, 244–65.
Konings, P. 2002. University students' revolt, ethnic militia, and violence during political liberalization in Cameroon. *African Studies Review*, 45(2), 179–204.
Krieger, M. 1994. Cameroon's democratic crossroads, 1990–1994. *The Journal of Modern African Studies*, 32(4), 605–28.
Kuper, A. 2003. The return of the native. *Current Anthropology*, 44(3), 389–402.
Li, T. 2000. Articulating indigenous identity in Indonesia: Resource politics and the tribal slot. *Comparative Studies in Society and History*, 42, 149–79.
Meyer, B. and Pels, P. (eds) 2003. *Magic and Modernity: Interfaces of Revelation and Concealment*. Stanford: Stanford University Press.

Moore, H. and Sanders, T. (eds) 2001a. *Magical Interpretations, Material Realities: Modernity, Witchcraft and the Occult in Postcolonial Africa*. London and New York: Routledge.

Moore, H. and Sanders, T. 2001b. Magical interpretations and material realities. An introduction, in *Magical Interpretations, Material Realities: Modernity, Witchcraft and the Occult in Postcolonial Africa*, edited by H. Moore and T. Sanders. London and New York: Routledge, 1–27.

Niehaus, I., Mohlala, E. and Shokane, K. 2001. *Witchcraft, Power and Politics: Exploring the Occult in the South African Lowveld*. London: Pluto Press.

Nyamnjoh, F. 2001. Delusions of development and the enrichment of witchcraft discourses in Cameroon, in *Magical Interpretations, Material Realities: Modernity, Witchcraft and the Occult in Postcolonial Africa*, edited by H. Moore and T. Sanders. London and New York: Routledge, 28–49.

Pelican, M. 2006. *Getting along in the Grassfields: Interethnic Relations and Identity Politics in Northwest Cameroon*. Martin-Luther Universität Halle-Wittenberg, Germany: unpublished dissertation.

Ranger, T. 2007. Scotland Yard and the bush: Medicine murders, child witches and the construction of the occult. *A literature review: Africa*, 77(2), 272–83.

Rowlands, M. 1987. Power and moral order in precolonial West-Central Africa, in *Specialization, Exchange and Complex Societies*, edited by E. Brumfield and T. Earle. Cambridge: Cambridge University Press, 52–63.

Rowlands, M. and Warnier, J.-P. 1988. Sorcery, power and the modern state in Cameroon. *Man*, 23, 118–32.

Stewart, P. and Strathern, A. (eds) 2004. *Witchcraft, Sorcery, Rumors and Gossip*. Cambridge: Cambridge University Press.

Takougang, J. and Krieger, M. 1998. *African State and Society in the 1990s. Cameroon's Political Crossroads*. Boulder: Westview Press.

Wendl, T. (ed.) 2004. *Africa Screams: Das Böse in Kino, Kunst und Kult*. Wuppertal: Peter Hammer Verlag.

West, H. and Sanders, T. (eds) 2003. *Transparency and Conspiracy. Ethnographies of Suspicion and the New World Order*. Durham and London: Duke University Press.

Chapter 9
Constitutionally Divine: Legal Hermeneutics in African Pentecostal Christianity

Thomas G. Kirsch

Introduction

One day during my research in rural Zambia, a clergyman of a small Pentecostal-charismatic church invited me to his homestead so that we could talk about the laws of his church. After exchanging some gossip, he solemnly placed the constitution of his church on the tabletop. I was curious. This was the first time I was to see the church constitution of which I had heard so much during the previous months. In front of me lay a yellowed, crinkled and creased copy of a typewritten document whose pages had been loosely fastened with a metal clip. Going through it, I first realized with surprise that its pages were not following the conventional order; when reading a clause which ran over two pages, one had to leaf back and forth in order to find the page with the second part. Then I discovered that there were two different church names mentioned in the constitution – each of them being employed as if it were the actual name of the church. My bewilderment must have been obvious. After a while, the clergyman, himself a prophet, gently touched my arm and removed the constitution from my hands. He said: "Don't worry. You cannot understand. You do not have the Holy Spirit."

This encounter, and others of a similar kind that I experienced during my field research among African Christians, puts doubt on a long-standing dichotomy in the social sciences and humanities. In line with Max Weber's characterization of charisma as a revolutionary force that breaks with traditions and formal laws, scholars have depicted the relationship between charisma and institutionalization through written laws as antagonistic. Reading the literature on religious charisma, for example, it appears that charismatic leaders have a penchant to burn books. Theirs, one is persuaded, are spoken laws with a short lifespan that cease being "charismatic" once being put down in writing. But what if this is not always and necessarily the case? What about empirical cases where charismatic leaders refer to and even compose formal laws in writing: How do they relate written laws to the source of their ascribed "extraordinariness" – such as the Holy Spirit?

In this chapter, I shall attempt to offer some answers to this question by examining the ethnographic case of a Pentecostal-charismatic church in present-day southern Zambia. In the Spirit Apostolic Church (SAC) – to which the clergyman, mentioned above, belonged – there were constant debates on how the church constitution was related to other recognized sources of religious laws, namely the Holy Spirit and the Bible. Yet, contrary to what one might expect given conventional perspectives on religious charisma, I show that the basic tension in this matter did *not* lie in the relationship between the Holy Spirit as an innovative spiritual entity, on the one hand, and written laws as the objectified products of institutional routinization, on the other. To the contrary, in this church and in various other Pentecostal-charismatic churches in the area of my research, the Holy Spirit was reckoned to be a force that bridges (seeming) contradictions by enabling religious practitioners to discover systematic unity in orally transmitted and written religious-legal diversity. The Holy Spirit was accordingly seen as an essential prerequisite for "legal hermeneutics" (compare Gadamer 1982, Leyh 1992).

In the case of the church constitution, which is the main focus in this chapter, legal hermeneutics was affected by language-related constraints.[1] I show that the constitution of the SAC partly is the outcome of a transnational diffusion of constitutional models that, in this specific case, started with a South African denomination in the early twentieth century. Yet, inadvertently, the adoption of such constitutional model implied that church elders had difficulties in comprehending the language of their own constitution: because it was composed in elaborate English, the "letter of the law" to them often appeared obscure. Given this situation, the Holy Spirit was not only assumed to bridge (seeming) contradictions but also played an important role in how the constitution was approached hermeneutically: The constitutional regulations of the SAC were not interpreted in a quest for "functional purpose", as defined below, but instead in a spiritually led quest for God's intention – the "spirit of the law".

I argue that this particular form of "spiritual legal hermeneutics" was bound to – and perpetuated because of – Pentecostal-charismatic processes of self-authorization. Religious authority in the SAC being grounded on the ascription of an outstanding relationship to the Holy Spirit, anyone who (allegedly) pursued a "secular" interpretation of constitutional regulations was suspected of being a "secular" person himself and thus spiritually incapable. To a certain extent, the idea that legal hermeneutics is a spiritual affair therefore remained unchallenged because it was assumed that the religious status of a person could be inferred by the way he inferred meaning from religious texts.

When now examining premises and modalities of religious legal hermeneutics with regard to my case study, the contents of church laws and the use of them cannot be discussed due to lack of space.[2] I rather focus on, firstly, local assessments concerning the relationship between different sources of religious regulations,

1 This chapter will mainly focus on *written* laws in African Christianity, not on orally transmitted principles of religious disposition and conduct (for example Engelke 2006: 71–4, 2007: 138–70).

2 The constitutional regulations for the greatest part pertained to organizational and administrative matters.

secondly, how religious practitioners related to written laws, and thirdly, how the latter aspects are linked to processes of religious authorization. In doing so, I combine the concern with "sources of laws" as found in the anthropology of law (see, for example, Gluckman 1955: 224–90, Moore 1978: 13–31) with the interest in sociocultural and politicized forms of text-reader relationships as developed in the anthropology of reading (Boyarin 1993) and the New Literacy Studies (Collins and Blot 2003, Street 2003). Addressing the issues outlined above not only promises to broaden our understanding of connections between religion and law in general and of the role of written laws in African Pentecostal Christianity in particular, but also sheds light on the hitherto disregarded question of how sociocultural dimensions and processes of self-authorization influence what in specific religious fields is implied when people talk about the "spirit" of laws.

The Spirit of Laws

In his book *De l'esprit de lois*, first published in 1748 as a contribution of enlightenment philosophy to the study of comparative law, Baron de Montesquieu distinguished between "natural laws", that are the transcendental creation of God, and "positive laws", that are man-made and therefore subject to "ignorance and error" (1773: 4). Arguing that the "spirit" of "positive laws" can be discovered by examining, for instance, the political institutions of the people subscribing to these laws, their "customs", religions, economies, and even the climate in which they live, Montesquieu formulated a critique of pre-existing approaches to law and replaced the theological *singular* ("divine law") with a secular, relativist and socioculturally contextualized *plural* ("laws"). It is therefore hardly surprising that, shortly after it was published, Montesquieu's *De l'esprit de lois* was placed on the Catholic Index of Forbidden Books, while, some centuries later, it has been appraised as a precursor to the anthropology of law (see, for example, Moore 2004).

Important for my argument of this chapter is the question what Montesquieu refers to when talking about the *spirit* of laws. He writes: "I do not pretend to treat of laws, but of their spirit"; then he continues by explaining that "this spirit consists in the various *relations* which the laws may have to different objects" (1773: 9; emphasis added), these objects being the factors, noted above, that frame the laws of a society such as political system, culture and economy. For Montesquieu, "the spirit of laws" therefore is something like the essence of a set of relations within a structural whole. It is an abstract principle that lies beyond the contents of laws or instances of their application.

But this is certainly just one way of putting it. Since many centuries, the phrase "the spirit of the law" has regularly been appealed to by actors in legal and religious domains, although with a broad range of different connotations. In order to develop an analytical terminology for my examination of the case study below, let me distinguish two of the most prominent variants. What is sometimes meant by the phrase "the spirit of the law" is the *abstract purpose* of a law. Here, the "spirit" is defined as *a functional orientation towards certain outcomes*. Alternatively, the "spirit of the law" is at times equated with the *intention of its creator(s)* – be it human authors or divine will. In this variant, the "spirit" of the law is determined by what is reckoned to be its originative moment.

These variants have in common that they relate to some "hidden reality" of laws that has to be inferred by going beyond surface appearances if the law is to be interpreted and applied properly. They differ, however, in how they specify the essence of this hidden reality: on the one hand, the "spirit of the law" is constituted by functional relations between a law and its context; on the other hand, it is the relationship between the law and the (personalized) will of its creator(s).

Spirit and Letter

The "*spirit* of the law" is usually contrasted with the "*letter* of the law" with which a different set of ideas is invoked, such as perspicuity and literalness. Reference to "the letter of the law" is most pronounced among advocates of literalism, a style of textual interpretation that, according to Vincent Crapanzano, is characterized by a set of features of which I will name a few:

> It focuses on the referential or semantic language … rather than on its rhetorical or pragmatic (that is context-relating) dimensions … It assumes a simple, unambiguous correlation of word and thing … It insists on the single, the essential, the 'plain, ordinary, commonsense' meaning of the word … It believes that the meaning of a text … is ultimately decidable … It finds figurative understanding distorting, even corrupting. (2000: 2–3)

Generally speaking, the distinction between the "letter" and the "spirit" of the law therefore concerns the interrelated questions of what characterizes the meaning of a text and of how it should (or can) be interpreted.

In the history of Christianity, the distinction between "the letter of the law" and "the spirit of the law" has often been made in theological debates about the relationship between the Old and the New Testament. With reference to the Pauline dictum that "the letter kills but the spirit gives life" (2 Corinthians 3: 6), some theologians, such as the bishop Marcion (c.110–c.160), argued that the Old Testament – here equated with the "killing letter" – should not be included into the Christian Biblical canon. Other scholars, however, opposed this view and contended that Jesus provided a spiritually led reading of Old Testament laws through which their full intent became evident or even fulfilled. According to this perspective, a "spiritual reading" thus serves as a bridge between different, (seemingly) contradictory covenants.

In addition, the distinction between "the letter" and "the spirit" in the history of Christianity is paralleled by another which concerns principles of scriptural interpretation. In the patristic period, for instance, Origen (c.185–c.254) distinguished between three different senses of the scripture: the literal, the moral and the spiritual sense. A truthful interpretation of the Bible, he claimed, would take account of all three senses while treating the spiritual – that is, the hidden and allegorical – sense as the most meaningful and most valuable for discerning God's will (compare Chau 1995). But this idea of distinct senses of the scripture is not just historical. In the second edition of the Catechism of the Catholic Church, published in 1997, the "spiritual sense" of the Bible is devoted a full paragraph. In this catechism, it is stated that "Thanks to the unity of God's plan, not only the text of Scripture but also the realities and events about which it speaks can be signs" (CCC, § 117). These signs pertain to spiritual realities. The catechism accordingly puts forward:

> In order to discover *the sacred author's intention*, the reader must take into account the conditions of their time and culture, the literary genres in use at that time, and the modes of feeling, speaking and narrating then current … But since Sacred Scripture is inspired, there is another and no less important principle of correct interpretation, without which Scripture would remain a dead letter. 'Sacred Scripture must be read and interpreted in the light of the same Spirit by whom it was written'. (CCC, §§ 110–11; emphasis in the original)

Here, "the spirit" pertains to the relationship between "text" and "reader", an idea we will encounter again when below examining the case study of a (non-Catholic) church in Africa.

This excursion into the history of ideas is illuminating when examining notions of law in religions of the book. It draws our attention to a variety of dimensions that might play a significant role when people in a religious context speak about "the spirit of the law", dimensions such as the opposition between "the manifest" and "the hidden", the question of how different religious covenants are interrelated, the relationship between "texts" and "readers", and the idea that "the Spirit" is important for interpreting religious texts.

In comparison to research in the fields of history and religious studies, however, the prevalent analytical approaches in anthropology appear quite impoverished when dealing with issues like those outlined above. It is true that there exist various social scientific studies on literalism, particularly with regard to American Protestant fundamentalists (Barnhart 1993, Boone 1989). And in a recent book, Crapanzano (2000) even treats literalism both among Christians and members of the legal profession. But the question what in particular socio-cultural fields is implied with the equally important references to "the spirit of the law" has in anthropology hitherto not been dealt with adequately.

It can be suggested that this neglect has to do with three legacies in the anthropological history of ideas. First, many anthropologists equate writings with ossification, hegemonic power, or the Weberian iron cage. I certainly do not deny that writings are and have been used to create, stabilize and objectify power relationships or to change the nature of (previously illiterate) legal systems and procedures (see, for example, Chanock 1985, Goody 1986: 127–70). But, as Brian Street (1984) and others have convincingly demonstrated, literacy is not an autonomous technology that has the same consequences all over the world and at all times. Instead, there exists a broad variety of socioculturally bound literacy practices of which "literalism" and Michel Foucault's disciplinary "network of writing" (1977: 201) are just examples. Yet, many of the references to the role of writings in society made by anthropologists are astonishingly naïve. They seem to blank out, for instance, that textual hermeneutics is inevitably contingent; they neglect what has steadily been pointed out in the field of literary criticism, namely that textual interpretation always is alive – even if it refers to (materially) dead letters.

The second legacy, which seems to have inhibited ethnographic analyses of the "spirit of the law" in the context of religions of the book, has to do with the fact that anthropological references to literacy still tend to follow certain outlines set by Jack Goody and Ian Watt in 1963. Despite the critique voiced against their approach (Finnegan 1970, Street 1984, 1993, Collins and Blot 2003), many subsequent anthropologists have implicitly assumed Goody's and Watt's conceptual framing of the problem, for example, by adopting the idea that "orality" and "literacy" are the most important categories for the ethnographic analysis of the use of writings. Alternative distinctions which might shed a new light on long-standing empirical and theoretical problems, such as "the letter" and "the spirit", continue to play only a minor role (compare Goody 1986: 165, but see Probst 1989, Kirsch 2008).

Third, the dichotomy of "orality" and "literacy" has – following Max Weber's work on types of authority – often been translated into another, namely "charisma" and "institution". In general, this parallelism attributes evanescent utterances to the unstable phenomenon of charisma, while objectifying writings are attributed to specific institutionalized types of authority. In this mode of reasoning, to think of a co-occurrence of charisma and writing appears problematic or even typologically impossible. And indeed, there are many instances in the history of religion that suggest that writing can restrict and transform charisma. Spiritual revelations are frequently turned into dogmas when being put down in writing. Yet all the same, to talk of an *intrinsic* antagonism of charisma and writing would be misleading, since the history of religion also abounds in cases where charismatic leaders deliberately refer to and make use of writings.

How Penetecostal-charismatic leaders relate to religious-legal writings is the topic of the remaining sections. Having been sensitized to a number of issues through the foregoing excursion into the history of ideas, I shall now concentrate on relational aspects of religious laws in two ways: the relationship between different religious-legal sources and the one between texts, readers and the Holy Spirit. But let me first introduce some basic information on the ethnographic setting of my case study.

The Ethnographic Setting

My research on African Christianity was mainly conducted in the area of the Bantu-speaking and formerly acephalous Gwembe Tonga in Zambia (Colson 1960, Scudder 1962).[3] In the Gwembe Valley – for a long time one of the most remote regions of sub-Saharan Africa – Christianity had been introduced by Western mission societies around the turn of the twentieth century (Luig 1997). Yet it was only after the mid-1950s that Christianity increased its impact in the Valley. The construction of the Kariba Dam and mining created new infrastructure (Colson 1971), which opened up the Gwembe Valley to the Central African Plateau and thus cleared the way for both Western and African indigenous churches to enter the area.

In the 1990s, most Tonga of the younger generation in my area of research were associated with a Christian congregation. A considerable number of Western and African-initiated churches co-existed in mutual competition for members. In 1999, for instance, 18 different churches could be found in the range of an hour's walk starting from the small rural township of Sinazeze, the main area of my field research. Out of these, eleven were prophet-healing churches, that is, churches where the divination and healing of afflictions played a "pivotal role with regard to doctrine, pastoral praxis and the recruitment of members" (Schoffeleers 1991: 2). In these churches, an attempt was made to employ the "life-transforming power of the Holy Spirit" (Hammond-Tooke 1987: 157) in order to treat bodily afflictions, cases of sterility, and mentally or socially odd behaviour. This implied that church members expected their leaders to be capable of divination and to have curative powers. Although church offices (*chuuno*) such as "bishop", "secretary" and "deacon" existed, the ascription of an outstanding relationship with the Holy Spirit (*muya usalala*) was crucial for the legitimacy of church leaders. If the leaders failed to stabilize their authority, the members just left the particular church for good. In general, the Gwembe Tonga are highly flexible in choosing the church of their liking, and churches did not have any means of exerting compulsion on their members. Thus, the church leaders had to struggle to maintain a following.

The existence of church offices makes clear that, in these churches, Pentecostal-charismatic dimensions co-occur with features of bureaucratic organization (Kirsch 2002, 2008: 183–242). This was particularly pronounced in the SAC, an African-initiated church that is the primary case study of the present chapter. Comparable to other churches in the area, this coexistence of charisma and formal organization in the SAC entailed that there existed three sources of legal regulations: the Holy Spirit, the Bible and the church constitution. Before I elaborate what each of

---

3 Fieldwork was conducted during a total of 17 months in 1993, 1995, 1999 and 2001 and was funded by the Free University of Berlin, the German Academic Exchange Service, and the German Research Foundation. The data presented in this chapter were collected through prolonged periods of participant observation, informal conversations, narrative interviews, and through the textual analysis of church constitutions and other religious documents.

these elements stood for and how their interrelation was conceptualized by the religious practitioners, a sketch of the historical development of this denomination is important for the analysis below.

In the early 1960s, a Tonga labour migrant returned from the mining towns of Southern Rhodesia (now Zimbabwe), where he had been a member of the Full Gospel Church of God in *Southern Africa*, which originated in South Africa.[4] He decided to form a branch of this denomination in his home village at the escarpment between the Gwembe Valley and the plateau, yet on the long run he lost contact with the headquarters. Eventually, he separated and transformed his church into the Full Gospel Church of God in *Central Africa* (FGCCA). This denomination still exists today, although a major schism occurred in 1991 when some of the church elders decided to break with their bishop. This was the group which subsequently initiated the SAC.

What is significant here are the reasons given for the separation: Besides mentioning a variety of other conflicts, my interlocutors mainly emphasized that the bishop of the FGCCA had failed to establish effective organizational structures and procedures. Working on the middle level of church hierarchy, the prospective founders of the SAC complained about their bishop's autocratic style of leadership, which put them into the awkward position of incessantly being forced to keep up with their leader's spontaneous decisions. Such spontaneity, for sure, was a by-product or even an essential feature of the denomination's spiritual practices. Yet, the separation from the FGCCA was not explained by referring to controversies about spiritual matters but by pointing out the lack of organizational formalism. Bureaucratization thus became a cornerstone for the founding myth of the SAC. And by actually bureaucratizing the church in subsequent years, the church leadership continuously attempted to fulfil what had been promised at the beginning – among other things as a strategy for distinction in those villages where a congregation of the SAC coexisted with a branch of the FGCCA.[5]

For the church elders in the SAC, the configuration resulting from this development required constant efforts in equilibrating what often appeared to be disparate dimensions: On the one hand, their religious authority depended on the ascription of an outstanding relationship with the Holy Spirit, while, on the other hand, the founding myth of the church relied on the idea of bureaucratic formalization. As will become clear below, this precarious configuration also had an influence on how religious laws were approached.

4 In 1909, an American missionary named George Bowie came to South Africa, where he formed the Bethel Pentecostal Assembly. He was soon joined by a former preacher of the African Faith Mission, Archibald H. Cooper. After conflicts, Cooper separated from the Bethel Pentecostal Mission and founded the Church of God. In April 1910, however, the two denominations joined up again under the name of the Full Gospel Church of God in Southern Africa.

5 In the year 1999 the SAC comprised eight congregations and an overall membership of about 1,200. Personal names and the name of the church have been kept anonymous.

Religious Sources of Law

Given the conventional scholarly perspective on religious charisma, one would expect that the basic tension concerning the religious-legal organization of Pentecostal-charismatic churches, such as the SAC, lies in the relationship between the Holy Spirit as an innovative and subjectively experienced entity, on the one hand, and formal written laws as objectified products of institutional routinization, on the other. Such perspective builds on Weber's work on types of authority where he states:

> Genuine charismatic domination ... knows of no abstract legal codes and statutes and of no 'formal' way of adjudication. Its 'objective' law emanates concretely from the highly personal experience of heavenly grace and from the god-like strength of the hero. ... Hence, its attitude is revolutionary and transvalues everything; it makes a soverign [sic] break with all traditional or rational norms: '*It is written, but I say unto you.*' (1968: 23–4; emphasis added)

But the situation is far more complex. As we shall see, taken together, the SAC referred to *three* sources of religious laws, namely the Bible, the church constitution, and the Holy Spirit.

According to statements made by my interlocutors, the Holy Spirit (*muya usalala*) represents a divine entity that *is* the law in the sense that its manifestations are expressions of God's will to regulate life on earth. During church services, for example, prophets explained what God had disclosed to them in visions or while speaking in tongues. These disclosures entailed statements about how Christians should lead a divinely ordained life. The Bible (*ibbaibbele*), in turn, was assumed to lay down general rules and moral principles on which a proper Christian life should be built; providing an overarching framework, it was envisioned as the prospective constitution for the ecumenical *ecclesia* many Christians in my area of research yearned for. Finally, church constitutions (*milawo wamuchikombelo*) were understood to be a consequence of denominational diversification; in contrast to the Bible, constitutions accordingly pertained more to specific religious groupings than to Christianity as a whole. As will be shown below, there was nonetheless the widespread idea that there once existed an original and archetypal church constitution of the very first Christians, of which later constitutions were derivates.

In principle, these three sources of religious laws were not ordered hierarchically; none of them preceded over the other, and each of them was invoked by religious practitioners according to circumstances. Actually, similar to what is stated in the Catechism of the Catholic Church quoted above, church elders assumed that there was a consolidative "divine truth" present in all of them. For them, pluralism of sources did not mean pluralism of regulations. All the same, there existed multidimensional tensions between these sources of religious laws. First, it was not always easy for my interlocutors to reconcile the idea of the Bible as the statutory *Urtext* of Christianity with the existence of subsequent denominational regulations in the form of church constitutions. Second, the relationship between the constitution of a given church and those of preceding denominations, from which the church had separated, occasionally gave rise to controversies. And last, there were tensions between expressions of "embodied law" as exemplified and promulgated by church elders while being in a state of possession by the Holy Spirit, on the one hand, and non-embodied legal regulations as exemplified by the Bible and church constitutions, on the other.

When now examining how these elements were related to each other, it will first be delineated the role of the Bible and its relationship to the Holy Spirit; then I will turn to the issue of church constitutions.

Scripture and Inspiration

Among churchgoers in the area of my research, the Bible was accorded the high status of representing the Word of God as witnessed by early prophets and the Apostles of the New Testament. These "authors" were ascribed the status of "divine secretaries": Since their writings had been guided or even dictated by God, the contents, ordinances and phraseology of the Bible were not of human but of divine and therefore infallible origin.

The acceptance of a religious organization as a "Christian church" was accordingly based on its recognition of the Bible as the *Urtext* of Christianity. As I was able to observe during my field research, renouncing or calling into question the Bible severely put into doubt one's status as Christian. In 1999, for example, a former bishop of the SAC claimed that he had thrown away his copy of the Bible because – as he declared in a letter to me – "The bible is finished, it is theory only". For many, this nourished the suspicion that he had stopped being a Christian. Even though the contents of his sermons resembled those performed by other church elders of the SAC, his disinclination to cite from the Bible was understood as representing a break with proper Christian practice.

Being Christian thus involved reference to a divine truth which had been revealed in the distant past and of which the Bible was an emanation and materialization. But the Scripture was also made significant for religious practitioners by being consulted as a contemporary source for divine truths and regulations. Among Pentecostal churches, what was assumed to connect these temporal dimensions was the Holy Spirit: On the one hand, the Bible was considered as having been written by divinely inspired "authors"; on the other hand, it was accepted that the Bible could only be actualized – that is, made relevant for the present by providing a divinely ordained reading of it – with the assistance of the Holy Spirit (Kirsch 2008: 125–54). Inspiring both "writers" and "readers", the Holy Spirit was therefore understood to create a transcendental connection between temporally separate instances revolving around the Bible.

Against this background, it becomes clear that the Holy Spirit can here not be said to leave "traditions" behind (see also Riesebrodt 1999). Instead, in the understanding of my interlocutors, the Holy Spirit guarantees sameness over time and space that accommodates (seeming) contradictions by uniting (written) past and (oral) present in the conciliative framework of divine will. The Biblical sentence "... it is written, *but* I say onto you ...", that is crucial to Weber's definition of religious charisma as an innovative force that breaks with traditions and routinized laws, therefore appears inappropriate for the analysis of cases like the one presented here. The leaders of Pentecostal-charismatic churches face the challenge of doing two things at a time: securing legitimizing linkages to Biblical traditions while simultaneously presenting themselves as spiritualized innovators, the latter being the basis of their ascribed charisma. Unless the leaders were ready to sever their association with Christianity, they had to proclaim "It is written *and* I say unto you" rather than accentuating a "... but ...". If they failed to equilibrate the two dimensions, either their status as Christians or their charismatic extraordinariness was abnegated.

When (seeming) contradictions between revelatory utterances, the Biblical text and/or the church constitution were critically pointed out to church elders, such equilibrium was attained through the argumentative construction of a *tertium comparationis* through which the (seeming) contradiction was resolved on a more abstract level (compare Kirsch 2004: 705–6). This strategy allowed to ascertain divine consistency over time. Those, however, who pointed out contradictions or who questioned the *tertium comparationis* were usually accused of lacking the Holy Spirit, the alleged prerequisite for a substantive and deep understanding of divine truth – as found in the Bible, but also in the church constitution.

Constitutional Precedents

In April 1993, members and local leaders of a congregation of the Divine Church in Sinazeze area felt in a limbo: The bishop of their church had died recently, and there were rumours that other congregations of the same church had dissolved – though they were not sure about this because contact with these congregations had ceased long ago. Some time later, this congregation associated with the SAC. When talking with members of the congregation about this development, I was told that joining the other church had not been an easy decision since the SAC officially decried herbalist treatment which, however, had always been an important aspect in the Divine Church. Asking why they had not formed their own independent church, it was explained that this had not been possible because there was no written church constitution at hand. Without constitution, they asserted, there was no alternative to uniting with another denomination.

This case is not exceptional. Even among other Pentecostal-charismatic churches in southern Zambia the existence of a church constitution (*milawo wamuchikombelo*) was usually assumed to be a prerequisite for setting up a new church. This perceived need for a constitution had to do with particular model conceptions of how "churches" should be organized, conceptions that can be traced back to historical mission Christianity (see Luig 1997) and at present-time were influenced by people's experiences with contemporary Western denominations in this area. In contrast to "traditional" herbalists (*bang'anga*) and *masabe* possession cults (Colson 1969), "churches" (*bachikombelo*) were perceived to require some formal organizational structure that, according to my interlocutors, had to be specified in written form and in English language.

Given the idea of an organizational model for "churches" and the fact that most of my interlocutors felt unqualified to reproduce it without exemplary, prospective church founders took recourse to already existing church constitutions. In addition, reference to already existing church constitutions provided a certain religious legitimacy to the new denomination. The ideal version of a constitution was widely deemed to be a derivate of the (ideated) archetypical church constitution of the first Christians which, in turn, had been connected to teachings in the Bible. The use of conventionalized constitutions was consequently regarded as an indication that church laws were not arbitrary and idiosyncratic creations but historically transmitted regulations that maintained links to divine truth.

Against this background, the "invention" of a new constitution was seen as unwarranted, since it nourished suspicions that the practices of the new church might not be of a truly Christian kind or that it might not be a "church" at all. Whoever gathered a following in order to establish a new denomination would therefore first of all try to obtain a copy of the constitution of the denomination he had previously belonged to. Those branches that planned to break away from their headquarters but had not secured a copy of the church constitution attempted rather to (however loosely) join another, already existing denomination rather than set up a church without a constitution.

Since constitutions were considered a precondition for setting up a new church, the unrestricted dissemination of church constitutions represented a potential threat to existing church leaderships. A common strategy to deal with this threat therefore consisted in restricting access to the church constitution. Before coming back to this point below, let me first elaborate by the example of the SAC how the adoption of church constitutions evolved and what particular constraints went along with it.

Intertextuality and the Search for the Archetype

The constitution of the SAC as devised in 1991 and amended in 1996 is the product of a transnational diffusion of constitutional models.[6] It has intertextual traces of three other church constitutions:

6 In recent years, the transnational dimensions of African Christianity, involving the diffusion of religious writings, have increasingly come to scholarly attention (see Hansen 1980, Hofmeyr 2004, Maxwell 2006, Kirsch 2007).

- The constitution of the Full Gospel Church of *Central Africa* (FGCCA) from which the SAC had separated in 1991;
- The constitution of the Full Gospel Church of *Southern Africa* which had been formally constituted in South Africa in 1910 and (most probably) represents the precursor of the FGCCA;
- The constitution of the Church of God with headquarters in Zambia's capital Lusaka, which in 1999 was interpreted by the SAC as being the contemporary successor to the Full Gospel Church of Southern Africa.

In 1999, the constitution of the SAC consisted of twenty typewritten pages and was composed in English. Its general outline was highly formalized, containing a *Preface*, several general *Declarations* and a list of six *articles*, which were subdivided in sections. Furthermore, its language was bureaucratic and formalistic in kind, for example, article 2: "The general mission of the [SAC] will meet as often as considered necessary, but at least three times per year in the general interest of the work and the pomp [sic!] despatch of the business of the affairs of the church."

Taken together, the structure and terminology of the constitution indicate historical influences that can be traced as far back as to the Full Gospel Church of God in Southern Africa, the earliest African precursor of the SAC. The first article of the constitution of this early denomination states: "Die naam von hierdie Christelike organisasie is 'Die Volle Evangelie-kerk van God in Suidelike Africa'" (Du Plessis 1984: 328). The same formulation can be found in article 1 of the constitution of the SAC: "The name of this Christian Dinomination [sic!] shall be: The [SAC]." Here is an example of the order of a resolution and its particular wording being transposed from the constitution of a Western denomination in the early twentieth century to an African indigenous church in the 1990s.

That the two quotations above had been carefully copied by the SAC from the constitution of the FGCCA, its immediate precursor, is indicated by the spelling mistakes ("pomp" and "Dinomination") that had also been reproduced. Yet other church regulations, which (apparently) belonged to the Full Gospel Church of God in Southern Africa reached the SAC indirectly. In 1995, a church elder, Miliot, by chance met a missionary of the Church of God, who gave him a small booklet entitled the *Constitution Book*. Upon studying the preface to this booklet, Miliot and Rabson (then vice bishop of the SAC) found the following sentence:

> This complete Constitution of the Church of God in the Republic of Zambia, contains *what was formerly in the Constitution of the Full Gospel Church of God*, therefore supersided and took the place of the constitution of the Full Gospel Church of God which was published in 1974. (Constitution Book; emphasis added)

From this sentence, Miliot and Rabson concluded that they had by chance obtained a constitution that was – like the constitution of the FGCCA – linked to the early Full Gospel Church of God in Southern Africa.[7] Noting the differences between the constitution of the FGCCA and the newly obtained *Constitution Book*, Rabson concluded that his former bishop had excluded certain laws when devising the constitution for the FGCCA. Since he assumed them to have the same constitutional "ancestor", Rabson thus used *both* constitutions as a model when amending the constitution of the SAC in 1996. Some of the features of the constitution of the Full Gospel Church of God in Southern Africa were thus introduced into the SAC through the back door. The first *Declaration of Faith*, for example, which in the Full Gospel Church of God in Southern Africa pertained to "Die Goddelike inspirasie van die Heilige Skrif – die Bybel" (Du Plessis 1984: 328), was missing in the constitution of the FGCCA. The amended laws of the SAC thus adopted the following phrase from the constitution of the Church of God: "We believe ... in the verbal inspiration of the Bible."

Although I do not know what influences other denominations might have exerted on the constitution of the SAC, it is remarkable that the deliberate appropriation of constitutional laws related to regulations that were considered to have a common historical source. In a sense, merging the constitutions was accordingly an attempt to reconstruct an "original" church constitution. The constitution represented a hybrid that had been generated by the merger of two – indirectly three – other constitutions, yet this hybridity did not mean a lack of discrimination in making choices. Instead, it emphasized a common line of descent and was informed by the idea that constitutional laws should have a systematic quality about them that reflects the original (divine) intention.

Interpretive Opacity

Given how the constitution of the SAC actually looked, however, it was not always easy to identify this divine intention. The protracted copying had led to mistakes,[8] as well as to deliberate alterations and abbreviations. Nonetheless, the constitution still retained the main features of its predecessors. On the one hand, this led to considerable incompatibilities between the constitution and the organizational practices of the church. Article 4, section 4a, for instance, declares

7 This assessment accorded with actual historical events. The name "Full Gospel Church of God in Southern Africa" originally indicated this denomination's geographical position within the world-wide fellowship of the "Church of God", which had its headquarters in Cleveland, US. In 1951 the two church bodies amalgamated, although the Full Gospel Church of God in Southern Africa retained autonomy in questions of church leadership (*Standard Encyclopaedia of Southern Africa*, 1972).

8 For example, as mentioned in the introduction, in some sentences of the constitution of the Spirit Apostolic Church the denomination's name is indicated as the "Church of God".

that "The President and the Deputy President shall ordain all ministers, probational ministers, evangelists during the time of the general conference as set forth in this constitution on page 3 article 2, which deals with the power of the general mission board." The designations "President" and "Deputy President", however, were not actually used in the SAC, nor did "probational ministers" exist. Consulting the constitution thus meant involving in acts of translation and selective omission: the "Deputy President" had to be understood as the "Vice-Bishop" and the term "probational ministers" had to be ignored.

On the other hand, the constitution reflected its historical Western predecessors in that it was composed in an elaborate English that was oftentimes beyond the comprehension of its readers who for the greatest part had only some years of formal school education (see Kirsch 2008: 72–9). This led to situations where church elders had to infer what a particular passage of the constitution actually meant. Due to their lack of proficiency in English, what was written in this constitution was all but "plain, ordinary, commonsense" language to them. Instead, the "letter of the law" was obscure; interpretation inevitably concerned the (hidden) "spirit of the law".

Yet, surprisingly, "plain language" was not always considered to be a necessary attribute of church constitutions. There was widespread agreement in the SAC that contriving and amending a church constitution requires the guidance of the Holy Spirit. It was part of the founding myth of the church, mentioned above, that Rabson had worked on the constitution in the early 1990s, and then again in 1996 after *spiritual sojourns* in the mountains. This claim was in line with the idea that spirituality represents the foundation of religious authority and was based on the assumption that divinely ordained church regulations could only be devised with God's assistance. In this respect, the act of composing and amending a church constitution was likened to how the Bible was conceived to have been created. The two thus shared certain features: Similar to the Bible, which was conceived to be characterized by indirect speech, the difficult language of the constitution was in principle not deemed problematic but was seen as something that – given the "divine authorship" – was to be expected.

Hermeneutics and Religious Authority

The relationship between the church constitution, the Bible and the Holy Spirit was the object of controversies in the SAC. There were different ways of relating these three elements to one another. At times, the messages contained in the constitution were interpreted as being an outflow of previous revelations, which had been obtained through spirit mediumship in order to *supplement* the Bible. At other times, they were said to *summarize* the laws in the Bible, which had been drawn up with the help of the Holy Spirit. But most importantly, as the following examination of arguments made during a conflict over the constitution exhibits, the debates regularly culminated in questions of "legal hermeneutics". The consensus that a reader of the constitution had to be spiritually capable in order to understand it properly had consequences for how the "spirit of the laws" was approached and, as I argue below, can also be conceived as a reason for why "spiritual legal hermeneutics" continued to prevail over other, more secular, types of constitutional hermeneutics.

In 1999, the bishop of the SAC, Rabson, had eight copies of the constitution, yet he repeatedly refused to distribute them. The constitution therefore became an object of conflict. The withholding of the constitution was triggered by Rabson's fear of schisms and by the awareness that his own actions did not always agree with the regulations of the written laws of the church. Although, for example, the constitution laid down that the "main board" had to be re-elected every three years, in 1999 Rabson was already in his fourth year of holding his own post.

Since several other members of the "main board" were in the same position as Rabson, they agreed with his desire to restrict the junior leaders' access to the constitution. Nonetheless, they opposed Rabson's efforts to curtail even their own access to it. Referring to the narrative concerning their separation from the FGCCA in the early 1990s, mentioned above, they maintained that the SAC had been founded in order to provide church elders with certainties concerning how to pursue religious practice and conduct church offices. For them, such certainties presupposed having access to the constitution of the church.

Rabson's line of reasoning when confronted with these arguments in July 1999 was based on different premises. According to him, the constitution was a divinely inspired ordinance, whose contents corresponded with the spiritual messages of the Holy Spirit. He insisted that church elders with genuine spirituality would know what was written in the constitution without ever having read it. At large, he depicted the "spirit of the law" to be *identical* with the Spirit. Through this argument, Rabson implied that requests to be provided with the church constitution could be taken as indicating a lack of spirituality on the part of his colleagues. In fact this was plausible enough to silence his adversaries, at least temporarily.

Some weeks later, however, Rabson's argument was countered by saying that the constitution and the type of knowledge attained through the Holy Spirit were different in kinds, thus associating the church constitution with the tradition of the Bible. As in the sermons of a preacher, it was argued, where the Bible *and* the Holy Spirit were both required, an acquaintance with the laws of the church presupposed both the written constitution and spiritual guidance. According to this argument, to which Rabson eventually succumbed, the "spirit of the law" represented an *amalgamation* of letters and the Spirit.

Taken together, the order of arguments made in the course of this controversy can be resumed as follows: The reference to bureaucratization was countered with a reference to the Holy Spirit. This argument temporarily brought the debate to a halt because it insinuated that anybody who questioned it was without spirituality himself. Then, the tension was resolved by declaring the need for the Holy Spirit *and* the church constitution. Thus, what was kept apart in the first two lines of argument, was brought together in the third: Bureaucratic dimensions were confounded with charismatic dimensions.

As I was able to observe, this process shaped how the constitution was approached hermeneutically. Church elders engaged in bureaucratic procedures and consulted the written constitution as administrators, yet as readers framed their interpretation of constitutional articles not as a quest for functional "abstract purposes" but for "divine intentions". Comparable to the interpretation of the Bible, this quest was assumed to presuppose spirituality.

Alternately, particular ways of identifying the "spirit of the law" of the constitution were seen as an indicator for spirituality. And this represents one of the main reasons for why "spiritual legal hermeneutics" persisted in the SAC despite conflicts over the constitution and its emphasis on formalized bureaucratization. It was taken for granted that the spiritual capabilities of the reader could be deduced by the way he inferred meaning from the constitutional text: *How* you interpreted the constitution was an evidence for *who* you were. Given that the ascription of spirituality was the basis of religious authority in the SAC, declaring that spirituality was irrelevant when dealing with a constitution would have put serious doubt on the religious legitimacy of the speaker. In short, challenging the notion of spirituality as a premise of legal hermeneutics would have been a challenge to one's own basis of authority.

Concluding Remarks

In the introduction to an interdisciplinary volume on legal hermeneutics, Gregory Leyh points out:

> To see the problem of reading the law in terms of law's history, the linguistic constitution of law, and the political implications of the way law is read and understood is to set legal interpretation squarely within the humanist tradition … This volume, then, points in the direction of a larger unity, a unity in which, as Hans-Georg Gadamer suggests, 'jurist and theologian meet the student of the humanities.' (1992: xi)

This chapter has been an attempt to develop some preliminary ideas on how anthropologists might meet the jurist, the theologian and the student of the humanities. It has been shown that "legal hermeneutics" in the context of charismatic religions might mean more that taking account of laws' history, the linguistic constitution of laws and the political implications of ways of reading laws, but also requires an examination of religious premises and modalities.

Summarizing some aspects of the ethnographic case discussed above, these premises entail, first, that there exists a unitary divine will behind the diversity of existing religious laws and, second, that the Holy Spirit not only represents one source of such regulations but also helps to bridge (seeming) contradictions between different sources of law. These premises were associated with particular modalities of legal hermeneutics: Concerning the constitution, for example, the Holy Spirit was instrumental in overcoming difficulties that arose from the transnational diffusion of constitutional models and the ensuant interpretive problems, described above. In addition, rather than interpreting constitutional articles in a quest for "functional purpose", what was sought for in the SAC was the divine intention – the "spirit of the law" – which, in turn, could only be discovered by a *spiritually* led reading of the law. As a whole, this case thus exemplifies what I have called "spiritual legal hermeneutics". The constitution was part of a formalized church bureaucracy and the object of controversies and conflicts. In the final analysis, however, these conflicts did not challenge the idea that spirituality represents a prerequisite for a proper interpretation of the constitution. Since hermeneutic practice was linked to Pentecostal-charismatic notions of religious authority, "spiritual legal hermeneutics" was perpetuated and not transformed into more secular forms of hermeneutics.

References

Barnhart, J.E. 1993. What's All the Fighting About? Southern Baptists and the Bible, in *Southern Baptists Observed*, edited by N.T. Ammerman. Knoxville: The University of Tennessee Press, 124–43.

Boone, K.C. 1989. *The Bible Tells Them So. The Discourse of Protestant Fundamentalism*. New York: State University of New York Press.

Boyarin, J. (ed.) 1993. *The Ethnography of Reading*. Berkeley: University of California Press.

Chanock, M. 1985. *Law, Custom and Social Order: The Colonial Experience in Malawi and Zambia*. Cambridge: Cambridge University Press.

Chau, W.-S. 1995. *The Letter and the Spirit. A History of Interpretation from Origen to Luther*. New York: Peter Lang.

Collins, J. and Blot, R.K. 2003. *Literacy and Literacies. Texts, Power, and Identity*. Cambridge: Cambridge University Press.

Colson, E. 1960. *The Social Organisation of the Gwembe Tonga*. Manchester: Manchester University Press.

Colson, E. 1969. Spirit Possession among the Tonga of Zambia, in *Spirit Mediumship and Society*, edited by J. Beattie and J. Middleton. London: Routledge and Kegan Paul, 69–103.

Colson, E. 1971. *The Social Consequences of Resettlement*. Manchester: Manchester University Press.

Crapanzano, V. 2000. *Serving the Word: Literalism in America from the Pulpit to the Bench*. New York: The New Press.

Du Plessis, I.G.L. 1984. *Pinkster-panorama. 'n Geskiedenis van die Volle Evangelie Kerk van God 1910–1983*. Irene: Volle Evangelie Kerk.

Engelke, M. 2006. Clarity and Charisma: On the Uses of Ambiguity in Ritual Life, in *The Limits of Meaning: Case Studies in the Anthropology of Christianity*, edited by M. Engelke and M. Tomlinson. Oxford: Berghahn Books, 63–83.

Engelke, M. 2007. *A Problem of Presence: Beyond Scripture in an African Church*. Berkeley: University of California Press.
Finnegan, R. 1970. *Oral Literature in Africa*. Nairobi: Oxford University Press.
Foucault, M. 1977. *Discipline and Punish*. New York: Pantheon Books.
Gadamer, H.-G. 1982. *Truth and Method*. New York: Crossroads.
Gluckman, M. 1955. *The Judical Process among the Barotse of Northern Rhodesia*. Manchester: Manchester University Press.
Goody, J. 1986. *The Logic of Writing and the Organization of Society*. Cambridge: Cambridge University Press.
Goody, J. and Watt, I. 1963. The Consequences of Literacy. *Comparative Studies in Society and History*, 5(3), 304–45.
Hammond-Tooke, W.D. 1986. The Aetiology of Spirit in Southern Africa. *African Studies*, 45(2), 157–70.
Hansen, H.B. 1980. European Ideas, Colonial Attitudes and African Realities: The Introduction of a Church Constitution in Uganda, 1898–1909. *The International Journal of African Historial Studies*, 13(2), 240–80.
Hofmeyr, I. 2004. *The Portable Bunyan: A Transnational History of The Pilgrim's Progress*. Princeton, NJ: Princeton University Press.
Kirsch, T.G. 2002. Performance and the Negotiation of Charismatic Authority in an African Indigenous Church of Zambia. *Paideuma*, 48, 57–76.
Kirsch, T.G. 2004. Restaging the Will to Believe. Religious Pluralism, Anti-syncretism, and the Problem of Belief. *American Anthropologist*, 106(4), 699–711.
Kirsch, T.G. 2007. Ways of Reading as Religious Power in Print Globalization. *American Ethnologist*, 34(3), 509–20.
Kirsch, T.G. 2008. *Spirits and Letters. Reading, Writing and Charisma in African Christianity*. Oxford: Berghahn Books.
Leyh, G. (ed.) 1992. *Legal Hermeneutics: History, Theory, and Practice*. Berkeley: University of California Press.
Luig, U. 1997. *Conversion as a Social Process. A History of Missionary Christianity among the Valley Tonga, Zambia*. Münster: Lit-Verlag.
Maxwell, D. 2006. *African Gifts of the Spirit: Pentecostalism and the Rise of a Zimbabwean Transnational Religious Movement*. Oxford: James Currey.
Montesquieu, C.L. de Secondat 1773. *The Spirit of Laws*. London: J. Nourse and P. Vaillant.
Moore, S.F. 1978. *Law as Process: An Anthropological Approach*. London: Routledge and Kegan Paul.
Moore, S.F. (ed.) 2004. *Law and Anthropology: A Reader*. Oxford: Blackwell.
Probst, P. 1989. The Letter and the Spirit: Literacy and Religious Authority in the History of the Aladura Movement in Western Nigeria. *Africa*, 59(4), 478–95.
Riesebrodt, M. 1999. Charisma in Max Weber's Sociology of Religion. *Religion*, 29(1), 1–14.
Schoffeleers, M. 1991. Ritual Healing and Political Acquiescence: The Case of the Zionist Churches in Southern Africa. *Africa*, 60(1), 1–25.

Scudder, T. 1962. *The Ecology of the Gwembe Tonga.* Manchester: Manchester University Press.

Street, B. 1984. *Literacy in Theory and Practice.* Cambridge: Cambridge University Press.

Street, B. (ed.) 1993. *Cross-Cultural Approaches to Literacy.* Cambridge: Cambridge University Press.

Street, B. 2003. What's "New" in New Literacy Studies? Critical Approaches to Literacy in Theory and Practice. *Current Issues in Comparative Education,* 5(2), 1–14.

Weber, M. 1968. The Sociology of Charismatic Authority, in *Max Weber: On Charisma and Institution Building*, edited by S.N. Eisenstadt. Chicago: Chicago University Press, 18–27.

Chapter 10
Religious Message and Transnational Interventionism: Constructing Legal Practice in the Moroccan Souss

Bertram Turner

Introduction

This chapter analyses how transnationally active propagators of religious messages transform the construction of legal practice in rural Morocco. It is based on the observation that Morocco's local economies, and the repertoires of legal practice connected to them, become reconfigured through the transfer of religious and moral messages. These reconfigurations affect the relationship between local economies and their social dimensions not only in Morocco but around the globe, while also reinforcing the involvement of rural worlds into trans-scale interactions.

I argue that the diffusion of moral and religious messages (those with hidden religious transcripts included) is connected to the expansion of neoliberal economic concepts by either supporting them or rejecting their impact. This is because religious and moral messages more or less implicitly contain a vision of economic behaviour. The spectrum of such religious concepts of economy may range from the obligation to abandon a monetary economy to a faith-based justification of extreme neoliberalism (cf. Coleman 2005). The economic adjunct of the religious message, I argue, affects the social negotiation of normative orders in rural settings.

The spatial diffusion of moral and religious messages takes a variety of forms. Transnational networks and religious movements function as propagators of such messages and, in doing so, affect local legal repertoires. I refer here mainly to missionary activities and transnational religious activism (particularly Evangelical Christian and Islamic movements) which exercise influence on local ways of life.

However, moral ("value-oriented") and religious ("faith-based") messages also find expression within the realm of developmental cooperation. They are disseminated by religious NGOs and FBOs (faith-based organizations) and even by those "non-religious" development agencies which subscribe to a (more or less explicit) religiously and morally loaded, salvation-oriented concept of development or use the rhetoric of universal ethics (Harper 2000, Tomalin 2006, Tyndale 2006, Hefferan 2007). It is beyond doubt that secular development actors and donor organizations, with the World Bank leading the way (Belshaw and Calderisi

2002, Marshall and van Saanen 2007), increasingly take recourse to religious phraseology. In face of the contested legitimacy of the Bretton Woods Institutions as an important provider of legal templates for transnational interaction and due to the weak position of UN institutions in transnational legal matters, an additional (or even alternative) legitimate substantiation for superordinated normative standardization is sought in trans-scale religion. This strategic approach itself appears to be driven by religious values and is often inspired by the search for partnership in development, be it among faith-based organizations in developed countries, or religious actors and communities in developing countries at the grassroots level.

As I show below, the religious impact of transnational actors becomes evident in the everyday life of rural populations in the Souss region, a rural area in southwest Morocco. Analysing the relationship between the different layers of religious-normative entanglements in this region, I argue that the exposure to such external impact does not inevitably result in an attachment of the local arena to a transnational model of salvation but rather in the reinforcement of local expressions of religion.

This analysis is carried out in several steps. In the first step, I discuss the economic relations of the Souss region, the regulation of access to natural resources, and the socio-legal framing of local modes of resource exploitation. In the second step, I contrast different modes of agricultural production, their respective religious-moral connotations and how they are connected to different socio-economic scales. I show how a local model of sharecropping arrangements, one which is based on religious parameters, became threatened through the intervention of transnational actors and the introduction of alternative and competitive models of production. One of these models was introduced by an Islamic movement whose adherents sought to adapt sharecropping to Islamic principles and to integrate the local economy into a transnational network of Islamic charity and social work. Another model was inspired by developmental concepts of "sustainability" and "women's empowerment" but also claimed "traditional" legitimacy. The competitive implementation of these different models caused controversies among different transnational actors, and between them and the local population of the Souss region.

In a third and final step, I focus on the reaction of local actors to the processes mentioned above, demonstrating that local actors did indeed intend to adjust to transnational economic relations and in so doing improved their ability to cope with the trans-scale entanglement of religious and legal matters with which they had been confronted.

I conclude by arguing that these (partly contradictory) transnational influences did *not* mean that global actors dominated people's lives in the rural areas (Gibson-Graham 2002, 2005, Edelman 2005, Edelman and Haugerud 2005, Scott 2005). On the contrary, the competition among different transnational actors, on the one hand, and between them and local communities, on the other hand, stimulated local actors to *rework* their local normative repertoires.

Broadly speaking, the methodological focus on scalar arrangements and trans-scale interaction pursued here helps understanding, first, the role of religious and moral dimensions in accessing and making use of natural resources (Tsing 2000, Herod and Wright 2002, Purcell and Brown 2005, but Brenner 2001), and second, the conjunction between local processes and transnational framings. In addition, it contributes to examinations of how a scalar re-adjustment creates room for social manoeuvring in which local actors reinforce their local normative sphere in order to cope with what they perceive to be the problematic side effects of transnational integration.

At the theoretical level, the chapter considers the phenomenon by bridging the gap between the local ("cultural") and transnational ("rational") readings (Rottenburg et al. 2000) of the religious embedding. The current process of reinforcing the religious-normative framework for the rural economy is regarded as a form of reformatting. This reformatting was triggered by the invention of alternative modes of production whose legal framework displayed locally developed religious loadings. It was designed to accomplish both participation in the capitalist market and to contain its inherent negative social consequences at the local scale. The process described in this chapter thus suggests an anthropological analysis of the consequences of transnational and competitive interventionism for the revitalization of a moralizing local religion which, in particular, normatively frames local strategies of resource exploitation and modes of production.

The Souss as Locale and Space

The Souss region – a plain in southwest Morocco that is bordered by the mountainous chains of the Atlas in the north and the Anti-Atlas in the south, their convergence in the east, and the Atlantic coast in the west – features a highly diversified agricultural production and a unique ecosystem. On the central plain, conventional agricultural production coexists with ultramodern cash-crop production; the landscape is dominated by large citrus and vegetable plantations and greenhouses. In addition, the Souss is home to the Argan woodland, a globally unparalleled ecosystem formed by the Argan tree, the emblematic tree of the region (*Argania Spinosa (L) Skeels*) and an endemic relict of the Tertiary period. These form the only forests in this semi-arid area that are able to curb the progressive desertification.

In the year 1998, the entire *Arganeraie* region was declared a UNESCO Biosphere Reserve (MADR 2001). At the same time, the Argan forest provides the essential means of livelihood for large parts of the local population and is integrated into the zone of agricultural activity (see, for example, El Aich et al. 2005, Nouaim 2005). Argan oil, extracted from the kernels of the fruits of the tree, is the most prestigious product of the Souss. In addition, as will be discussed below, the uniqueness of the ecosystem of the *Arganeraie* and the conjuncture of conventional and modern agrarian production have recently been attracting the attention of different transnational actors.

Generally speaking, most local Souassa, the people of the Souss region, are *fellahin*, peasants.[1] More particularly, the majority are Tashelhiyt-speaking Berbers who refer to themselves as *Ishilhayen*. However, there is also a high proportion of Arabic speakers concentrated especially in the urban centres and in some enclaves in the countryside. The political organization of these populations is loosely structured at the village level and oscillates in practice between tendencies of centralization and the dissemination of power. This concerns both official and informal institutions: In some villages, the political scene is dominated by a few prominent political figures or elitist oligarchies of wealthy landholders. In others, informal collective organizations, known as village councils (*jma'a-s*), take responsibility for leading and organizing the local community. These village councils are the arena in which the events and developments discussed in this chapter have been debated and negotiated, and in which people from the Souss voice their opinions.

At large, the political organization in the Souss region mirrors the local social stratification differentiating (a) a rural elite that emerged in the post-independence era after 1956, from (b) a small and relatively instable middle class, and (c) a majority of small peasants and day labourers.[2] This rural social fabric is also reflected in the involvement of the Moroccan state at all levels, notably in local administration and the organization of agriculture that relies on a network of agricultural agencies and interactions with transnational actors (Turner 2006).

The Legal Framing of Local Access to Natural Resources

The analysis of the influence of transnational religious and moral messages on local regulations relating to access to economic resources and agricultural production has to take account of, first, the variety of religious framings, regulations and normative orders involved in this process, and second, locally dominant ideas on social rights and obligations. In the Souss region, this normative repertoire is an amalgamate of customary law (*'urf*), state legislation, and Islam (be it in its orthodox, *sufi*, or popular form). The people's access to natural resources in the Souss region is, therefore, framed by an ensemble which includes and combines elements from various religious and normative regimes.

---

1 Proper names and toponyms are transcribed in the commonly used orthography; Arabic terms are in simplified transcription without diacritical marks.

2 The data on which this chapter is based has been anonymized. Fieldwork on the transnational moral-religious impact on a local moral economy was carried out for several weeks each year between 1996 and 2005. Data from different settings and concrete constellations on the Souss plain is included in the analysis. Since 2001, the fieldwork has been part of a project of the Legal Pluralism Project Group at the Max Planck Institute for Social Anthropology in Halle, Germany, on "Sustainable Development and Exploitation of Natural Resources, Legal Pluralism, and Transnational Law in the 'Arganeraie' Biosphere Reserve".

In this section, I give a brief outline of these normative repertoires as they pertain to natural resources. The first thing one has to consider in this context is that we are dealing here with a complex system of classification that integrates different types of property and access rights, and that ranges from individual private property (*melk*) and temporary or permanent collective property to various regulations concerning usufruct and use rights.

On the one hand, Moroccan state law itself represents an amalgamation of various normative orders. It draws on the legislation of the French protectorate (1912–1956), on Islamic law of Maliki orientation, and – in the form of generalizations – on customary regulations which stem from diverse historical epochs and have local variations. Islamic law, on the other hand, is generally not considered to be favourable to the interests of rural populations (see, for example, Bouderbala 1999).[3] This has to do with the fact that the basic understanding of rural life in Islamic law is inspired by commercial and contract law, which means that it classifies rural social conditions less in terms of "property" and "production" but, instead, in terms of "taxes" and "levies". Moreover, the different modes of *collective* agricultural production contravene the Islamic interdiction of a risk economy. The (allegedly) speculative character of such collective arrangements raises suspicions that they are driven by usurious interests (Turner 2003). Further, the Islamic law of succession is a point of contention since it leads to a fragmentation of land and of the means of production and, in doing so, interferes with the persistence of access rights and the passing on of rural property.

Finally, with regard to "customary law" at the local level, regulations emanating from national law have been adapted to traditional practice (Leveau 1985, Swearingen 1987, Bouderbala 1997). Depending on the circumstances, such adapted legal practices may then be legitimized either as secular tradition or as being rooted in popular Islam. In addition to this, there exists a unifying version of "customary law" which has been codified by the state but which is creatively interpreted in everyday life. This illustrates that "customary law" is not fixed, but always in a process of a transformation that reflects the needs of those invoking it. For example, the state version of "customary law" plays an important role in the legislation of the Argan forest; adapted traditional law, by contrast, is usually invoked in cases concerning leasing and renting, and the management of collective resources and sharecropping arrangements.

In fact, all these different repertoires combine to form a plural legal sphere that allows individuals to choose from a varied ensemble of rights and obligations. Depending on the specific circumstances, the respective choice then results in different combinations of rights concerning the access to and exploitation of natural resources.

It is important to note with regard to the analysis pursued here that, first, the families of a village in the Souss region usually combine their economic resources,

3 See also Sait and Lim (2006) on property in Islam in general and within the context of buzzwords such as poverty reduction, property and human rights issues.

and second, that these resources are classified as either "individual private property" (such as irrigated fields and livestock) or access rights to "shared resources" (such as forest or collective land used as pasture). Moreover, villagers have individual usufruct rights. This means that, since the era of the French protectorate, the totality of the Moroccan forest is classified as "statal domain", meaning that local residents have only limited use rights. Customary use rights were first codified by the French in 1911 in legislation that is still operative in modified form today (MADR 2001) and that – together with the diversity of local customary regulations – shapes present day legal practice.

A particular section of this legislation concerns the Argan forest: In the central Souss region, local residents have individual access to defined plots for the exploitation of Argan fruits; they also may use the land for agriculture. The pasturing of animals in the Argan forest, by contrast, counts as a temporary and collective right. The regulation also prescribes a closure time and periods of obligatory collective activities, such as for the collection of Argan fruits.

Religious Embedding as a Local Strategy

An examination of the local model of sharecropping associations and of its revitalization in the Souss region can help us understand what was at stake for locals when the transnational Arganmania company seized the region.

Beginning in the 1940s, the appropriation of vast stretches of land in the Souss plain by French colonists triggered a fundamental transformation of rural life in general, and of property relations in particular (Popp 1983, Swearingen 1987). Despite the French protectorate law prohibiting them from becoming active in this part of Morocco, which was referred to as "*Maroc inutile*" (that is the useless part of the country), colonists established large plantations for citrus fruits and, later, for vegetables. In the Souss region, this period initiated an agricultural production that was oriented towards external markets.

This development continued after Moroccan independence in 1956 and led to a handover of French-owned farms to the new Moroccan rural elite in the 1970s. Apart from this emerging rural elite, only a small number of local investors with relatively meagre budgets and close contact to the economically destitute part of the population succeeded in acquiring agricultural land. This process also involved a stratification of rural society in which villagers, who had sold their land (or most of it) since the time of the protectorate, became day labourers for wealthy and influential farmers (see also Turner 2003).

The data in Table 10.1, collected over a period of ten years of regular research stays in the central Souss plain, gives an impression of the uneven distribution of landed property:[4]

4 The data refer to a rural district in the central Souss. This administrative unit is composed of about 20 villages and hamlets and has a population of approximately 22,000 inhabitants.

Table 10.1 Uneven distribution of landed property in the Souss region

Percentage of Land Owners	Percentage of Cultivation Area
3	33
7	21
11	20
79	26

At the time when landed property was transferred into the hands of Moroccan citizens, opportunities for wage labour were plentiful due to the high demand for agricultural labour on large farms. This was, in turn, especially the result of the irrigation systems.[5] As an unforeseen effect of the modernization of agriculture, however, the constant overpumping of the groundwater reserves in the Souss region raised the costs for irrigation tremendously. Therefore, since the early 1980s, farmers started rationalizing the irrigation system by means of new water saving technologies such as drip irrigation. As a consequence, a great number of wage labourers have been laid off.

During this period in the early 1980s, a further transformation took place in the Souss region when the tomato was introduced as a new cash crop designated for the international market. In view of the new situation, the impoverished peasants reactivated a traditional model of collective agricultural production (*chr 'ka*). This sharecropping arrangement is based on a contract of cooperation between a land owner with sufficient resources to assume the role of an investor, and a peasant. The latter often has nothing to offer but his manpower, which in fact often entails the peasant's "extended" manpower because all family members, women included, contribute to the fulfilment of the contract.

In principle, the division of responsibilities between the two contractual partners is subject to negotiations. The most common version is called *khammessat* and stipulates that of the five (*khamza*) components of agricultural production, four are to be provided by the investor (fields, seeds, other materials used for planting (fertilizer included), and water); while the fifth one, manpower, remains the contribution of the "active associate". At the end of an agricultural cycle, the two partners share the benefits according to the negotiated arrangements. In case

5 Traditional irrigation technology had the reputation of being a highly sophisticated craft and its mastery was a source of local self-esteem: "*We are Souassa, fellahiyya (agriculture) is in our blood and we are masters of irrigation*", as the head of a local village explained it to me in 1996. (All literal quotations in this chapter [*in italics*] are translated from recorded interviews and discussions with local informants – villagers, peasants, farmers, nomads, development brokers, Islamic activists, and state officials – held during fieldwork in the years 1996–2005.)

of a *khammessat*, the investor takes four parts of the earnings while one part is due to the labourer. The fields used for cultivation are usually the property of the investor or rented by him; in a few cases the labourer provides his own fields which allows him to claim two parts of the benefits.

However, the farmers who are willing to act as investor in such arrangements are *not* part of the rural elite. The latter regard wage labourers and peasants as an obstacle to modern agricultural production. "*We do not need them* [the peasants]. *They prevent the formation of large real estates, a prerequisite for modern agriculture. And very soon farms will be run fully automatic and we don't need wage labourers anymore.*"

During the French protectorate era, sharecropping associations of this kind had disappeared because they were reportedly based on relationships of dependency and exploitation to the disadvantage of those offering their manpower. Nevertheless, for people in the Souss region, this sharecropping model promised to work for tomato production, and it also allowed those deprived of landed property to take part in the modern agricultural market. This was because, in this model, investment was low when compared to that required by citrus plantations which had dominated the region until then. "*The tomato became the poor man's citrus fruit. We small peasants could from then on also profit at least a bit from the* '*grand souk*' [world market]."

Furthermore, because the cultivation of tomato necessitates fertile fields, it was essential to cyclically rent new lands. This is why, over time, large parts of arable land fell fallow which, in turn, resulted in the gradual extension of tomato production into forest areas where peasants held individual usufruct rights. In this situation, peasants began to offer these rights to investors as part of their contribution to sharecropping arrangements. This brought about a considerable transformation of the system of collective production. The production now focused on the forest, placing the "active associates" in a much better situation as they could now use their usufruct rights as the land component of a *khammessat* contract.

It is important to point out, however, that this system poses multiple risks for those involved in it. In a sharecropping association like the one described above, production and cooperation does not have any legal protection. Accordingly, sharecroppers operate in a permanent state of legal insecurity. The Moroccan state, in fact, views this mode of production to be an "outmoded" and "backward-looking" relic of the past that resembles Oriental "rentier capitalism". Moreover, the state-run agricultural agencies and state agricultural administration are expressly in favour of a concentration of landed property in the hands of the post-independence rural elite and consequently do not adopt measures that are favourable to the survival of small agricultural producers in rural areas (see also Turner 2003).

Against this background, state agents (even those in the judiciary) keep a low profile in disputes between sharecroppers. In addition, as mentioned above, orthodox Islamic law does not provide legal protection for modes of production based on risk and "illicit" and "immoral" speculation. The speculative character of this mode of production is relevant to cooperation in agricultural production in general because the outcome of such cooperation is always unknown at the moment when a contract is made; but speculation appears even more accentuated in the case of cash crop production where extremely high profits can be expected if production and timing meet the demand of the market (Turner 2003); in case of oversupply or crop failure, both partners have to bear the consequences.

Thus, all in all, it is noteworthy, on the one hand, that sharecroppers are in a situation of legal uncertainty. On the other hand, however, it has to be emphasized that people in the Souss region consolidated their sharecropping model by taking recourse to repertoires of social and religious values. They integrated this model into their local normative order and in this way created a social space of mutual trust that is necessary for economic transactions between unequal partners.

Coping with Legal Insecurity

Of course, both parties to the arrangement show a propensity to interpret the sharecropping partnership to their own advantage, and the prospect of shared profits does not serve to prevent fraud. Given this background, the only reliable juridical reference for resource management and cooperative production is the one legitimized by consensus and rooted in a moral conception of popular Islam. The reestablishment of sharecropping arrangements therefore led to a positive reevaluation of what was called "local morality". Practically speaking, this means that, in order to establish trust in the cooperation, the sharecropping partners agree upon a contract that is orally concluded in front of the village assembly and accredited by, first, local institutions such as the *fqih*, the religious expert, and secondly, the *muqqadim*, the official village leader who acts as a local notable in this context. The conclusion of the contract is, moreover, accompanied by religious practices such as the sharing of a blessed meal.

The interdependence of the partners in a sharecropping arrangement becomes apparent when looking at the religious obligations linked to the respective arrangement. On the one hand, the producing partner avers his commitment to the contract with a religious oath which is seen to be a proof of his agricultural capacity and reliability. On the other hand, the investing partner stakes his personal reputation as a pious and honest person in order to guarantee his fulfilment of the contract. My local interlocutors emphasized that recourse to religion assures the protection of the producing partner, who is vulnerable, from his investing partner.

Thenceforth, the sharecropping association interconnects the two partners in an asymmetrical constellation: The producing partner obtains as a guarantee for the investing partner's correct behaviour nothing but the investor's reputation. This reputation and credibility, in turn, in most cases implies that the investor should preferably be a *hajj* – meaning that he should have accomplished the pilgrimage to Mecca. This is because there is a general understanding that a *hajj* cannot allow himself a compromising comportment, and that he is attentive *not* to endanger his spiritual capital. As a consequence, a potential investor, whose reputation has become questionable, will no longer find potential partners.[6]

The obligations of the investing partner towards his sharecropping partner are, however, limited and restricted to precisely defined occasions. The investor invites his partner on the occasion of the conclusion of contract to have a dinner at his home, a social act with significant ritual meaning. He will grant a small credit during the growing period of the crops. He may consent to conclude an additional small cooperation contract, for instance, for the breeding of goats, even if this will not provide him with a great yield. He will also offer small presents on the occasion of the high religious holidays. Cooperative relations based on such grounds may last for decades.

At the same time, the comparatively weak position of the labourer becomes especially apparent when a contract ends. It is, for instance, the responsibility of the investing partner to sell the harvest. Yet, this enables the investing partner to illegitimately make an extra profit by pretending that the crops generated much lower profits than they actually did. In such cases, the producing partner, who has the contractual right to his share of the benefits, has no other option than to appeal to the reputation of the investor.

As this shows for the context of sharecropping associations, local religion is more than a makeshift in a standby modus or a repertoire in reserve that is only to be revaluated and activated when the legal repertoire seems unlikely to provide sufficient security on its own. Local religion is fundamentally associated with the legal sphere in the region, an arrangement that generates legitimacy and trust. This religious embedding of sharecropping and its concomitant legal register, however, does not involve existing religious ideas of how natural resources should be dealt with adequately. Almost to the contrary, sharecroppers acted in accordance with the principle of attaining a maximal profit to the detriment of the sylvan environment. This problematic increase of use pressure on the Argan forest proved to be at least partly responsible for the developments described in the following section.

6 As the local *fqih* explained to me, a Souassa as a religious individual is in fact defined by the adoption of a local moral identity which he or she has to prove constantly through appropriate behaviour, symbolic acts and a conduct in everyday life that is suited to inspire confidence within his social environment. A man should invest, for instance, a part of his wealth in the social infrastructure of his community and in mutual aid (*tou'iza*). He also should comply with the rules of the redistribution of benefits and perform religiously defined acts of solidarity. He should thus regularly distribute alms (*sadaqa*; lit. charity), support the poor, contribute to the organization of local rituals or otherwise show his intention to let his compatriots participate in his revenues to a degree.

Transnational Competitive Interventions

In addition to the introduction of modern agriculture, there were other factors contributing to the accelerated incorporation of the Souss region into large-scale contexts. Since the 1990s, local phenomena increasingly interacted with global processes, also involving juridical processes on a transnational scale.[7] This meant that the local model of a religiously formatted economy with its specific legal regulations of access to natural resources was put to the test.

These processes of transformation set in as development projects increasingly focused on the sustainable use of natural resources, environmental protection, and the conservation of natural heritage, and when, in doing so, transnational agencies began to "discover" the importance of the *Arganeraie* as a unique ecosystem. Having identified the Argan forest as a promising field of intervention for transnational donor machinery, projects to modernize agriculture and to fight rural poverty were established. It was at this time that the Souss region welcomed an armada of development agencies, among them the *Gesellschaft für Technische Zusammenarbeit* (GTZ – German Association for Technical Cooperation), the US Agency for International Development (USAID), Oxfam Canada, and the *Agence Française de Développement* (AFD), in addition to powerful donor organizations such as the World Bank, the International Monetary Fund (IMF), the European Union (EU), and UNESCO.

The basic set of legal regulations that were brought to bear in the interventions of these organizations in the Souss region was laid down in the UNESCO programme "Man and the Biosphere" and in the UN programme to combat desertification (PAN/LCD). The wider framework has been set up in international conventions such as the "Rio Convention" of 1992 (CNUED-Rio 1992) and the "Convention to Combat Desertification" (CCD-Paris 1994) (see also Turner 2006).

The policy approaches that legitimize this transnational intervention support, in so doing, the diffusion of universalized "commodities of globalization", such as "democratization", the bringing into being of "civil society", "regionalization", administrative "decentralization", "good governance", "sustainable development" and the protection or safeguard of "biodiversity" (Jenson and Santos 2000). The global actors mentioned above encouraged the adoption of these "commodities of globalization" at national scale and, in doing so, were committed to a programme that can be seen as an attempt to tacitly moralize the Moroccan population.

This is connected to the fact that, since the turn of the millennium, the discourses of transnational interveners have increasingly been coloured by an emphasis on faith-based and moral values. This tendency can hardly be disconnected from

---

7 This chapter does not take into account the impact of migration on the re-moralization of access to resources at village level. The reinforcement of informal legal security within the realm of property seems inspired by an exchange of ideas between migrants who regularly visit the villages and Souassa on the spot, an exchange from which the rural elite remains excluded (cf. Lacroix 2005).

the development goals mentioned above, namely the conditioning of developing countries for their integration into neoliberal economy. Therefore, in seeming correspondence with the religious formatting of local legal sharecropping arrangements, this externally introduced religious or moral discourse may be seen as a pre-formatting code, paving the way for the expansion of economic globalization (cf. Rottenburg et al. 2000: 27).

Yet, the interaction of the Moroccan state and particularly of the Souss region with transnationally promoted forms of legislation was not without difficulties. Though the government incorporated transnational legal templates into its national law, not all aspects of this legal reform reached rural areas (Cohen 2003, Desrues 2005). Moreover, because the process of legal harmonization stagnated at national scale, actors in the development sector and donor organizations adopted a strategy of making these standards operative in local contexts in the form of "project law", and in so doing, bypassing the state by establishing intermediary institutions and local NGOs.

Salafiyya Intervention

At a time when the Souss region became entangled in processes of globalization that had an impact on local notions of property and access to natural resources and also influenced the moral and religious dimensions of forest sharecropping, another transnational actor, an Islamic movement named "Salafiyya" entered the scene. With a general reorientation toward an "authentic", "original" and consistent Islam throughout the Muslim world, the movement began missionary activism in the Souss region in 1999 (Turner 2007).

However, although profoundly convinced of their duty to give religious advice to the local population on all sorts of rural matters, the Salafis – that is the adherents to the Salafiyya movement – were badly prepared for this task. In fact, Salafi theology seems hardly geared to rural life. Nevertheless the Salafis incessantly criticized the Souassa for everything they regarded as violations of Islamic prescriptions. The movement's adherents propagated a legal approach that included a universal Islamic vision of the management of property and of the regulation of access to natural resources and that stood in direct opposition to the neoliberal project.

What the two approaches sketched so far have in common is their weak compatibility with the exigencies of rural societies. Neoliberal ideology and the Salafi mindset are both objects of a forced introduction triggered by external interested parties, and yet the Salafi approach eventually turned out to be *irreconcilable* with other transnational impacts. This has to do with the fact that the Salafis mobilized local adherents with a social work approach involving the establishment of a charity network in accordance with Islamic prescriptions. They thus stood in sharp contrast to the local model of pious solidarity, a model they rejected as pagan.

Faith-based Local Economy in the Face of Transnational Challenges

In the course of the economic processes described above, the religion-based legal underpinnings of sharecropping in the Argan forest were the subject of criticism by external interventionists. Transnational actors involved in the environmental protection of the forest considered the sharecropping associations responsible for the degradation of the biosphere. One has to point out, however, that they knew nothing about the socio-religious basis of cooperative agricultural production in the Souss region. The fact that relations between members of local communities rest upon the cross-linkage of distributive obligations and shared rights, as outlined above, slipped their attention, so that they concentrated their efforts solely on the devastating effects of this mode of production.

For their part, agents from the GTZ, Oxfam Canada, and other development agencies launched an alternative economic strategy to exploit the Argan forest, namely the creation of women's cooperatives for the production of Argan oil for the global organic goods market. This model would take into account all exigencies of development cooperation:

- the legal implications of the UNESCO Biosphere Reserve established in 1998
- a focus on ecology
- the wish to fight poverty
- the empowerment of rural women

After 1998, therefore, the Souss region experienced an explosive increase in women's cooperatives of different types which were initiated by different developmental partners, and all of which claimed to be a development of "traditional practices" (Turner 2005).

Many Souassa understood the critique of their model of agricultural cooperation as a critique of their local social networks and religiosity. Against this background, some Souassa suspected that the development agents attempted to infiltrate their local beliefs in the manner of the Salafi, in this case, however, using the rhetoric of "Christian-neoliberal" religiosity. This perception influenced the interactions between the Souassa and the development actors. For the Souassa, this transnational interventionism had a religious-moral flavour despite the fact (or, as some suggested, *because* of the fact) that the development agents had themselves never made references to local Islam. A common strategy of the external experts was in fact not to interfere with religious matters in order to avoid any accusations of partiality or proselytizing (cf. Harper 2000).

And indeed, the transnational environmental discourse to some extent appears inspired by neo-spirituality and a sort of "secular theologization" of the nature (see also Tucker and Grim 2001, Taylor 2005). This discourse emphasizes the global responsibility for a prudent exploitation of natural resources and often finds its expression in a kind of moral paternalism.[8] Therefore, what can be observed is an interaction between, on the one hand, a global religious morality that increasingly affects the discourse on development and, on the other hand, the complexities of a legal pluralism that derives its legitimacy from the ideals of a local rural religiosity.

One has to point out, however, that the combination of messages with a hidden religious transcript (respect for "divine creation"; the idea of "environmental sin") and a certain altruism characteristic for some representatives of development organizations did *not* facilitate the acceptance of the latter. On the contrary, the Souassa mistrusted any sort of altruism because they assumed that a purely altruistic moral code, one divested of reciprocal social commitments and commercial incentive, had to be interpreted as a sign of mental deficiency. In fact, the local concept of morality cannot be dissociated from the underlying notion of reciprocity and from how it manifests materially. "*It's not necessary to always respond immediately, sure, but at the end, your account should be balanced*", as the organizer of a *sadaqa* distribution in a village explained it to me (2001).

Meanwhile, what for the one side was seen as a means in the fight against rural poverty and a scheme for the empowerment of rural women, represented, for the other side, a serious threat to the last stronghold of Islam: the family. The Salafis strongly opposed women's cooperatives. They continued criticizing those cooperatives in harsh ways, arguing that women in such cooperatives would enjoy a kind of liberty that, in the final instance, would constitute debauchery. Yet, the development partners in these projects, such as Oxfam Québec and Oxfam Canada, refused to take notice of this criticism and turned a blind eye to these polemics circulating in the villages.

The Salafis, in contrast, took no action against the "traditional" sharecropping arrangements despite the ambiguous position of such arrangements in Islamic law, insisting instead on reforms. In so doing, they were less concerned with questions of risk economy and the rooting of the sharecropping arrangements in popular Islam (with the specific spiritual connotations, mentioned above) but with the protection of working women. They propagated a "correct dress code" for women doing agricultural labour, involving, among other things, a veil and gloves. Furthermore, they insisted that the reed fences that had been installed as windbreaks around tomato fields should be higher. In other words, they insisted on modifying the function of these fences from "windbreaks" to "screens", thus also increasing the costs of production to be borne by the investing partner in the sharecropping cooperation. Moreover, according to the Salafis, everybody (even investors) was required to shout when approaching the fields; this, however, was inconsistent with the controlling function of an investor. Finally, another demand concerned the forbidding of traditional singing during work in the fields, which, in the final analysis, in the eyes of the majority of Souassa lent little credence to the Salafi religious approach.

---

8 See also the articles on this issue in Taylor (2005); cf. Hefferan (2007) for examples of directly faith-based NGOs.

Updating Local Morality

Taken together, all these factors profoundly affected local economic practices and intensified the sense of contradiction within the region's fabric of normative and moral pluralism. The processes outlined above reinforced the local religious-legal matrix in the face of diverse transnational intervention. NGOs and development actors, local representatives of the state, and Islamic activists all compromised the previous, rather informal management of access to natural resources which was based and legitimized with reference to the locally prevalent repertoire of values. This perturbation of local orders motivated the Souassa to enact an essentially passive form of resistance which found expression, for instance, in the refusal to accept the establishment of a women's cooperative in their immediate neighbourhood. And yet, they were able to deliberately adapt some developmental innovations to local conditions.

The adjustment of the local legal repertoire was facilitated through a reference to "custom", the importance of which was also emphasized by development organizations. The transnational discourse concerning the "revitalization of local tradition" therefore turned out to be helpful for people in the Souss region (see also F. and K. von Benda-Beckmann and Turner 2007) – as it has been elsewhere: The implementation of programmes for the revitalization of "good traditions" has become one of the principal strategies of transnational actors, an approach that entails that these actors themselves define what "good tradition" means. In other words, the process in which transnational legal standards are implemented locally progresses through the instrumentalization of those elements of local regulations of resource management that seem compatible with the normative requirements of environmental protection and sustainable development. Accordingly, the definition of "tradition" eclipses all those practices and regulations that are categorized as detrimental to the intervention of transnational activism.

This configuration relies on the idea that most of those normative structures which development agents plan to make operative at the local scale are already preexistent or pre-formatted in local knowledge. Against this background, "local knowledge" becomes a crucial argument which the Souassa mobilized in their negotiations with state authorities and development organizations. The complex web of rights and obligations relevant to local resource management was an integral part of this local approach. It aimed at the valorization of popular (or "tribal") Islam as a resource, spiritual capital, intellectual property, local knowledge, and cultural inventory. Thus, in this approach, the specificities of local versions of religion such as pilgrimages, the role of religious congregations, the rites of social integration, and simply the manner of performing prayers, are markers of Souassa identity.

In this way, external influence was responsible for a return of "custom" at local scale. It encouraged the formation of updated versions of local normative repertoires that became adjusted to the needs of Souassa communities. It would be mistaken, however, to assume that this local reorientation was in harmony with transnationalized and global values.[9] In enacting passive resistance, for instance, the Souassa referred to the very fundamental rights that transnational actors in their region mentioned so often. For example, the Souassa pointed to the discourse on minority rights and emphasized the "*berbérité*" of local culture including the traditional model of collective agricultural production (*chr'ka*) and the specificities of local popular Islam.

Broadly speaking, the Souassa thus presented a rather diffuse mixture of arguments in favour of fundamental rights with a religious/moralizing discourse and a plea for the revitalization of those "traditions" which, to them, seemed advantageous in defending their economic model. They also instrumentalized discourses on "rural women". Just as "strikes" were organized among women members of Argan oil-producing cooperatives, the Souassa resisted attempts of the Salafis to exercise control over the female sphere by pretending that the nearby cooperatives would lead to progress. They thus developed a strategy of playing off one transnational actor against another whereby the external threat was transformed into an *opportunity* for a gradual emancipation from Western interveners, Salafi and state agents, all at the same time.

Conclusion

This chapter's point of departure was the analysis of a particular "traditional" model of collective resource exploitation in rural Morocco that follows an informal legal code, one that is constituted with reference to the legislation of the nation-state, various versions of religious law, and customary regulations. This juridical arrangement guaranteed people a certain legal security with regard to the management of natural resources due to its association with local religion. When rural areas became involved in processes of globalization, however, transnational actors began to affect this complex legal arena. The latter did not criticize the legal repertoire as much as the local mode of production that it assures. In so doing, however, some transnational actors implicitly, some overtly, questioned the religious reference of that legal arrangement. At the same time, their own messages were understood locally as either being clearly missionary in nature and directed towards religious change (as in the case of the Salafiyya), or, if not openly religious, then at least transporting a "hidden" religious message (as in the case of development cooperation). Thus, the involvement of development actors was considered not to be one free of faith-based notions, but to have incorporated a "religion" of neoliberal economy or an anti-neoliberal moral paternalism.

For the people of the Souss region, encounters with the ideas propagated by these transnational actors made it necessary to re-format their legal frameworks whereby, as I have tried to show, they gave priority to the reinforcement of their

9 See Tomalin (2006) on the absence of research programmes on "religion and development" and the human rights and civic rights approach.

existing legal repertoires and institutions. In so doing, moreover, they benefited from the incompatibility and competition between different external providers of legal and religious-moral templates. They thus also ensured the persistence of a mode of agricultural production that combines a market orientation with religious reference – or, in other words, ideas of morality with material interests.

Therefore, the analysis of this configuration provides an apt opportunity to examine religious-legal interplay in scalar arrangements. The religious and moral discourses that arose in the Souss region, accompanied the implementation of alternative models of agricultural production such as, on the one hand, women's cooperatives as a specific form of a new worldwide economy in solidarity (cf. Allard et al. 2008) and, on the other hand, an Islamic economy of care. Both models connect the region with the transnational scale whereby the religious messages and normative standardization complement each other. In local spheres, these external impacts encounter a configuration wherein popular religiosity supports the continuance of the legal arrangement upon which the local mode of collective resource exploitation is based.

The resistance of the people of the Souss region to a possible reemergence of legal insecurity caused by this external intervention and their strategy to keep control over local natural resources was inspired by arguments from various scales. Their approach therefore consisted in a "scalar arrangement" (Purcell and Brown 2005) which resulted in the maintenance, even expansion, of the room for manoeuvring of local actors while the scope of external interveners was restricted. The group, whose scope of action has benefited from such development, has remained local nevertheless. Thus, in all, the stabilizing effects only involve the network of users of this sylvan resource who agree to cooperate and accept a body of religious and moral implications in legal practice.

References

Allard, J., Davidson, C. and Matthaei, J. (eds) 2008. *Solidarity Economy: Building Alternatives for People and Planet.* Chicago: ChangeMaker Publications.

Belshaw, D. and Caldrisi, R. (eds) 2002. *Faith in Development: Partnership between the World Bank and the Churches of Africa.* Oxford: Regnum Books and World Bank Publications.

Benda-Beckmann, F. von, Benda-Beckmann, K. von and Turner; B. 2007. Umstrittene Traditionen in Marokko und Indonesien. *Zeitschrift für Ethnologie*, 132, 15–35.

Bouderbala, N. 1997. La modernisation et la gestion du foncier au Maroc. *Options Méditerranéennes*, 29, 155–64.

Bouderbala, N. 1999. Les systèmes de propriété foncière au Maghreb. Le cas du Maroc. *Cahiers Options Méditerranéennes*, 36, 47–66.

Brenner, N. 2001. The limits to scale? Methodological reflections on scalar structuration. *Progress in Human Geography*, 25(4), 591–614.

Cohen, S. 2003. Alienation and globalization in Morocco: Addressing the social and political impact of market integration. *Comparative Studies in Society and History*, 45, 168–89.

Coleman, S. 2005. Economy and religion, in *A Handbook of Economic Anthropology*, edited by J. Carrier. Cheltenham: Elgar, 339–52.

Desrues, T. 2005. Governability and agricultural policy in Morocco: Functionality and limitations of the reform discourse. *Mediterranean Politics*, 10(1), 39–63.

Edelman, M. 2005. Bringing the moral economy back in ... to the study of 21st-century transnational peasant movements. *American Anthropologist*, 170(3), 331–45.

Edelman, M. and Haugerud, A. (eds) 2005. *The Anthropology of Development and Globalization: From Classical Political Economy to Contemporary Neoliberalism*. Malden, MA: Blackwell Publishers.

El Aich, A., Bourbouze, A. and Morand-Fehr, P. 2005. *La Chèvre dans l'Arganeraie*. Rabat: Actes Editions.

Gibson-Graham, J.K. 2002. Beyond global versus local: Economic politics outside the binary frame, in *Geographies of Power. Placing Scale*, edited by A. Herod and M. Wright. Malden, MA: Blackwell Publishers, 25–60.

Gibson-Graham, J.K. 2005. Surplus possibilities: Post-development and community economies. *Singapore Journal of Tropical Geography*, 26(1), 4–26.

Harper, S. (ed.) 2000. *The Lab, the Temple, and the Market: Reflections at the Intersection of Science, Religion, and Development*. Bloomfield: Kumarian Press.

Hefferan, T. 2007. Finding faith in development: Religious non-governmental organizations (NGOs) in Argentina and Zimbabwe. *Anthropological Quarterly*, 80(3), 887–96.

Herod, A. and Wright, M. (eds) 2002. *Geographies of Power. Placing Scale*. Malden, MA: Blackwell Publishers.

Jenson, J. and Santos, B. de Sousa (eds) 2000. *Globalizing Institutions. Case Studies in Regulation and Innovation*. Aldershot: Ashgate.

Lacroix, T. 2005. *Les Réseaux Marocains du Développement: Géographie du Transnational et Politique du Territorial*. Paris: Presses de Sciences Po.

Leveau, R. 1985. Public property and control of property rights: Their effects on social structure in Morocco, in *Property, Social Structure and Law in the Middle East*, edited by A.E. Mayer. Albany, New York: State University of New York Press, 61–84.

MADR (Ministère de l'Agriculture, du Développement Rural et des Eaux et Forêts) (ed.) 2001. *Etude du Plan Cadre d'une Réserve de la Biosphère Arganeraie. Partie IV: Finalisation du Plan Cadre*. Rabat: Agroforest.

Marshall, K. and van Saanen, M.B. 2007. *Development and Faith: Where Mind, Heart, and Soul Work Together*. Washington: World Bank Publications.

Nouaim, R. 2005. *L'Arganier au Maroc: Entre Mythes et Réalités*. Paris: L'Harmattan.

Popp, H. 1983. *Moderne Bewässerungslandwirtschaft in Marokko*. 2 vols. Erlangen: Erlanger Geographische Arbeiten 15.

Purcell, M. and Brown, J.C. 2005. Against the local trap: Scale and the study of environment and development. *Progress in Development Studies*, 5(4), 279–97.

Rottenburg, R., Kalthoff, H. and Wagener, H.-J. 2000. In search of a new bed. Economic representations and practices, in *Facts and Figures. Economic Practices and Representations. Jahrbuch Ökonomie und Gesellschaft 16*, edited by H. Kalthoff, R. Rottenburg and H.-J. Wagener. Marburg: Metropolis, 9–34.

Sait, S. and Lim, H. 2006. *Land, Law and Islam: Property and Human Rights in the Muslim World*. London: Zed Books.

Scott, J.C. 2005. Afterword to "moral economies, state spaces, and categorical violence". *American Anthropologist*, 170(3), 395–402.

Swearingen, W.D. 1987. *Moroccan Mirages: Agrarian Dreams and Deceptions, 1912–1986*. Princeton, NJ: Princeton University Press.

Taylor, B.R. 2005. Introduction, in *The Encyclopedia of Religion and Nature*, edited by B.R. Taylor. London et al.: Thoemmes Continuum, vii–xxvi.

Tomalin, E. 2006. Religion and a rights-based approach to development. *Progress in Development Studies*, 6(2), 93–108.

Tsing, A.L. 2000. The global situation. *Cultural Anthropology*, 15(3), 327–60.

Tucker, M.E. and Grim, J.A. 2001. Introduction: The emerging alliance of world religions and ecology. *Daedalus*, 130(4), 1–22.

Turner B. 2003. *Chr'ka* in southwest Morocco: Forms of agrarian cooperation between *khammessat* system and legal pluralism, in *Legal Pluralism and Unofficial Law in Social, Economic and Political Development. Papers of the XIIIth International Congress, 7–10 April 2002, Chiang Mai, Thailand*. Vol. III, edited by R. Pradhan. Kathmandu: ICNEC, 227–55.

Turner, B. 2005. Der Wald im Dickicht der Gesetze: Transnationales Recht und lokale Rechtspraxis im Arganwald (Marokko). *Entwicklungsethnologie*, 14(1–2), 97–117.

Turner, B. 2006. Competing global players in rural Morocco: Upgrading legal arenas. *Journal of Legal Pluralism*, 53/54, 101–39.

Turner, B. 2007. *Islamic Activism and Anti-Terrorism Legislation in Morocco*. MPI for Social Anthropology, Working Paper No. 91.

Tyndale, W.R. (ed.) 2006. *Visions of Development: Faith-based Initiatives*. Aldershot: Ashgate.

PART IV
Registers of Argumentation and the Negotiation of Order

Chapter 11
Playing the Religious Card: Competing for District Leadership in West Sumba, Indonesia

Jacqueline Vel

Introduction

One of the central themes in this book concerns the normative force of religious orders and their interplay with other legal orders (F. von Benda-Beckmann 2002). How are religious ideas invoked as justifications for political and legal action, as tools of power and competition, as the basis for social stratification and as markers of identity? What role do religion and religious ideas play in legitimating (or not) schemes of morality and regulation? This chapter discusses how religious ideas and symbols are used as tools of power and competition at election rallies in Indonesia. District head elections take place in the context of legal pluralism: while the rules and procedures of the elections are set by state law, and the contest concerns the highest local state office, the election campaigns submit many arguments for legitimizing leadership that are derived from other legal orders. Candidates address their audiences at rallies and through the media, using symbols and specific language that provoke ethnic and religious identities. Studying this form of competition through election campaign strategies offers an overview of the normative repertoire available to politicians and opens up opportunities for the analysis of the candidates' assessments of the relative strengths and weaknesses of each of the normative orders in the local repertoire.

The empirical data in this chapter are from Sumba, the area in Indonesia where I have been involved in development work and research since 1984. Sumba is an island in Nusa Tenggara Timur, Indonesia's poorest province. Administratively, Sumba consisted in 2005 of two regencies, East Sumba and West Sumba with about 200,000 and 400,000 inhabitants respectively. Having lived in West Sumba for six years (1984–1990), I have been returning frequently since 1998, when Suharto's authoritarian rule gave way to democracy in Indonesia. Studying the district head elections in 2005 was part of my larger project of analysing the process of democratization in the local context (Vel 2008a). My long-term relationships with many Sumbanese have allowed me access to networks and thus information about political strategies and easy access to all kinds of events and informants. A small video camera and tripod turned out to be the perfect research tool for election rallies in Sumba, as the rally organizers welcomed any video recording, inviting me to the best spots for filming and encouraging me to interview candidates. Local newspapers that have started up since 2000 constituted an additional source of information.

West Sumba is not the average Indonesian district. It is populated relatively sparsely, it is poor in resources, agriculture is the main economic activity for 85 per cent of the population, and there is no large urban centre. And still, it is well integrated into the national processes of democratization, administrative decentralization (Vel 2008a: 237–48), and more recently even the globalization of its economy (Vel 2008b). In Sumba these national processes can be studied in the context of a normative repertoire in which both the local, traditional religion and a universal religion (Christianity) are prominent.

This chapter begins by explaining how democratization in Indonesia made room for the inclusion of religious elements into regional politics and legislation. Changes in the election laws made politicians more dependent on their local constituencies, thus encouraging identity politics. The second section discusses the type of identity politics most suitable for winning elections under circumstances as found in Sumba. Candidates for election try to find identity markers that unify as many voters as possible into a single constituency of which they are the legitimate and accepted leaders. For a deeper understanding of the normative repertoire on Sumba, the fourth section elaborates on its historical background and describes characteristics of Sumbanese Christianity. Following these sections depicting the background and context, the chapter continues with a description of the election campaigns in 2005. The case study concentrates on the two main competitors. One played the religious card by stressing his Protestant Christian identity and including many symbols from the traditional local religion in rallying rhetoric and style. The other candidate opted for the image of a clean and competent bureaucrat and chose a popular Catholic medical doctor as his deputy. In both strategies, religious arguments – or at least religious affiliation – were very important tools in competition for the most powerful district state office. In 2005, it seems like the boundaries of law, religion, and culture were actively blurred by the local politicians, who sought to derive authority from whatever was available in the total normative repertoire in Sumba. The chapter concludes with a section on the election results and the general conclusion that democratization in Indonesia created preconditions for identity politics in which religion has been the major identity marker.

Religion and Politics in Indonesia

In countries with pluralistic societies like Indonesia the link between religion and politics is potentially divisive from a national perspective. With over 80 per cent of its population registered as Muslim, the prominent role of Islam in politics has posed a chief threat to pluralism since the independence of Indonesia. Turning

Indonesia into an Islamic state would have encouraged secession movements in predominantly Christian areas and could also have restricted the rights of non-Muslim citizens and been harmful to business interests.

The regime of President Suharto (1966–1998) banned most political activities and allowed only a small number of nationally unified and controlled political parties. All civil servants were obligatory members of the regime's functional organization Golkar (Golongan Karya, Functional Groups) which also acted as a political party, mobilizing support for the authoritarian regime during all elections from the 1970s to 1998. Local political activity, the freedom to assemble and to openly connect religious (or indeed ethnic, race, or class) arguments to local interests were seen as threats to the priorities of the Suharto regime: national unity, economic growth, foreign investment, and stability (Smith-Kipp 1993: 109). The state recognized five different religions: Islam, Protestantism, Catholicism, Buddhism, and Hinduism, to which Confucianism was later added (Hosen 2005: 419). All citizens were supposed to adhere to one of these recognized religions, and their membership was printed as a marker on their identity card. Other religions, like the traditional ancestral religion on Sumba, were not recognized and regarded as either backward or suspicious. "No religion" is not an option for Indonesian citizens and, during the Suharto regime it was to be equated with communist sympathies.

Once the regime fell, ethnicity and religion were immediately used for labelling contesting parties in regional power struggles (van Klinken 2005). For several Muslim groups and political parties, regime change in 1998 provided the opportunity to propose the introduction of *sharia*, Islamic Law, into the Constitution (Hosen 2005: 419). Up to 2007 these proposals have not been accepted, but the debate about the role of religion in law and in politics has become much more intense than during the Suharto regime. Regional autonomy presented opportunity for district governments to include religious elements into their legislation. Of these, the best known are the *perda sharia*, regional regulations that introduce Islamic law in some districts (Hasan 2007: 10–13).

With the fall of Suharto two major changes in the relation between politics and religion would follow. First, there was a new freedom to speak about religion in political contexts since the ban on publicly discussing ethnic, religious, race or class issues was lifted and human rights came under legal protection. Second, decentralization led to a new type of local politics, in which primarily the regions (the provinces and their constituent districts) and their inhabitants were central, and national interests only became political issues when they restricted regional ambitions. Within the autonomous districts, the relation between politics and religion varies depending on the pattern of religious adherence and the religious identity of the district elite. Religious identity is one of the markers of political leaders, so if they represent the majority of the district population regarding religious affiliation their electoral prospects improve. Religious affiliation is an important criterion in differentiating between societal groups in the local context. Fellow Christians or fellow Muslims visit the same houses of worship, are members of the same organizations, and contribute to the same projects (building new churches or paying for pilgrimages to Mecca). It is this social aspect of religious affiliation rather than any theological issue that matters in local politics. This chapter argues that, for local politicians, religion is a force that unites large constituencies within the boundaries of their districts.

The difference between national and regional/local perspectives on the role of religion in elections is the major reason why this chapter argues against Liddle's and Mujani's (2007) conclusion concerning voting behaviour in Indonesia based on a national opinion survey: "Bivariate and multivariate analysis of our data confirm the significance of leadership and party identification and the non significance for the most part of the other variables tested, including religious orientation, long the most popular explanation for the Indonesian case" (Liddle and Mujani 2007: 832).

This conclusion generalizes the research findings for "explaining voting behaviour in Indonesia". Yet the data do not cover district head elections, and define ethnicity only in large categories that are eventually compressed into only two categories: Javanese and other; while religious orientation was operationalized as Muslim religiosity (Liddle and Mujani 2007: 852–4). These simplifications make the conclusion inapplicable to more locally oriented elections in non-Muslim areas, as well as in areas where political parties are not well developed. There, social leaders use religious orientation to increase the size of their constituencies and to strengthen their legitimacy as leaders. Decentralization has created over 400 autonomous districts in Indonesia since 2001 and therefore it is very important to analyse the progress of democratization on the basis of local dynamics and realities.

Identity Politics

Identity politics describes a wide variety of actions that serve to create constituencies, including groups that experience a shared identity, whether caused by shared injustices, by marginalized ethnicity, or by threatened religious affiliation. Essential is the understanding of distinctiveness (Heyes 2007 [2002]). It indeed often requires a politician to create this type of group consciousness. Audiences then in turn view the politician as a person who represents them, and who can be their leader. In a full democracy, political parties would function as groups uniting people with similar political ideas. When political parties are not (yet) strong enough for voters to identify with, there is room for forms of identity politics that use ethnicity and religious affiliation as shared identities that can be conveniently turned into political identities by politicians looking for voters. Ethnicity is central to social and political discourse and in social competition. A group is deemed to be "ethnic" because of its "subjective symbolic or emblematic use of any aspect of culture, in order to differentiate themselves from other groups" (Eller 1999: 8). Identity politics stresses the marginalization of the group within national or global developments and is phrased as an expression of local resistance against threatening global flows (Castells 1997: 2).

In the context of Sumba, ethnicity is not a self-evident marker of certain groups. A division in traditional domains leads to island-internal ethnic distinctions on Sumba. These domains are vague geographical areas – 16 in West Sumba and 8 in East Sumba – which were autonomous "kingdoms" in the pre-colonial era. The integrating force within a domain is the hegemony of the main village and of the leading clan of that village (Needham 1987: 8). Ancestry was the unifying principle in these domains. From the earliest accounts, Sumba is described as an island with permanent internal warfare between domains (Hoskins 1993: 44). At present, the domains still function as sub-ethnic distinctions, which can be used as political identities. The administrative division in sub-districts roughly follows the lines of traditional domains. Also the election areas, created for the general elections in 2004 and 2005 resemble (groups of) traditional domains.

For politicians in Sumba who sought to use ethnicity to create a political constituency, identities related to traditional domains constituted the only possibility. In the past, identities based on traditional domains were used to divide rather than to unite. In 1998, rivalling district politicians used ethnic identity politics to invoke mass violence in West Sumba's capital as a means in their power struggle (Vel 2008a: 125–47). From 2002 through 2008 there was a political campaign for creating new districts in West Sumba, and backstage (sub-) ethnic arguments were often voiced as a reason to create Central Sumba (Vel 2007). In these cases ethnicity was turned into a political identity by politicians who delineated the boundaries that separate "us" from "them", and (re-)constructed stories about those boundaries (Tilly 2003: 32).

Candidates running for the position of district head (*bupati*) do not require a political identity that divides, but instead benefit from identification with identities that are shared by as many potential voters as possible. Religion can be such a uniting political identity (Castells 1997: 13). In Sumba Protestantism and Catholicism are the two world religions that unite people across the borders of traditional domains. What were the historical forces that brought these religions to Sumba, how were they connected to the state, and how did they shape socio-political stratification and normative pluralism on Sumba?

Traditional Leadership and Marapu Religion

In pre-colonial times, the Sumbanese polity was based on kinship and rank, and leadership confined to members of the noble houses. Sumbanese worshipped their ancestors and lived with their traditional *Marapu* beliefs. This belief system provided guidelines for social behaviour, explained the features of nature and every-day life and provided everyone with a sense of belonging by linking them to venerated ancestors in the spiritual world. It brought with it the authority of the "eternal yesterday" (Hoskins 1993: 307). The past defined the position of those living in the present. The past itself was regarded as a shared heritage, "an array of established sequences, like the stages of a ritual, which can be instantiated in various forms" (Hoskins 1993: 308).

Traditionally, there was a strong connection between leadership and religion, and a division of labour between ritual and temporal leaders. The temporal leader was someone of noble descent with excellent rhetorical skills (Hoskins 1993: 44), and wealthy enough to be able to organize large feasts. A nobleman, *maramba*, could become a political leader only when appointed by spiritual leaders of his clan who held a higher position in the traditional hierarchy. These spiritual leaders maintained contact with the ancestors, guarded the sacred houses, and held the ultimate responsibility for fertility.

Part of the traditional normative order, this social organization is made up of patrilineal clans. Each clan is connected to a founding father, who in turn became the *Marapu*, the deified ancestor. Within the patrilineal clans there is a distinction according to social rank. Nobility is hereditary, and confirmed by the possession of slaves (Forth 1981: 214). Many contemporary leaders are of noble descent, and people of slave descent will usually still be members of the lowest class in present-day social and economic terms. The middle class, who are referred to as *tau kabihu*, the commoners, are more or less still subjects of the noble rulers, who in the past could be called upon to join in warfare, and to provide labour and materials for the renovation of noble houses and the harvesting of wet rice fields (Forth 1981: 229). Marriage alliances on Sumba can be regarded as the cement between the *kabihu*, stating the rules and extent of social, economic and political solidarity (Keane 1997: 51–6). These alliances are asymmetric, which means that a long chain of clans are tied to each other though marriage bonds. In this chain the bride-givers, *yera*, have special power over their bride takers, *ngaba wini* (Keane 1997: 54).

In summary, a good traditional leader would be of noble descent, have the blessing of the ancestors to be the temporal leader, be wealthy enough to organize large feasts, and maintain a social network through kinship and a marriage affiliation that guarantees support. Traditional charisma is evidenced, moreover, in the leader's rhetorical style (Kuipers 1990: I, Vel 2008a: 184).

State Formation and Christianity

During the nineteenth century, Sumba became incorporated into the Dutch East Indies, with the colonial state creating a superstructure over traditional domains. In 1845, Resident Sluyter from Kupang offered a contract to several prominent Sumbanese leaders, who by signing acknowledged the authority of the Dutch Indian government over their area on Sumba. Those who signed were rewarded with precious gifts, gold and silver staffs of office that symbolized their appointment as *raja* (ruler) and *raja kecil* (sub-ruler) (Hoskins 1993: 50). Patrimonialism (Weber 1964: 341) on Sumba thus came up when the colonial government appointed one among the *maramba*, noble leaders, of a certain traditional domain as *raja*, its highest local leader.

The *raja* was the colonial government's local ruler, and was expected to combine his traditional leadership with compliance to the colonial state's normative order. The colonial government placed the kings of domains within a larger structure, creating a new hierarchy while their style could remain traditional. The relations of subordinates to the chief were not impersonal obligations of office, but personal loyalties to the chief.

Christianity and the state are intertwined on Sumba. The colonial government brought a central state to Sumba, while European missionaries introduced the world religion (Kapita 1976: 39). In 1866, Roman Catholic missions opened a post in West Sumba, and the first Dutch Protestant Christian missionary arrived in East Sumba in 1881. Education and health care are usually regarded as state services, but these services were also part of the missionaries' work on Sumba. The Catholic missions opened the first school, where teaching the Gospel went hand in hand with teaching the idea of "state", as Christian missions supported colonial rule by educating the local elite to be colonial administrators (Hoskins 1993: 282).

With the "Flores-Sumba Contract" of 1913 the colonial government tried to prevent competition between Catholic and Protestant missionaries, giving Flores to the Catholics and Sumba to the Protestants (van den End 1987: 160). The Protestant schools on Sumba received government subsidies and official approval. From this time onwards the traditional Sumbanese elite's children were educated in Christian schools. The connection of Christianity with schools made literacy an attribute of Christianity. Some of the elementary school's pupils were selected for further studies, and entered boarding school at the missionary house. Christianity was seen as an entrance to the wider world, and the Sumbanese just combined two religions. Hoskins (1993: 287) wrote that, in the late colonial period, Sumbanese made a distinction between their own social and geographic spheres of the ancestral village where they worshipped their spirits, whereas the wider world beyond the island and everything pertaining to government offices, hospitals and schools belonged to the realm of the foreigners and the Christian religion. The link between Christianity and education had, as an effect, that the educated elite of Sumba is now Christian.

Some elite children pursued further education outside Sumba, sponsored by their relatives. The consequence was twofold: they got detached from their villages of origin and became more "Indonesian" than Sumbanese, and second, with their migration to other Indonesian islands they created new networks or links within those networks. Since career opportunities on Sumba are few, many educated Sumbanese do not return after graduation, but still maintain links with their home villages. Their migration does not alter their position within the kinship system, nor does it affect obligations within the reciprocal economy, especially in times of weddings and funerals. For the well-educated Sumbanese who return home the state is the most important employer.

This brief overview of state formation and religious reform depicts the contours of the normative orders that remain valid on Sumba: the "traditional complex" linked with *Marapu*, the national Indonesian state with its bureaucratic rules and state law, and the religious order – either Protestant or Catholic – with its own practices, institutions, moral imperatives, values and habits. In his book "Christian Moderns" Webb Keane describes how a separation between these normative orders was part of the project of modernity in the nineteenth century, when Christian missionaries came to Sumba. "Religion, in these narratives of modernity … finds its proper place confined to the private sphere of individual belief, individuals, and the congregations they voluntarily form. For religion to maintain its proper place requires a vigilant policing of conceptual and, often, juridical boundaries" (Keane 2007: 84). In 2005, it seemed as if the boundaries of law, religion and culture were actively blurred by local politicians, who sought to derive authority from whatever was available in the total normative repertoire in Sumba.

Sumbanese Christianity

The indigenization of world religions facilitates the use of religion as a political identity. By 1987 there had been discussions in Kodi among indigenous Protestant reverends:

> Although some Church leaders insist on a narrower interpretation on the content of 'religion', many followers clearly wish to accept Christianity *along with* traditional practices. They want someone to develop an argument for syncretism that makes sense to its real judges – the ambivalent and divided villagers of the region, who do not want to abandon their ancestors yet still seek to move into a newer and wider world. (Hoskins 1993: 303)

All these discussions took place under the repressive Suharto regime that promoted adherence to one of the religions the regime recognized. After Suharto's demise, Indonesians were again free to decide on their religious adherence. Recent statistics in West Sumba do not show a decline in numbers of Christians, however. By contrast, their number is increasing. The increase in registered adherents of Protestantism is partly due to growing popularity of Evangelical churches which are relatively new to Sumba[1] (See Table 11.1).

The number of Muslims, Buddhists and Hindus is very small; most of them are immigrants from other areas in Indonesia. In coastal areas of Sumba there are Muslim communities, including Sumbanese who have become Muslims, usually as the result of intermarriage with Muslims from other islands. There are many Muslims among civil servants of the central government, who mostly live in the capital of West Sumba, Waikabubak.

By 2005, being Protestant or Catholic was a part of Sumbanese identity for many of the island's inhabitants. Due to a growing membership in the Christian Church of Sumba (Gereja Kristen Sumba, GKS) the character and content of the services and

1 Interview with U. Dingu, secretary general of the GKS, February 2004.

Table 11.1 Religious adherence in West Sumba according to government statistics in 2000 and 2002

Religion	Islam	Protestant Christian	Catholic	Hindu	Buddhist	Other, mostly Marapu	Total population
Number of adherents in 2000	8,161	154,425	90,986	327	5	96,802	350,706
In 2002	11,224	197,888	105,385	327	5	69,157	
As percentage of total population in 2000	2	44	26	0	0	28	100
In 2002	3	52	27	0	0	18	100

Source: Sumba Barat dalam Angka 2000 and 2002, Badan Pusat Statistik (2001, 2003), Kabupaten Sumba Barat, Provice NTT.

the type of ceremonies held outside church buildings have gradually changed from the prescribed forms set by European missionaries – particularly austere forms of Dutch Calvinism (Keane 2007: 61–7) – to a Sumbanese version of Christianity that includes new types of rituals and emphasizes those parts of Christianity that appeal to the traditional Sumbanese religious feeling, abolishing rules and practices that were perceived as too foreign. Such a process facilitates turning religious identity into political identity, and studies about comparable situations in Indonesia stress this argument. Lorraine Aragon described in her book "Fields of the Lord" how the Tobako in Central Sulawesi created their own version of Protestantism. They regard themselves as true and committed Christians, who modified Christianity to fit local conditions and local philosophy into Central Sulawesi Protestantism, which is not just a Christian-coated style of animism (Aragon 2000: 36).

Aragon connects the indigenization of Christianity with state intervention. At first Christianity was instrumental in the colonial process: In converting, missionaries created bridges of inter-ethnic relationships and support for colonial rule. After independence in 1945, Indonesian nationalism was formulated in terms of modernity and economic development. Modernity was strongly associated with Christianity. Under the Suharto regime, the pressure to convert to one of the officially recognized religions became even stronger. After 1965 being "without religion" could be equated with communist sympathy, a label that would end all career perspectives at the very least.

On Sumba, the history of conversion to Christianity can be compared to that of Central Sulawesi. In both regions, ethnic minorities – as seen from the national perspective – converted, and the missionaries concentrated major efforts on the fields of education and development. One difference between Sulawesi and Sumba however is that there is no Muslim majority on Sumba, which would require a distinctive identity for minorities. A Protestant identity does not make sense in Sumba as a strategy of distinguishing oneself from the inhabitants of neighbouring territories. Christianity as a uniting characteristic of modern, educated Sumbanese, who are well connected to the Indonesian state, does, however, make sense. In this way, it can be used as a means of political identity, as described below in the election campaign.

Contesting Leadership in West Sumba

The district head elections in West Sumba in June 2005 illustrate how religion can be made instrumental in politics. How are religious ideas invoked as tools of power and competition, as the basis for social stratification and as markers of identity?

In the absence of strong political parties, electoral candidates cannot rely on the party's identity or programme, but instead have to find the best way to be regarded as legitimate leaders. Sven Cederroth (2004: 104) argued, based on his research about traditional power and party politics in North Lombok, that the political system can be seen as consisting of layers of patrons and their clients in concentric but also overlapping circles – from petty officials on the hamlet level all the way up through the village, sub-district, district and provincial levels. In such a context, district politicians can either act as traditional leaders, or introduce modern political identities such as religion or ethnicity. This raises the age-old general question of political leadership. Weber (1921) distinguished three ideal types of legitimacy upon which domination may be embedded – traditional, charismatic, and legal-rational. The normative repertoire available to the politicians in West Sumba in 2005 consisted of the religious – Protestant and Catholic – the traditional, and the national Indonesian comprising state law and organization, and modern culture. Politicians could choose elements of various normative orders as arguments or debating styles and symbols to support their legitimacy as leaders, stressing one or combining all Weberian types.

During the June 2005 district head elections in West Sumba, the candidates appealed to these types of legitimacy stressing the types that they considered to be their strengths. There were three types of candidates (see Table 11.2).

- Bureaucrats who were chiefly of Sumbanese nobility and who would boast about the importance of their (fore)fathers as *raja* or *bupati* (4 of 10).
- Successful and wealthy Sumbanese living elsewhere (Jakarta, Kupang) who promised to bring prosperity – business and industrialization – to Sumba (3 of 10).
- Well-educated, relatively young politicians from a lower social status who stressed their competence in delivering public services to the population of West Sumba (3 of 10).

Table 11.2 West Sumba *pilkada* electoral tickets, June 2005

	Candidate for District Head	Candidate for Deputy	Political Party	Previous Position
1	Jubilate Pieter Pandango, SPd (son of Raja Tana Righu)	Markus Dairo Tallu SH	PPDK, PNI, PDI, PPelopor	Head Transport Department Sumba Barat – Army officer in Jakarta
2	Julianus Pote Leba, M.Si	Kornelius Kodi Mete	Golkar	Last Deputy District Head – Director General Waikabubak Hospital
3	Julius Bobo, SE, MM	Umbu Dedu Ngara	PDI-P	Businessman Jakarta- Parliament member SB, before Bappeda Kupang
4	Umbu Sappi Pateduk (=Umbu Bintang) (son of Raja Anakalang)	Imanuel Horo, SH (son of Raja Kodi)	PKPI, PKB, PPDI	Staff District Government (Assistant II) – Head of Transport Department East Sumba
5	Thimoteus Langgar, SH	Agustinus Niga Dapawole (grandson of Raja Loli)	PAN, PDS, PBB, PKBP, PPP, PD, Patriot Pancasila, PNU, PPD	Last District Head Sub-district Head

Weber's types of leadership legitimacy do not include wealth. Yet, economic capital is very important in election campaigns. Economic assets on Sumba are traditionally measured in terms of land, livestock, and labour, and this traditional economic capital is the type of wealth associated with the higher nobility, to which Umbu Bintang and Imanuel Horo belong. Yet, their economic wealth was very small in comparison to the two candidates from Jakarta who earned their fortunes in trade (Julius Bobo) and the security business (Markus Dairo Tallu). The candidates from Jakarta had strong networks outside Sumba: Markus Dairu Talu was, among other things, the chairman of the Union of Sumbanese in Jabotabek, the region surrounding Jakarta, and Julius Bobo had been a member of the National Parliament with the PDI-P (Partai Demokrasi Indonesia Perjuangan, Indonesian Democratic Party of Struggle) since 1999. What these candidates lacked was strong networks on Sumba. By contrast, the candidates who had lived on Sumba most of their lives had sufficient social capital on Sumba, but lacked necessary active connections outside the island (Vel 2008a: 216–18).

The two electoral tickets that eventually gained most votes used contrasting election strategies. Ticket 4 consisted of two sons of former *rajas*, Umbu Bintang and Imanuel Horo. Their heritage became their hallmark and they stressed their knowledge of the culture and needs of the people of West Sumba. Ticket 2, Julianus Pote Leba and Kornelius Kodi Mete presented themselves as modest and competent; their slogan was *dari rakyat untuk rakyat* (from the people for the people) to distinguish themselves from their aristocratic competitors. Both tickets used religion as a competitive tool: Umbu Bintang manipulated both Protestant and *marapu* symbols as a means of convincing the audience, whereas Pote Leba – supported by the only experienced political party Golkar – cleverly mobilized Catholic identity. The next two sections elaborate on these differences between the two tickets.

Election Rally of the Protestant Prince

On 21 June 2005, Umbu Bintang and Imanuel Horo held their largest rally in Umbu Bintang's home village of Kabunduk. The campaign programmes in West Sumba district head elections consisted of: a welcome by the organizing local committee; the performance of popular songs by a band; speeches of political party representatives; a speech by a member of the local elite; a speech by the candidate for deputy district head; and, lastly, a speech by the candidate for district head. Sometime during the events a meal of rice and meat was served, preferably at the end. These campaign meetings were open to anyone who wished to attend.

Kabunduk is a *paraingu*, a traditional village, and home to one of the main clans of the traditional domain, with about ten large traditional houses, built in two rows along a rectangular square, three hundred metres in length. In the middle there is a road. A smaller structure at the entrance of Kabunduk covers the huge tomb erected for Umbu Remu Samapati, Umbu Bintang's father and former *raja* of Anakalang and district head in West Sumba. Umbu Bintang's ancestral house can be found immediately behind the structure, where his father's youngest wife still resides. Each house in Kabunduk was assigned a special task on 21 June to host one of the groups representing a specific part of election area five. These groups began to arrive early in the morning, singing songs just like adat groups on their way to a traditional ceremony.

Although Umbu Bintang was actually the host for this event, he only arrived from his residence in the capital Waikabubak around midday, when two thirds of the visitors had already arrived. He left his car outside the gate and walked up to his house, together with his wife and children, dressed in traditional costume, including a sword. He entered the house to greet his mother, while weeping. There he awaited the arrival of his running mate, Imanuel Horo, who would come with his own following of people from Kodi.

This took a long time, and youth members of the coordinating committee persuaded Umbu Bintang to entertain the crowds. Umbu Bintang started with some popular songs, which, on Sumba, have mainly Christian lyrics (in Bahasa Indonesia). He then went on to sing, with his wife, their campaign song, encouraging the audience with the chorus of "vote for number four". In Indonesia, good election campaigns include singing performances, and the best campaigners can sing songs themselves. With Umbu Bintang's wife joining in, their performance conveyed an image of harmonious family life and love for the Lord and the people. Moreover, Christian pop songs are symbols of modernity on Sumba, associated with mass media and modern electronic equipment.

Horo came to Kabunduk in traditional style, *secara adat*, bringing a pig and presenting his following, in terms of kinship politics, as wife-givers. This gift exchange underlines the alliance between the two extended clans, reminiscent of the exchange ceremonies that take place at weddings and funerals between members of these groups. This exchange was purely symbolic, since it was only a fragment of a ceremony that should last much longer and consist of negotiations between the parties. The message conveyed was that "Kodi and Anakalang are allies, and we can count on popular support". Umbu Bintang and Imanuel Horo also wanted to stress how Sumbanese they were and how well they knew the people, especially when compared to other candidates who had lived most of their lives in Jakarta or Kupang, or who were bureaucrats who never left their offices.

After that, Imanuel Horo and his following walked over to Umbu Remu's tomb to meet Umbu Bintang. They performed a short ceremony of ritual crying, calling the name and spirit of his venerated father. Then they said a short prayer, placing a hand-woven cloth on top of the tomb as a sign of respect, and scattering flower leaves. All those in the core group in this ceremony lit a candle for Umbu Remu and put it on the inner stone of the tomb, believing that this reference to their fathers would underscore their claims to "natural" leadership. The ceremony before Umbu Remu's tomb was a compromise ritual. For those who adhere to *Marapu* beliefs it was a ritual asking the consent of the deified ancestor, especially the ceremonial weeping part and the presentation of woven cloths. For Christians it could be interpreted as paying respect to the memory of the deceased by burning a candle on the tomb. In political terms, however, it constituted the appropriation of the heritage of a powerful leader, claiming succession and the support of the deceased leader's followers.

Subsequently, Reverend Foni Papilaya was invited to open the official meeting with a prayer, in which she asked that God guide people to vote for the right candidates on 30 June, and prayed for him to bless the two candidates. She thanked the Lord for bringing so many people to Kabunduk to attend the meeting, and for bringing the two families of Umbu Bintang and Imanuel Horo together. The prayers underlined the Protestant Christian identity of the candidates. Horo additionally mentioned the fact that his father started his career as a village Evangelist in order to demonstrate his Christian education. The shared history of going to Christian schools created an alliance among the nobility of different regions in Sumba. They were classmates, and subsequently some of them became fellow members of the Christian Student Movement of Indonesia (Gerakan Mahasiswa Kristen Indonesia, GMKI), broadening the alliance network to include members from other parts of Indonesia. The GMKI functions as an "old boys' network" that helps members from outer regions to get access to power holders in Jakarta, the centre of the country. Umbu Bintang and Imanuel Horo were both students at the Gadjah Mada University in Yogyakarta, where they even shared a room and where they both were board members of (GMKI). Being a good Christian on Sumba is still associated with being modern, educated, and having access to the larger world of which Sumba is only a small part.

A teacher from Kabunduk was subsequently invited to lead the audience in singing the national anthem. The next item on the agenda was a short memorial ceremony for the national heroes, an obligatory programme item for every public meeting during the Suharto regime. This was led by Umbu Bintang, seeking to appear as an obedient servant of the nation, who, however, shortened the ceremony to only two minutes. This was followed by the usual programme of election meetings, including the speeches held by the party representative and the candidates themselves. Umbu Bintang began his speech with another song, half spoken and half sung, to stress his love for the people of West Sumba. He sang that "only thanks to the Lord can Imanuel Horo and I be candidates in this election". During his speech that followed the song, he spoke in a loud staccato style and accelerating rhythm of the shame that there were still so many hungry, unhealthy, and illiterate people in West Sumba and that that would change if he were district head. A vibrant form of ritual speech is required in all ceremonial events on Sumba (Kuipers 1990: i), and Umbu Bintang considered election campaigns to fall into that category. While no master of ritual speech, he adopted its style: fierce, competitive and masculine. He responded to his opponents' accusation that he misused the fame of his father by saying: "I am his son, his blood, so it is my right to refer to the great Umbu Remu!" The audience shouted and applauded and Umbu Bintang unsheathed his sword and danced a few steps of the traditional war dance. Then he went on to warn that if people scolded, hated or cursed him, they would surely be punished by God. He concluded with promises not to focus on fancy buildings or ways of enriching himself, and proclaimed that love and concern for the people of West Sumba was his only motivation to become district head.

In this election rally Umbu Bintang had appealed in a symbolic way to all the elements of the normative repertoire that could be able to support his legitimacy as district leader, with an emphasis on both modern and traditional religious symbols. His main competitor, however, would use religious adherence differently.

A Competent, Clean and Calculating Bureaucrat

Neither Julianus Pote Leba nor Kornelius Kode Mete belongs to Sumba's nobility. Pote Leba was the deputy district head over the previous term, and was known as a competent and modest man. He was not a flagrantly charismatic leader, and he did not organize large campaign feasts like Umbu Bintang did. Pote Leba's father was a policeman from Loli, the domain in which the capital Waikabubak is now located, and had served as a sub-district chief of police for a long time. Pote Leba studied at the Nusa Cendana University in Kupang and, after graduating, became a lecturer in public administration at that same university. Pote Leba was involved in Christian networks and Golkar in the 24 years he lived in Kupang, where one of his main organizational positions was being chairman of the Kupang branch of the Christian Student Organization GMKI (1979–1981).

After the demise of the Suharto regime in 1998, the national atmosphere in Indonesia required clearing away the old political elite and replacing them by new leaders who were "clean" in the sense of not involved in corruption, collusion or nepotism that were associated with the Suharto regime. Pote Leba fit that image and the fact that he originated from Loli was an important argument for his selection as deputy district head, alongside Thimotius Langgar from Wewewa, thus representing two areas, and serving as a public symbol of reconciliation between the two sub-ethnic groups that had been involved in an episode of mass violence in 1998 in Waikabubak (Vel 2008a: 147).

During the June 2005 elections, Thimotius Langgar's banner said "remember all my achievements in the last five years for West Sumba", but whenever I asked people on the street to give examples they could not mention much. Moreover, negative aspects, like the uncooperative attitude in the process of creating new districts were usually accorded to Langgar, while Pote Leba kept up a reputation of being a competent and clean bureaucrat. Therefore, it was not surprising that, leading to the district head elections in June 2005, Pote Leba was mentioned as one of the main candidates alongside Langgar and Umbu Bintang. His own political party PDI-P dropped former Bupati Langgar and opted for a wealthy candidate, Julius Bobo, a businessman and politician in Jakarta who was originally from Wewewa. Golkar had supported Umbu Bintang's candidacy for district head in two previous terms, and both times he lost. In 2004, Golkar decided to choose Pote Leba as its candidate, and Umbu Bintang had to assemble a coalition between smaller parties.

Pote Leba chose Kornelius Kode Mete, better known as Doctor Nelis, as his deputy. Doctor Nelis was the director of the General Hospital in West Sumba's capital of Waikabubak. He was – just like Pote Leba – relatively young and "clean". His political capital lay chiefly in his charisma and reputation as a medical doctor, and his religious and sub-ethnic identity as a Catholic from Kodi. With his choice of Doctor Nelis, Pote Leba gained the support of many Catholics in Sumba. The only other Catholic candidate was the not very well-known Markus Dairo Tallu. The number of Catholics in West Sumba had increased over the previous five years and, according to the chairman of the General Election Committee, 50 per cent of the voters in this election were Catholic. The distribution of free rice by a Catholic Foundation[2] certainly helped increase sympathy for the church among poorer people in Sumba, with a vote for a Catholic candidate an easy choice of a reciprocal gift. The electoral ticket thus became associated by the poor with health

2 Food aid distributed by Karitas in Waitabula, 300,000 kg in 2005 according to information obtained in an interview with a Chinese trader in agricultural commodities in Waikabubak, 1 September 2006.

and food, reflecting both the Catholic food aid, and Doctor Nelis' position as the hospital director. Doctor Nelis was also a good choice in the face of ethnic voting tendencies. His home area Kodi is one of the western domains of this district (see Map 11.1) that is relatively populous.

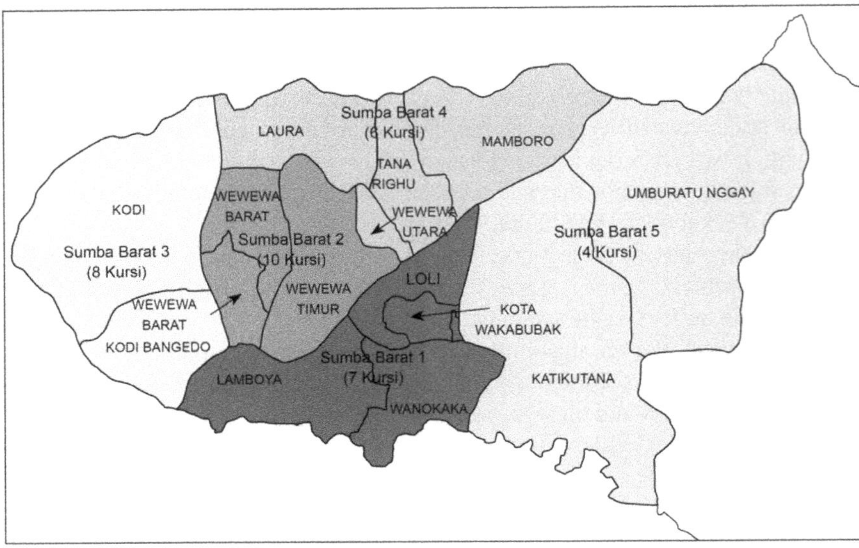

Map 11.1 Electoral districts in West Sumba during the general elections in 2004/2005

Source: Komisi Pemilihan Umum: http://www.kpu.go.id/peta/peta_dprd_kota2. php?propinsi=Nusa%20Tenggara%20Timur&prop_id=18&peta=Daerah [accessed: 26 June 2006] (Courtesy KITLV).

The Election Results

In the elections there was strong tendency to vote for candidates originating from the voter's own traditional domains. All candidates – except for one – won in their own home area, with four of the ten candidates earning more than two thirds of the votes. Yet, this type of ethnic voting would never be sufficient for an election victory in the total district, and to win votes outside one's home area candidates had to adopt other political identities.

Pote Leba and Doctor Nelis won the elections with 34 per cent of the votes and a third of their votes came from Kodi. Doctor Nelis indeed proved his ability to win votes with his charisma: not a traditional type of leadership charisma, arising from loud and angry speeches, but the charisma of a sociable, caring doctor who visits his patients. Umbu Bintang received only 17 per cent of the votes in West

Sumba, although in his "home election area" he earned 75 per cent. Pote Leba also won clearly in the capital Waikabubak (60 per cent) and the surrounding domain of Loli (46 per cent). This is an area in which many civil servants reside and, being loyal to the network of people with powerful positions in the district, they tend to vote for Golkar candidates.

Umbu Bintang used Protestantism as a very important unifying political identity. A candidate that could be regarded as the leader of Christians on Sumba should be able to gather sufficient votes to be elected. Eight of the electoral ticket's competitors were, however, Protestants, and were thus all fishing in the same pond. Being Catholic turned out to be the greatest political asset in a field of competition where only two of the ten candidates, but some 50 per cent of the electorate were Catholics.

Conclusions

Democratization in Indonesia opened up room for the inclusion of religious elements in regional politics and legislation. Decentralization and direct elections encouraged politicians to use identity politics in their struggle to be elected to the highest office in their autonomous districts. As long as political parties do not function well enough to be recognized as institutions that represent voters' interests, religion remains a resource for identity politics. The voters in the district elections assess the strength of the candidates as leaders in accordance with their social distance, which becomes clear in the sub-district breakdown of the elections results. Religious adherence is a form of social organization that bridges differences between ethnic groups and classes. Reduced social distance can also be defined as adherence to the same religious group. In 2005, the boundaries of law, religion, and culture were actively blurred by local politicians, who seek to derive authority from whatever is available to them in the total normative repertoire in Sumba.

The chapter's conclusion does not support Liddle and Mujani's (2007: 832) argument that religious orientation is insignificant in explaining voting behaviour in Indonesia. Direct district elections are by definition local affairs. Local social leaders are the prominent candidates in these elections. Their leadership is not only a matter of personal qualities but also one of their recognition as representatives of a constituency that can have an ethnic, class and religious identity. Only when political parties are trusted completely in taking over this function of representing the voters, and have a programme for which they are accountable and are supported by the media that informs the voters, can the preconditions for replacing identity politics be fulfilled. This part of the democratization process will take many years, especially in relatively isolated parts of Indonesia.

References

Aragon, L. 2000. *Fields of the Lord: Animism, Christian Minorities and State Development in Indonesia*. Honolulu: University of Hawai'i Press.

Badan Pusat Statistik 2001. *Sumba Barat dalam Angka 2000*. Waikabubak: Badan Pusat Statistik/Kabupaten Sumba Barat.

Badan Pusat Statistik 2003. *Sumba Barat dalam Angka 2002*. Waikabubak: Badan Pusat Statistik/Kabupaten Sumba Barat.

Benda-Beckmann, F. von 2002. Who's afraid of legal pluralism? *Journal of Legal Pluralism*, 47, 37–82.

Castells, M. 1997 *The Power of Identity* (Volume 2 of *The Information Age: Economy, Society and Culture*). Oxford: Blackwell.

Cederroth, S. 2004. Traditional power and party politics in North Lombok, 1965–99, in *Elections in Indonesia: The New Order and beyond*, edited by H. Antlöv and S. Cederroth. London and New York: Routledge Curzon, 111–32.

Eller, J.D. 1999. Ethnicity, culture, and "the past", in *From Culture to Ethnicity to Conflict: An Anthropological Perspective on International Ethnic Conflict*, edited by J.D. Eller. Ann Arbor: University of Michigan Press, 7–48.

End, T. van den 1987. *Gereformeerde Zending op Sumba 1859–1972*. Alphen aan de Rijn: Aska.

Forth, G.L. 1981. *Rindi – An Ethnographic Study of a Traditional Domain in Eastern Sumba*. The Hague: Martinus Nijhoff.

Hasan, N. 2007. *Islamic Militancy, Sharia and Democratic Consolidation in Post-Suharto Indonesia*, Working Paper 143. Singapore: Rajaratnam School of International Studies. Available at: http://www3.ntu.edu.sg/rsis/publications/Working Papers/WP143.pdf [accessed: 27 September 2008].

Heyes, C. 2007. Identity politics. *Stanford Encyclopedia of Philosophy*. [Online]. Available at: http://plato.stanford.edu/entries/identity-politics/#9 [accessed: 3 July 2008].

Hosen, N. 2004. Religion and the Indonesian constitution, a recent debate. *Journal of Southeast Asian Studies*, 36(3), 419–40.

Hoskins, J. 1993. *The Play of Time; Kodi Perspectives on Calendars, History and Exchange*. Berkeley: University of California Press.

Kapita, O.H. 1976. *Sumba di dalam Jangkauan Jaman*. Waingapu: Gunung Mulia.

Keane, W. 1997. *Signs of Recognition: Power and Hazards of Representation in an Indonesian Society*. Berkeley: University of California Press.

Keane, W. 2007. *Christian Moderns, Freedom and Fetish in the Mission Encounter*. Berkeley: University of California Press.

Klinken, G. van 2005. New actors, new identities: Post-Suharto ethnic violence in Indonesia, in *Violent Internal Conflicts in Asia Pacific: Histories, Political Economies and Policies*, edited by D.F. Anwar, H. Bouvier, G. Smith and R. Tol. Jakarta: KITLV/Yayasan Obor Indonesia and LIPI, 79–100.

Kuipers, J.C. 1990. *Power in Performance: The Creation of Textual Authority in Weyewa Ritual Speech*. Philadelphia: University of Pennsylvania Press.

Liddle, R.W. and Mujani, S. 2007. Leadership, party, and religion: Explaining voting behavior in Indonesia. *Comparative Political Studies*, 40(7), 832–57.

Needham, R. 1987. *Mamboru: History and Structure in a Domain of Northwestern Sumba*. Oxford: Clarendon Press.

Smith-Kipp, R. 1993. *Dissociated Identities; Ethnicity, Religion and Class in an Indonesian Society*. Ann Arbor: The University of Michigan Press.

Tilly, C. 2003. *The Politics of Collective Violence*. New York/Cambridge: Cambridge University Press.

Vel, J.A.C. 2007. Creating a New District in West Sumba, in *Renegotiating Boundaries: Local Politics in Post-Suharto Indonesia*, edited by H. Schulte Nordholt and G. van Klinken. Leiden: KITLV Press, 91–120.

Vel, J.A.C. 2008a. *Uma Politics: An Ethnography of Democratization in West Sumba, 1996–2006*. Leiden: KITLV Press.

Vel, J.A.C. 2008b. Miracle solution or imminent disaster? Jatropha biofuel production in Sumba, East Nusa Tenggara. *Inside Indonesia [Online], 91*. Available at: http://insideindonesia.org/content/view/1052/47/ [accessed: 29 September 2008].

Weber, M. 1921. Politik als Beruf, in *Gesammelte Politische Schriften*. Munich: Duncker and Humblot, 396–450. Originally a speech at Munich University, 1918, published in 1919 by Duncker and Humblodt, Munich. Available at: http://www2.pfeiffer.edu/~lridener/DSS/Weber/polvoc.html [accessed 18 May 2005].

Weber, M. 1964. *The Theory of Social and Economic Organisation. (Introduced by Talcott Parsons)*. New York: Free Press.

Chapter 12

Beyond the Law–Religion Divide: Law and Religion in West Sumatra

Franz and Keebet von Benda-Beckmann

Introduction

Discussions on the relationship between religion and law tend to oppose the view of religion and law as distinct normative orders based on different sources and legitimation. Tension and conflicts between the two are often deduced from the substantive contradictions in their demands on social organization and conduct. But such a perspective on the law–religion divide and its contestations generates a simplified and distorted interpretation of conflict and change. In this chapter we argue that, hidden behind "law and religion", lies a much more complex set of relations, which demands a much more differentiated analysis.[1]

First of all, the field of relations and interactions is too restricted. The concept of "law" in these discussions chiefly denotes exclusively state and sometimes international law, notably human rights law. Other types of rules and institutions are referred to as customs, religion, or culture. The analysis of the relationship is then limited to the ways in which state law deals with religion and the space religions or a specific religion is granted within the state legal structure. However, in many states such as Indonesia, traditional ethnic laws, called adat law, and religious laws are part of a pluralistic legal constellation. Their substantive content, political objectives, and position within the hierarchy of co-existing legal orders are often contested by the main proponents of the legal orders. In addition, neither state law, religious law nor adat law is a homogenous entity. As part of colonial and post-colonial transformations different versions of such legal systems may co-exist. Moreover, the relationship between law and religion entails more than relations between religion and non-religious bodies of law. Islam, for example, comprises much more than Islamic law because it is both a belief system involving the supernatural and a legal organization of social, economic, and political relationships in the here and now. Beneath the overarching umbrella of "religion" there may be tensions concerning the precise role of Islamic law (*shari'a* or *fiqh*). Studying the relation between law and religion thus also involves the relation between Islamic law and religion *within* Islam.

1 See also Mehdi et al. (2008) for some of the complexities in the relationship between law and religion.

Secondly, one cannot easily infer specific forms of conduct and consequences from such constellations. The plural repertoire of beliefs, moral, and legal orders form part of the contexts in which social practices take place. They form distinct sources of inspiration, provide guidance for conduct, and serve to legitimate social, economic, religious, and political organizations, interactions and decisions. They are resources upon which actors can draw to form regulations, to define relationships as legal, to seek solutions to specific problems, and to determine whether a marriage is valid and who is to be an heir. In general ideological and political discourses, they provide the basis to propose the superiority or even sovereignty of one legal order over the other. We therefore suggest distinguishing two sets of phenomena when speaking about this "relationship". On the one hand, relationship is an explicitly socially and also legally constructed scheme about how different elements, in this case the symbolic universes of law and religion relate to each other. This is an emic and empirical social construct. On the other hand, we talk about relationship as an analytical construct that juxtaposes the reproduction of adat, Islam and the state as properties of certain social processes in fields of interaction that are defined analytically or theoretically, independent of whether local people interpret it as a relation. At any given time, contestations over the relationships between the normative orders are embedded in context. They take place in different arenas, with reference to different domains of social organization, at different levels of political and administrative organization, and by different categories of actors and at different layers of social organization. Pragmatic accommodation in one context may go hand in hand with sharp contestation in another. The relationship may be negotiated in legal terms in one context, and in terms of morality in others. Moreover, all these different sets of relationships change over time. They may pass from violent confrontation to peaceful co-existence, accommodation, harmonization, hybridization and back again. We argue that we need data from all these different contexts in order to grasp the complexity of the relationships, their social significance in any given society, and for comparative purposes.

Indonesia, the state with the largest Muslim population in the world, provides interesting counterpoints to the history of Islamic law in Arab and Middle Eastern states and the contemporary relations between Islam and state, international (human rights), and traditional legal orders, which so strongly dominate current discussions over what Islam is or is said to be.[2] While roughly 80 per cent of the population is Muslim, Christianity, Buddhism and Hinduism form parts of its religious landscape as well. Indonesia's history is rich in the variety of ways major religions relate to other belief systems and legal organizations, prominently including the local ethnic legal orders commonly known as adat, a category that encompasses customs, law and morality. Within Indonesia, the Minangkabau of

2 Hefner (2000: 6). For legal pluralism in the Arab world, see Dupret et al. (1999).

West Sumatra[3] stand out because of the striking contradictions between Islam and the Minangkabau adat of matrilineal heritage that provides structure to social, economic and political organization.[4] For a long time, Minangkabau has been considered "a remarkable paradox in the sociology of Islam" (Bousquet 1938: 241), and the fact "that the antithesis of Minangkabau and Islam could lead to a synthesis that became the foundation of the Minangkabau character" (Van Ronkel 1916: 2) has intrigued foreign observers and Minangkabau people alike (Abdullah 1966: 1). Minangkabau religious leaders, adat experts, local politicians, and intellectuals have been very active in expressing their views about the relationship between Islam and adat.[5] Several authors have warned against too formalistic interpretations of the abstract contradictions between adat and Islam. They were seen to be based on Western legalistic thinking, based in the fact that "that the colonial authorities reified the distinction between adat and Islam".[6] The Minangkabau example is also interesting due to the many – well-documented – changes in the relationships between adat, Islam and state government. As we shall demonstrate with the example of the Minangkabau, understanding the transmutations of the relationships between "religion and law as contested sovereignties" calls for a differentiated and multi-contextual analysis. After providing some background information on religion and law in Indonesia, we focus on the historical changes in the relationships between law and religion. We then use the problems concerning property and inheritance in Minangkabau as a classic case to demonstrate the multi-contextual nature of the reproduction and change in these relationships. We then discuss how the relationships between adat, Islamic law and state law have been redefined in different contexts since the fall of the Suharto regime in 1998.

Religion and the Indonesian State

Legal pluralism has been a common condition in the Indonesian archipelago as the consequence of the co-existence of religious legal notions, mainly Islam and Hindu, with the various ethnic legal orders usually referred to as adat. With Dutch colonization, state law and judicial institutions complicated the legal constellation by introducing new legal orders and affecting the existing adat and religious legal orders. More recently the plural legal order has been enriched by international and transnational law. The issues of the Islamization of Indonesian law, the introduction of the *shari'a*, and the establishment of an Islamic state have

3 The term Minangkabau designates an ethnic group of about 10 million people, of which more than half live in the province of West Sumatra. It is also used for the region of West Sumatra.

4 In the realm of the supernatural, Islam has largely superseded pre-Islamic beliefs.

5 See also Kahn (1993), F. and K. von Benda-Beckmann (2007). Bowen (2003: 253ff) suggests this "irreducible pluralism" is a general Indonesian phenomenon.

6 Abdullah (1966: 23), Kato (1982), Hefner (2000: 33).

always been important topics in Indonesian politics.[7] The various governments have all had a somewhat ambiguous attitude towards religion, oscillating between embracement and containment. According to its constitution and the *Panca Sila* (Five Pillars) state ideology, a belief in "one god" is one of the five pillars of the Indonesian Republic. It does not necessarily have to be the god of the Muslims but has to be one of the five religions legally recognized. The state consciously fosters multi-religiosity but at times branches of the government have been involved in the suppression of non-Muslim religious communities. It has controlled religious social and political organizations quite strictly and banned political parties such as Masjumi that, in contrast to the two large Islamic mass movements, Nahdatul Ulama and Muhammadiah, tried to establish a more pronounced Islamic state. The government's main administrative arm for religious issues is the Department of Religious Affairs which maintains offices down to the sub-district level.

Since independence, Islamic organizations have become increasingly influential. The late 1970s and 1980s saw a general resurgence of Islam, a steep increase in the numbers of pilgrims, and in the building of new mosques and prayer houses. However, reservations against too strong an influence of Islamic forces remained and the ban on Masjumi was not lifted. The government tried to contain Islamic aspirations by establishing an Indonesia-wide Council of Islamic Authorities (MUI) with provincial and district branches in all Indonesian regions, as well as the network of Islamic Intellectuals (ICMI). The state granted some room for religious law, but only in the field of family law. In 1989 the government broadened the jurisdiction of religious state courts, allowing but not mandating that inheritance issues be decided according to Islamic law. Through Presidential Instruction No. 1 of 1991 it also issued a "Compilation of Islamic Law" (*Kompilasi Hukum Islam*) a set of guidelines for decision making by religious courts, covering marriage law, inheritance and gifts, and *wakaf* (Djakfar and Yahya 1995). This codification-like text, to some extent, clarifies and simplifies standard Islamic law, but also provides compromise formulations for instances in which state law, Islamic law and adat are not compatible. It is explicitly not meant to constitute "law" in the formal legal sense, leaving it to the judiciary and individual parties how to proceed.

During the Suharto regime, Islam came to play an increasingly important role as a standard for a critical evaluation of governmental practices, of corruption and administrative arbitrariness, and as "an ethical compass" (Hefner 2000: 17), in local as well as in national politics. In the same period, adat was increasingly marginalized as a political force, though its role in family and property matters continued to be prominent. When the era of *Reformasi* started after the fall of the Suharto regime, a process of liberalization and decentralization was set in motion. An Indonesian-wide revitalization of adat emerged in which adat became a prominent political factor. Religious parties obtained more political freedom and there was an upsurge of religious politics as well. Negotiating the relations

7 See Bourchier and Legge (1994), Ramage (1995).

between state, adat, and religion started anew.[8] But while the government allowed for additional space for religions, Salim (2006) argues that it is more appropriate to speak of an "Indonesianization of Islamic law" than of an "Islamization of Indonesian law".

Adat, Islam and State in Minangkabau History

Ever since the Minangkabau embraced Islam, they have had to accommodate a host of contradictions. Initially, this entailed contradictions between the formerly autonomous Minangkabau village republics with their adat tradition, and Islam, and later between those and the laws of the colonial and the Indonesian state. However, this has not necessarily and at all times led to corresponding legal and political struggles.[9] They have found different ways to deal with the contradictions throughout history (Abdullah 1966: 23). These range from violent civil war in the early nineteenth century to co-existence and harmonization after the colonial period and independence. After a long period of peaceful Islamization the bloody Padri War (1813–1837) emerged between adat-minded and fundamentalist Wahabist Minangkabau forces trying to establish a theocracy. When Dutch military intervention broke down all resistance and ended the war, the region was incorporated into the colony of the Dutch East Indies. In this period, the core of the "Minangkabau consensus" was formulated: "Adat is based on the *syarak* [Indonesian: *shari'a*], the *syarak* is based on adat" (Francis 1839, Abdullah 1966, F. von Benda-Beckmann 1979, Amir 2003: 118). Adat and *syarak* were seen as two equal foundations of Minangkabau morality, religion, and social and political structures. What was initially formulated as a relationship of equality, changed in the 1970s into a more hierarchical relationship. This was expressed in that "adat is based on the *syarak*; *syarak* is based on the Koran", or in the Minangkabau language "*adat basandi syarak, syarak basandi kitabullah*" summarized in the acronym ABSSBK. This period was also the beginning of a chiefly triangular relationship between Islam, adat and the state, which has also since become part of Minangkabau identity. Minangkabau speak of this unity as the "interwoven three ropes" (*tali tigo sapilin,* TTS) or "the hearth with three legs" (*tungku tigo sajarangan*, also TTS).

The symbolic universes of adat, Islam and the state each have their own main protagonists, who speak for "their" systems, based on the legitimation that their system provides them, such as state officials and government lawyers for state law, religious scholars for the *shari'a*, and adat experts for adat. Yet other actors also

8 Sakai (2002), Aspinall and Fealy (2003), F. and K. von Benda-Beckmann (2006a, b, 2007), Schulte Nordholt and van Klinken (2007).

9 As Abdullah (1966) pointed out there have always been other ideological and political conflicts taking place within and/or cross-cutting these categories, such as conflicts within religion, adat and the state.

partake in interpreting, applying, and changing concepts and rules in decision-making processes or in designing organizational structures and institutions. Islam and Islamic law are taught, preached, and applied by Islamic legal scholars; local religious leaders and villagers develop folk Islam, parts of Islamic law have been incorporated and re-regulated in state legislation, and Islamic religious courts "are constituted by the state".[10] Likewise, adat is interpreted by adat authorities, by state officials, and by religious leaders who all compete for the most authoritative version.[11]

As a consequence of these processes, elements of different orders have affected each other in various ways throughout the long history of their co-existence. Starting in pre-colonial times, Arabic words such as *hibah*, *hak*, *milik* and *wasiyat*, which are also Islamic legal concepts, were incorporated into Minangkabau Malay (and later into Indonesian), and in this way into the conceptual world of adat, and later into state law as well. Many such compounded or hybrid forms have been institutionalized. These Islamic legal institutions were mainly "adatized" and came to denote older adat categories and institutions. The *warith*, denoting the Koranic heirs, became in adat, for example, the *warih* (*waris*), the matrilineal heirs and group members. In contrast with other Islamic societies, where adat or *urf* concepts are reinterpreted as Islamic legal terms, there has been less semantic traffic in this direction in West Sumatra.[12] The one major exception has been the reinterpretation by Islamic scholars of matrilineally inherited property complexes. Realizing that the complete elimination of such property was not realistic, but trying to find a way out of the moral dilemma of choosing between adat and Islam, it was reformulated in terms of Islamic law as *waqf*, a kind of property trust.[13] As a result of these developments, the same term could be used in adat, in Islamic law, and in state law, and yet denote very different legal institutions and lay understandings. For example, in Minangkabau adat, *hibah* is a property transfer that takes effect after the donor's death and can be recalled as long as one lives. In classical Islamic law it is a complete and irrevocable donation made during the lifetime of the donor. In the regulation of *hibah* in Compilation of Islamic Law, the strict Islamic legal meaning is softened by providing some room for adat elements.[14] *Hibah* is also the concept for gifts or donations under Indonesian state law.

We find similarly hybrid judicial and administrative institutions as well. The religious courts, for instance, are established by state regulation and staffed with judges appointed by the state, and according to qualifications laid down by state law.

---

10 See Coulson (1964), for Morocco, see Rosen (1999), Turner (2006), in this volume.

11 See K. von Benda-Beckmann (1984), F. and K. von Benda-Beckmann (1985).

12 Abdullah (1966), F. von Benda-Beckmann (1979), F. and K. von Benda-Beckmann (1993, 2006a).

13 Prins (1954: 145), Anas (1968: 107), Huda (2003).

14 Sections 210, 211, 212 of the *Kompilasi Hukum Islam*, see Djakfar and Yahya (1995).

However, they are legitimated by reference both to religion and to state law, while procedural law is largely state law. In uncontested cases, in which a declaratory judgment on heirship is requested, the substantive rules applied are those of the Compilation of Islamic Law, while the reasoning in the judgments resembles the style of civil courts. Thus, depending on which of the features of the courts are examined, and in which relational context they are situated, religious courts can be seen either as exponents of "religion or religious law" or as "state courts". They appear to be "religious courts" when compared with civil courts, which apply state or adat law. But from the perspective of a village decision-making body such as a village adat council, an *ulama* issuing a *fatwa* or desiring the establishment of *kadi* courts, both religious and civil courts are just "state courts". Likewise, state civil courts are usually contrasted with village justice, which is associated with adat. However, they can theoretically also be seen as exponents of adat in contrast with Islamic law, as they apply adat in inheritance issues. In the same way, the substantive law that religious courts apply can be hailed as Islamic law, as distinct from adat law or state law, or be denigrated as adulterated government regulation, if compared with the strict interpretations of religious scholars. Similarly, but with different political and emotional undertones, hybrid institutions such as the village adat council, are considered adat institutions by some, while others see them as part of the state legal system. In the final analysis, however, they derive legitimacy from both normative systems (K. von Benda-Beckmann 1984, F. and K. von Benda-Beckmann 2007).

Most Minangkabau are "multi-legal" and take this plural constellation to be a natural state of affairs. They are quite comfortable with this sort of mix, however great a concern this may be for lawyers, judges and politicians. Yet despite these hybrid institutions, most Minangkabau also continue to see a clear distinction between adat and Islam as normative universes, underlining the distinct religious or adat elements when it seems appropriate and often postulating legal institutions in "undiluted" adat or Islamic versions to stress the predominance of either religious law or adat, as the case may be. While the different systems are thought of as distinct repertoires, they cease to be so once they are embodied in an institution, a decision, a regulation. Many negotiations and conflicts therefore deal with the question of how much of one system can be inserted into another. In early history, this mainly concerned the relation between adat and Islam. With the growing importance of state organization and its law, most of these struggles concern the question of to what degree religion and religious legal elements should be incorporated into state regulations and institutions. This plays at all levels, from the constitution to provincial regulations, district and village regulations, and in a variety of contexts. The history of the inheritance of self-acquired property illustrates the multi-contextuality of these processes.

Property and Inheritance Law in Minangkabau

Minangkabau adat distinguishes three major categories of property: self-acquired property, which originally was inherited matrilineally and after death became inherited property within the person's matrilineage; inherited lineage property, devolved on the basis of lineage-internal mechanisms of distribution and inheritance; and *ulayat*, the village commons, land and forest not permanently used for sedentary agriculture and horticulture. This "adat of matrilineal heritage", of inalienable material and immaterial lineage properties, formed the basis for the entire social organization, regulating kinship, group affiliation, access to property, and political village authority. These categories pose the most striking difference with Islam legal thinking, and urban Minangkabau traders often found it more convenient to adopt Islamic inheritance rules for their self-acquired property. Yet the hold of adat inheritance rules was difficult to break precisely because of the implications for Minangkabau adat as a whole. They remained a source of intense conflict.[15]

The matrilineal social order was mainly challenged by orthodox Islamic Minangkabau. Unable to eradicate the entire matrilineal property and inheritance complex, they singled out the inheritance of a man's self-acquired property. According to Islamic inheritance law, such property has to be inherited by Koranic heirs, with male heirs receiving twice as much as females. According to adat, such property was inherited by the matrilineal relatives, and in the case of land, especially nieces. Other dispositions were possible but only with the consent of the matrilineal relatives. In the 1930s it became acceptable that a man could dispose of his self-acquired property during his lifetime even without the consent of his matrilineal relatives. From the 1960s onwards, it became gradually accepted by the population, and supported by state courts, that a man's self-acquired property could be inherited by his children in intestacy as well.

These "classic" inheritance conflicts between a man's children and matrilineal nephews and nieces ebbed away with the growing consensus about the new inheritance rules for self-acquired property. There was, however, no consensus about the question of what this meant for the applicable inheritance law. According to many local interpretations, Islamic inheritance law, *hukum faraidh*, stipulated merely "inheritance by the children", and not according to the shares which official Islamic law prescribed. In this interpretation, this constituted a change from adat to Islamic law. Others saw the change in inheritance rules as a change within adat. To make things more complicated, a 1968 decision of the Supreme Court of Indonesia stated that self-acquired property was inherited by a man's children *according to changed adat law*. The court thus confirmed the substantive content upon which the protagonists of both sides in the political conflict had agreed, while at the same

15 On historical developments, see Abdullah (1966, 1971), F. and K. von Benda-Beckmann (1988), Kahn (1993), Kahin (1999), Huda (2003). On Islamic courts and the significance of inheritance for the adapt-Islam relationship, Lev (1972), F. and K. von Benda-Beckmann (1988, 2006a).

time authoritatively stating that this was to be seen as a change within adat, not as a change from adat law to Islamic law.

The issue was no longer a matter of which rule determined individual inheritance cases but, instead, what was to be the superior legal and legitimating universe in general. At stake was – and still is – the authority of the masters of the respective symbolic universes, of adat, religious leaders, and state officials. These struggles have taken place at different levels of organization, and have been highly contextual, depending on the arena and issue at stake. In everyday life situations, solutions have had to be found: Who has the authority to give a person into marriage, to succeed to an adat title, or to hold property? In the case of disputes, village institutions and state courts have had to make the necessary decisions; professors at Islamic and secular law faculties have had to teach the law of inheritance; and Minangkabau politicians have been concerned about social unrest. At the instigation of the provincial government, province-wide conferences of adat leaders, religious experts, politicians, judges, and academics were held in 1952 and 1968 to discuss the issue of inheritance law. The outcome was a compromise that was met with a broad consensus: Inherited property would further be inherited according to adat and matrilineal lines, but self-acquired property according to *hukum faraidh*. During our research in 1974–1975 this compromise was persistently restated in interviews with judges.

However, putting this political consensus into practice was an entirely different matter. While the Association of Judges persistently subscribed to the consensus, no judge in a civil court ever actually applied Islamic law in issues of inheritance of self-acquired property, instead applying the new adat law. Religious courts, if approached at all in inheritance cases, were generally reluctant to accept such "adat matters" (F. von Benda-Beckmann 1979, K. von Benda-Beckmann 1984).

The relationship between state, adat and Islam (law) as distinct sets of inheritance rules belonging to different legal orders has not only and not even primarily been reproduced in courts. Minangkabau men and women have long found a range of ways for navigating between the legal systems, in many instances making decisions using combinations of adat and Islamic elements without being overly concerned by possible inherent contradictions. Some individuals follow Islamic rules strictly when dividing their estates, but this is an exception. Others follow the recommendations of Islamic law when making their testaments, usually leaving all their property to their children. Such a testament would be in contradiction with and invalid in official Islamic law but accepted in the new adat law (Tanner 1969, F. von Benda-Beckmann 1979).

Religion and Law in the *Reformasi* Era

The recent political and constitutional changes have rekindled these debates once again. Since the fall of the Suharto regime in 1998 and the increased freedom of political action, relations between religion and the different laws involved have been reconstituted (see F. and K. von Benda-Beckmann 2006a, 2007). With the provincial policy of returning to neo-traditional village (*nagari*) organization as a basis for local government, alongside the general revitalization of adat, the interpretations of ABSSBK and TTS have regained importance. The inheritance consensus still is the core of ABSSBK, regularly restated for instance during our research in 2005.[16] Religious courts, which now apply Islamic law in the sense of the Compilation when approached in inheritance disputes, are still generally reluctant to accept such "adat matters". Despite all social, economic and political changes this has not changed during the past 30 years.[17] As our long-term research on the use of civil and religious courts has shown, disputants consistently turn to civil courts in inheritance disputes where they are decided on the basis of adat. In the urban religious court of the provincial capital Padang, the number of contested court cases seems to be on the rise, but the numbers are still negligibly low.[18] On the other hand, civil courts in West Sumatra have tried more than 1,200 inheritance disputes, about 22 per cent of all civil cases, since 1980. The difference between what is said and decided in different contexts, however, remains.

The inheritance issue has, however, lost much of its iconic character. The dominant place of the struggle over inheritance law has been largely replaced by the struggle between the state (agrarian and forestry institutions) and adat-based village communities for legitimate control over village commons (F. and K. von Benda-Beckmann 2006b). Generally, the contemporary discussions have evoked a wider debate and self-reflection by the Minangkabau population at large and by Minangkabau intellectuals in particular. The major issues to be resolved have remained the same: They concern the final authority in the realm of religious beliefs, law and morality; the prevailing or superior law in particular social domains; the substance of state law and the extent of including substantive adat or Islamic law within it. Some regard adat as the embodiment of past and outmoded ways of life and thought, while others see it as a dynamic order readily adapting itself to the demands of present or future requirements. Some see it as a distinct set of norms and values that exists side-by-side with but separate from Islam and the state, while others emphasize the unity of adat and Islam. Yet others point at the fact that Minangkabau identity is based on a combination of adat, Islam, and the state. Similar differences in opinion exist from the perspective of Islam. Islam in Minangkabau has strong traditionalist and modernist roots. Some consider Islamic law to be pure

16 For example in an interview in 2005 with the head of the provincial Council of Religious Authorities (MUI), and in books published by the Association of Adat Councils and other authors, see LKAAM (2002), Salmadanis and Duski Samad (2003).

17 Research on the registers of all state courts and Islamic courts in West Sumatra from 1980–2005 was carried out in collaboration with the Centre for Alternative Dispute Resolution at Andalas University. We are grateful for the support of Dr. Takdir Rahmadi, Tasman, Yuliandri, Zulheri, Mardenis and the late Narullah Dt. Perpatih nan Tuo. For the 1970s, see K. von Benda-Beckmann (1984).

18 K. von Benda-Beckmann (2009).

religion, providing standards for good Islamic social structures and behaviour, while others emphasize its compatibility with matrilineal principles. Islam can be interpreted as being fully compatible with secular, originally European notions of democracy, or, in contrast, as inevitably tied to an Islamic state (see Abdullah 1971). The relationship between the legal orders and religion can be presented as conflictive or harmonious, and as functioning in subordination or equality.

Balancing ABSSBK and TTS in the Political Arena

The significance of ABSSBK and TTS remains central to these debates. But the political field has changed in which the ideological debates have been carried out. Over time the number and kind of persons and organizations engaging in these public discourses has increased, and the arenas in which this occurred, have become more complex. In the 1970s, there were many experts in the adat of their village, but only a few were recognized as pan-Minangkabau adat experts and there were only a handful of social scientists and law teachers at Universitas Andalas interested in and knowledgeable of adat issues. The LKAAM, the Association of Minangkabau Adat Councils, was originally established by the provincial government and closely linked to the government. The present landscape is more varied. The number of Minangkabau intellectuals, university lecturers and journalists, politicians and migrants with a critical or supportive interest in adat had increased. From 1998 onwards, decentralization and the return to a neo-traditional village structure have further intensified the search for adat knowledge. New publications on adat and reprints of older books and booklets are flooding the market.[19] A series of books on adat and its history has been published for use in primary and secondary schools (Azrial 1994). The ritual formula ABSSBK is on everybody's lips. Posters displaying one Minangkabau couple in proper Islamic dress, one in adat dress, one in military attire, and one in civil service uniforms, all against the background of an adat house and a mosque symbolize the renewed public interest in the relationship between adat and religion. The text runs: "Let us make the movement back to the *surau* a success. Implement the philosophy of ABSSBK. Let us start from the *surau*." Traditionally the *surau* was a house for unmarried men, situated at the fringe of the village. Over time it was Islamized into a prayer house where young men received religious and adat instruction. The slogan itself emphasizes the central role of religion in the current political negotiations (see Figure 13.1).

The LKAAM has developed into a rather independent and very vocal adat law lobby and provides ABSSBK interpretations with a strong bias towards adat. It has published books and teaching materials, and for some time a *Buletin Seri Alam Minangkabau* in Minangkabau language, and it offers training courses in adat. But

---

19 For example Hasbi et al. (1990), Erizal (2000), LKAAM (2002), PPIM (*Pusat Pengkajian Islam dan Minangkabau*) (2003), Salmadanis and Duski Samad (2003). For further sources, see F. and K. von Benda-Beckmann (2007).

Figure 13.1 Street poster in Lubuk Sikaping

Source: Photo by F. von Benda-Beckmann, 2005.

today the LKAAM is only one organization out of many extolling the significance of ABSSBK. The major religious position is taken by the MUI. Besides, a number of religious and secular NGOs have entered the scene. The government sponsors a number of organizations in the field of adat-Islam-culture, such as the Study

Centre for Islam and Minangkabau (*Pusat Pengkajian Islam dan Minangkabau*, PPIM). Other activist groups, such as the Legal Aid Bureau (*Lembaga Bantuan Hukum*, LBH) and the Forum of Concerned West Sumatrans (*Forum Peduli Sumatera Barat*) fight by and large for the same issues as the adat lobby. But while the members of the LKAAM fully identify as champions of adat and call for adat rights and a strong role for adat leadership, other organizations fight for the recognition of adat rights without implying an extensive role for an adat leadership, of which they are extremely critical (F. and K. von Benda-Beckmann 2007). The government, moderately inclined towards adat, is an important and active player within this political arena.

While each of the actors has positioned itself in the discussion of the relationship between Islam, adat, and the state, each has done so from a different perspective. During the late Suharto period, Islam was a prominent forum for the criticism of public behaviour and corrupt state practices, while adat had been almost reduced to mere folklore in public discussions. This would, however, change radically: During the first post-*Reformasi* years, most public debate focused on the revitalization of adat structures in which religion did not play a dominant role. With the slogan "back to the prayer house", Islam returned to the fore in public debate, which emphasized the importance of Islam in the current reconfigurations. All actors are acutely aware that no less than the restructuring of relationship between the three normative orders is at stake. The question is who has the authority to define this relationship. In careful negotiations, the various actors compete for recognition of their particular defining authorities, and by doing so for potential funding by the government and donor agencies without which they would lose power. Protagonists of adat and Islam encroach more or less subtly on the traditional home terrain of each other, engaging in different strategies of universe maintenance (Berger and Luckmann 1966: 133). The LKAAM no longer positions itself as the protagonist of adat alone but also claims authority to speak for Islam, while according to a member of the LKAAM, the MUI "only" speaks for religion. The chairman of a provincial branch of the MUI, who was not very interested in adat during the Suharto era, now emphasizes that "of course, *ulama* are capable of teaching adat. After all, they are Minangkabau". Islamic Universities have started to offer courses in adat law. In adat-minded publications, such as LKAAM (2002), Islamic kinship terms and rules are translated into adat, while religious scholars redefine the adat category "adat that is truly adat" as religion (Salmadanis and Duski Samad 2003).

Law and Religion in Rule Making

Since ABSSBK and TTS are so deeply ingrained in the collective and individual sense of Minangkabau identity, and their ideological force is so strong, there are few contexts in which the maintenance of one legal order can occur without implicating others. This also became clearly evident when, in 2000, the province of West Sumatra reorganized village government and "returned" to the *nagari* as the lowest unit of local government, a move that was generally regarded as a return to adat.[20] The Village Adat Council was officially recognized as an important village institution and authorized to settle disputes in adat matters. In these processes, adat is highly visible in the public rhetoric, identity matters, and claims to village property, though its influence is more ambivalent in the formation of the new village administration. By contrast, religious organizations have always played a marginal role in village administration and were severely curtailed in the political arena. Adat has been far more prominent than Islam in the realm of village organization.

While adat has acquired greater prominence in political and administrative terms, Islam was able to gain prominence by calling for a moral revival. The "return to the *prayer house*" movement mentioned above was an answer to the discourse on a "return to the *nagari*". It stressed that Minangkabau moral values had to be defended against a corrupt bureaucratic state and a largely immoral process of cultural and economic globalization. It was an attempt to reclaim a position within public discourse that had been dominated by political issues such as land claims, but for which Islam, in contrast to adat, could not provide solutions. These moral values and concerns were in tune with a national and indeed global Islamic moral revival calling for more modesty and abstinence from worldly pleasures, which therefore provided a powerful alternative to the adat concern with its focus on village government and land rights. However, with claims that a true return to adat implied a revival of the prayer houses where the male youth traditionally acquired knowledge of Islam and adat, Islamic protagonists gave the discourse a pronounced Minangkabau flavour. While nobody envisaged a literal revival of such prayer houses, the slogan was understood as a call for more strict public moral behaviour and for the need of the youth to respect the knowledge and authority of the elderly. Gambling, narcotics, prostitution and indecent dress were considered problematic before, but their incidence was increasingly dramatized as a "societal illness". Pressure by Islamic parties forced the provincial parliament to adopt the hotly discussed Regulation 11 of 2001 on "Societal Illnesses", prohibiting women from walking on the streets at night without a male escort. This regulation had great symbolic and ideological value and was discussed intensely in the provincial parliament and the local media, but it has not been implemented. However, many urban women fear this regulation might stimulate police harassment.

The moral crusade has also been followed at the district and village levels. Many districts have made regulations demanding Islamic dress for its staff and for school children, either limited – or indeed not limited – to Fridays. Some have issued regulations that demand knowledge of the Koran as a precondition for men to marry. This has, however, not gone uncontested. One top district official, for example, did not want to issue a dress regulation, despite heavy pressure from the ranks of his staff, believing that this should be a personal choice for every woman and that the government had no business interfering. His deputy, however, made it

20 F. and K. von Benda-Beckmann 2007; Afrizal 2005; Sakai 2003.

a point to ask women in the office whether and when they would start wearing this Islamic dress. While the district leader did not agree, he did not dare discourage this either.

As a sign of their newly gained autonomy, villages have experienced a virtual legislative explosion. In addition to regulations directly related to the operation of village government, some villages also have started regulating issues traditionally covered by adat law and Islamic law. Regulation No. 6 of *nagari* Sungai Batang, for instance, threatens people who marry within their clan or outside their religion, and those who leave their religion with heavy adat sanctions such as various degrees of ostracism and, if committed by an adat leader, with withdrawal of his adat title. Some villages have banned "societal illnesses" in response to "the outside influences on adat and religion". Some require women to wear Islamic dress, but other regulations state that "women must be dressed in accordance with adat and *syarak* norms". Sanctions can be quite heavy, even reaching ten million rupiah (roughly USD 1,000; Regulation No. 3/2002 of *nagari* Taram).

Adat and Islamic principles are both used in shaping this new form of local village law. Protagonists of Islamic values have been quite successful in their "march through the institutions" of adat and state, and it is difficult to escape the recent tendency toward "Islamic correctness". Adat protagonists, however, do not leave the field to Islam and stress the unity and importance of adat values as an important part of the discourse concerning a "return to the prayer house". They join the moral crusade, presenting it as "good adat" besides being "Islamically correct". This imposition of a more orthodox and prudish Islam on public behaviour through village regulations in terms of adat can be seen as the ultimate fusion of state bureaucratic regulation, adat-state authority, and Islamic influence.

Conclusions

The illustrations from Minangkabau show that equating "law" with state law and other normative rules and institutions with customs, religion or culture, does not capture the full range of possible relationships in plural legal contexts: Adat and religion law form only part of the equation. We have also shown that simple distinctions between state law, adat law and religion are insufficient in characterizing the full range of phenomena that make up a legal system. This becomes particularly clear when looking at the varying degrees of hybridization of local state, adat and religious principles and legitimations, as for example in *hibah*, *nagari* and its authorities and religious courts. To adequately characterize such rules and institutions, several criteria are needed, including the legal order constituting the institution, the authority providing the legitimation of the institution, and the kind of procedural and substantive content of rules used.

The relationships between state, religion and adat in West Sumatra are the result of complex processes of negotiation and struggles by different actors in different arenas. While normative systems compete for dominance, this competition is fought out in the understanding that no one party can fully prevail. All discussions and new regulations depart from the asserted unity of TTS and ABSSBK. Interpretations also vary depending on which aspects of the relationship are discussed. At the political level, this is a matter of subordination, superiority or equality between the normative orders. With regard to concrete decision-making processes it concerns the clarification of the significance of the relationship in concrete cases of inheritance, donations, parental authority, or village organization.

We have argued for a *multi-contextual* analytical approach to highlight this diversity. Legitimate inheritance for instance has been negotiated in such diverse arenas as state courts, national and regional political arenas, media and publications, and through village decision making and inheritance practices, with quite different outcomes in each of the arenas. It would be misleading to infer "the relation" or the respective social and political significance of the respective orders from only one of these contexts. The political consensus is indeed very different from court decisions, and actual inheritance practice is then again largely different from what is said to be in the political arena or decided in the courts. Yet while the ABSSBK and TTS discussions have a mantra-like quality they have also been seen as preventing conflicts from erupting in which the legal orders are pitted against each other wholesale. As the provincial chairman of MUI emphasized in an interview, "Minangkabau is quiet as long as there is ABSSBK".

The examples discussed in this chapter show that, while the critiques of "Western" interpretations that have been alleged to take a legalistic view of the abstract contradictions between the normative orders (Abdullah 1966: 23, Kato 1982, Hefner 2000) may carry some truth, they are, on the whole, overly simplistic. Abstract contradictions may of course – but do not necessarily need to – emerge in social life as social conflicts, and the Minangkabau are certainly masters in defining the relation as harmonious if and when it suits them. The ideological unity should not prevent us from recognizing that social, economic, and political conflicts may be viewed as conflicts between legal orders. The examples discussed in this chapter, however, demonstrate that it is the various Minangkabau actors, and not Western or Indonesian scholars, who present the legal orders in legalistic terms, distinctly, and in conflict. While such an understanding and use of law in interaction is undoubtedly influenced by the colonial and post-colonial history, emphasizing distinctness or hybridity as a resource in social interaction constitute standard ways of mobilizing law in plural legal orders. The same persons may use hybrid legal institutions in one context, while pointing out that religion, adat and state law are completely distinct legal systems in another context. And they may argue in strictly legalistic terms in one context, while accepting workable compromises or constructing hybrid forms in another. Our analysis showed that neither insurmountable contradictions nor a peaceful co-existence are entirely dominant.

Moreover, the example of Minangkabau also shows that references to religion sometimes serve to criticize immoral behaviour within state institutions or within the realm of adat, and to call for more Islamic morality within adat or state law. But that does not necessarily imply the invocation of religious law or, by implication, the introduction of *shari'a*. Thus, the relationship between religion and law also includes the various ways in which religious authorities and other religious actors assign a place for religious law within the religious domain and for religion in other domains. As a result, the boundaries between religion and law are not always clear, but some of the perceived blurring and contradictions may be an effect of glossing over the analytical distinctions presented in this chapter. One can only identify where the boundaries are actually drawn and where mixing occurs when looking at the full range of contexts in which law and religion are used. In a more general sense, our analysis suggests that comparisons between regions, ethnic groups, or even states need to be informed by data from all major contexts, lest they miss the complexity of these relationships.

References

Abdullah, T. 1966. Adat and Islam: An examination of conflict in Minangkabau. *Indonesia*, 2, 1–24.

Abdullah, T. 1971. *Schools and Politics: The Kaum Muda Movement in West Sumatra*. Ithaca, NY: Cornell University, Modern Indonesia Project.

Afrizal 2005. *The Nagari Community, Business and the State: The Origin and the Process of Contemporary Agrarian Protest in West Sumatra, Indonesia*. PhD Thesis, Flinders University.

Amir, M.S. 2003. *Tanya-jawab Adat Minangkabau. Hubungan Mamak Rumah Dengang Sumando. Cetakan ke-2*. Jakarta: PT. Mutiara Sumber Widya.

Anas 1968. Masalah hukum waris menurut hukum adat Minangkabau, in *Menggali Hukum Tanah dan Hukum Waris Minangkabau*, edited by M. Naim. Padang: Center for Minangkabau Studies, 95–108.

Aspinall, E. and Fealy, G. (eds) 2003. *Local Power and Politics in Indonesia: Decentralisation and Democratisation*. Singapore: Institute of Southeast Asian Studies.

Azrial, Y. 1994. *Budaya Alam Minangkabau. Kurikulum muatan lokal Sumatera Barat 1994 untuk sekolah dasar Untuk kelas 3, 4, 5, 6*. Padang: Angkasa Raya.

Benda-Beckmann, F. von 1979. *Property in Social Continuity: Continuity and Change in the Maintenance of Property Relationships through Time in Minangkabau, West Sumatra*. The Hague: Martinus Nijhoff.

Benda-Beckmann, F. von and Benda-Beckmann, K. von 1985. Transformation and change in Minangkabau, in *Change and Continuity in Minangkabau. Monographs in International Studies, Southeast Asia Series Number 71*, edited by L.L. Thomas and F. von Benda-Beckmann. Athens, Ohio: Ohio University Center for International Studies, Center for Southeast Asian Studies, 235–78.

Benda-Beckmann, F. von and Benda-Beckmann, K. von 1988. Adat and religion in Minangkabau and Ambon, in *Time Past, Time Present, Time Future. Essays in Honour of Professor P.E. de Josselin de Jong*, edited by H.J.M. Claessen and D.S. Moyer. Dordrecht: Foris Publications, 195–212.

Benda-Beckmann, F. von and Benda-Beckmann, K. von 1993. Islamic law as folk law, in *Liber amicorum Mohammad Koesnoe*, edited by H. Slaats. Surabaya: Airlangga University Press, 19–37.

Benda-Beckmann, F. von and Benda-Beckmann, K. von 2006a. Changing one is changing all: Dynamics in the adat-Islam-state triangle, in *Dynamics of Plural Legal Orders. Special Issue of the Journal of Legal Pluralism 53/54*, edited by. F. von Benda-Beckmann and K. von Benda-Beckmann. Berlin: Lit-Verlag, 239–70.

Benda-Beckmann, F. von and Benda-Beckmann, K. von 2006b. How communal is communal and whose communal is it? Lessons from Minangkabau, in *The Changing Properties of Property*, edited by F. von Benda-Beckmann, K. von Benda-Beckmann and M.G. Wiber. Oxford and New York: Berghahn Books, 194–217.

Benda-Beckmann, F. von and Benda-Beckmann, K. von 2007. Ambivalent identities: Decentralisation and Minangkabau political communities, in *Renegotiating Boundaries. Local Politics in Post Suharto Indonesia*, edited by H. Schulte Nordholt and G. van Klinken. Leiden: KITLV Press, 417–42.

Benda-Beckmann, K. von 1984. *The Broken Stairways to Consensus: Village Justice and State Courts in Minangkabau*. Dordrecht, Leiden, Cinnaminson: Foris Publications, KITLV Press.

Benda-Beckmann, K. von 2009. Balancing Islam, adat and the state: Comparing Islamic and civil courts in Indonesia, in *The Power of Law in a Transnational World: Anthropological Enquiries*, edited by F. von Benda-Beckmann, K. von Benda-Beckmann and A. Griffiths, Oxford and New York: Berghahn Books, 216–35.

Berger, P.L. and Luckmann, T. 1966. *The Social Construction of Reality*. Harmondsworth: Penguin Books.

Bourchier, D. and Legge, J. (eds) 1994. *Democracy in Indonesia: 1950s and 1990s. Monash Papers on Southeast Asia, vol. 31*. Clayton: Centre of Southeast Asian Studies, Monash University.

Bousquet, G.H. 1938. Introduction à l'étude de l'Islam Indonésien. *Revue des Etudes Islamiques*, II–III, 135–259.

Bowen, J.R. 2003. *Islam, Law and Equality in Indonesia: An Anthropology of Public Reasoning*. Cambridge: Cambridge University Press.

Coulson, N.J. 1964. *A History of Islamic Law*. Edinburgh: Edinburgh University Press.

Djakfar, H.I. and Yahya, T. 1995. *Kompilasi Hukum Kewarisan Islam*. Jakarta: Pustaka Jaya.

Dupret, B., Berger, M. and al-Zwaini, L. 1999. *Legal Pluralism in the Arab World*. The Hague, London, Boston: Kluwer Law International.

Erizal 2000. Adat basandi syarak, syarak basandi kitabullah, in *Minangkabau Dalam Perubahan*, edited by A. Chandra, A.R. Rizal, Erizal and Ronidin. Padang: Yasmin Akbar, 106–11.

Francis, E.A. 1839. Korte beschrijving van het Nederlandsch grondgebied ter Westkust van Sumatra. *Tijdschrift Nederlandsch Indië*, 2, 28–45, 90–111, 203–20.

Hasbi, M., Naim, M. and Damciwar (eds) 1990. *Nagari, Desa dan Pembangunan Pedesaan di Sumatera Barat*. Padang: Yayasan Genta Budaya.

Hefner, R.W. 2000. *Civil Islam: Muslims and Democratization in Indonesia*. Princeton, NJ: Princeton University Press.

Huda, Y. 2003. *Islamic Law versus Adat Debates about Inheritance Law and the Rise of Capitalism in Minangkabau*. PhD Thesis, University of Leiden.

Kahin, A. 1999. *Rebellion to Integration. West Sumatra and the Indonesian Polity 1926–1998*. Amsterdam: Amsterdam University Press.

Kahn, J.S. 1993. *Constituting the Minangkabau: Peasants, Culture, and Modernity in Colonial Indonesia*. Providence, Oxford: Berg.

Kato, T. 1982. *Matriliny and Migration. Evolving Minangkabau Traditions in Indonesia*. Ithaca, London: Cornell University Press.

Lev, D.S. 1972. *Islamic Courts in Indonesia: A Study in the Political Bases on Legal Institutions*. Berkeley, Los Angeles: University of California Press.

LKAAM 2002. *Adat Basandi Syarak, Syarak Basandi Kitabullah. Pedoman Hidup Banagari*. Padang: Sako Batuah.

Mehdi, R., Petersen, H., Reenberg Sand, E. and Woodman, G.R. (eds) 2008. *Law and Religion in Multicultural Societies*. Copenhagen: DJØF Publishing.

PPIM 2003. *Reaktualisasi Adat Basandi Syarak di Minangkabau*. Padang: Pusat Pengkajian Islam dan Minangkabau (PPIM) Sumatera Barat.

Prins, J. 1954. *Adat en Islamietische Plichtenleer in Indonesië*. 's-Gravenhage, Bandung: N.V. Uitgeverij W. van Hoeve.

Ramage, D.E. 1995. *Politics in Indonesia: Democracy, Islam and the Ideology of Tolerance*. London, New York: Routledge.

Rosen, L. 1999. Legal pluralism and cultural unity in Morocco, in *Legal Pluralism in the Arab World*, edited by B. Dupret, M. Berger and L. al-Zwaini. The Hague, London, Boston: Kluwer Law International, 89–95.

Sakai, M. 2002. *Beyond Jakarta: Regional Autonomy and Local Society in Indonesia*. Adelaide: Crawford House Publishing.

Sakai, M. 2003. The privatisation of Padang Cement: Regional identity and economic hegemony in the new era of decentralisation, in *Local Power and Politics in Indonesia: Decentralisation and Democratisation*, edited by E. Aspinall and G. Fealy. Singapore: Institute of Southeast Asian Studies, 148–63.

Salim, A. 2006. *Islamizing Indonesian Laws? Legal and Political Dissonance in Indonesian Shari'a, 1945–2005*. PhD Thesis, Faculty of Law, University of Melbourne, Australia.

Salmadanis, H. and Duski Samad, H. 2003. *Adat Basandi Syarak: Nilai dan Aplikasinya Menuju Kembali ke Nagari dan Surau*. Jakarta: Kartika Insan Lestari Press.

Schulte Nordholt, H.G. and Klinken, G. van (eds) 2007. *Renegotiating Boundaries. Local Politics in Post Suharto Indonesia*. Leiden: KITLV Press.

Tanner, N. 1969. Disputing and dispute settlement in Minangkabau. *Indonesia*, 8, 21–67.

Turner, B. 2006. Competing global players in rural Morocco: Upgrading legal arenas, in *Dynamics of Plural Legal Orders. Special Issue of the Journal of Legal Pluralism 53/54*, edited by F. von Benda-Beckmann and K. von Benda-Beckmann, Berlin: Lit-Verlag, 101–39.

Van Ronkel, P.S. 1916. *Rapport Betreffende de Godsdienstige Verschijnselen ter Sumatra's Westkust*. Batavia.

Chapter 13
Negotiating Custody Rights in Islamic Family Law

Nahda Shehada

Introduction

The following examines the application of Islamic family law with regard to custody and custody rights in the Gaza city *shari'a* courts.[1] Four objectives are pursued in the paper. First, it identifies areas of gender asymmetry in the legal code, which distinguishes female-oriented physical care of the ward (*hadana*) from male-oriented guardianship (*wilaya*). Second, while examining the strategies adopted by men and women in claiming (or refraining from claiming) custody rights, the paper identifies areas of tension between the textually prescribed custody rights and their highly differentiated social construction. Third, in fulfilling these objectives, it demonstrates the ways in which judges deal with various aspects of custody, and how, in the process, a knowledge of social norms overshadows the text; it will argue that today's judges are still loyal to the heritage of Islamic jurisprudence, which asserts the concepts of fairness, consideration of the context, and protection of the weak. Finally, the conduct of judges is elaborated with reference to the notion of *ijtihad* (independent reasoning) in the contemporary application of Islamic family law. An illustrative case is presented to argue these points.

Theoretical Underpinning

The paper draws on the theoretical insights of Moore (1978, 2000, and 2005) who has been acknowledged for changing the paradigm of law and society in her seminal work, *Law as Process* (1978). In her book, Moore examines the duality of order and change in the social working of law. Order (law) always exists, but it

---

1 This chapter was written prior to the 2008–2009 Israel–Gaza conflict. It will not touch upon changes that took place in the Palestinian society since the withdrawal of Israeli troops from Gaza (September 2005), nor does this chapter analyze the impact of the Hamas victory (January 2006) on the operation of *shari'a* courts. This does not underrate the importance of the ongoing process of spatial and social fragmentation within Palestinian society since the eruption of the second intifada (2000).

never fully prevails. It leaves gaps of indeterminacy, which make adjustment, that is, change, necessary. The interplay between order and change provides people with sufficient space to adjust the law to meet a variety of objectives.

Custody, the focus of this study, is subject not only to the order of law, but also to the particular matrix of social relations within which individuals operate. In this context, it is important to emphasize the fact that unlike legislation, which purports clarity and universality, social relations are full of ambiguities, inconsistencies, and discontinuities (Moore 2000). The temporality of social relations is essential, which entails that indeterminacy exists as a pervasive quality of social and cultural order. Thus, people's behaviour might be interpreted in two ways. On the one hand, they try their best to control their lives by furthering the rule of order and working to fix and crystallize social reality. Such attempts at "social regularizations" would ultimately produce what Moore calls "conscious models", which are meant to organize and systematize people's "customs and symbols and rituals and categories and seek to make them durable" (Moore 2000: 50). This fixed model has its own merits; it allows people to live in relative stability and predictability, thus enabling them to plan their lives and interact with others on the basis of reasonable expectations of behaviour. However, when the "conscious model" becomes constraining, people tend to search for gaps in the model to counter its curtailments. They may even generate such gaps to accommodate new circumstances that have not been foreseen by the model, and thus engage in "processes of adjustment". The ambiguous area between the previous order and the new adjustment is the area in which indeterminacies occur. Moreover, Moore's framework does not regard the determinate and indeterminate as fixed states, but rather as ever-changing processes. What is fixed is only the continuous renewal. If "situational adjustment" is adopted, repeated, and becomes a pattern in people's lives, then it is likely to be part of processes of regularization; this implies that each process "contains within itself the possibility of becoming its schematic opposite" (Moore 2000: 51).

In the *shari'a* court, litigants often search for such gaps of indeterminacy, ambiguity, or uncertainty in the interplay of codified law, social customs, and the multi-referential framework of judges, in order to find space to express and materialize their needs and interests.[2] In the course of their attempts, litigants often manoeuvre and manipulate these structures and sometimes succeed in turning them to their benefit.

2 The first attempt to codify the *shari'a* in Islamic history, as Botiveau (1997) points out, took place as early as 1534. Three centuries later, the Ottomans introduced commercial and civil laws in a process known as Tanzimat through the adoption of codification based on the European model. Later, the *majalla* appeared (1869–1876) as a compilation of Hanafi civil law regulations (Welchman 2000). At the beginning of the twentieth century, ten years after the restoration of the 1908 constitution, the Ottomans introduced the first personal status code of its kind, known as "The Ottoman Law for Family Rights", for the application in the *shari'a* courts.

Moore also stresses the importance of investigating the context within which the law operates and thus within which familial disputes are resolved. The source of the law used in dispute settlement does not matter, analytically, as much as the context within which the process of "amalgamation" takes place.

In the particular context of Gaza, judges and litigants operate in "multiplex relationships". These relationships "endure through the lives of individuals and even generations" (Gluckman 1955: 20–21). Each relationship is part of a complex network of multiple bonds. The implications of any dispute between spouses reach far beyond their "private" life in the sense that the social relations between their respective families are strongly involved. What makes the picture more complicated is the fact that these familial relationships (between the spouses' families) are also part of the larger social setting of Gaza, in which the boundaries between kinship, politics, and economy are often blurred. The effect of any disruption in one aspect of these multiplex relationships causes equivalent or greater disruption throughout a series of other relationships. Therefore, it is often observed that the judges not only investigate the particular dispute beforehand, but also expand their investigations to include other ties that embrace many interests, and which may have further implications in the future.

Furthermore, within the context of Islamic family law, the duality of customary practice and codified law raises the question of how we should define law; or indeed what law is. Moore's concept of a "semi-autonomous" social field, which deconstructs the single legal field into several arenas, was a revelation for sociologists interested in law (see Chanock 2000: xi). Moore points out that we should not apply the term *law* only to those binding rules enforced by governments or states. For sociologists, law is better seen as a social phenomenon that indicates "every form of rule pertaining to an organized group in any society" (Moore 2000: 18). In her view, any form of rule that entails authority, an intention of universal application, obligation, and sanction should be deemed to be *law* (see also Pospisil 1971). The dichotomy between codified law and "other" laws does not in fact reflect social reality. This applies to both industrial and less-developed societies. In the former, as Moore observes, although a presumed "rational" state law is applied, it is smoothly sidelined on some occasions. Thus, in both settings, formal laws can work only partially; they have never controlled (and perhaps never will be able to control) every social activity.

In Palestine, customary practice, as Welchman (2000: 6) contends, "constitutes a stronger controlling force than the [family] 'law'". Customary practices are customs defined by anthropologists as describing "patterns of behavior of a particular group" (Gluckman 1955: 236), or simply put, the primary forms of maintaining social harmony. They manifest particular ethical values of certain groups, but are nonetheless often based on hierarchical distribution of power and resources. Rights and obligations in the context of applied Islamic family law thus become subject to both. This is evident when considering the historical development of Islamic family law, which shows that it has not been entirely imposed from above, but has rather arisen from below, from communities that practised rights and obligations, thus leading to their recognition (see Hallaq 1984, 1996, Gerber 1994, 1999, Esposito 1982).

When applying Islamic family law, judges not only use customary codes but also other "Islamically informed legal concepts". Goals such as the public interest (*maslaha*), equity (*istihsan*), protecting vulnerable members of society, and similar matters serve to ensure that the litigants receive what they identify as "justice". Unlike the codified law, these are unwritten codes and require the discretion of the *qadi* to be realized. Sometimes, in its application, codified law may come into conflict with the judges' objective of providing "justice". When such a paradox arises, the judge works it out by employing the "legal concepts". Unlike law, which is supposed to be clear, particular, and decisive, "legal concepts" are flexible, permeable, unspecific, unwritten, and used by the judges to manipulate the code and surmount situations in which paradoxes between the written code and social reality are inevitable (see Gluckman 1955). Hence, the judges' flexibility is generated from this multiplicity of references, or combinations of rule-binding law and imprecise principles, which in fact provide the grounds for the application to be flexible.

The Legal Text

Having introduced the theoretical framework of this study, let us now move to the legal text to review its gendered nature. The *shari'a* courts in the Gaza Strip rely on two legal references for the application of family law: the Law of Family Rights (LFR) of 1954 and the Book of Personal Status Rulings According to the School of Abu Hanifa compiled by Qadri Pasha (BPSR) of 1875. The LFR provides fewer details than the BPSR on how judges should treat custody cases. This makes judges more reliant on the BPSR for their rulings. In organizing custody rights, the BPSR reflects a particular world-view regarding the status of the person: Gender, age, lineage, religion and morality are all important, but gender is the fundamental axis along which custody rights and responsibilities are distributed. The BPSR divides custody rights into *wilaya* (guardianship, authority, decision making and maintenance), which is exclusively the domain of the father or male agnates, and *hadana* (care, feeding, clothing and bodily hygiene), which is assigned to mothers or female relatives (see Welchman 1999, Layish 1975). This hierarchical division of custody into different domains is consistent with the gendered philosophy of law, which identifies fathers as the final decision makers while mothers may or may not be viewed as care providers.

Thus, the concepts of *wilaya* and *hadana* cannot be conveyed accurately using the blanket term "custody". The most salient feature of *hadana* is that it does not entail major decision making regarding the child. Its Arabic root *hadana* means to hold in one's arms, to embrace and to place on the lap. The *Lisan al-'Arab* gives a broader definition of *hadana*: "to nurse, to bring up or to raise a child" (quoted in Zahraa and Malek 1998: 156). According to Samara (1987: 368), *hadana* means "taking physical care of the child who is still unable to do so by itself. The one who has the right to do this is the *hadin* (the carer)". In contrast, *wilaya* refers to notions of authority and decision making. It is divided into two aspects: guardianship of a person and guardianship of property (*wilaya 'ala al-nafs wa wilaya 'ala al-mal*). The guardian (*wali*) has the right to exercise authority over both the person and the property of the ward.

The division of custody into *hadana* and *wilaya* is distinctly gendered. While mothers cannot transgress this gender boundary, men may cross the limits established by the law, as we shall see later in this section. The BPSR devotes one full chapter of 14 articles to custody issues while the LFR has only one such article. Article 118 of the LFR specifies one matter of importance: Permission is given to the *qadi* to allow mothers to extend the period of their *hadana* over boys until they reach the age of nine and over girls until they reach the age of eleven, if "the *qadi* believes that [the child's] interests will be served by that". In this way, the LFR stretches the time limit of mothers' *hadana* by two years beyond the period previously stipulated by article 391 of the BPSR.

Litigating Custody

The above review was made not only for its relevance to the sections below, but also to contrast the ideological construction of law with its highly differentiated applications. Let us now turn to the court to see how the law is applied in concrete situations, how rights are claimed and negotiated. How does the social context within which litigants file claims influence the process of litigation and ruling? The following ethnographic material was collected during 14 months of fieldwork in 2001–2003 and is grounded in the observation of the legal and social universe of *shari'a* courts.[3]

---

3 I conducted this research between 2001 and 2003 in the Gaza Strip, one of the two sections that make up the Palestinian territories occupied by Israeli military forces in 1967. The occupation has made travel both extremely difficult and hazardous, especially due to multiple checkpoints and frequent Israeli raids on Palestinian towns and cities. Initially, my intension was to explore the strategies developed by the Palestinian women's movement to achieve family law reform. But Israeli-imposed restrictions on movements hindered this undertaking. I decided to make only a few visits to the *shari'a* courts to explore the possibilities to save my research. The first visits fascinated me to such an extent that I could sit for hours just listening to the daily encounters between the judges and litigants. Gradually, I grasped the necessity of understanding family law dynamics before considering reform. I obtained permission from the chief judge to carry out my research in the court and started attending the hearings regularly. To try and blend in, I began wearing a headscarf and sat in the section reserved for the litigants' family and friends. The change in the research focus was a blessing, for it was only then that I understood the difference between the making of law from above and the dynamics of its remaking from below. I was struck by the discrepancy between the dominant public discourse on Islamic family law and its practical, less ideologically

In litigation over custody, the legal text operates in a social context in which various complex webs of relations determine the outcome of the case. As in all family disputes, custody cases do not reach the court unless all other avenues for resolving the conflict have failed, indicating the degree of disagreement and bitterness between the spouses and their respective networks. As has been noted in a variety of studies (legal and anthropological), certain factors discourage individuals from going to court: Financial cost, a lack of information or time, and the shame attached to revealing one's own private life to public institutions are only some of the factors that account for such patterns. In matters related to custody, the socio-economic circumstances constitute crucial elements in deciding the fate of the children since custody involves not only physical care (by the mother's side of the family), but also financial responsibility (on the father's side of the family). Some fathers (or agnates) default on the children's *nafaqa* because of their (alleged or actual) financial difficulties. Instead, they offer to take the children to be raised in their homes, which they believe to be the more economically efficient option. As one claimant said: "My children will not cost me more than what I currently spend; they will eat from my dish and sleep on my mattress."

The picture is further complicated when a *hadana* case concerns widows; they become subject to pressure emanating from different sides. If widows aspire to keep their children with them, they have to maintain a positive relationship with their in-laws, for the law alone does not guarantee them *hadana*. Various court cases indicate that some in-laws file suit against mothers just because of their embittered relations. If the mothers are young, with a few children, their own families also exert pressure on them to hand over the children to their in-laws, since children would curtail the mother's prospects of remarriage. Given their economic dependency on their families, widowed women show little resistance. The rationale behind this

charged application. The encounters with the judges, lawyers and female litigants, as well as the process of continuous negotiation and bargaining inside the courtroom, led me to re-examine my biases and assumptions. After a few weeks, it became obvious to me that the social construction of law differs significantly from the law as published in books. I was particularly struck by the flexibility of the judges; they play a significant role in protecting women from abuse by their male relatives. Judges show sympathy and consideration; they do not hesitate to reprimand men for treating their wives badly, citing Quranic verses that call for women to be treated with respect and compassion. After deciding to continue to explore the application of Islamic family law in its entirety, I combined a partially open-ended ethnographic approach with semi-structured interviews with judges, lawyers, litigants and court personnel. Litigants' life-histories and those of relevant other actors were generated in order to gain more insight into the backgrounds and positions of those concerned. In particular, while processing the cases, I constructed some individual life-histories, recorded ideological positions, investigated occupational or economic circumstances, composed the dispute history, and gathered information on norms relating to specific actions. The qualitative data were combined with an analysis of the text of family law and its various interpretations. This chapter presents only parts of the data and analysis generated in the course of the research trip. The full research is published in Shehada 2005.

behaviour is that sooner or later the mother will be legally or "socially" forced to give up her children (see also Moors 1995). Moreover, keeping the children with the mother would, in most cases, mean additional expense for her family. And due to the conformity between the agnatic responsibility set by Islamic family law and people's perceptions regarding the distribution of rights and duties between agnates and the mothers' relatives, her family would be reluctant to cover the expenses of a child belonging to "another" family.

Unlike the formulation of the code, in which gender is the most informative characteristic, the actions of judges are based on principles related to serving the best interests of the child, given the socio-economic context in which litigants operate. Sometimes they conclude the case at the expense of fathers' legal rights, sometimes at the expense of mothers' legal rights, but in all cases, the eyes of the magistrate are focused on providing the child with the "particular justice" that s/he deserves.

The following case illustrates how the deputy *qadi al-qudah* had to intervene personally when a divorced woman was faced with two difficult choices: to give up her children or to renounce their maintenance rights.[4] The *qadi al-qudah*'s advice to her, which was situationally embedded and socially informed, helped her to keep both, the children and their maintenance. Although she had to compromise over parts of their financial rights, the overall result was in her favour.

Adala, a 35-year-old primary school teacher, had recently been divorced from Ziyad when I met her. He had left her with ten children, the eldest being a 15-year-old girl and the youngest a three-year-old boy. Ziyad married another woman who also worked as a school teacher. Adala teaches at an UNRWA[5] school, which pays a higher salary than government schools. After the divorce, she filed a *nafaqa* suit for her children and won it. Ziyad had to pay JD 25 (Jordanian dinars) for each child, the total amounting to more than 60 per cent of his salary. The court had the authority to deduct the *nafaqa* directly, since he was a government employee. After a few months, Ziyad tried to escape this financial burden by filing a case for custody over the two eldest girls. His aim was to put pressure on Adala to stop claiming the *nafaqa*. Although Samahir and Ilham were aged 15 years and 14 years, which meant they could legally be placed in their father's custody, Adala was worried that her daughters would become servants in a household where the wife was not their mother. Adala did not want to give up her daughters, nor did she accept the father's dependence on her to finance her children. In order to keep the children as well as receive the *nafaqa*, she went through many difficulties.

First, she had to prove that the father was ineligible to be a custodian. She hired Khalid al-Tayyib, who is reputed to be one of the best lawyers in Gaza, who acted on behalf of the eldest daughters and chose a strategy based on an incident in which the father had beaten his daughter in the street and torn off her headscarf. Khalid al-Tayyib brought witnesses to prove the veracity of the incident. He told the court:

---

4 *Qadi al-qudah* could be translated as "chief judge".

5 United Nation Relief and Work Agency.

> The father is not eligible to be a custodian because he has beaten his daughter twice in the street. The most disgraceful act was that he took off her headscarf and uncovered his daughter's hair. Samahir [the daughter] is a mature Muslim woman and it is forbidden for her hair to be seen in public [*'awra*]. That was not the act of a protective father. Men have to provide the female relatives who are in their custody with the protection that Allah has asked us to afford them. Failing to do so means that the father is not eligible to be a protector and should therefore not be allowed to get his daughter.

Ziyad's lawyer interpreted the incident differently. He told the court:

> My client's daughter is 15 years old now and she has reached the age at which the custody of men is needed. I agree with my colleague that Ziyad had beaten his daughter in public twice but he did not exceed the limits of disciplining children. The beating did not cause anguish. This is part of his role as a father. He wants to continue his duty of supervising his daughters, and to provide them with the best Islamic education. If her hair became visible during the quarrel, that happened accidentally, of course. Therefore, I request the court to implement the law in this regard and allow my client to get his daughters back.

The case was heard by *qadi* al-Karmi. After hearing testimony over several sessions, al-Karmi made up his mind:

> In view of article 386 of the Personal Status Law, the father is not eligible for custody over his daughter Samahir.[6] This decision may be submitted to the Court of Appeal. Custody is something that cannot be divided. Therefore, the father who is ineligible for custodianship over Samahir is also ineligible for custodianship over her sister for the same reason.

The matter did not end there because the father appealed to the higher court. The Court of Appeal did not accept *qadi* al-Karmi's judgment and sent the case to *qadi* Muhammad al-Ansari, who ordered Adala to hand over Samahir and Ilham to their father:

> The daughters are of the age to be placed in men's custody … in accordance with articles 16, 18, 38, 39, 46, 48, 81, and 83 of the Code of Islamic Jurisprudence

6 Article 386 (of the Book of Personal Status Rulings According to the School of Abu Hanifa compiled by Qadri Pasha of 1875) states that if there is no legitimate guardian, or if the guardian is insane, dissolute, or unsafe, the child should not be transferred to him. The article also stipulates that, in such cases, girls should be transferred to their (*muhram*) male kin; that is grandfathers, uncles in the mother's line, and so on. *Qadi* al-Karmi, however, did not pronounce his ruling in accordance with this article. He settled the case in a way that would serve the interests of the girls and their mother.

and article 391 of the Family Law, we have decided to order the mother Adala to deliver Samahir and Ilham back to their father. We took into consideration the following facts:

- The father's right of custody should not be jeopardized by the fact that he did not file a legal case earlier.
- The witnesses have testified that the father is an ordinary, reliable and protective Muslim. Therefore, he is eligible to take his daughters under his supervision.
- The testimony concerning Ziyad's beating of his daughter seems to have been magnified by some witnesses.
- The most important thing is that his daughters have become mature (*baligh*) and need the guardianship of men. Therefore, we give the father the right to take them back and we oblige the mother to deliver them to their father so that they can be taken care of as stipulated by the *shar'ia.*

Khalid al-Tayyib, the daughters' lawyer, did not accept the new judgment. He had to devise another strategy to allow the girls to stay with their mother. He exploited all the legally available routes. One semi-formal option was an intervention by the deputy *qadi al-qudah,* so the lawyer arranged a meeting with him for Adala. She and six of her children went to the deputy *qadi al-qudah*'s office accompanied by Khalid al-Tayyib.[7] The lawyer explained the case to the deputy *qadi al-qudah* and made it clear that Ziyad was not seeking custody because of his willingness to care for his daughters; rather, his action was intended to put pressure on the mother to forego her demand for *nafaqa*. The deputy *qadi al-qudah* sympathized with the mother and gave her the following advice:

> I will order the court to reassess the case despite the decision of the Court of Appeal. The case will be heard by al-Karmi because, obviously, he is very familiar with it and his initial judgment was more in line with the *shari'a* than the second one. You have to give your former husband the impression that you are willing to give up your children. When the hearing takes place, let your daughters ask him to take them all. On our part, we will put pressure on him to take all the children. He has remarried and his wife is unlikely to accept your 'army', fearing they would ruin her house and life, especially your youngest 'monsters'. They are not hers. The best thing we can do is to send them to her and give her an unpleasant surprise. She has to get mad. This depends on your children's behavior. Once they are there, they should be noisy, break plates, play football indoors, and switch the TV on and off all the time. In sum, they have to drive the wife crazy. Your children will return to you the next day.

7 There is an important difference between the conduct of the deputy *qadi al-qudah* and other PA officials: despite his ministerial rank in the PA hierarchy, the deputy *qadi al-qudah* office is known to be easy to approach.

On the day of the hearing, the father and daughters were present in court. The girls stood in front of *qadi* al-Karmi and played the role assigned to them by the deputy *qadi al-qudah*:

> We do not want to leave our brothers and sisters. Our father should not choose whom to take and whom to leave. You should help us to continue living together. We would love to go to our father's place but he should take us all. We will not go alone, either he takes us all or leaves us all.

Qadi al-Karmi turned to the father and told him: "Now you have an excellent opportunity to take all your children to live with you. Your ex-wife does not object to that and the children want to live with you, so what is your decision?" The father had no option but to tell the *qadi*: "Yes, of course, they are my children and I will take them all." Adala sent all her children to their father's house the same day. There, they followed the instructions of the deputy *qadi al-qudah*. Within an hour of their arrival, they were returned to their mother's house.

The deputy *qadi al-qudah* also informed Adala that it was unfair to deduct 60 per cent of Ziyad's salary. She had to compromise in order to keep her children with her. She decided that it would be enough for her to receive JD 100 instead of JD 250. That was not the best deal, but she has to accept it as part of the comprehensive bargain.

Synthesis

The law operates on the supposition that both agnatic and maternal kin act in good faith with equal degrees of responsibility and decency. Yet, when examining its application, we find that it is more dependent upon people's circumstances and motives than of any intentions. In practice, the agnates generally try to use their legal precedence to further their personal interests. While claiming their rights to guardianship, what is significant in the agnates' behaviour is their attempt to manipulate the law, both by keeping the rights assigned to them and by evading the duties attached to these rights. In particular, family law ensures the custody right of agnates and links it with their financial duties. However, in practice, agnates always adjust this provision to meet their objectives, which often do not match the intentions of the law. It is in this ambivalent area between fixity (of the text) and indeterminacy (of people's behaviour) that men manipulate their fixed rights. Agnates misuse the advantages assigned to them through the law's gendered distribution of rights and instrumentalize children, either to gain benefit or to minimize their financial losses.

Mothers, who are severely disadvantaged by the text, struggle to correct its asymmetry by holding men (fathers or agnates) responsible for their legal duties. They do this by using the means at their disposal. There is no normative vacuum between text and practice (Griffiths 1992); rather, a social space exists, and it is within this space that people generate and manipulate it. The fate of children's *hadana* is a result of negotiation and social struggle between the actors, including the judges, who have to be accountable to a variety of ethical, social, political, and occupational domains.

Lawyers, for their part, do not limit themselves to the letter of the law; they also blend idioms from the *shari'a* with cultural norms to be used as reference points while presenting their cases. That was the situation in the case of Adala, with the lawyer employing religious and cultural norms to disqualify the father's claim of custody over his daughter. Since the headscarf is considered an essential aspect of women's public appearance, the lawyer argued that the father would not be a suitable custodian because he had torn the headscarf from his daughter's head, exposing her hair to public gaze.

The central objective of judges is to provide people with what they view as "justice" (*haqq*). Judges, as argued, have several references at their disposal. Codified law is the written reference, while "legal concepts" are unwritten. This study has identified concepts such as public welfare (*maslaha*), equity (*istihsan*), protecting the weak, customarily acceptable practices, and others which serve this purpose. These concepts are flexible, permeable, ambiguous and unspecific. Judges, using diverse strategies, exploit the characteristics of these concepts to arrive at a correct and "just" (*haqq*) solution. The legal concepts used by judges do not operate in a vacuum; they are part of the historical, economic, social and political context of their operation. They are also permeated by the interests, values, and perceptions of judges as well as of people. As demonstrated, the judges view themselves and are viewed (by litigants) as representing not only a legal institution but also moral and religious authority. In the case of Adala, they plot with a female litigant to devise a strategy to keep her children. In this case, the judge not only reinterpreted the law, but disregarded its relevance.

The *qadi al-qudsh*'s strategic advice to Adala is insightful with regard to the degree of the judges' embeddedness in the social fabric of Gaza. He is not merely implementer of the law; rather he exercises a degree of discretion informed by his self-perception as members of his community. Moreover, judges in general are well informed about "who is who" in the community and have strong contacts with the community leaders and other influential social and political figures. Their decisions depend not only on the history of cases filed, but more importantly, on the potential consequences of their judgments on the individual litigants and the larger community behind them (Rosen 1989). The *qadi al-qudah*'s ability to predict the second wife's response and his willingness to provide "justice" to the children enabled Adala to keep her children.

The criterion of litigants' "rightness" or "wrongness" depends on the context within which the dispute takes place. The *qadi* assesses the wrongdoing of a litigant against that which is defined by society as normal behaviour. Interestingly, the same trend, that is, placing the transgression of social norms within the framework of socially accepted behaviour, can also be observed among litigants. When they communicate with the *qadi*, they often refer to his moral and religious authority instead of his legal position. Women frequently address the *qadi* as the father of Muslims, the protector of God's worshippers, and so forth; and men do the same. Even when protesting the *qadi*'s interventions, they frame their objections in religious and moral idioms. There is a dialectic relation between the ethical requirements of *shari'a* in which the judges are well-trained, and the legally sanctioned principles of gender asymmetry. When judges find that strict adherence to the written code would lead to an unjust outcome, they strive to interpret the law in a way that makes it more in harmonious with its objectives.

The case of Adala is also relevant in discussing issues related to women's agency. The concept of "agency" is a powerful analytical tool for understanding and theorizing on how women subvert or resist their domination; and whether, how, and in which ways women contribute to the continuation of their own subordination. If agency means choices to be made as a means of realizing one's own well-being, does this imply that the direction of women's action should be "fixed a priori" (Mahmood 2001: 212)? In other words, when a woman decides, for example, to present herself as helpless and capitalizes on the judge's empathy and his notion of protection, does such an action imply that she is contributing in some way toward reinforcing her state of subjection? Acknowledging women's agency entails taking into account the specific historical and cultural context that creates the conditions within which women operate and make their choices. This practical notion of agency refers to their ability to cultivate their capabilities in order to attain their goals, despite (or perhaps due to) the injustices they have experienced.

The action of filing a suit, regardless of its outcome, is an empowering step. This was shown in the case of Adala, who used the action of going to court as an integral part of her strategy and not just as a procedural action. Astonishingly, the judges, the very figures whose function is assumed to be to safeguard the law, supply women with the means of overcoming their difficulties and thus assist them in strengthening their bargaining position *vis-à-vis* the children's guardians. Women, moreover, carefully choose which norms to invoke and in what forum to do so.

The most striking feature of the observed case is that nothing was registered in the court record except a brief statement outlining the final ruling. In Adala's case, the *qadi al-qudah*'s strategy was communicated behind closed doors. Under the circumstances, the only way to trace the daily "*ijtihad*" (independent reasoning) of judges is to observe it on the spot. The protection of the child's best interests stood in conflict with codified law, and therefore the *qadi* had to ignore the latter in order to carry out his duty as the provider of "justice". Some might argue that this behaviour is expected of those who have authority in the legal system. Yet the question remains as to what would be the impact of recording these interventions on the development of Islamic legal theory. If the legal system acknowledged such interventions and required the judge to put them down in writing, then the extent to which daily "jurisprudence" contributes to Islamic legal theory would be greater.

This takes us to another point related to the debate on codification and *ijtihad*. The process of codification produced a written legal corpus that is poorer than those of the four *madhahib* (schools of Islamic jurisprudence), in which contradictions are a built-in aspect of jurisprudence and thus allow for the adaptation of the legal judgments to the existing needs of society. The movement towards codification has confronted judges with an irresolvable problem: If, on the one hand, they apply the codified law as is, they inevitably injure both litigants and the moral principles of the *shari'a* through "unjust" judgments. If, on the other hand, they go beyond the scope of the codified statutes, they can be held responsible for violating the law. To resolve this dilemma, judges rely on orality. Most of their actions, reactions, interventions and "violations" of codified law are, understandably, not recorded anywhere. The fact that they have the authority to dictate the written record allows them to decide on the exclusion or inclusion of certain material; oral negotiations, the devices of certain judgments, out-of-court solutions, and in-court propositions appear nowhere in the court record. Thus, no one can trace the judges' exercise of *ijtihad*. In view of this reality, the argument put forward by Tucker (1998), namely that the codified law has come to affect the subjectivity of judges, holds true as long as the evidence studied is confined to written texts or archival material. Codification forces jurisprudence to resort to orality, which means that there is no way to reconstitute the entire picture unless the researcher adopts an appropriate methodology based on the observation and recording of the daily practice of *ijtihad*. Another consequence of orality is the judges' inability to rely on precedents. The lack of written precedents makes every case "new" and to be dealt with not on the basis of what has been accumulated through court history, but on the basis of the accumulated experience of the individual *qadi* alone. Contemporary *ijtihad* is obscured by the recourse to orality. Innovations are covered up and changes in the system concealed. Every *qadi*, therefore, is a universe unto itself, whose judgments are made subjectively and transmitted orally. *Ra'y* (subjective reasoning), which is one of the foundations of *ijtihad*, is obscured through orality and thus no legacy (*turath*) is allowed to accumulate. This leads to stagnation of the text on the one hand, and proliferation of oral *ijtihad* on the other.

Conclusion

This chapter has reviewed how the gender-based double standard of *hadana* is articulated in the text. However, when we turn to the practice we attain greater insight into how the law is socially constructed. This requires considering people's counter-consensual actions, for law is not transmitted from legal authorities to litigants by "cables". Communication between the legal authorities and citizens is rarely unmediated (Griffiths 1992). How, the paper inquired, did the actors in the court perceive the law? What sorts of accommodations or modifications were made by actors in the court, be they decision makers or litigants? In which areas did adjustment or non-adjustment occur, and why? Which ambivalences in codified law allowed people to adjust situationally? How do gender, social status and class play out, together or separately, in the process of adjustment? Which historical or temporal indeterminacies allowed and still allow people to adjust the law? In particular, the paper, while comparing the relevant text with its practice, did not seek to examine whether family law is effectively applied or obeyed; rather, the main aim was to investigate how it worked sociologically. It was in this examination that the law appeared less influential than assumed by social engineering theorists.[8] Moreover, the people's conduct not only suggests a difference between text and practice but also directs our attention to the quality of this difference: The text is often more conservative than the practice. This confirms the argument put forward by Dwyer (1990), which emphasizes the importance of reading the text through the eyes of the people rather than through an ideological presentation of Islamic law. Rules, as Moore (2005) points out, do not always rule. The sociology of law acknowledges that law operates in a culturally specific domain and within a context of social relations full of inconsistencies, ambiguities, and discontinuities. This approach has indeed been useful in Gaza. Recognizing the temporality of people's circumstances is essential in light of the indeterminacy that exists as a pervasive reality for people who endure enormous instability under the brutal and continuous Israeli occupation. The ethnography on the judicial reasoning in this particular corner of Palestine may prove useful, to the extent that it illustrates the capacity of judges to create a legal framework that can encompass multiple sources of law, amid litigants' shifting strategies. The disparity between the discretion of the judges and the purported binding code raises a double question: In whose interest does the judge rule in family law cases? What does it mean to adhere to the notion of rule of law when the judge decides as he sees fit? The answer – as the case of Adala indicates – is that the judges' discretion is able to serve the best interests of the weaker party and the rule of law is once again a notion that requires careful revision.

References

Anleu, S.L.R. 2000. *Law and Social Change*. London and New Delhi: Sage.

Botiveau, B. 1997. *Al-shari'a al-islamiyya wa al-qanun fi al-mujtama'at al-'arabiyya. [The Islamic Shari'a and Law in Arab Societies]*. Cairo: Sienna.

---

8 Anleu (2000: 2) argues that "during the twentieth century, there is increasing reliance on the law as a route, or resource, to implement desired social change. In part this reflects the aspiration for the welfare state and its social reform agenda, which rely on the statutory implementation and bureaucratic administration of social programmes". However, recent socio-legal commentators have started questioning the meaning of legal change, especially with growing inequalities in societies (Frohmann and Mertz 1994: 829). The main point is that legislation cannot change society alone; change is greatly influenced by cultural factors such as the institution of family, kinship, descent system, religion, and other socio-economic variables (Singh 1989).

Chanock, M. 2000. *Introduction in Law as Process: An Anthropological Approach (1978)*, edited by S.F. Moore. 2nd Edition. Hamburg: Lit-Verlag and James Currey, xi–xxx.

Dwyer, D.H. 1990. "Law and Islam in the Middle East: An introduction", in *Law and Islam in the Middle East*, edited by D.H. Dwyer. New York: Bergin and Garvey, 1–15.

Esposito, J. 1982. *Women in Muslim Family Law*. New York: Syracuse University Press.

Frohmann, L. and Mertz, E. 1994. Legal reform and social construction: Violence, gender and the law. *Law and Social Inquiry*, 19, 829–51.

Gerber, H. 1994. *State, Society, and Law in Islam: Ottoman Law in Comparative Perspective*. Albany: State University of New York.

Gerber, H. 1999. *Islamic Law and Culture 1600–1840*. Leiden: Brill.

Gluckman, M. 1955. *The Judicial Process among the Barotse of Northern Rhodesia*. Manchester: Manchester University Press.

Griffiths, J. 1992. Legal pluralism and the social working of law, in *Coherence and Conflict in Law: Proceedings of the 3rd Benelux-Scandinavian Symposium in Legal Theory*, edited by B. Brouwer, T. Hol, A. Soeteman and A. de Wild. Amsterdam and Deventer: Kluwer Law and Taxation Publisher, 151–76.

Hallaq, W. 1984. Was the gate of Ijtihad closed? *International Journal of Middle East Studies*, 16, 3–41. Also in *Islamic Law and Legal Theory: The International Library of Essays in Law and Legal Theory*, edited by I. Edge (1996). Aldershot: Dartmouth, 287–325.

Hallaq, W. 1996. "Ifta" and "Ijtihad" in Sunni legal theory: A developmental account, in *Islamic Legal Interpretation: Mufis and their Fatwas*, edited by K. Masud, B. Messick and D. Powers. Cambridge: Harvard University Press, 33–43.

Layish, A. 1975. *Women and Islamic Law in a Non-Muslim State*. Jerusalem: Tel Aviv University. Shiloah Center for Middle Eastern Studies.

Mahmood, S. 2001. Feminist theory, embodiment, and the docile agent: Some reflections on the Egyptian Islamic revival. *Cultural Anthropology*, 16(2), 202–36.

Moore, S.F. 1978. *Law as Process: An Anthropological Approach*. London: Routledge and Kegan Paul.

Moore, S.F. 2000. *Law as Process: An Anthropological Approach (1978): New Introduction by Martin Chanock. 2nd Edition*. Hamburg: Lit-Verlag and James Currey.

Moore, S.F. 2005. Certainties undone: Fifty turbulent years of legal anthropology, 1949–1999, in *Law and Anthropology: A reader*, edited by S.F. Moore. Malden, Oxford and Victoria: Blackwell, 347–67.

Moors, A. 1995. *Women, Property and Islam: Palestinian Experiences 1920–1990*. Cambridge: Cambridge University Press.

Pospisil, L. 1971. *Anthropology of Law: A Comparative Theory*. New York: Harper and Row.

Rosen, L. 1989. *The Anthropology of Justice: Law as Culture in Islamic Society*. Cambridge: Cambridge University Press.
Samara, M. 1987. *Ahkam wa athar al-zawjiyya: sharh muqaran li-qanun al-ahwal al-shakhsiyya* [Rules and Consequences of Marriage: Comparative Commentary on the Law of Personal Status]. Jerusalem: (no publisher).
Shehada, N. 2005. *Justice without Drama*. PhD Dissertation, The Hague: Shaker.
Singh, I.P. 1989. *Women, Law and Social Change in India*. London: Sangam Books.
Tucker, J. 1998. *In the House of Law: Gender and Islamic Law in Ottoman Syria and Palestine*. California: University of California Press.
Welchman, L. 1999. *Islamic Family Law: Text and Practice in Palestine*. Jerusalem: WCLAC.
Welchman, L. 2000. *Beyond the Code: Muslim Family Law and the Shar'i Judiciary in the Palestinian West Bank*. The Hague: Kluwer Law International.
Zahraa, M. and Malek, N.A. 1998. The concept of custody in Islamic law. *Arab Law Quarterly*, 13(2), 155–77.

Legislation

Laws Applied in the Shari'a Courts of the Gaza Strip

BPSR. 1875. "*Kitab al-ahkam al-shar'iyya fi al-ahwal al-shakhsiyya 'ala madhhab al-imam Abu Hanifa*" [The Book of Personal Status Rulings According to the School of Abu Hanifa] compiled by Muhammad Qadrii Pasha, in Dahduh et al. 1996, pp. 2–107.
LFR. 1954. "*Qanun huquq al-'a'ila*" [Law of Family Rights] regulated by the Egyptian Governor General of Gaza Strip by order number 303 (special official *Gazette* 22/5/1965), in Dahduh et al. 1996, pp. 108–22.

Index

For Product Safety Concerns and Information please contact our EU
representative GPSR@taylorandfrancis.com
Taylor & Francis Verlag GmbH, Kaufingerstraße 24, 80331 München, Germany

www.ingramcontent.com/pod-product-compliance
Ingram Content Group UK Ltd.
Pitfield, Milton Keynes, MK11 3LW, UK
UKHW020013200926
475702UK00014B/1866

* 9 7 8 1 1 3 8 2 7 6 4 0 6 *